The D...

SIMON GRAY

IV

ff

faber and faber

LONDON · BOSTON

This collection was first published in 1993
by Faber and Faber Limited
3 Queen Square London WC1N 3AU

Photoset by Wilmaset Ltd, Birkenhead, Wirral
Printed in England by Clays Ltd, St Ives plc

Simon Gray is hereby identified as author of this work in accordance with
Section 77 of the Copyright, Designs and Patents Act 1988

Hidden Laughter was first published in 1990 by Faber and Faber Ltd. This
revised edition first published in this collection.
The Common Pursuit was first published in 1984 by Methuen London Ltd.
The Holy Terror was first published in 1990 in a volume entitled *The Holy Terror/
Tartuffe* by Faber and Faber Ltd. This revised edition first published in this
collection.
Screenplay *After Pilkington* was first published in 1987 by Methuen London Ltd
Screenplay *Old Flames* was first published in 1990 in a volume entitled *Old
Flames and A Month in the Country* by Faber and Faber Ltd

All professional and amateur rights in these plays are strictly reserved and
applications for permission to perform them must be made in advance to
Judy Daish Associates Limited, 83 Eastbourne Mews, London W2 6LQ
Telephone 071–262 1101

A CIP record for this book is available from the British Library
ISBN 0–571–16659–8

2 4 6 8 10 9 7 5 3 1

Contents

Hidden Laughter

For Sarah

Sudden in a shaft of sunlight
Even while the dust moves
There rises the hidden laughter
Of children in the foliage
Quick now, here, now, always –

T. S. ELIOT, 'Burnt Norton'

Hidden Laughter was first presented by Michael Codron on 12 June 1990, at the Vaudeville Theatre, London. The cast was as follows:

HARRY	Kevin McNally
LOUISE	Felicity Kendal
BEN	Richard Vernon
RONNIE	Peter Barkworth ～ vicar
DRAYCOTT	Sam Dastor
NATALIE	Caroline Harker
16 NIGEL	Samuel West
NAOMI	Jane Galloway
Director	Simon Gray
Designer	Robin Don
Lighting	Rick Fisher

ACT ONE

SCENE I

*Summer 1980. Evening. Country cottage and garden. The wall of
the cottage invisible. There are two rooms connected by
passageway. Stage left the kitchen and stage right the room that
becomes the sitting room/Louise's study. There are entrances to the
garden and through the front door at the sitting room end. Both the
kitchen and the sitting room contain minimal furniture which is
shrouded in dust sheets.*

*The garden is well kept, but there is an anomalous and very ugly
tree stump prominent. There is also visible, at the end of the
garden, a 'For Sale' sign.*

There is music over: 'The Paradise Duet' from Haydn's Creation.
*This is played at the beginning and end of every scene in the play.
It is twilight. As the curtain rises,* RONNIE *is finishing the planting
of a trough of geraniums. His task completed, he picks up his
shopping basket, looks round with satisfaction, and exits.*

LOUISE *and* HARRY *appear in the house. As they wander through
it:*

LOUISE: What an awful smell – as if it's rotting.

HARRY: Yes, well it is, I think. The walls upstairs –
(*Stumbling*) and the bloody floorboards!

LOUISE: (*As they enter kitchen*) I suppose this was the kitchen.

HARRY: Or the bathroom. We haven't seen a bathroom yet. Or
even a lavatory –

LOUISE: We haven't seen a kitchen either.

HARRY: Darling, there's no point. Let's go on to the next. It's
in Lower Mudge. (*Consulting estate agent particulars.*)
About a five-mile drive – and there are two more after
that – we want to see them before the light goes –

5

(LOUISE, *meanwhile, has opened door to garden, steps out. Stares around her in wonderment.* HARRY *joins her.*)

LOUISE: Oh, darling! Oh, Harry darling! Look at it – look at the roses. All of it!

HARRY: Yes – it's – it's beautiful, isn't it? Nearly as beautiful as you. (*Looking at her.*)

LOUISE: Oh, it's much more beautiful. And almost as lovingly looked after!

HARRY: Yes, that's strange – the estate agents said it belongs to some old woman that's had to be put into a home – yes, I made a note – (*Looking at particulars.*) Ivy Cottage, Great Yarcombe. Owner ga-ga.

LOUISE: We could fix the house, couldn't we?

HARRY: It would cost a bit.

LOUISE: More than we can afford, you mean?

HARRY: Well, with luck. And faith – and a decent mortgage. We could probably swing it.

LOUISE: Oh, I have all the faith in the world, my darling. In you. And we'll have luck. We'll *make* luck. Touch wood. (*Touching branch of tree.*)

HARRY: Then that only leaves the mortgage. (*Laughing.*) And Daddy might help with that. And the deposit. And if anything goes wrong we can always sell. House prices are bound to go up and up in this little corner of Devon.

LOUISE: Oh, Harry, isn't it extraordinary? We trudge through that filthy little cottage, hating it. Then step into the garden and we're claimed. It's – it's as if it had been waiting for us, keeping itself trim and beautiful and serene until the moment that you and I find it and fall head over heels, hopelessly in love with it. That's why it's glowing – glowing away at us.

HARRY: Saying 'buy me, buy me, buy me.'

LOUISE: Because it wants to go to the right couple. Who'll look after it. And love it for itself. I could start down here, you know.

HARRY: Start? Start what, Lou?

LOUISE: My life. My writing life.

HARRY: Ah. It's come back again, has it? The old urge?

LOUISE: It's never left. I only stopped because the children were so young – I wasn't ready to – to settle down. (*Little laugh.*) But now, here, in all this I know that I am. Ready. Oh, darling, don't look so – so troubled. That very first piece I showed you. The autobiographical piece. You said I had talent. That was your professional opinion.

HARRY: Well, you had. And *have*. I'm sure. But it cost you an awful lot, remember? Sleepless nights, headaches – it's so lonely, a writer's life – you found that. Cutting yourself off, then facing rejection – and it's harder than ever, these days. The market's so odd –

LOUISE: I know, darling. And I know you understand about writers better than anybody in the whole world, probably. I won't be lonely down here. Not with you, the children. Just us. What could be less lonely? (*Little pause.*) I have to do it, darling. I have to *try*, at least.

HARRY: Then if you have to, you will. I know that look only too well.

LOUISE: My look? What does it look like?

HARRY: The look of someone who's determined to have a go at being a writer. And there it is. On the face of my beloved, God help me! (*Laughs.*)

LOUISE: If I'm no good you'll tell me, and I'll stop, I promise. If you'll promise to tell me.

HARRY: I promise I shall never tell you anything but the truth.

LOUISE: And you'll be patient? Until I've done something I'm ready to risk with you?

HARRY: Very patient, darling. I'm famous for my patience with writers.

LOUISE: And with wives.

HARRY: As long as the wife is mine.

LOUISE: Oh, Harry darling. Thank you. And for this. (*Looking *around garden.*) And thank you, garden, for being here this afternoon –

HARRY: Lou, my love. They may not accept our offer. (*Looks at her face.*) Yes, they will. I'll make them one they can't refuse.

LOUISE: (*After a little pause*) Now make me one I can't refuse. (*Seductively.*)

HARRY: (*Staring at her, smiling*) What?

(LOUISE *begins to dance, humming, directing herself in an intimate and sexy manner at* HARRY.)

LOUISE: Remember?

(HARRY, *laughing in delight, hums, begins to do the dance.* LOUISE *whirls herself gently into his arms. They embrace, then begin kissing with increasing passion.*

BEN, *meanwhile, is coming through the house. Lets out an exclamation of disgust, kicks out at something unseen, goes through kitchen into garden, stops on seeing* HARRY *and* LOUISE, *clears his throat.*

HARRY *and* LOUISE *break, embarrassed.*)

HARRY: Ah, Daddy. Everything all right?

BEN: Yes, yes, perfectly all right. Fine. Fine.

LOUISE: And Nigel and Natalie –?

BEN: Perfectly safe, Lou, perfectly safe. Don't worry. Good God, look at that old monster! (*Pointing to tree stump.*) What's the point of it?

HARRY: Oh, don't worry about him, Daddy. I'll have him up in no time.

BEN: What? What do you mean? You don't mean – you don't mean you're going to buy this dump! Do you know what I saw inside? A rat! Great brute of a rat! Just trudged past me, didn't even bother to hide! And the smells! The smells everywhere! And there's damp rot, dry rot, holes in the roof, holes in the floors – ! Harry, you can't buy it! Lou, you mustn't let him!

LOUISE: (*Goes to* BEN, *takes his arm*) Ben, Ben, look at this –

(*Indicating garden*) this is what we want, this is what we're buying!

BEN: (*Looking around him, not understanding*) What? I don't see anything – just a garden – oh, to build on, I see! Well, now that's a different matter! If you can get planning permission –

HARRY: (*After exchanging glances with* LOUISE) No, no, Daddy, it's the garden we want. Just as it is.

LOUISE: It would be sacrilege to build on it. Don't you love it, Ben? How can you not?

BEN: (*Clearly taking garden in for the first time*) It is rather lovely. Now you mention it. Yes. Very lovely. Very – and it does have something about it, doesn't it? Extra. Something extra. (*Clearly becoming more entranced, and moved.*) And those – what are they? (*Peering towards flowers that aren't hollyhocks.*) Hollyhocks, aren't they? Yes, I do believe they're – they're hollyhocks. (*Turns suddenly away, his shoulders shaking.*)

(HARRY *and* LOUISE *exchange another look.*)

LOUISE: Oh, Ben. (*Goes over, put her arms around him.*)

HARRY: Daddy. (*Goes to him uncertainly, puts a hand on his shoulder.*)

BEN: Sorry. Sorry. (*Wiping his eyes.*) Bloody grief. Bloody grief. Just leaps up when I'm least expecting it. Like a lump – damn it, damn it – (*Sobs more violently.*)

LOUISE: It's all right, Ben. It's all right. You can cry or scream or shout – anything you want – with us.

HARRY: Yes, Daddy. It's nothing to be ashamed of.

BEN: (*Attempting to compose himself*) Well, nothing – nothing in my experience, I suppose. Prepared me for it. Your mother's death. Couldn't imagine a life without her, you see. Forty-seven years we were together. Forty-seven years. Most of my whole life, adult life. And of course I keep thinking that in some way it's my fault, if I'd taken better care of her –

9

HARRY: You were a wonderful husband, Daddy.

BEN: Was I? Was I? How do I know whether I was? I was her only husband, perhaps some other man –

LOUISE: Oh, Ben, she was always telling me about her luck in the two men in her life. The two men she loved –

BEN: Two men! Two! What do you mean, two!

HARRY: I think the other one was me, Daddy.

BEN: Oh. Oh, yes. I see. You. Of course it was. Don't know why I thought for a second – even for a second – always trusted her, you know. Trusted her completely. Just as she always trusted me. At least I hope she did, hope to God she did. Because I never got up to anything – but then why would I want to? With a woman like your mother. The soul of kindness, gentleness –

HARRY: I know, Daddy.

BEN: – never asked for anything for herself. Never anything big, anyway. Except once. Only that once. (*Begins to tremble again.*) And I refused her.

HARRY: What did she ask for, Daddy?

BEN: This! (*Sweeping arm.*)

LOUISE: *This*, Ben? You mean you've been here before? You know it?

HARRY: I expect it was Mummy that knew it. She came from this part of Devon – is that it, Daddy?

BEN: (*Temporarily absorbed in grief*) What, what? (*Looking from one to other.*)

HARRY: Mummy brought you here.

BEN: Here. (*Bewildered.*) No, she didn't. Who said she did?

HARRY: But Daddy, you said she asked you for it – this garden.

BEN: No, no, not this one. Not this particular one. But something like this. A cottage – a *clean* little cottage she'd have wanted – with a garden. Yes, a garden – she hungered for a garden, you see. An English garden. After all those years abroad – just before that damned sickness took hold of her – a couple of months before, it must have been – and do you know what I said? I said, sorry, Emily old girl, can't really afford both London *and* Devon, which is it to be? And of course she chose to stay in London, to be near the grandchildren – and here I am, here I am, with all the money from her life insurance – enough to buy her her cottage and some to spare, isn't that a joke? (*Laughs.*) Of course I keep thinking, I could have found a way to get her what she wanted, get my Emily what she wanted and perhaps down here, with a garden and the good air, she wouldn't have been taken sick – how could I have said no, how could I – (*Stands, shoulders shaking, sobbing helplessly.*)

HARRY: Daddy, Daddy, you mustn't blame yourself – nothing could have saved Mummy –
(RONNIE *enters through gate, in dog-collar, etc., carrying shopping basket, now full.*)

RONNIE: Um, hello – I do hope you don't mind – I was just coming back from the shop and heard voices. I'm, um, Ronald Chambers, the – the local – (*Taking in scene.*) I'm so sorry. I'm intruding. (*Makes to go.*)

HARRY: No, no, we were just –

BEN: I've a touch of hay-fever, 'fraid. (*Blowing his nose.*) Must be the hollyhocks.

RONNIE: Hollyhocks? Oh, the geraniums –

LOUISE: We were wondering who keeps the garden up – we understand the old lady who used to live here left some time ago.

RONNIE: About six months ago. Dear old May. She loved it, you know. It was all her creation. Even when she was past it she'd come out and scrabble away with a trowel – she was actually deep in one of the flower beds – (*Points.*) that one – when they came to take her away. She made me promise to keep it up for her. Almost her last words. She's scarcely spoken or moved since, I understand. So of

course I come in whenever I can – to tell you the truth it
suits me – my own garden, the vicarage garden, it's on the
small side, and my housekeeper, a wonderful woman
called Mrs Mossop – wonderful – but she's insisted on
growing vegetables everywhere, every available inch, for
her soups and such, she's a marvellous cook, my Mrs
Mossop – but it's been such a – a pleasure to have a real
garden to tend. Without a possible bowl of soup in sight.
(*Laughs*.) Are you interested? In – in purchasing. Most
people just take a few steps inside the door – and then go
straight back out to their cars. You're the first I've seen
come this far – (*Gestures*.)

LOUISE: Which is why we're going to buy it.

RONNIE: Are you really? Are you really? Well, that's the best
news – to think old May's Ivy Cottage is going to be
inhabited again –

BEN: (*Turning*) What?

HARRY: We're just saying we're going to buy it, Daddy. This
place.

BEN: Of course we are! Of course we bloody are!
(*To* RONNIE) Think I'm going to let him make the
same mistake with Louise that I made with Emily!
Like hell I am! Like bloody hell I am! Every penny,
every penny of that damned blasted insurance – oh,
excuse my language, Father – reverend, um, I was in
the Diplomatic, you see, more Ministry of Trade as a
matter of fact, had to be so polite in public that in
private we used to let go – even my wife, my Emily,
wasn't above the occasional 'damn' and 'bloody', he
(*pointing to* HARRY) knows – he knows – ask him.
Remember, Harry, that time we were just off to Peru,
we'd come to school to say goodbye, and your mother – at
the thought of leaving you all over again – her language –
not fit for your ears, fa – rev – she let loose, didn't she,
Harry, let loose – let loose –

HARRY: (*Laughing awkwardly*) Yes, she did, Daddy. In front of the matron, too.

BEN: Yes, in front of the matron – (*Tries to laugh, turns away again, overcome.*)

(*There is a pause.* RONNIE *glances again at* BEN.)

RONNIE: Um, um, (*Turns back to* HARRY) may I – um – may I ask – what line *you're* in?

HARRY: I'm an agent. A literary agent.

RONNIE: A *literary* agent! Really! Who would have thought of our little village as a place for a literary agent to – to set up shop in – but of course with the telephone, these days, and all the technology – fax machines – word processors –

LOUISE: No, no, we want to come down here to get away from all that, don't we, darling?

HARRY: Yes, my office is in London. It has to be.

RONNIE: Oh, so it'll be a weekend cottage, holiday cottage sort of thing – how delightful, how delightful for you and – and – well, look, if you need someone to look in during the week, keep an eye on things, water the garden, do a bit of sowing and weeding and whatever – I'd be happy, *most* happy –

LOUISE: Thank you. We'd be very grateful –

HARRY: Yes, we would. Especially during the winter. Thank you.

RONNIE: Not at all. I can't tell you how pleased I am after all these months on the market – I've longed for a family to come here – and children in the garden – oh, oh, I don't mean – you haven't children, I take it, but a young couple –

(HARRY *and* LOUISE *look at each other, laugh.*)

HARRY: As a matter of fact, we can provide children too. A boy and a girl.

BEN: (*Re-entering conversation*) What, Harry?

HARRY: We're talking about the little terrors, Daddy.

BEN: Oh, they're not terrors, no, no, just mischievous, a

couple of mischievous charmers, that's what they are, aren't they, Lou, Nig and Nat, never know what they'll get up to next! No different from you, Harry, when you were that age!

RONNIE: Oh, how – how! And they'll love it down here, I'm sure, how old are they?

BEN: Nat is nine and Nig is eight.

HARRY: (*Laughing*) Nearly right, Daddy, except it's the other way around.

LOUISE: Yes, Nigel is eight and Natalie is nine, Ben.

HARRY: No, darling, the other way around again. Natalie is eight and Nigel is nine.

LOUISE: (*Confused*) What? Oh yes, yes of course – (*Laughs.*)

RONNIE: Lovely age, whichever way around it is. I suppose you left them in London, did you, while you – you – (*Gestures.*)

HARRY: No, no, we brought them down. They're here. At least I hope they are. (*With a little laugh.*) They *are* still in the car, aren't they, Daddy?

BEN: Yes, yes. Well no, actually, I let them out into the field.

LOUISE: The field?

BEN: Well, there's not much they can get up to in a field, Lou, is there, fa – reverend?

RONNIE: Oh, do call me Ronnie. Please.

HARRY: Ronnie. Harry Pertwee. Louise (*Indicating*) and my father –

BEN: Ben. Ben Pertwee.

(*They nod and smile at each other.*)

RONNIE: (*To* BEN) Which field did you leave them in exactly, um?

BEN: Oh, the big one just up the road, to the left.

RONNIE: Ah. (*Looks worried.*) That'd be old Tomalin's, I expect. A rather – rather ferocious old character.

LOUISE: You mean he may not like our two being in his field.

RONNIE: No, no – I'm sure – quite sure – well, I mean, two

young lives, even old Tomalin – he'll keep an eye on old
Dan.

HARRY: Who's old Dan?

RONNIE: He's the bull.

BEN: Bull? What bull? There wasn't a bull!

RONNIE: No, he generally lies a bit low until Tomalin
brings the cattle down – about now – so if you are
worried – you'd probably be there in time to get
them out –

LOUISE: Come on, darling, let's go! (*Making towards the house.*)

RONNIE: It'd be quicker if you go by the gate, the little path
takes you straight to it.

HARRY: Oh, right.

LOUISE: (*Following*) I do wish you hadn't left them alone,
Ben.

(LOUISE and HARRY *hurry off.*
There is a pause.)

RONNIE: I wonder if I should go with them. As I know the
terrain, so to speak.

BEN: No, don't worry, no need for a hue and cry. To tell you
the truth, old Lou's a charming girl, dead right for Harry,
but she's a slight tendency to fuss and fret. Anyway,
where the children are concerned. Where most things are
concerned. I'm always trying to get her to take a leaf from
my Emily's book, straightforward, no nonsense, never
flustered – I'm Emily's widow, as I expect you've
gathered. Not widow. Wife, I mean. Dead wife. I'm
Emily's – no, no, I'm a widower is how I intended to put
it. Died four months ago. My wife, that is. Emily.

RONNIE: I'm very sorry.

BEN: Don't be! Don't be! I'm not! At least I try bloody hard
not to be! After all, she had a good life. A damned good
life, my Emily. And it was quick. Mercifully quick. Her
death, I mean. Not her life. Though that was quicker
than it should have been – only sixty-five. Looked and

behaved twenty years younger. God, I miss her. I'll admit to that.

RONNIE: I'm sure you do, I'm sure you do.

BEN: I mean, there we were in our nice little retirement flat in Fulham, only just bought it before she – she – hardly had time to get used to it, and suddenly I'm left in it all by myself – thinking what am I doing here without Emily, how's it happened? How? (*Nearly breaks down again, manages to control himself.*) And you? You married?

RONNIE: Yes. Yes, I am. Well – in the sense that I have a – have a wife. If you follow. But she – she – it's rather hard to explain precisely – um –

BEN: Ah. I see. She left you, did she? (*Sympathetically.*)

RONNIE: Oh, no. No. Not that. No. But she's not – not altogether – she's been ill on and off for quite a few years. Since the year after we got married, in fact. She spends a lot of the time in a – a – rather special – rather special – um –

BEN: Wheelchair, is that it? A paraplegic –?

RONNIE: No, no, not that sort of illness. No. In a – in a special *home*. So to speak. *Mentally* ill, you see. Mentally.

BEN: Oh. Oh, dear. I'm sorry.

RONNIE: No, no, don't be. Some of the time she's very happy. In fact, a surprising amount of the time. Well, it's a private home, you see – her name's Wilemena.

BEN: Wilemena. Odd name. German, is she?

RONNIE: No, no, quite English. So's the name, really. Wilemena.

BEN: Must be difficult for you. Very difficult.

RONNIE: No, no – an exceptionally nice woman comes in from the village, looks after me – Mrs Mossop. In fact, I was telling your son and daughter-in-law. Mrs Mossop's a widow herself.

BEN: No, I mean believing in God. Difficult to believe in a God who condones madness, death –

RONNIE: Oh, quite. Almost impossible.

BEN: I have to tell you, been a life-long atheist. Fervent.

RONNIE: Oh, I – I don't blame you. I quite understand. Most
of my parishioners are like that. They don't believe a
word of it. Can't blame them either. As really the whole
thing is so – so preposterous, isn't it? In this day and age.

BEN: You mean you don't believe in God! (*Angrily*.)

RONNIE: Well, Ben – I wouldn't put it quite like that.

BEN: Well, how would you put it?

RONNIE: I don't know – well, who can say – but – but – the
point is – you see, there's no point in believing in Him
unless it's impossible to believe in Him, if you follow,
because if He existed, and we all knew He existed there'd
be no difficulty at all in believing in Him and what'd be
the point of *that*. (*Little pause*.) No, I've put that rather
badly too, Ben, all I mean is that faith is – is – a matter
of believing what's impossible to believe. Do you – see?
Otherwise it's not faith. It's certainty. If you follow.

BEN: The certainty's all I've got to believe in. The certainty
that this impossible bloke of yours, that you call God,
allows people like my Emily and your – your – your –
Brunehilda –

RONNIE: Wilemena, actually. Her name –

BEN: To go mad. To die. So I'd prefer it if He wasn't there to
be responsible for it. Otherwise all there is to believe in is
a nasty piece of work.

RONNIE: But – but if He does exist, impossible though it may
be to believe, then whatever He's up to would be
impossible to understand. That's all I – I – that's my
whole – the mystery of it. If there is a mystery. If it turns
out that there isn't, then you're right, of course, Ben.

BEN: But for God's sakes, how can you – how dare you – if
that's as far as you can go, how do you expect the rest of
us, me, for instance, if *nobody*, including types like you
who are paid for it – I mean, it's your bloody job to
believe in God, damn it! If you don't, who will?

RONNIE: I know, I know. But we do try, you see, and quite a few of the other chaps actually manage it, I suppose. Really do believe in Him on a day to day basis. And the rest of us – those of us who find it impossible, well, we just have to make the leap – the leap into the – (*Gestures*) dark!

(HARRY *and* LOUISE *appear at the gate.*)

HARRY: (*With suppressed urgency, to* RONNIE) Would you mind – the field is full of cattle and a bloody great bull and that lunatic of a farmer won't let us in to look for the children – or even look himself – so perhaps you'd come and have a word with him?

BEN: What? (*Uncomprehendingly.*)

LOUISE: They'll be trampled, you see.

RONNIE: Oh, yes, of course I'll come. But – but really old Tomalin – I'm quite sure, when it comes to it – now, where's my shopping? (*Looking round for it.*)

LOUISE: Oh hurry, please hurry! Before something awful – awful happens!

RONNIE: Ah, yes, here it is!

LOUISE: (*Out of control*) For God's sake, hurry!
(*They go to gate.*)

LOUISE: (*Almost to herself*) Oh, please don't let them be hurt, God, please don't let them be hurt –
(*Sudden laughter of children. They all stare towards shrubbery.*)

HARRY: There they are! There they are! (*In joyful relief.*)

LOUISE: (*Her face radiant*) Oh, you naughty – you naughty, naughty – oh, you two!

BEN: There you are. I said all the time they'd be all right, didn't I, Harry?
(*Laughter gets louder.* HARRY, LOUISE, BEN *and* RONNIE *join in as:*
Lights and curtain.)

SCENE 2

Three years later. Late afternoon. Full sunshine. The inside of the house is now visible. A small sitting room, with minimum of furniture – small table, a door stage right, that leads to stairs up to bedrooms. A door, stage left, that leads to a short hall (not visible on stage) that leads to a kitchen, not yet fully equipped, but with an oven, a fridge, table and chairs. A chair, stage left, below stump, with scattered typescript on it.

LOUISE *is sitting at the table, typing with minimum fingers but with great speed and controlled energy. On the radio at her side, a magnificently excited piece of music is playing – preferably Brahms, 'The Academic Festival Overture'.*

HARRY *is in the garden, in which there is now a swing. He is digging with controlled energy at the unsightly stump. A travel rug and cushion are on the lawn.*

As LOUISE's *typing accelerates to a kind of climax, unconsciously following the music,* HARRY *accelerates his digging, almost as if in time to the typing and the music, to a point of demented ferocity.*

LOUISE *concludes a sentence as the music achieves an appropriately triumphant flourish. She switches radio off mid-phrase, rips paper out and reads it.*

HARRY *glances towards* LOUISE, *frustrated that music has stopped, then throws down his spade and starts to grapple with the stump, swaying and levering it this way and that.*

LOUISE *reads the page in increasing despair.*

LOUISE: It's no good, it's no good – it's no bloody good!
(*Crumples it into a ball, throws it into wastepaper basket, full and surrounded by discarded pages.*
HARRY *continues to grapple with stump, swearing at it, almost* sotto voce *initially, but his swearing getting louder and louder.*)

HARRY: Come on, you sod, come on, you bastard, come on, come on, oh, you brute – you swine – you – you – (*Reels back, having lost his footing, then lurches forward again, as if*

19

about to assault a human enemy.) You – you shit! (*Grapples with it ferociously, then collapses on top of it as:*)

LOUISE: (*Comes out into garden. Looking around*) Ah, an inspiration at last. Little Paradise.

HARRY: Mmmm? (*Still collapsed.*)

LOUISE: Well, we've taken down the Ivy Cottage sign, but we still haven't given it a new name. In London we always say we're going down to Devon, or to the cottage. Time we said we were going down to Little Paradise. Because that's what it looks like. What do you think?

HARRY: Little Paradise – yes, yes – fine, fine. (*Gives the stump a vicious kick, winces.*) I like it. Little Paradise.

LOUISE: You know, I wish we'd brought the children after all. Every time I come out I expect to find one of them on the swing.

HARRY: Or both of them squabbling about whose turn it is.

LOUISE: I even miss that. Well, at least it's better than worrying about what they're up to when I can't see them.

HARRY: Daddy's perfectly capable of looking after them, you know.

LOUISE: Yes, but – well, darling, you know I adore Ben – adore him – I couldn't have hoped for a nicer father-in-law – in fact the only thing wrong with him is he never listens to a word I say. At least about anything to do with the children. He always thinks he knows best – I mean – I mean, when I tried to explain about all the meals I'd left in the fridge, his eyes just glazed over, and I know he doesn't really believe dairy produce brings on Nigel's headaches – in fact he said as much – and then when I got on to Ophelia and the boiled fish, he just kept shaking his head and saying, 'It'll be all right, Lou, it'll be all right, don't you worry, I'll look after everything' – as if I were demented or something. And I'll bet you he feeds Ophelia scraps every time she miaows and then she won't want the fish with the worm powder and she'll go around the house

crapping out those frightful creatures again – *and* he'll
ignore all the rules about television watching, they've both
got school projects –

HARRY: (*Interrupting soothingly*) Darling, darling, it'll be all
right. We're back tomorrow – (*Gently.*) You're blocked
again, aren't you?

LOUISE: (*Nods ruefully*) I don't understand it – it's always the
same place – and it ought to be so simple. It *feels* simple
when I'm writing it, simple and exciting. But when I read
it back it's – it's hopeless. I keep running up to it, you
see, as if I'm going to hurdle over it, and leap – leap –
take a terrific leap, an exhilarating leap, and when I land
it's on my bottom. In a ditch. That's what the process
feels like.

HARRY: So my wife is currently on her bottom, is she?

LOUISE: In the ditch. (*Nodding, looks at him appealingly.*)

HARRY: Would you – would you like me to read it?

LOUISE: (*After a little pause*) No. We made an agreement. Only
when I'm sure it's worth your reading.

HARRY: Yes, but – well, things do change, darling. You've
been stuck there in your ditch – well, for *weeks* now, isn't
it? Isn't that true?

LOUISE: But once I get through it – over it – perhaps I
shouldn't run and jump – try trotting down into
the ditch and up the other side – very gently and
methodically –

HARRY: Yes – or. Take a little break, perhaps? (*Watches her.*)

LOUISE: (*Prickling*) What do you mean?

HARRY: A rest, Lou. That's all. Perhaps going at it again and
again, without giving yourself any chance to see it
freshly –

LOUISE: (*Goes to him*) You're not asking me to give it up, are
you? Or hoping I will? (*Looks at him seriously.*)

HARRY: Lou, my darling, I love you and I love the way you
stick at it until you think you've got it right – why, if that

bugger Draycott had a fraction of your determination I'd have something a lot better than *Fuck All*, wouldn't I? (*Pointing to typescript.*)

LOUISE: Still, he finished it. *And* it's going to be published. I've got to go on. If I let go of it I might never get it back – the thought of that fills me with panic! The thought of it! It does, Harry. Please be patient, my love.

HARRY: I told you – I'll be as patient as you want, darling. It's nothing to do with *me*, my – my concern. It's for *you* – your health – look (*Gives a sudden laugh*) by break I mean – I only mean – a very little one. (*Takes her in his arms.*) With me. (*Kisses her on the lips.*) Actually, for my sake. (*Kisses her again.*) Not yours. (*Kisses her again.*) I need you, Lou. (*Kisses her again.*) My love.

LOUISE: (*Becoming excited*) Oh, you're so hot.

HARRY: Am I? Yes, I am. (*Begins to unbutton her dress.*)

LOUISE: And you smell.

HARRY: Yes, I expect I do. That damned stump. Do you want me to wash?

LOUISE: No, no, it's delicious. Delicious. Manly. Lovely and manly. It makes me want to swoon. I could gobble you up.

HARRY: Why don't you then? (*Pulling her to the grass.*)

LOUISE: What, here, you mean?

HARRY: Why not? We haven't done it outside since the children were born. (*Goes on unbuttoning her dress, kisses her on her body.*)

LOUISE: Oh – ! Oh – !
    (RONNIE *appears at the gate on his bike. He dismounts, props bike beside gate.*)

HARRY: Oh, Christ! Would you believe it? (*Getting up.*)

LOUISE: (*Also getting up, desperately buttoning up her dress, half-laughing*) If we'd gone inside –

RONNIE: Oh, hello. I heard you were down so – so – as I'm on my way to Lower Mudge – I'm doing evensong there –

22

I thought I'd just pop my head over the gate and say –
um – say hello. I hope you don't mind.

HARRY: Of course not, Ronnie.

(*There is a pause.*)

RONNIE: Well – well, that's all really – I'd better –

LOUISE: (Sotto voce *to* HARRY, *turned away, still buttoning up.*)
Ask him in.

RONNIE: Perhaps I'll – um – see you later, then.

HARRY: Right, Ronnie. Let's hope so.

LOUISE: But can't you come in now, Ronnie? It would be such
a pity if we missed you.

(HARRY *shoots her a dagger's glance, frustrated.*)

RONNIE: No, no, I really must be – well, perhaps for a minute
or two. (*Entering garden.*) Actually, I'm so glad you asked
me because to tell you the truth I'm in a bit of a state,
you see – something's on my mind that I really need to –
well, to unburden. That's really why I took a little detour
– in the hope that you were briefly – um, available – so I
could do my duty in Lower Mudge in a fitting – fitting –
slightly more fitting – well, unburdened anyway. Unless,
of course, you'd rather I didn't –

LOUISE: No, no, Ronnie. You must tell us. If it'll help.

HARRY: Yes, Ronnie, fire away.

RONNIE: It'll probably strike you as awfully trivial –
(*Stops.*)

LOUISE: (*Helpfully*) Is it something to do with Hildegard?

RONNIE: Hildegard?

HARRY: Isn't that your wife's – um – ?

RONNIE: Oh, Wilemena, you mean – no, no, not Wilemena.
Though actually she's been very – um, active recently,
phoning a lot with some rather strange – obscene
propositions – yes, that's what they are, obscene
propositions – but – but no, it wasn't her at all. (*Little
pause.*) It's Mrs Mossop.

HARRY: Mrs Mossop?

LOUISE: Oh, your housekeeper – isn't she? But I thought you
    had a wonderful relationship.

RONNIE: Yes – yes, we have. That's just it, you see. I
    wouldn't hurt her for the world – yet that's just what I've
    done – hurt her. Hurt her most grievously.

LOUISE: Why, what did you do?

RONNIE: It isn't what I did, it's what she thinks I did. She
    thinks that in my sermon this morning I – I denounced
    her from the pulpit in front of the whole congregation –
    well, the whole congregation, there were only the usual
    dozen or so – but of course they all know Mrs Mossop,
    have known her for years – so from her point of view, her
    thinking that I was attacking her personally – *personally* –
    from the pulpit of all places – (*Stops, stricken.*)

HARRY: (*At last interested*) Well, what did she think you were
    attacking her about?

RONNIE: About being a bigot. You see, my sermon was on
    racial prejudice – rather effective for once, I thought – in
    fact so effective that after the service I went for a long
    walk and considered – yes, actually considered – making a
    paper out of it. Isn't that an irony? Because when I got
    back, there she was, my poor, dear Mrs Mossop, in the
    kitchen in floods of tears trying to make my Sunday
    lunch. Roast beef. And she said, 'Oh, Reverend, how
    could you do that to me? – Oh, Reverend!'

HARRY: But why did she think it was her?

LOUISE: Yes, why?

RONNIE: Because the other day, apparently, I'd reprimanded
    her for something she happened to say about a Jewish
    family her nephew works for in Axminster. In their cheese
    shop. I'm sure I did it very gently – at least I hope I did
    – because the truth is I'd completely forgotten – and still
    don't remember very clearly. There's so much prejudice in
    a small community like ours that it becomes almost
    routine to try to check it – in fact, that's why I decided to

give my sermon, because it suddenly struck me that it was
so routine that we'd all stopped taking it seriously, unless
I made some kind of issue – Christian issue –

HARRY: (*Losing interest*) Well, I'm sure she's over it by now.

RONNIE: No, no, she isn't. We had this dreadful conversation,
you see, quite dreadful. Nothing I said could persuade her
that it was all an unfortunate – unfortunate coincidence,
really – and that the last thing I intended – but she didn't
believe me, she was still crying and going on about how
she couldn't face anyone in the village again – and – and
in the end I couldn't cope, I'm afraid. I just gave up, said
I had to get to Lower Mudge – and remembered I'd heard
you were here – what do you think I should say to her to
put it right? Have you any suggestions? Anything?

HARRY: Well, Ronnie, firstly I think –

(SAM DRAYCOTT *appears at the gate.*)

DRAYCOTT: Oh, here you are at last!

HARRY: (*Momentarily appalled*) Sam, what are you doing here?

DRAYCOTT: Come to see you, of course. (*Entering.*) Had a bit
of trouble as nobody in the bloody village seems to have
heard of any Pertwees. I suppose because you're only
weekenders. (*He is obviously in a state of controlled tension.*)
I've driven all the way down from London –

HARRY: But why? We're meant to be having lunch next week.

DRAYCOTT: Because this is urgent. I want you to find me a
new publisher, Harry. This isn't just the best thing I've
ever done, we both know it's that, but it's by far the most
commercial thing.

HARRY: Yes, I know. I was just re-reading – (*Gestures to
typescript.*)

DRAYCOTT: Thirty thousand isn't good enough. Not for *Fuck
All*. I want sixty thousand for it.

HARRY: (*Stares at him in disbelief*) Well, that's quite a jump, Sam –

DRAYCOTT: It isn't only a question of money, bloody hell, you
know that better than anyone, Harry. People get to hear

25

about the advance, it even gets into the newspapers. *Fuck All* is a major achievement. I want recognition for it. It's time I was up there with the big names. I'm sick to death of hearing and reading about the kind of money dished out to little buggers like Julian Belp and Roger Rigg – and that bitch, Lucinda Darkon. Well, now my time has come, Harry. That's what I've come down to say. My time has come. (*He is shaking, every so often slapping the side of his neck.*)

HARRY: Look, let's just calm down, Sam – and I'll – um – I'm sure we could all do with a drink, I'll go in and get a bottle of wine.

LOUISE: I'll get it, darling.

HARRY: (*Hurrying into house*) No, I will.
(*There is a pause.*
HARRY, *meanwhile, has paused in the kitchen, then sits down in chair in some ferment.*)

LOUISE: I'm Louise, Harry's wife. (*Goes to* DRAYCOTT, *holding out hand.*)

DRAYCOTT: How do you do?

LOUISE: I'm so looking forward to reading *Fuck All* – Harry's been speaking so highly of it – oh, and this is Ronald Chambers, our vicar – Ronnie, this is Sam Draycott, one of Harry's most distinguished clients.

RONNIE: How do you do? (*Shaking his hand.*) Such an honour to meet a living author –

DRAYCOTT: You've met some dead ones, have you?

RONNIE: (*Laughs nervously*) No, no, how silly of me – I only meant – what I mean is down here one doesn't have a chance to meet actual writers – the people who do the creating – oh, apart from Louise, of course.

LOUISE: (*Hurriedly*) Oh, I don't count. I've never been published and I don't expect I ever will be, I just do it as a hobby – really.

RONNIE: Oh, I'm sure that one day you'll produce the most

wonderful – the most wonderful – (*then to* DRAYCOTT)
actually, I've just started building up a parish library so
I'm on the look-out for any interesting – and I gather
you've just finished a new one?

DRAYCOTT: It's called *Fuck All*.

RONNIE: Yes, I heard – I hope you don't mind, I couldn't
help it –

DRAYCOTT: So I doubt if it would fit into your parish library,
would it?

RONNIE: Oh, I don't know – some of the folk around here are
quite fearless readers, old Mrs Durrant, for instance, she
actually enjoyed the Old Testament, said it made her
laugh aloud – and I'd make sure it didn't get into the
wrong hands, of course.

DRAYCOTT: The wrong hands – oh, censor it, so to speak.

RONNIE: Well, no, not exactly censor – but only recommend it
to – to people who care for that sort of thing.

DRAYCOTT: What sort of thing?

RONNIE: Well, like your novel. *Fuck All*.

DRAYCOTT: What do you think it's like, my novel?

RONNIE: Well, I'm assuming – given its title – that it's pretty
strong meat.

DRAYCOTT: And you wouldn't want strong meat to go down
the wrong throats, eh?

RONNIE: Well, I wouldn't want anyone who might be upset by
it to – well, to be upset by it.

DRAYCOTT: You don't believe in people being upset by art
then?

RONNIE: Not if they don't want to be. I mean, some people
like being upset, and I'd press it on them, of course, and
some people aren't really upset by anything, are they? So
I'd press it on them.

DRAYCOTT: Press it on them? Like a leech, you mean, to draw
blood? One of your old country customs, is it?

LOUISE: (*Looks from one to the other*) Oh, I'd better go and find

27

out whether Harry's found the wine – I put it in the cellar and forgot to tell him – (*Hurrying off.*)

RONNIE: I do hope I haven't given you offence.

DRAYCOTT: Yes, I expect you're against that too, eh?

RONNIE: Well, yes. As a matter of fact I am.

DRAYCOTT: Yes, you would be, wouldn't you?

(RONNIE *makes to say something, gives up.*
Meanwhile in the house, LOUISE *has stopped to draw breath,*
pull herself together, etc., then goes into kitchen.)

LOUISE: What are you doing? Where's the wine?

HARRY: What, darling? (*Recollecting himself.*) Oh. I was just trying to sort out what's the best thing to do about Sam – leaving his present publishers is about his worst possible move –

LOUISE: But darling, we can't leave Ronnie out there alone with him. He's being so offensive – is he drunk, do you think? (*Taking wine out of fridge.*)

HARRY: No, I wish he were. He's quite sweet when he's drunk. But sixty thousand – sixty thousand – how can I possibly ask for sixty thousand for *Fuck All*? Because that's what it is. No, it isn't – (*As if talking to himself*) but there's not a publishing house in London that would even consider –

LOUISE: You *must* go back out, darling. It's not fair on Ronnie.

HARRY: Bugger Ronnie! Can't you see this is a crisis, for God's sake? I need a moment to think. To think. Is that too much to ask? I thought I'd done my stint with aspiring geniuses for the day – (*Stops.*)

LOUISE: Do you mean me?

HARRY: Well frankly, darling, one of the reasons I like coming down here is to get away from writers and their perpetual needs – and I find myself having to cope with first you, and then him –

LOUISE: (*Barely able to speak*) To hell with you. (*Slams bottle*

28

on table. She turns, goes through passage into sitting room, sits down on chair.)

RONNIE: (*Abruptly, he is shaking*) I simply don't understand.

DRAYCOTT: What don't you understand?

RONNIE: How you can be so purposelessly rude. There's enough rudeness in the world, cruelty, people do such things to each other – often they think they've got a reason – they feel something – something – powerful – or drink – who knows, who knows where it comes from, the why of it, but you – you had no reason – you just see a chap – a vicar – and you think, why not have a bit of fun, sneer at him – to – to do what? Why? Does it make you feel better? Bigger? Stronger? A more important writer, and I'm just a vicar – no consequence – a joke, feeble, polite – eh? Is that it?

DRAYCOTT: Look, I drove all the way down here to have an extremely important conversation with my agent about changing publishers – and I end up having an absolutely asinine conversation with you about how *you're* going to decide which of your bloody parishioners you'll allow to read my novels, how do you expect me to feel? (*Slapping the back of his neck.*) These bloody things, what are they?

RONNIE: Oh, it's a kind of midge, I think.

DRAYCOTT: Why the hell don't they go for anyone else?

RONNIE: Oh, I expect they do, but there's been such a plague of them this summer that we don't notice them any more. Or they don't notice us, eh? (*Gives a little laugh which* DRAYCOTT *ignores. After a little pause.*) Look, I'm afraid I didn't quite understand how – how strongly you'd feel – as far as I'm concerned anybody can read your books. Anybody who wants to, that is.

HARRY: (*Crosses to sitting room*) Darling, I'm sorry, so sorry. I don't know what came over me. I didn't mean a word I said. Not about you, anyway. I love you. And I love it that you write. Perhaps I'm a little envious, eh? Or jealous, even? That you have something that takes you away from me so completely. So often.

LOUISE: No, you're right. You should be able to come down here and be completely safe from the likes of me. I should really give it up – yes, I must! I can't bear to think of it coming between us.

HARRY: Don't you dare! I'm longing for the day when I'm *your* agent. And then I'll have you to myself twice, won't I?

LOUISE: Is that true?

HARRY: (*Seriously*) Absolutely true, you'll be my wife and my author, my Louise twice over. (*Takes her in his arms.*)

LOUISE: I don't care about being your author, just your wife, your Louise will do – oh, my Harry!
(*They kiss.*)
Oh, my darling! We'd better go back out. Oh, the wine!

HARRY: To hell with the wine! Let's just get rid of them as quickly as possible. (*Grabs her, kisses her again.*)

RONNIE: Is it any good my trying again?

DRAYCOTT: To do what?

RONNIE: To apologize.

DRAYCOTT: Not really, as I don't want you to. I'd just like silence until I can conclude my conversation with Harry, and be on my way. All right?
(RONNIE *nods, makes to sit down, then suddenly hurls himself across at* DRAYCOTT, *seizes him by the lapels, shakes him about.*)

DRAYCOTT: (*Incredulously, half-laughing*) What the – what the hell! (*Struggles with* RONNIE, *overpowers him easily, getting him into a half-Nelson as* RONNIE *continues to flail feebly.* LOUISE *and* HARRY *step outside.*)

HARRY: (*Stands staring as* DRAYCOTT, RONNIE *struggle*) Good God! (*He hurries across garden.*) Get your hands off him – for God's sake, Sam – leave him! (*Pulls at* DRAYCOTT.) What the hell do you think you're doing?

(LOUISE *stands watching, shocked.*)

DRAYCOTT: Me doing – he – he – he attacked me!

(RONNIE *has partly collapsed, drags himself to chair.*)

HARRY: Are you all right?

RONNIE: (*Nods*) My – my fault – I – I –

(HARRY *turns, looks at* DRAYCOTT.)

LOUISE: (*Runs down*) How dare you! How dare you! You – you contemptible bully! (*Slaps* DRAYCOTT.)

(*There is a moment of shocked silence.*)

HARRY: Yes, I think you'd better clear off, Sam. You had no bloody business coming down here and muscling in on our Sunday anyway, and there'll be no need for you to do it again, you can find a new agent to find your new publisher for you, (*Slaps typescript into his hand*) and I'll give you my last bit of professional advice, you haven't a hope in hell of getting sixty thousand for your book, your publishers wouldn't have come through with the thirty thousand in the end anyway, because frankly, Sam, the book's OK now that I've got you to cut and rewrite large parts of it, it'll get by, no more than that! (*Opens gate for him.*)

(*Pause.*)

DRAYCOTT: And I thought – I thought you were meant to be good with writers. (*Turns, goes through gate.*) And you – (*To* RONNIE) you're just a little shit! A little shit in a dog collar! (*Slams gate.*)

(*There is a pause.*)

LOUISE: How are you feeling?

RONNIE: Better. Better thank you – thank you so much, both of – both of – I'm terribly sorry – it really was all – all my fault.

LOUISE: Nonsense, Ronnie. I heard the way he was talking to you.

HARRY: Yes. He was obviously provoking you.

RONNIE: Yes, but he was an important client of yours, I could tell, and he's quite right – in a way – a shit in a dog collar – I mean, I mean, how can I speak of all the things I'm meant to speak of – if I can't myself – the Lord knows, my influence is feeble enough but if I can't restrain myself – and it wasn't anything to do with him really – I was already in such a state – because of Mrs Mossop – so I had no patience, no tolerance – couldn't bear to have him speak to me like that. Vanity. Vanity and self, yes. Self, you see, self, self, self. So yes, my fault. Yes. Yes. A little shit in a dog collar. I'm deeply sorry. Sorry.

LOUISE: Oh, poor Ronnie. Nobody could be less like a little shit – and you've got absolutely nothing – nothing – to be sorry about! Darling – (*To* HARRY) do let's have a glass of wine to cheer Ronnie up with.

HARRY: (*After a fractional pause*) Yes, of course. (*To* RONNIE) Would you like a glass of wine?

RONNIE: Yes, I'd love – oh, what's the time – oh, good God, Lower Mudge! I can't go looking like this, even in Lower Mudge, as if I've been in a brawl, which I have, got to get back and change – oh, I hope – I do hope Mrs Mossop's not waiting for me – or that she's recovered a bit at least. And we haven't even had a proper talk – and I expect you're off tomorrow as usual – and I've been so looking forward – it's been months – and how is everyone? Old Ben?

LOUISE: He's fine, Ronnie.

RONNIE: And Nigel and Natalie?

HARRY: They're fine too.

RONNIE: Well, please give them all my – my – (*Hurries towards gate*) my – (*Stops, turns at the gate.*) I'll write you all my other news, did you get my last letter before you left?

LOUISE: Yes, we did, Ronnie. We did so enjoy it as usual.

RONNIE: Good, good. Well – goodbye – goodbye. (*Hurries out.*)

HARRY: What letter?

LOUISE: He writes to us. Once every three weeks, about. They go on for pages and pages and they're full of parish gossip and even excerpts from his sermons. So I've spared you. As a good wife should. The awful truth is that I haven't even bothered to open the last two or three, so I've been sparing myself. Self, self, self, you see. (*Laughs but is clearly upset.*) Oh, Harry – Harry, I haven't hit anyone – never – not since I was a child. I don't understand it, I didn't even know I was going to do it until I'd done it. I'm so ashamed.

HARRY: (*After a little pause*) You needn't be, darling. If ever anyone deserved it, he did.

LOUISE: But people can't go around hitting people just because they deserve it. Otherwise we'd be hitting people all the time. And they'd be hitting us. (*After a little pause.*) But I suppose it's quite serious for you, isn't it, losing a client like Sam Draycott? And you wouldn't have thrown him out if I hadn't hit him, you'd have found some way of patching it all up, I know you would. How serious is it?

HARRY: Not serious at all, darling. I'll still get my ten per cent of whatever I finally get for *Fuck All*. And I won't have to see him while I'm doing it. How's that for a bargain? On top of which, my giving him the chuck for brawling with the vicar will enhance my professional reputation for rectitude. So you see, my love, I emerge a clear winner – and what's more, I thought you were magnificent. Absolutely magnificent.

LOUISE: (*Smiling*) Did you really?

HARRY: And sexy with it. (*Goes to her.*)

LOUISE: And I thought you were terrific. So – so commanding. And sexy with it.

HARRY: (*Taking her hands*) Well then, why don't we get back to doing what we were doing before we were interrupted?

LOUISE: Yes. But first – (*Claps her hands and dances away from him backwards.* HARRY *laughs, claps his hands, dances*

33

*backwards. They begin to hum, clap, dancing in a stately
minuet, coming towards each other slowly.
The telephone rings.*)

HARRY: Oh, damn! That'll be Daddy, he said he'd ring about
now. (*Runs to kitchen.*)

(LOUISE *remains in garden, taking a few dance steps by
herself as:*)

HARRY: (*On phone*) Hello? Yes, hello, Daddy, everything all
right? Good. Yes, we are, thanks, very much – where are
they, by the way? Oh, well don't let them watch too
much, they know the rules, an hour an evening – what?
Oh, yes, that's right, two hours at weekends. Well, give
them our love, Louise sends hers to you – what? I'll tell
her – (*Shouting to* LOUISE) his compliments to the chef.
The fish concoction was especially scrumptious.

LOUISE: (*Still dancing to herself*) Oh, good. (*Suddenly realizing.*)
The fish! But that was for Ophelia. It had worm powder
in it! (*Comes towards kitchen.*)

HARRY: (*On phone*) Daddy – Daddy, listen carefully but don't
panic. That fish had worm powder in it so you'd better
call the doctor – it isn't funny, Daddy! Listen to me!
What? (*To* LOUISE) He says it was just a joke. Nigel's and
Natalie's actually. (*On phone.*) Well, thank God, Daddy,
just tell them – no, don't tell them anything – give them
our love, see you tomorrow. Goodbye. (*Hangs up.*)

LOUISE: (*Staring at him, transfixed*) Harry –

HARRY: Darling, what is it? Everything's all right, everything's
fine. Just as I said.

LOUISE: Darling, would you – would you excuse me for a
moment? I've just had the most wonderful idea. I know
exactly – *exactly* how to do it. (*She hurries into sitting room,
sits down at typewriter, begins to type very soberly, carefully.
HARRY walks to the door, stands looking at her. Makes to
speak, then wanders angrily back out, through the kitchen,
into the garden. Suddenly spots stump. Aims a kick at it,*

34

checks himself, remembering consequence of previous kick.
Stands for a second, then hurls himself on to stump, embraces
it, wrestling with it in fury.)
HARRY: Come on then, you shit, come on, I'll do you – I'll do
    you this time – I will – I bloody will –
    (LOUISE *is still typing very seriously.*)
    (*Lights and Curtain.*)

SCENE 3

Four years later. Mid-morning. In the sitting room, Louise's
typewriter, typescript piled beside it. There are additional bits of
furniture. In the kitchen various smart items added.
In the garden a few more pieces of light garden furniture – i.e. deck
chairs, etc. The tree stump has been sawed level, and a round piece of
wood attached to it, to make it into a table, on which coffee cups, etc.,
evidence of breakfast, newspapers scattered around.
NIGEL, *about sixteen, is on the swing, reading a book.* NATALIE *is*
sketching him. Suddenly, NIGEL *stands up on the swing and*
swings to and fro.

NATALIE: Stop it, you bugger, I'm trying to draw you. Christ,
    I'm bored already. What are we going to do for the rest of
    the day?
NIGEL: I'm going with Grandad on one of his walks.
NATALIE: How exciting.
NIGEL: Well, actually it is, because do you know what he's
    started doing? Those sugar lumps he takes in case we
    come across a field of horses – what he really does with
    them is drop them into the petrol tanks of threshers,
    tractors – any machine he thinks is helping ruin the
    countryside.
NATALIE: Sugar lumps? Why sugar lumps? What do they do?
NIGEL: Well, they bugger up the petrol, of course. And choke
    the engine.

NATALIE: And you let him?

NIGEL: How can I stop him?

NATALIE: Well then, why do you go with him?

NIGEL: To look after him of course. And if he's caught I can explain that he's – you know – (*Taps his forehead.*)

NATALIE: Yes, I suppose he is, isn't he? Poor old Grandad. God, if only we could get a television set down here at least.

(NIGEL *screams.*)

NATALIE: What?

NIGEL: You know who gets back today, the Reverend Ronald Droopy-bum. I'll have to hear all about his travels through China – with long discussions about Communism and faith and – oh God, God.

NATALIE: Why do we call him Droopy-bum?

NIGEL: Because it seemed funny when you thought it up ten years ago or whenever it was. Very childish. We really ought to show him more respect.

NATALIE: Yes, it's horrid, isn't it? What about – (*Thinks*) the Very Reverend Ronald Dribble-Cock?

NIGEL: Yuck.

NATALIE: Oh God, oh God – listen – I *knew* they'd play it, I love it! (*Running to transistor, turns it up.*)
(*During this,* LOUISE *has entered sitting room, taken off her straw hat which she tosses aside. Stands for a moment listening, then forces herself to the desk and begins to work.*)

NIGEL: Hey, be careful! She may hear it.

NATALIE: Frankly, my dear, I don't give a damn.

NIGEL: Turn it down!

(NATALIE, *ignoring him, begins to move to the music, cigarette hanging from her lips.*)

NIGEL: Turn it down! (*Quietly but severely.*)

(NATALIE *looks at him, turns down transistor, continues to dance. The doorbell goes.*

LOUISE, *during this, has lifted her head as if hearing
something, but goes back to her typing.
The doorbell goes again, unheard by* NIGEL, *who has gone
back to reading, and* NATALIE, *still dancing.*
LOUISE *stops, and exits.*)

LOUISE: (*Offstage*) Oh, hello.

NAOMI: (*Offstage*) Hello, I'm Naomi. From the office. For Mr
Pertwee.

LOUISE: (*Offstage*) Oh – oh, really? (*Pause.*) Well then, please
come in –
(LOUISE *re-enters sitting room, followed by* NAOMI, *who is
carrying an electric typewriter and a briefcase.*)
– to tell you the truth, I had no idea that my husband had
someone coming down today or I would have cleared my desk
– here – (*Picking up her typescript*) have to be careful that
they're in the right order – I never number the pages until
I've finished a draft – Harry says that's very silly of me but
really it's a superstition and as important as any religious –
there you are! Now I'll go and work in the kitchen.
(NAOMI *puts her typewriter down in Louise's place. She is
rather gauche, flustered.*)

LOUISE: You did say Melanie, didn't you?

NAOMI: No, Naomi. Naomi Hutchins.

LOUISE: Oh, yes, aren't you the girl that went off to get
married, Harry said was irreplaceable?

NAOMI: Well, no, that was Angela.

LOUISE: Oh, so you're Angela's replacement?

NAOMI: Well no, Angela's replacement is Debbie, she was
going to come down today but her mother was taken ill –
so I'm replacing her, really. I've never worked for Mr
Pertwee before but – but she told me everything I had to
do so I – is there a plug, by the way?

LOUISE: A plug?

NAOMI: I mean a – a socket. For the plug. For the typewriter.
It's an electric –

37

LOUISE: Is it? Oh I see. Well, here's one, it's the nearest – here – (*Getting on her hands and knees.*) I'll take the lamp out – (*Takes lamp plug out, while* NAOMI *looks increasingly desperate.*) Now if you give me the plug – (*Holding up her hand.*) The plug.

NAOMI: Oh, damn.

LOUISE: What?

NAOMI: I've – I've – I forgot it. It comes separately, you see, and I just – just picked up the typewriter without thinking.

LOUISE: So what will you do then?

(*There is a pause.*)

NAOMI: Can I borrow that one? (*Indicates Louise's typewriter.*)

LOUISE: (*Fights a brief battle with herself*) Oh, it's rather old-fashioned, I'm afraid, but it's the only one I've ever had down here – actually it's rather personal – like a fountain pen really. I've written great chunks of all my novels on it, you see.

NAOMI: (*Obviously relieved*) Oh, I don't mind honestly, I've done lots of work on machines just as old as that.

LOUISE: Well then – (*Gets it, puts it on the table*) there you are. Is there anything else? (*Controlling crossness.*)

NAOMI: No, I'm ready as soon as Mr Pertwee is.

LOUISE: Oh, well he's gone to Honiton to do some shopping – he'll be back any moment –

NAOMI: Well, there are one or two things Debbie gave me to type up – I'll get on with those. (*Opening briefcase.*)

LOUISE: Right. Well, I'll leave you then.

(*She goes to door, left, turns and glances in pain as* NAOMI *sits down at her table, lifts lid off Louise's typewriter, opens briefcase, puts sheet of paper in, takes out document, begins to type.*)

Is it all right?

NAOMI: (*Looks at* LOUISE) It's fine, thanks.

LOUISE: Good. (*Goes into kitchen, stands for a moment dealing with anger, frustration, etc. with the typewriter clacking away on right; music coming from garden, left, where* NATALIE *is dancing sexily around and over* NIGEL.

NIGEL *suddenly turns the transistor off*.)

NATALIE: (*Turns, looks at him*) Bloody hell!

NIGEL: (*Almost as if bewildered himself*) Sorry. Sorry, Nat. It was – was – my head. Doing one of its things. Or something.

NATALIE: Probably because I'm so sexy. (*Putting transistor back on, low*.)

NIGEL: (*Grins*) Yes, you are, aren't you? In your way.

NATALIE: Do you remember that time she caught us messing about in the bath and she said, 'Now Nigel, little boys really shouldn't put their fingers up little girls' wee-wees and Nat darling –'

LOUISE: (*Goes on to porch, attempting calm manner, smiles with warm reproof*) Natalie darling, you're not actually smoking, are you? And with the transistor on.
(*There is a pause*.)

NATALIE: (*Putting out cigarette*) Sorry, Mummy. (*Turns transistor off*.) It was so low we didn't think anybody could hear it.

LOUISE: It was right underneath my concentration, you see. Banging away. Like a headache. And anyway, we come here to get away from all that – pop and London and fashionable noises – we all had an agreement that we wouldn't – but *why* are you smoking? Apart from your health you know what'll happen to you at school if they catch you – Nigel, have you been?

NIGEL: Yes, Mummy. 'Fraid I have.

LOUISE: Oh, it's so depressing, so depressing –
(NATALIE *has shot* NIGEL *a grateful glance*.)
– you know that Daddy and I would never dream of issuing prohibitions and orders, there's just been an agreement between us all, that's how we work as a family,

39

through agreements, Daddy gave up smoking – not that
he ever smoked much – but he couldn't bear the thought
that he could be responsible for your taking it up –

NATALIE: Sorry, Mummy. You take them.

LOUISE: (*Makes to take them, resists*) No, I can't do that.
They're yours. Bought out of your pocket money.

NATALIE: But I want you to take them, really I do. I don't
want to smoke.

NIGEL: Yes, take them for *our* sake, Mummy. Please. (*Taking
package from* NATALIE *and passing it to* LOUISE.)

LOUISE: All right. I will. If that's what you really want. But if
you want them back –

NIGEL: We'll just ask – fair enough?
(NATALIE *grimaces*.)

LOUISE: Fair enough. (*Takes cigarettes, looks into package.*)
There aren't any.

NIGEL: No, but it'll be a symbol, Mums. Keep it as a symbol.

NATALIE: (*Getting up*) And I'll do a drawing now, shall I? Of
that oak by the river. (*Picks up sketch pad, pencils,
transistor.*)

LOUISE: A good idea, darling, it's the only way, practise,
practise, practise – especially these days when the
competition for art schools – but why are you taking that
with you? (*Indicating transistor.*) You're not going to play
it out on the river –

NATALIE: No, no, of course not, Mums – I'll leave it here –
(*Bangs transistor down, runs angrily off towards the gate.*)
(*There is a pause, as* LOUISE *stares after* NATALIE.)

LOUISE: Why did she do that? We're not against her playing
anything she wants to listen to, even pop – after all, we
gave it to her, it was our birthday present – it's only down
here we objected to. And she agreed. Because of other
people –

NIGEL: (*Fiddles with the controls, switches it on, lets it play a
second*) There you are, plays perfectly. (*Switches it off.*)

You know, Mums, you really shouldn't worry about everthing so much.

LOUISE: I know, I know. I wish I didn't, too. (*Smiles at* NIGEL.) But I bet – I bet anything you like –

NIGEL: What, Mums?

LOUISE: That you didn't smoke a single half of a fraction of a cigarette, did you?

NIGEL: (*After a little pause*) But if people just let people do and be what they want –

LOUISE: But if you love them –

NIGEL: Well, that's why you have to let them, I suppose. I mean, if you don't everybody just gets more upset and then things get worse, don't they?

LOUISE: You sound just like your father. (*Turns away, upset.*)

NIGEL: I'm sorry, Mums. We're all jolly pleased you worry so much about us – well, love us so much, anyway.

LOUISE: (*Voice trembling*) But you're right. I know you're right, you and Daddy. I don't know why I get so – so – feel so – all the time – just at the moment. (*Stares at* NIGEL *pleadingly*.)

NIGEL: (*Puts his arms around her*) Everything's all right, Mum. Really it is.

(*During this,* NAOMI *has been typing steadily but uneasily.* BEN *enters sitting room. Sees* NAOMI *at typewriter.*)

BEN: Top of the morning, Lou, old girl! (*Goes on into kitchen, singing 'Hey-ho, Hey-ho, it's off to walk we go.'* NAOMI *stares after him, then sits slumped over typewriter.* BEN *comes out into garden, singing.* LOUISE *pulls herself together, separating from* NIGEL.)

BEN: Hey-ho, hey-ho, it's off to walk we go, with a la-la-la and a la-la, la – (*Stops, stares at* LOUISE *in amazement.*) Good God, what are you doing out here, old girl?

LOUISE: What do you mean?

BEN: Well, I saw you at it – inside – just a second ago –

LOUISE: What do you mean 'at it', Ben?

BEN: Well, at your typewriter. Firing away on all cylinders (*Clearly genuinely shaken.*)

LOUISE: No, no, it's just a girl from the office for Harry –

BEN: Oh, well that explains it! (*Relieved.*) Thought for a moment I must have seen a ghost back in there – though I suppose as you're alive you couldn't really have a ghost yet, could you?

NIGEL: How do you know (*Indicating* LOUISE) the one out here isn't the ghost –

LOUISE: (*Laughs*) Oh, stop it. Nigel – I may not feel perfectly real today, but I'm here – it's such a pity we have to have office people down though –

BEN: Especially on a day like this! Have you ever known such a summer, eh? On and on, day after day –

LOUISE: (*Interrupting*) Well, to tell you the truth, Ben, it's beginning to get on my nerves a bit. It's – it's so unEnglish. And all the poor farmers are in despair.

BEN: Oh, don't worry about them, they're always pretending to be in despair, old girl. That's how they get their subsidies to spend on those damn machines for destroying our countryside. Yes, vandals on tractors – and they dare to moan about the rest of us having a lovely summer – I'll tell you what I'd like to do to them – get every farmer in the neighbourhood into the church hall and then blow them across the landscape, so you'd find a head or a foot in every ditch, that'd start the birds singing again! Eh, old girl?

LOUISE: (*Clearly bored*) Oh, Ben, I do wish you'd stop going on about the farmers. They've got a living to make after all, and they're always perfectly nice to us.

BEN: Perfectly nice? Like that old brute, Tomalin, you mean, Lou? Who actually set a bull – yes, a mad bull on our Nig and our Nat –

LOUISE: Oh, for heaven's sake, Ben, that was years and years ago – and besides, they were in the garden all the time. Perfectly safe.

BEN: But he didn't care whether they were safe or not, did
   he, Lou? Oh, he's one I'd like to get, eh, Nig? Old
   Tomalin!

NIGEL: (*Hurriedly*) Yes, well, um – let's get going, shall we,
   Grandad?

LOUISE: But you'll be back in time for lunch, won't you?

BEN: It's already half-eleven, Lou. Don't worry, we'll pass by
   way of the Yeoman for cottage pie, and a tankard of – of
   good brown Coca-Cola, eh, Nig? Hey – don't forget the
   horses.

LOUISE: Horses? What horses?

NIGEL: Sugar lumps for the horses. I'll get them, Grandad.

LOUISE: And get a hat, darling. You know what the heat does
   to your head

NIGEL: Yes, Mums (*Goes into kitchen.*)

LOUISE: I do hope you're careful when you give them sugar.
   Horses bite sometimes, you know.

BEN: Not the ones we bump into, Lou. We know how to deal
   with them, they never bite. (*Laughs.*) How's it coming
   along, Lou? The new novel.

LOUISE: What? (*Suddenly spots one of Natalie's cigarette ends.*)
   Oh, I do wish she wouldn't do that – (*Picking it up,
   looking for others*) with her damn cigarettes. (*Proceeds to go
   around garden looking for cigarette ends.*

   BEN *stares at her for a second, then sits on swing, begins to
   swing.*

   NIGEL, *meanwhile, has taken sugar lumps from bowl, put
   them into his pocket. Finds a hat.*

   NAOMI, *who has been sitting over typewriter with her head in
   her hands, gets up, takes out packet of cigarettes, lights one,
   inhales deeply, begins to walk agitatedly up and down.*

   As NIGEL *comes out of kitchen,* NAOMI *hears him at last
   moment, looks desperately around for ashtray, puts cigarette
   behind her, sits down.*)

NIGEL: (*Enters, carrying hat*) Oh, hello.

43

NAOMI: Hello. (*Relieved.*)

NIGEL: Do you mind if I just look for another hat –

NAOMI: Of course.

NIGEL: I think my sister had it last – oh no, there it is, must have been Mummy – (*Picks hat up.*) There we are. I'm Nigel, by the way, Nigel Pertwee.

NAOMI: I'm your Dad's secretary. Temporary, that is. Naomi Hutchins.

NIGEL: Is there anything I can get you, Miss Hutchins?

NAOMI: No, thanks – oh, well, if there's an ashtray?

NIGEL: Um, well – (*goes to Toby jug on mantelpiece*) what my sister does is she spits into this and then just drops them in – if you follow.

NAOMI: Thanks. (*Gratefully.*)

NIGEL: Well – um. (*Goes out.*)

LOUISE: (*Who has been irritably conscious of Ben's swinging, is suddenly unable to stop herself*) Oh, do be careful on that swing, Ben. You're much heavier than the children and I'm sure it's weakening the rope.

NIGEL: (*Comes out into garden, carrying hats*) There you are, Grandad. (*Handing him hat.*)

LOUISE: What, no, no, I meant for you, darling –

NIGEL: I've got one, Mummy. (*Putting other hat on his head.*) Come on then, Grandad, hey-ho, hey-ho, it's off to walk we go, with a tra-la-la, and a tra-la-la, hey-ho, hey-ho, hey-ho –

(NIGEL *and* BEN *march down the garden, singing.* LOUISE *stares after them, calls out.*)

LOUISE: Please be back in time for tea – or I shall worry! (*After a little pause, as their voices recede, looks down at butts in her hand, makes to go to kitchen, looks towards sitting room, exasperated, throws butts into the bushes, goes to sit on swing with back to audience as:*
NAOMI *spits into Toby jug, drops cigarette in.*
HARRY *enters sitting room, his arms full of shopping.*)

HARRY: Hello, darling, going well? I'll just put these in the kitchen.
(*He goes past* NAOMI, *then stops, turns around, stares at her.* NAOMI *looks towards him apprehensively.*)

HARRY: Oh, my God! (*Then, in a frantic whisper.*) What the hell are you doing here?

NAOMI: It's all right, I'm replacing Debbie. Her mother's been taken ill suddenly and she's gone to spend the weekend –

HARRY: Debbie's mother lives in Australia.

NAOMI: No, I mean that's what I told your wife. You're angry with me, then. (*Stares at him.*) I'm sorry, Harry. I *had* to see you. I thought I'd go mad if I didn't. (*Stares at him pleadingly.*)

HARRY: Where's everybody else?

NAOMI: Don't know. They keep coming in and out.

HARRY: Who?

NAOMI: Well, your son and – and – your wife. And her father, I suppose it was.

HARRY: *My* father. So they're all here then!

NAOMI: Do you want me to leave?

HARRY: Yes, yes, you must – no, you mustn't, of course you mustn't, how could I explain – we'll just have to – have to –

NAOMI: I'm sorry, I couldn't help it, when Debbie said she was coming down it seemed like – like a gift, you see – a chance to – to – (*Looks at him yearningly.*)

HARRY: (*Suddenly realizing*) What on earth did you tell Debbie?
(NAOMI *looks at him miserably.*)

NAOMI: She understands, Debbie understands, I made her swear, swear, cross her heart, honestly, I promise!

HARRY: Sssh! Ssssh! They'll hear.
(*There is a pause.*)

NAOMI: (*Bursts out in a whisper*) I don't understand it, any of it, you couldn't keep your hands off me, you even said

45

things, wonderful things, you said you'd never known anything like it, you said it was as if you'd been smitten, smitten by the hand of God, you said every time you looked at me, thought about me even, it made you go all hard –

HARRY: I know, I know, yes, I know, I'm sorry, Debbie – Naomi. Sorry. The thing is it was all true – it really was – as if I'd been smitten by something outside my – myself – but you've seen for yourself why I can't any longer, why I had to stop – my wife, my son, my father – and I have a daughter – Natalie –

NAOMI: And me! You've got me too! Because I'm not going to let you go. I've never loved anyone before in my life. It wasn't just you that was smitten, it happened to me too, but for me it wasn't God. It was you! You can't just do all that to me and then shove me aside, something shameful that never really happened. It did happen! I'm in your life and – and I'm not going to leave it! (*Stares at him, then starts to cry.*)

HARRY: (*Puts shopping down*) Oh, Christ – don't cry, don't cry, please don't cry!

(NAOMI *fumbles in briefcase, takes Kleenex out, wipes eyes, blows nose.*)

Look, they're probably all in the garden – my family – and the vicar too, if I know him – they're bound to come in in a minute, any minute, we can't, we really can't talk now, not like this, listen, my – love – when I get back to London we'll talk properly, I promise, we'll have dinner even. All right? We'll really – really –

NAOMI: (*Snivelling, nods*) I don't want to hurt you, you know. I don't want to hurt you.

HARRY: Of course you don't, of course you don't. I know that. But we'll sort everything out in London, don't you worry.

NAOMI: (*Pulling herself together, with sudden determination*) No, no, we can't go on. We mustn't go on.

46

HARRY: Why?

NAOMI: We've got to stop. For my sake. As well as yours.

HARRY: (*As if not hearing her and seeing her sexually for the first time.*) God, you're so – so – (*Goes over, takes her in his arms.*)

NAOMI: (*Struggles*) Don't!

(HARRY *persists.* NAOMI, *almost in spite of herself, responds. They kiss each other greedily.*)

LOUISE: (*Getting up, walking towards house*) I'm not putting up with it for another second! Not another second! It's my room, my work – (*Stops, subsides, goes back to swing, sits down.*)

HARRY: You see – you see, the hand of God!

NAOMI: (*Shaken*) I've got to go, got to get away.

HARRY: (*Urgently*) I'll see you in London.

(NAOMI *looks at him, picks up her things, goes out.*
HARRY *stands for a moment, then looks around, sees groceries. He picks them up, carries them into kitchen, puts them on the table. Looks towards porch as if to go out, then collapses into kitchen chair.*)

HARRY: Oh God, why do I do it?

LOUISE: (*Gets off swing*) Yes, I will, damn well will! (*Begins to walk angrily towards house.*)

RONNIE: (*Appears at the gate*) Hello, Lou.

(LOUISE *turns around, stares at* RONNIE, *as if not recognizing him.*)

RONNIE: Sorry – did I – did I alarm you?

LOUISE: No, no, I was – expecting Harry, you see. Back with the shopping. (*Goes to him, kisses him.*) How lovely to see you, Ronnie. (*Still rather absent.*) Um – well, how are you?

RONNIE: Very well. Very well indeed.

LOUISE: Oh, good. Good. Yes, you look – (*Gestures*) splendid.

RONNIE: And how are you?

LOUISE: Oh, fine, thanks. Well, actually (*Laughs*) I'd just worked myself up into having a scene with Harry's little secretary – she's rather taken over the sitting room – and my – my – actually dreadfully trivial of me – I can't bear the thought of her using my typewriter and thinking I can hear it is driving me – (*Gestures.*) So your turning up at the right moment has probably saved me weeks of embarrassment.

RONNIE: Well, that's the first time I've been able to see myself as – as in any way providential. Actually I've only popped over briefly, to welcome myself back, so to speak, and to let old Nigel know I hadn't forgotten our date – I promised him the first thing I'd do when I got back was to show him that little church in Lower Midgley – and the graveyard, they say Thomas Hardy once actually wrote a poem there.

LOUISE: Oh well, he's gone for a walk with Ben.

RONNIE: What, in this heat? Is that a good idea? What with Nigel's headaches.

LOUISE: Really, Ronnie, I think as his mother I know what's best. And I made him take a hat, of course.

RONNIE: Yes, yes – sorry, Lou, none of my – none of my – it's just that now I'm back I was so looking forward to one of our little expeditions, Nigel's and mine and – and –

LOUISE: No, my fault for snapping – anyway, it's wonderful you're back. And how was – (*Thinking desperately*) Japan?

RONNIE: Um, actually it was China. Though as a matter of fact I didn't quite make it all the way to China, either.

LOUISE: Oh. Well, where did you go?

RONNIE: Well, um, just a few miles down the coast, as a matter of fact, a little place called Bidscombe. Have you ever been there? (LOUISE *shakes her head.*) Oh, well, charming, very charming. You see, I rather stupidly told Wilemena my plans – she'd phoned me up a week before I was due to leave for Hong Kong and I was so excited that I just blabbed it out without thinking of the consequences, and so she – suddenly insisted that she

48

would come too – I got the hospital to veto that of course,
but they did say she was up to a little holiday on the coast
so I had to scrap China. And book Bidscombe instead.

LOUISE: Oh, what a pity. But at least with this wonderful
weather –

RONNIE: Yes. Oh yes. Lovely. It was all quite um – (*Lets out
a sudden whinny of laughter*) sorry, Louise! (*Then laughs
again.*) It was a nightmare, actually, an absolute
nightmare! You see, it turned out that what poor
Wilemena had in mind was a second honeymon. And so
first we spent a day in London buying a rather –
(*Gestures.*) She knew about these special shops – she'd cut
out advertisements from some – magazines, I must find
out how she got hold of them – as they have such an
inflammatory effect on her imagination – and you can
imagine some of the – hideously embarrassing. I was
terrified I'd be glimpsed by one of my parishioners –
coming out of one of those shops accompanied by a rather
eccentric trollope – well, that's what she looked like, as
she'd had her hair hennaed. It was such a relief to get her
to Bidscombe, into the hotel – behind locked doors, so to
speak. Though on the other hand the intimacy – she
spent most of the first day parading around in those
undergarments – and trying to make the implements
work. Fortunately she didn't realize that they required
batteries – and I didn't tell her – but in the end I
managed to get hold of one of her doctors, one of the
more sensible ones, who sent some pills down on the train
– so from then on it was really comparatively calm –
except once or twice, but the manageress was really
remarkably understanding. It turned out her own
daughter had been a manic-depressive, thank God.

LOUISE: Oh Ronnie, how dreadful for you. I'm so sorry. So
sorry.

RONNIE: Anyway, anyway, here I am, back to sanity again,

back with my dear old Mrs Mossop again – and back in
this garden again. (*Looks around garden, drinking it in.*)

LOUISE: (*Absently, almost automatically*) Yes, yes, you've kept it
up beautifully, Ronnie. We've hardly had to touch it
while you've been away.

RONNIE: Heavens, I love it, Lou! I've always loved it, but
just before I left something – something rather special
happened in it – the memory of it kept me going during
the worst times in – in – Bidscombe. It was evening, you
see, and I was – well, in that corner, over there, where
the hollyhocks are, doing a spot of weeding – (*Points*)
and I stood up – rather too quickly, I suppose,
momentarily a touch dizzy – a touch *something* or
touched *by* something – and the house – the garden –
well, you remember that first afternoon when we all met,
and Nigel and Natalie were hiding all the time, but you
were frightened and thought they'd been trampled to
death by old Tomalin's cattle – and then we suddenly
heard them, their voices, they were laughing – and you
and Harry – I don't think I've ever seen such joy on
human faces – well, that evening I heard it all again.
Seemed to hear it all again, their laughter, and the sun
suddenly – in the twilight – it was suddenly so strong –
and I felt your joy again, and I thought, yes I thought,
there is a spirit. A human spirit, a divine spirit even,
they meet sometimes, by accident, if you're lucky. Or a
touch dizzy. In an English garden.

LOUISE: Thought they were dead? Yes, yes, Ben was just
talking about it. It was a terrible moment, terrible – and
then the children laughing. And our joy and laughter –
just as you said. So we must have been happy! All of us.
Even though everything was so uncertain – but then it
always îs, isn't it? – the future, I mean. But we didn't
mind then – we liked it even, not knowing what was
going to happen next or how things were going to turn

out. When we first started we had nothing – straight out
of university with no money and no plans even. Then
there was Nigel on the way and so much to worry about –
and do you know what we used to do instead – instead of
worrying – ? We used to dance.

RONNIE: Dance? Really? You mean in the halls? Ballroom
dancing?

(HARRY *gets up, goes on to porch to go to garden, stops,
seeing and hearing.*)

LOUISE: No, no, just Harry and me. To each other. It was our
dance – we made it up. For no reason at all really, we'd
suddenly look at each other and break into it – our dance.
And now we've stopped. It's gone out of our lives. All the
dancing and the joy and the laughter. And something –
something else has crept in instead – and Harry keeps
telling me not to worry so much, it's bad for me and bad
for him and bad for everybody. But it isn't worry,
Ronnie, it's worse than that. It's dread. And I don't know
what it is I dread – oh, Ronnie, I'm so frightened! (*Lets
out a sob.*)

(RONNIE *goes to put his arms around her, as* HARRY *turns
away, ashamed and appalled, puts his hand to his face.*)

RONNIE: My poor, poor Louise – I'm sure everything's all
right really –

LOUISE: (*Breaking from him*) Yes, that's what everybody always
says – it's all right really, everything's fine.

(HARRY, *bracing himself, comes out into garden.*)

HARRY: (*Attempting cheerful nonchalance*) Hello, you two.

LOUISE: (*Attempting to pull herself together, with false brightness*)
Oh, hello, darling. When did you get back?

HARRY: A while ago. Very irritating – some secretary was
waiting for me – nobody from the office had bothered to
warn me she was coming of course – and she turned out
to be absolutely useless – I've had to send her packing.
But good to see you again, Ronnie – and now on to your

51

adventures in Japan or have you already been through them together?

RONNIE: (*Evidently flustered*) Yes, yes, Louise will fill you in on everything – um, I'd better get back or Mrs Mossop will be furious with me again – she's trying out a soufflé, her first ever – and I have strict instructions to be on time – (*Going out of garden*) so see you later – tomorrow possibly, eh?

HARRY: What's the matter with him?

LOUISE: Oh, he's a bit upset. He was just telling me all about poor old Wilemena – poor old Ronnie. Quite funny, really, in a hideous kind of way.

HARRY: (*Watching her.*) But he seems to have upset you. You know, for all his virtues, Ronnie should think about the effect it has on other people, dumping his miseries on them.

LOUISE: No, no, it wasn't that. It was just – just that he brought some things back to me – things I'd forgotten.

HARRY: Really? What things, darling?

LOUISE: About us. About when things were different between us.

HARRY: But darling, I don't understand. What sort of things?

LOUISE: I don't know, I don't know. That's the point, you see, I don't know what I mean. It could be anything. (*Looking at him, it suddenly striking her.*) It could be somebody else. Is that it? Is there somebody else? Please tell me. I need to know.

HARRY: (*Incredulously*) Somebody else?

LOUISE: But things do go wrong between people. Even people who think they love each other. It happens, doesn't it, all the time? We know people in London –

HARRY: (*Interrupting*) People? People in London? People? We're not people, darling, we're us. (*Takes her hands.*) You're my Harry. I'm your Louise. (*Realizes, laughs.*) The other way round of course. (*Gently.*) I'm your Harry and you're my Louise. Till death, remember.

LOUISE: (*Stares into his eyes searchingly*) So everything really is fine, everything really is all right?
(NIGEL *appears at gate. His jeans are badly torn on the right leg and his leg is covered in blood.* BEN *follows him in.* HARRY *and* LOUISE *run to* NIGEL.)

NIGEL: Sorry, Mums, sorry, Daddy.

LOUISE: Oh, my God, oh my darling – what happened, what happened?

BEN: I don't understand – it wasn't even a bull. Just a cow. One of old Tomalin's bloody cows. Just ambled up and gave him a butt – and he fell on something sharp – broken glass, it must have been –

NIGEL: I'm all right, Mummy. I'm all right, Daddy. Honestly. (*Faints.*)
(HARRY *catches him, struggles to lift him up.*)

LOUISE: Oh, my darling, my darling.

BEN: There was this damned tractor, you see – we were just dropping a few sugar cubes in the tank – to immobilize – and then the cow – the cow came up and – he'll be all right, Lou. He'll be all right.

LOUISE: Oh, you bloody old fool. I always knew you'd be the death of someone!
(NATALIE *appears at gate, stares in shock.*)

HARRY: I'll get him inside. (*Begins to carry* NIGEL *towards house, suddenly looks down in horror at him.*) He's still! He's gone very still! Oh God!
(*Lights and curtain.*)

ACT TWO

SCENE I

Two years later. Mid-morning. BEN *is in kitchen in a posture of despair, newspaper beside him unread, sipping tea.*
NATALIE *is on the swing, swinging.*
LOUISE *enters kitchen, carrying a carrier bag. She smiles frigidly at* BEN, *who smiles awkwardly back, shifts his position clumsily.*

LOUISE: Excuse me a moment, Ben.
> (*She takes out a couple of chickens from the carrier bag, looks at them in disgust, turns on the oven, puts the chickens into a baking dish, smears butter over them, sprinkles salt, shoves them into the oven, all this at slapdash speed. She turns towards the door, to go to the sitting room, suddenly remembers, and turns back to the oven. She takes chickens out, scoops inside them, brings out the giblets in plastic bags, shudders, tosses them into the fridge, shoves the chickens back into the oven, rinses her hands, and goes into the sitting room, sits down at her typewriter, stares blankly at the page in it.*
> RONNIE *comes into the garden, sits down on stump which has now been converted into a garden seat, almost as if not noticing* NATALIE, *who is still swinging. He is clearly depressed.*
> NATALIE *sees him, sings* 'Bugger, bugger' *to the tune of* 'Glorious Things of Thee are Spoken', *then swings down.*)

NATALIE: Aren't you at least impressed? Or shocked even? A well-brought-up young lady chanting obscenities at the vicar!
RONNIE: What? Sorry – oh, (*Attempts a laugh*) actually it looked really quite – quite gymnastic.
NATALIE: It's what they call therapy, innit? You know, get rid of all the bad feelings and stuff.

54

RONNIE: And did you?

NATALIE: No. I've just had some disgusting news. (*Gets up.*) Can I practise breaking it? On you?

RONNIE: If you think I should be the first to know.

NATALIE: I'm pregnant, Ronnie. (*Pause.*) So what are your views on abortion?

RONNIE: Um, well, there are two views really. The official Church of England view and – well, mine. They're slightly contradictory but I try to hold them both. You see, Natalie, I do believe – do believe – that on the one hand all life is sacred. And that on the other – well – we have to think, however painfully, what's best. Best for you, best for the child, best for all the people who love you.

NATALIE: It's all right, Ronnie. You don't have to believe anything. I'm not pregnant really. It's far worse than that. I've just heard that I've failed all my A levels. Every fucking one of them.

RONNIE: Oh. (*Laughs in relief.*)

NATALIE: I mean the whole fucking lot. And that's not funny, Ronnie.

RONNIE: No, of course it isn't – I was just relieved – all of them? Oh dear, did you really? All of them!

NATALIE: (*Lighting cigarette.*) Well, I passed a few, but not enough to get into Cambridge. Not getting into Cambridge is failure in this family, Ronnie.

RONNIE: But you don't want to go to Cambridge, do you?

NATALIE: Good Christ, no!

RONNIE: What *do* you want?

NATALIE: Screw around, shoot up in loos all over London, then get myself knocked up, live in a council house off state hand-outs, with three kids by different dads. That sort of thing.

RONNIE: Well, you won't achieve all that lolling about in a garden in Devon, will you?

(NATALIE *laughs.*)

RONNIE: Who's down this time – ?

NATALIE: So far just Mummy and Grandad and me on the train.
    Last night.
RONNIE: Ben – so your grandfather's – down again at last! That's
    good! I've missed him –
NATALIE: Yes, well, we didn't know what he was up to for months
    and months, he wouldn't answer the phone and whenever
    Daddy went round to Fulham he either wasn't in or
    pretended he wasn't because he blamed himself for what
    happened to Nigel, and then suddenly last week he rang up
    and – and anyway, he'll tell you himself, don't worry, he's
    longing to, you especially.
RONNIE: Oh. Well, I'll look forward to – to hearing – your
    mother's working, I suppose?
NATALIE: She went down to the butcher's to get the chickens –
    listen!
    (LOUISE *has suddenly started typing.*)
    She's back. The typewriter. Can't you hear it?
RONNIE: No.
NATALIE: Sometimes I'm not sure whether I can actually *hear* it
    either. It's just something that I know is happening. Perhaps
    because it usually is. Like a mild headache. Why don't you go
    in and stop her?
RONNIE: No, no, I wouldn't dream – wouldn't dream –
NATALIE: Good. Then you can answer another question, Ronnie.
    Do you think there's a chance I'm adopted?
RONNIE: (*After a little pause*) I can't hold out much hope, I'm
    afraid.
NATALIE: (*Laughs*) Nigel always says you're quite funny
    sometimes – if people would only bother to listen to you. But
    the point is that I'm not like them, you see. I could never be
    like her, turning out novel after novel, sometimes I think
    there's almost one a month, like the curse. And not like him,
    with all his – his sense of responsibility. Except – except the
    wanting-to-screw-around bit, I suppose. Yes, that could be
    Daddy's genes all right. I've seen him at it, you know. I

dropped in on his office once and there they were, him and one of his secretaries or something, on the desk. I could even see his erection. It was sticking up against his trousers. He looked sort of crazy. I hear him on the phone at night when he thinks we're asleep. Hear him creep down, then his voice – daddying away at his latest. Being responsible. What I don't understand is why I hate her for letting him get away with it and not him for doing it. But the truth is I do hate her, I hate her for everything, everything.

RONNIE: Why – why are you telling me all this?

NATALIE: Don't know. Wanted to tell someone who wouldn't gossip and I expect you've taken vows of silence – anyway, you're not allowed to gossip about what your parishioners confess.

RONNIE: I don't think you qualify as a parishioner. (*Clearly upset.*) You've never once set foot in my church during service, not a single one of you. And it wasn't a confession. Which we don't really go in for in the C. of E. It was telling tales, Natalie.
(NATALIE *looks at him in shock, turns away.*)

RONNIE: (*Stands helplessly, looking towards her.*) Natalie, my – my dear – I – I –

NATALIE: I'm sorry. I didn't mean to make you angry.

RONNIE: No, I'm sorry. My response was – utterly selfish. Completely unpastoral. What's worse, unfriendly.

NATALIE: I don't see why you should have to be bothered – (*Lights a cigarette.*)

RONNIE: Yes. I bloody well should be bothered. Simply because I find it upsetting – but you've said so much I scarcely know where to – to –
(LOUISE *appears around side of house, unseen by* RONNIE *and* NATALIE, *hears rest of conversation.*)
– but I think probably the most important thing is what you said about your mother. I don't believe, whatever you think you feel, that you really do hate her.

NATALIE: Yes, I do. But don't worry. It's quite mutual. She

57

thinks I'm shallow, boy-mad and selfish. All true. While I
think she's – she's interfering and – and negligent and
blinkered and just as selfish as me. More selfish. Because –
(*Suddenly realizing that the typewriter is silent.*) It's stopped!
(*Turns, sees* LOUISE.)

RONNIE: What? (*Looking around, sees* LOUISE.)

LOUISE: Ronnie! I didn't know you were here – why didn't you
come in and announce yourself?

RONNIE: Oh, I was just about to. But then Natalie and I found
ourselves having a bit of a – bit of a gossip –

LOUISE: (*Seeing cigarette end, picks it up*) Natalie darling, I thought
we had an agreement that if you *are* going to smoke in the
garden you'd bring some sort of ashtray out with you –

NATALIE: Yes, sorry Mummy. (*Takes stub from her.*) I'll put it in
the rubbish.

LOUISE: Thank you, darling.

(NATALIE *goes up garden to kitchen as:*
RONNIE, *deeply embarrassed*, LOUISE *watching him.*
BEN, *starting to false life with mug and paper as* NATALIE *enters,
then sees it's* NATALIE *relaxes slightly.*)

BEN: Ah, hello there, Nat. What have you been up to?

NATALIE: (*Throwing butt into rubbish*) Just talking to Ronnie.

BEN: (*Excited*) Ronnie – he's here then! (*Getting up.*)

NATALIE: Yes. In the garden. Talking to Mummy.

BEN: Ah! (*Re-sits.*)

(NATALIE *goes on into sitting room, stands for a second looking in
despair, goes out stage right.*
BEN *stands uncertainly, yearningly, as:*)

RONNIE: (*Approaches* LOUISE) My dear Louise – my dear, dear
Louise – I don't expect she meant a word of it, really.
Natalie – girls of her age – not that I know much about them
but – but I expect. You know. Hormonal – (*Gestures*)
changes.

LOUISE: That comes earlier, Ronnie. And later. At the moment
Natalie's hormonally at her most harmonious.

RONNIE: Ah.

LOUISE: But she's perfectly right – I'm not patient with her. Not as patient as I should be. I do get irritated by her – her obsession with boys. I hear her on the telephone for hours, you know, and at all hours – and it doesn't sound like her at all. She puts on a different voice, manner – and so I probably say things I shouldn't – but then – but then – (*Stops*) she's also perfectly right about my being just as selfish and obsessed as she is.

RONNIE: Well, I expect it's hard, being a writer as well as a wife and mother –

LOUISE: I've finished *The Daffodil Corner* at last, by the way. Apart from two immensely difficult lines, that is. Did Natalie tell you? I expect not.

RONNIE: No. Why, Louise, that's – that's – congratulations!

LOUISE: Thank you. It was prompted by you, you know, Ronnie.

RONNIE: By me, really?

LOUISE: The story you told me – do you remember? How you were weeding around the daffodils over there.

RONNIE: Wasn't it the hollyhocks?

LOUISE: Yes, and how you thought you heard children dead – but in some way happy – sublimely happy, wasn't it?

RONNIE: That's not quite how I remember it, Lou.

LOUISE: Yes, well anyway, that was the seed – it's a kind of ghost story, but more than that, I hope.

RONNIE: Why, Louise – I'm sure it is, I'm sure it's – it's – Lou – Lou, that letter I sent you – my last one – what did you make of it?

LOUISE: Your last letter? Well, Ronnie – I – Harry and I – um, we – we – thought it um – (*Clearly not remembering.*)

RONNIE: I apologize – apologize, Lou. But it didn't occur to me until after I'd posted it that there you'd be, opening it quite casually over breakfast, expecting just another of my gossipy little newspieces, with an excerpt from my latest sermon – so your horror and distress when you read the first sentences –

the way I just went straight into it without at least warning you, finding some way of leading into it gently – but you see, Lou, you see, it wasn't just that she died! No. Nor that she died so – so abruptly! No. It was the grotesqueness. The grotesqueness of her death. Like a mockery. Almost a blasphemy. And so I just seized my pen and spilt it out to you. Because you Pertwees are the only people I know who could understand all my feelings. However ugly. And – and – what did Harry say? Was he angry with me? For being so thoughtless? And violent?

LOUISE: Oh no, Ronnie, no – he felt for you! Really felt for you. Actually he should be here any moment, he's driving down – but of course the traffic at this time – (*Looking around with desperate vagueness.*)

RONNIE: Anyway, the thing is Lou, I've quieted down quite a bit you'll be glad to hear. I mean, now it's more a matter of raising my arms to the heavens – the sky anyway (*Little laugh, as he raises his arms*) in a spirit of religious enquiry, you see, rather than – than that terrible, enraged – (*Shakes his fist angrily, the anger suddenly, in spite of himself, becoming almost demented, accompanied by a howling noise.*)
(BEN *appears.*)

LOUISE: Oh, Ben, there you are. Out at last.
(BEN, *who has made several tentative moves towards appearing on the porch, has gathered himself together, surges on to it as* RONNIE *is in mid-shake and mid-howl.* BEN *stands staring at* RONNIE.)

RONNIE: Hello, Ben – hello, old – I was just showing Wilemena – Louise, Louise – what one of our farmers does every morning when there's sunshine instead of rain – or the other way round. Depending on which there is, eh? (*Laughs.*)

BEN: Not their fault, Ronnie. They are what they are! Innocent devils. Like the rest of us. Innocent devils. Mustn't blame them. Threaten them with everlasting what's-it!

RONNIE: Um? (*Stares at* BEN, *slightly perplexed*.) Yes, well –
um – yes. That's true. Wouldn't want to do that, Ben.
Under any circumstances.

LOUISE: Would you two excuse me for a – there's something I
must finish before Harry and – I'll see you later. (*Hurries
off, through to sitting room, stage right. Sits in chair at desk.*)

BEN: You see, Ronnie, you see – all a matter of understanding.
Even types like old Tomalin with his bulls and cows.
Nobody had any choice. That's the key and clue to the
whole business, Ronnie. But you know all that. In fact,
you're the one who put me on to it. Without you I'd
never. No, never. Your words came back to me at my
hour of darkest need.

RONNIE: Well, I'm so glad – what words exactly, Ben?

BEN: Just after my Emily died. That first evening, before we
bought the place, Harry and I. You told me that God was
looking after her. That she was on Abraham's bosom.
Asleep.

RONNIE: I said that, did I?

BEN: Yes.

RONNIE: Abraham's bosom?

BEN: Yes.

RONNIE: I must say it doesn't sound quite – quite my –

BEN: All came back to me. Not only *your* words but bits and
pieces from across my life – a phrase here from Singapore, a
prayer in Chile – something my Emily said to me one
summer's leave in Gosport – and when little Harry – three
years old he must have been, asked me about the sun
coming up, why it bothered to come up – oh, I'm not
making great claims for myself, Ronnie, no enormous
religious conversion, I know my place in the scheme of
things, you see. Just another little dot of a chap who's had a
– a tiny glimpse of the light, all very humble, boring even
some might say. I mean, there I was skulking about in my
little flat in Fulham, couldn't face people, not even my own

son because of what I'd done to his son – spent hours –
whole hours – day after day – down on my knees, jabbering
out what prayers I could remember from when I was a child
– or bellowing out those hymns from school – (*Suddenly
bursts into song: 'The Lord's My Shepherd, I'll not want/He
makes me down to lie', laughs*) you know the sort of thing –
your sort of stuff, eh, Ronnie? But all the time I was
sobbing away inside. Desperate to give up my life. But of
course nobody came and asked for it, did they? Well, what
could they do with it? Even worse than what I'd done with
it, for all I know. (*Laughs.*) So it gradually dawned on me,
all this penance and praying and whining and hymn-singing
was a lot of nonsense. Self-pity. And what was worse,
arrogant. Yes, arrogant. I – I – little Benjamin Pertwee –
trying to make it seem as if it was all my fault! The sheer
effrontery of it! Who am I to think I can blame myself for
His decisions? Absolute bloody blasphemy, when you think
about it! – Pardon my diplomatic language. (*Laughs.*) But
through all this I kept remembering what you'd said –
Emily asleep on Abraham's bosom. Do you see? (*Stares at
him intently.*) Emily. On Abraham's bosom. Yes. That's
when it hit me – slowly hit me – bong, bong, bong (*Thumps
his head slowly but powerfully.*) And except for you, Ronnie,
without benefit of clergy. Of course I went around to my
local vicar in London, decent enough little blighter in his
way, but I could see he didn't understand a word I was
saying, but then he's got a drinking problem – anyway reeks
of alcohol – to Hell with him, eh? – now I'm not saying I've
solved all the world's problems – not a bit of it – what I do
say is that if we take God's view then there aren't any
problems to solve. They're all His problems, and He can
solve them any way he wants to, as long as we all end up on
Abraham's bosom. There it is, in a nutshell. Along with my
thanks. That's what I came down here to say. To you.

RONNIE: Well, thank you, Ben. Thank you for coming down.

But look – I think there's been a bit of a – a
misunderstanding here –
(NIGEL *appears at gate, leans on it to rest. He is carrying a
stick. His gored leg is in a calliper. He is wearing dark glasses.*)
– you see, I don't really think we can just shove all human
responsibility – *our* responsibility on to –
(BEN, *meanwhile, has seen* NIGEL, *stares at him in shock, then,
recognizing him, lets out a kind of scream.*)

BEN: Oh, no.

NIGEL: (*Enters*) Grandad! How good to see you at last – I've
missed you. (*Limping over to* BEN, *puts an arm around him.*)
And you – (*Turning*) Ronnie. Can't imagine coming back to
Little Paradise without finding you in the garden.
(BEN *stands unable to speak, staring at him.*)

HARRY: (*Appears at gate, carrying a leg-strengthening contraption
and a mattress, which he drops over side of gate*) Hello, everyone
– I wonder if someone can give me a hand – (*Goes off.*)

RONNIE: Yes, of course, of course – (*Goes to take leg contraption,
mattress.*)

BEN: Here, let me! (*Hurries over, seizes contraption and mattress
from* RONNIE.)

RONNIE: No, I'm – I can –

BEN: I've got them, I've got them. (*Wrestling them away from*
RONNIE, *gives him a push so that* RONNIE *staggers backwards,
glances furtively at* NIGEL, *almost runs up the garden.*)

HARRY: (*Reappears, carrying suitcase, groceries, etc.*) Careful,
Daddy – there's no rush, you know. (*Enters through gate.*)
You coming in for a lie-down, Nigel?

NIGEL: Oh, no, thanks, Daddy. Not yet anyway. A bit of fresh
air – perhaps a stroll with Ronnie.

HARRY: Right. I'll just go and tell Mummy we're here.

NIGEL: Would you mind a little stroll?

RONNIE: Love one.

NIGEL: Good. Just give me a minute to – (*Lies down, puts his
head back.*

63

BEN *enters sitting room, carrying* NIGEL's *things, attempting to recover emotionally. Stares at* LOUISE. LOUISE *rips sheet of paper out, puts another one in, turns, looks at* BEN *almost blankly.*)

BEN: Where shall I put these?

LOUISE: Oh, Nigel's room I should think.

BEN: What is this thing exactly? Can't quite make it out.

LOUISE: It's to help strengthen his leg muscles.

BEN: Ah. (*Looks at it in a kind of horror.*)

HARRY: (*Entering*) Sure you can manage, Daddy?

BEN: Yes, yes – (*Struggles out.*)

HARRY: Hello, darling.

LOUISE: (*Finishing typing*) How's Nigel?

HARRY: A bit peaky from the journey. He's going for a little walk with Ronnie.

LOUISE: As long as Ronnie takes it easy – oh, God, darling, Ronnie! Wilemena's dead.

HARRY: Oh, really! How?

LOUISE: I haven't the slightest idea, that's the trouble. He thinks we know all about it because he told us in his last letter. Which we didn't open as usual. So I just had to bluff my way through.

HARRY: Well, I'll have to do the same, I suppose. Still, it must be a relief for him, really. (*Picks up bags.*)

LOUISE: Yes, I'm sure it is. Although he didn't seem particularly relieved. (*Turning back to typing.*)

HARRY: Well, of course he wouldn't, being Ronnie. (*Makes to go out, turns, watches her for a second, then goes out.*
LOUISE *looks at what she's written, pulls out paper, crumples it, throws it into wastepaper basket. Puts in new sheet, types a few words, shakes her head, then sits perplexed.*)

NIGEL: Right. Now let's give ourselves a whirl, eh, Ronnie?

RONNIE: Are you sure you're really up to – you really do look a little –

NIGEL: Shaky. Yes I am, actually. But I wouldn't mind a go on the swing. (*Rising with difficulty*.) I need a bit of support, I'm afraid. Pins and needles in my good leg.

RONNIE: Of course. How – um – how –

NIGEL: Let me do this. (*Puts an arm around* RONNIE's *shoulder*.) And off we go.

RONNIE: (*After a pause, awkwardly*) Quite comfortable?

NIGEL: (*With a little laugh*) More comfortable than you, I expect. (*They walk a few steps*.) Isn't it lucky that you never did anything to regret in those days when you used to take me church-visiting.

(RONNIE *stops*.)

NIGEL: Don't stop.

RONNIE: You knew then?

NIGEL: Well, you used to look at me with such sad eyes – there were times when I thought, oh well, if he really wants to do whatever it is he wants to do, let him do it. It probably won't hurt. (*They continue towards swing*.) But if I had let you you probably wouldn't be able to hold me up now, when I really need it, would you? From embarrassment, guilt – the usual stuff.

RONNIE: It wasn't sexual, you know. Not really. Nothing like it ever happened to me before. Or since. But I was – was hopelessly in love with you. Loved you. And sometimes the need to express it – somehow! I'd hate you to think I'm just another Church of England vicar who – who gropes choir boys.

NIGEL: Don't be ridiculous, Ronnie – I've never thought of you as anything but the nicest man I've ever met. Of course you could still be that and grope choir boys, couldn't you? But you'd never permit it. Forgive in others what you'd never permit in yourself is virtually your life's principle. (*Little pause*.)

RONNIE: Did you get my letter?

NIGEL: About Mrs Mossop's death? Yes, I'm terribly sorry. I

know how devoted you were to each other. It must be a
dreadful loss.

RONNIE: Thank you.

NIGEL: I would have written back but –

RONNIE: But what? (*Little pause, then almost a cry.*) I longed for a
letter from you!

NIGEL: Yes. I should have. Even – well, the truth is, Ronnie, I
couldn't have written without telling you the truth.

RONNIE: And what would that have been? Something smart and
Cambridge?

NIGEL: Well sort of. Tit for tat anyway.

RONNIE: Tit for tat?

NIGEL: Well, your tat was how shocking it was that you should
have had such trivial thoughts at a time like that.

RONNIE: I remember perfectly well – the point is those *were* my
thoughts – my real thoughts – I mean, there she was, my
poor dear Mrs Mossop, lying there dead in my kitchen, with
a soup ladle in one hand, an onion in the other – she'd just
keeled over while I was in the middle of one of my – bloody
lectures on her attitude to an Irish Catholic family that had
moved in –

NIGEL: (*Almost testily*) Yes, yes, I know. You described it all
quite brilliantly – you made it perfectly clear that she died
from boredom.

(NIGEL *laughs.* RONNIE *looks at him indignantly, then also
laughs.*)

RONNIE: You could have written back making fun of me. I
wouldn't have minded. I'd have been grateful – what did
you mean, tit for tat?

NIGEL: There's a simple thing you don't understand. That's the
tit.

RONNIE: About – about death?

NIGEL: Exactly.

RONNIE: And you understand it, do you? (*Sarcastically.*)

NIGEL: Yes.

RONNIE: And what is it, pray tell, this – this – ?

NIGEL: Tit. Let me think how to put it. (*Pause.*) Yes. That the living – that's not it. That it's only the dying who – no, (*laughs*) that's not it, either. Oh well – what it amounts to is that without death we wouldn't know how to live.

RONNIE: And that's your – your –

NIGEL: Tit.

RONNIE: That old cliché! So why all this fuss and bother and grief over the likes of Mrs Mossop. Well, thank you. I'm glad you didn't write that to me! I'd have – I'd have –

NIGEL: I'm sorry, Ronnie, I was really only trying to find a way of – well, communicating something rather particular. Rather personal. To you. Without making too much fuss and bother.

RONNIE: What do you mean? (*Stares at* NIGEL.) It's not – true!

NIGEL: I'm afraid it is. My head's getting worse and worse – and I've always known – sensed – from when I was very young – that it – had a purpose. An ultimate purpose. To keep me alive to the thought of how close, how very close I always am to death. And the thought of that has made all my other thoughts more real. I've loved that, Ronnie. I really have. The something wrong with my head, *in* my head, growing and growing to kill me, is what's made everything, *everything*, so valuable. (*Grins.*) I wish I'd had some sex, though. Proper sex, I mean. God, I'd have enjoyed it, I know I would. Especially with someone I loved. But apart from that one major regret, I'm grateful –

RONNIE: But the doctors – are they so sure?

NIGEL: Oh, it's far too late for doctors and such.

RONNIE: But you must see one, you must!

NIGEL: It's too late, I tell you, Ronnie. And if I go to one now Mummy and Daddy will find out and I couldn't endure all their – their fussing – no, that's not fair – their fussing kind of loving – when all I want to do is to concentrate on the things that really matter.

RONNIE: Then why are you telling *me* this?

NIGEL: Well, because of Grandad, you see. After it's happened they'll want to blame somebody, people always do, and he's the obvious candidate. He's already taken the rap for turning me into a cripple. Although actually it was all my fault. I was much the older and more responsible party at the time. (*Little pause.*) But when I've snuffed it, I want *you* to tell them it was inevitable. Nothing at all to do with Grandad and that ridiculous accident with the cow and the broken bottle. You see?

RONNIE: Now this – (*Almost to himself*) is intolerable. *This* is intolerable!

NIGEL: Oh, come on, Ronnie, think of the world – the horrors it sups on every minute of every day and every night. Children dying of starvation, children shot to death by grown-ups, or other children even. And here I am, having had a wonderful life and having already exceeded the life expectancy of millions by years, and years, loafing about in the midday sunshine of an exceptional summer in an English garden – here, in Mummy's Little Paradise – (*Gestures around it*) consulting with a close friend and civilized soul (*Smiles*) on how best to leave him and – and the others I love –
(NATALIE *appears at the gate.*)
– so really to hell with me. And Mrs Mossop even. We're the lucky ones. She went in the middle of one of your sermons. I'll go full of – full of – (*Looks suddenly toward gate*) life. Hello.

NATALIE: Hi. Back then, are you? (*Coming in.*)

NIGEL: Yup. Back.

NATALIE: (*To* RONNIE) She heard everything I said, didn't she, Ronnie?

RONNIE: No, no, she – just a little bit of it, the last part of it.

NATALIE: That was the worst part. (*To* NIGEL) I said I hated her.

NIGEL: Did you now? (*Laughs, over-brightly.*) Well then she should know it. Do her no harm.

NATALIE: You all right?

NIGEL: Yes, yes – but I need to get in – lie down for a bit –

RONNIE: Oh. Well, can I – shall I – (*Goes to put his arm around him.*)

NIGEL: No, Nat. Nat can do it. Can't you, Nat?

NATALIE: I suppose so. Come on then. (*Helps him up, gives him her shoulder. They move slowly towards the porch.* RONNIE *stands watching.*
NIGEL *is helped into kitchen by* NATALIE. *He begins to collapse.* NATALIE *helps him into chair.*)

NIGEL: Oh God, my head, my bloody head! I don't want to, Nat, I don't want to die.

NATALIE: I know you don't. (*Then fiercely.*) I won't let you. (NIGEL *attempts to smile at her, then bursts into tears, puts arms on table, head on his arms.* NATALIE *sits beside him, stroking his head.*
HARRY *enters sitting room from right.*)

HARRY: He's being a bit odd again.

LOUISE: Who?

HARRY: Daddy. He's curled up on the bed clutching Nigel's things. He pretended to be asleep. But I'm sure he isn't.

LOUISE: Oh. Well, I expect he's – he's upset. After all, it's the first time he's seen Nigel since – (*Gestures*) the accident.

HARRY: Well, darling, that may be true but –

LOUISE: Just a minute – (*Types furiously, then takes paper out of typewriter, hands it to him*) here you are. I've been struggling with it all afternoon. The two most difficult and important sentences of my life. And they've just come to me at last.

HARRY: (*Reads out*) 'The Daffodil Corner is dedicated to my Harry. Faithful to a fault.'

LOUISE: I wanted to wait until I'd done something you wouldn't be ashamed to be named in.

HARRY: Thank you, darling.

LOUISE: Don't you like it?

HARRY: Yes – it's lovely. Lovely.

LOUISE: There is something – what is it?

HARRY: Well, only that – well, perhaps 'my' Harry's a little – a
little too – well, too 'between us'. I mean, something we
don't really want to share with your public.

LOUISE: Oh. Yes. Yes, I see, it does sound rather – rather
possessive. More for an infant son –

HARRY: Yes, or a dog even. Just 'to Harry' is fine, isn't it? And I
wonder if – well –

LOUISE: What?

HARRY: Well, something else instead of 'faithful'. Um –

LOUISE: Why, what's wrong with it? Nobody could have been
more supportive and loyal over my last seven novels –

HARRY: Yes, well, those are the words, aren't they, darling? I
mean faithful is used in such a – such a – limited sense,
these days – um, I think that word you used – not 'loyal, the
other one – 'supportive'. '. . . who has been so supportive' –
or 'for all his support'. Yes, that sounds really – really,
doesn't it? 'To Harry. For all his support.' If you think I
deserve it, of course.

LOUISE: Can't I add – 'over the years'? 'To Harry. For all his
support over the years.'

HARRY: Absolutely. And I have deserved it, haven't I? (*Kisses
her lightly.*)

LOUISE: Oh, my darling, without you as my agent I'd be
nothing. I know that.

HARRY: And without you as one of my leading writers I wouldn't
be much of an agent.

LOUISE: Wouldn't you? (*Looks at him, then shakes her head.*) No,
that's not true. You don't need me as a writer really –

HARRY: Don't need you? Oh, darling! I don't do it just for love,
you know. (*Laughs.*) I do it for the money as well.

LOUISE: Harry – kiss me. (*Runs to him.*) Please kiss me.
(HARRY *holds her awkwardly, kisses her.*)

LOUISE: (*Attempting lightness*) You can do better than that. Come on – come on. (*Begins to dance.* HARRY *tries, awkwardly, to dance back to her.*)

NIGEL: (*Pulling himself together*) I'd better go and say hello to Mummy, hadn't I? And then get to bed. (*Gets up shakily, helped by* NATALIE.
Enters sitting room. LOUISE *dances backwards into* NIGEL, *knocking his leg.*)

NIGEL: Ow! Sorry, Mummy – my leg's feeling a bit awkward. Need to lie down really.

LOUISE: Oh – sorry, my love! Daddy and I were just – (*Laughs, then, seeing his face*) But you look so – you look so – have you been crying? Was it Ronnie? Has he upset you going on about grief and God in that way of his?

NIGEL: No, Mums, no. I've simply got a touch of hay fever. That's why I came in. And my leg hurts. Otherwise I'm perfectly all right. Perfectly.

HARRY: Come on, I'll help you upstairs. Get you to bed. (*Puts his arm around* NIGEL.)

NIGEL: (*Struggling slightly to get free.*) Well, Nat can – Nat can manage, can't you, Nat?
(HARRY *hesitates.*)

LOUISE: Let Nat do it, darling, if that's what Nigel wants.

HARRY: She won't be able to manage him on the stairs, darling.

NIGEL: I can manage the stairs by myself, thanks. (*Goes out of room.*
There is a pause. LOUISE *looks at* HARRY *who avoids her eyes.*)

HARRY: Still, I'll go behind him in case he falls. (*Goes out.*)
(NATALIE *begins to go to kitchen.*)

LOUISE: Darling – would you mind checking on the oven, see how the chickens are doing – and peeling the potatoes? And oh, darling – whatever your feelings about me – and I think I understand them – I wouldn't be a writer if I didn't, after all (*Gives a little laugh*) – do you think you could try not to share them with one of our closest friends?

NATALIE: Sorry. Didn't mean it. Didn't mean you to hear.

LOUISE: I know, darling, but we ought to think of Ronnie too. He's got quite enough to cope with – Wilemena, his poor wretched wife, has just died, you see.

NATALIE: But he didn't tell me.

LOUISE: Well – darling, I don't expect you gave him the chance. Did you?

NATALIE: No. I'll do the potatoes then. (*Goes into kitchen.*) (LOUISE *stares after* NATALIE, *suddenly stricken. Makes to go into kitchen, hesitates, sits down at table instead. Her eyes stray to page. She starts to type furiously. She finishes, tears out page, crumples it up and throws it on the floor. As she does so:*)

LOUISE: Disgusting, disgusting, disgusting! (*Nods to herself.*) And so am I. (*Gets up, goes into kitchen. To* NATALIE.) Darling, I'm sorry, you're absolutely right. I've been a rotten mother.

NATALIE: No, you haven't, Mummy.

LOUISE: I love you.

(*She puts her arms around* NATALIE. *They embrace. Shakily.*) Here, I'll give you a hand.

(*They begin to peel potatoes together in awkward silence.*)

NATALIE: I phoned up the school today – the office.

LOUISE: Oh?

NATALIE: They got my A-level results. Two Cs – one for history and in French.

LOUISE: (*Attempting cheeriness*) Really? A C in French? I'm quite surprised, your French always seemed so good to me. What about the others? Any As or Bs?

NATALIE: No, Mum, the Cs were my best. I failed the others.

LOUISE: Ah. Well, darling, let's not worry about it now. Let's just all enjoy being together again in Little Paradise and leave everything troublesome until we get back to London, eh? (*Smiles at her.*)

NATALIE: (*Attempting to smile back*) Right, Mum.

(*They continue to peel potatoes.* HARRY *enters sitting room. Picks up crumpled paper on floor.*)

HARRY: (*Reads out*) 'The Daffodil Corner is dedicated to my faithful agent, Harry Pertwee, for all his support over the years. And also to Harry Pertwee, my faithless husband, whose humiliating and insulting philandering over the years has made it possible for me to become the writer and the woman that I am. Over the years.'

BEN: (*Enters*) My fault, Nigel.

HARRY: I'm Harry, Daddy.

BEN: Forgive me, will you? Oh, please forgive me, Nigel. (*Sinks to his knees, lets out a howl.*)

HARRY: I'm Harry, Daddy! (*Goes to him.*)

BEN: I did it – I did it – all my fault. Oh God, forgive me, please forgive me – help me, God, little Ben, little Ben – didn't mean it, didn't mean it, Nigel! (*Begins to sing 'The Lord's My Shepherd, I'll not want.'*

NIGEL *enters in underpants, a leg-brace.*)

(*Seeing him, to* NIGEL) Harry, Harry – forgive me – sing with me, sing with me –

(*Starts again 'The Lord's My Shepherd, I'll not want', stares pleadingly at* NIGEL. NIGEL *joins in, as he goes over to* BEN *bends down laboriously, puts his arms around him.* BEN *and* NIGEL *continue singing, watched by* HARRY, *appalled.*

LOUISE *and* NATALIE, *hearing singing, look towards sitting room.*

RONNIE, *in garden, lifts his head as if perplexed by what he is hearing as:*

Lights and slow curtain.)

SCENE 2

A year later. Garden at twilight. There is a 'For Sale' sign up, very new. LOUISE, *in raincoat, scarf, is typing. The rest of the furniture is covered, as at the beginning of the play.*

RONNIE *enters garden with basket and trowel. Looks around him, delighting in garden, puts down basket. Takes out plants in a pot, goes over to one of the beds, puts plants in various places, shaking his head.*

RONNIE: (*On hands and knees*) No – no, not right – ah – ah, there – that looks – that looks –
(LOUISE *stops typing, looks at the sheet of paper, gets up wearily, goes into kitchen, and on to porch.*)

LOUISE: Hello, Ronnie. You look as if you're seeing a ghost.

RONNIE: No, no, it was just that I had no idea that anyone was here.

LOUISE: Nor had I.

RONNIE: I had a spare hydrangea, you see – and thought how beautifully it would go in here somewhere – so I popped in to – to pop it in. (*Laughs.*) I hope you don't mind.

LOUISE: Oh, don't be ridiculous, Ronnie, (*Affectionately*) of course I don't mind. In fact, from the state of the garden, you've obviously been popping in fairly frequently.

RONNIE: Yes – well, I have. But not really since the 'For Sale' sign went up last week. Except once. On Sunday. After service.

LOUISE: Yes, that awful sign. Odd, isn't it, that people can do that to their past. Stick a 'For Sale' sign up on it.

RONNIE: But I suppose – as you don't get down any more – and it's such a distance from London – it's amazing that you managed so often for so long.

LOUISE: Still, I'm going to ask him not to sell. I've been in there writing him a letter. It's hard to find the right words –

RONNIE: You came all the way down here just to write Harry a letter – ?

LOUISE: Not exactly. I found out from his secretary – *one* of his secretaries – that he was coming down himself. To give the estate agents hell for not getting on with it, she said. So on an – an impulse, I suppose it was, I decided to

74

get the train and – discuss it with him properly. And
then I saw the typewriter in its old place. And the
usual box of paper – so I couldn't resist. I don't
expect it'll do any good. He's probably quite determined.
But at least I can look at it properly one last time. Say
goodbye.

RONNIE: Things aren't going too well, then?

LOUISE: Between Harry and me, you mean?

RONNIE: No, no – I meant financially. If Harry needs to sell –

LOUISE: Oh, we've got the money. Between us and
independently. (*Laughs.*) I suppose I could always offer to
buy it from him, come to think of it. But the idea of that –
that sort of transaction – my buying our past from him, that
would be worse than his just putting it on the market, I
think. Don't you?

(RONNIE *says nothing.*)

Especially as the money would come from royalties he'd
negotiated for *The Daffodil Corner*.

RONNIE: I'm glad – so glad – that *The Daffodil Corner*'s been
such a success – a best seller, isn't it? I know how hard you
worked on it, how much it meant to you –

LOUISE: Thank you.

RONNIE: And such nice reviews! One particularly – by that
novelist-friend I met once years ago – the one I had a bit – a
bit of a – the one who wrote *Fucking About – Fuck Off* – no,
Fuck All.

LOUISE: Oh yes, Sam Draycott. I expect Harry fixed him in
some way. After all, he's one of Harry's other stars.

RONNIE: You mean he's back with him?

LOUISE: Back with him? Oh, of course! That horrible afternoon
when he came down. No, Harry didn't let him go. Harry
never lets go of any of his writers. And gets them to review
each other – usually favourably.

RONNIE: Oh, come, Lou. I'm sure he loved *The Daffodil Corner*.
After all, I did. Very much. Even the bits that struck a little

– a little close to home, like the comic vicar and – and – they still made me laugh. And the children, the ghosts –

LOUISE: (*Interrupting.*) Harry and I are going to separate. Actually in practice we're separated already. As he spends most nights in a flat he's organized for himself in his new offices. So that he can be completely free to get on with his own life.

RONNIE: Oh. Well I – I – I'm very sorry. And – surprised, of course. I mean, when I noticed your dedication in *The Daffodil Corner*, I thought how moving it was that you could announce your feelings – I mean – I mean – I assumed that you were both still very much – 'To my Harry. Faithless to a fault', wasn't it? No, that doesn't sound quite –

LOUISE: (*With a little laugh*) It was faithful. Faithful to a fault. And it's only there because I knew it was the last thing he wanted. In literary circles it's earned me the reputation of being something of a wit, at last.

RONNIE: Oh. Then it's all – all very sad. So you've made the decision, have you? Both of you?

LOUISE: Oh, we don't talk enough to make a decision about anything. Just a few awkward conversations on the telephone. So it's better to acknowledge that we're losing touch completely, then we might become friends again, at least. Although I suppose his trying to sell this off amounts to a step towards a decision. So – so perhaps that's what I've really come down here – to our Little Paradise – to talk about. The end of our marriage. Yes. Thank you, Ronnie. You've helped clear things up, a little.

RONNIE: Oh, I hope I haven't – I wouldn't dream of interfering – it would be – be – but – but – how is everybody else, how's old Ben?

LOUISE: The other Sunday he phoned Harry up and invited him around to hear him give the sermon at his local church.

RONNIE: Ben gave the sermon!

LOUISE: Well, nearly. He raced the vicar to the pulpit, and

would have got there first if Harry hadn't caught hold of him. They had quite a tussle – Harry got him on to the street eventually. Since then he's been reasonably calm – but Harry will have to get him into some sort of home soon, I suppose.

RONNIE: Oh, dear. And Natalie? How's she?

LOUISE: She seems quite happy. She's got a place in art school which she's going to give up because she's pregnant. She won't say who the father is. In fact, she refuses to let us help in any way. She's living in a kind of hostel or perhaps it's a squat – she phones up from time to time and seems – quite happy.

RONNIE: So you're going to be a grandmother!

LOUISE: Dear Ronnie, always finding something to celebrate! Though this time I can't think what I've done to deserve it. (*Gives a little laugh.*) And I'm not sure Natalie will want me to get much joy from her child. Or see it, even.

RONNIE: Oh, I'm sure she will, in the end, I'm sure she will – and Nigel, how's Nigel? (*Waits in terror.*)

LOUISE: You don't know then?

(RONNIE *shakes his head.*)

No, I suppose you wouldn't, how could you? Those headaches of his, they'd been getting worse and worse – but he kept it from us – from everybody. Until one night at Cambridge they heard him screaming. That's when it began – scans, probes, test after test – then chemotherapy. And his hair falling out – (*Stops, at the memory.*)

RONNIE: (*Nodding fatalistically*) He's dead, then?

LOUISE: At the moment he feels quite well. He's gone back to Cambridge to take his finals. They call it remission. He's in remission. And of course Nigel's line is that everybody in the world is in remission. It just takes different forms. You'd think – you'd think, wouldn't you, that something like that would bring us closer, Harry and me, instead of making us worse – I think – I think the truth is we blame

each other – as well as ourselves – as if – if as a couple we'd
brought him his cancer, you see?

RONNIE: Nigel would hate that!

LOUISE: Yes, he would, wouldn't he? But still we didn't see how
serious it was – we didn't *see*, neither of us – and they think
– they think that if it had been detected a few months earlier
– if only we – or some of his friends – anybody who knew
what was going on in him, his head – he might have been –
he just *might* have been –

RONNIE: Oh, God!

LOUISE: Yes, that's the hardest part to take. And I suppose why
I can't forgive Harry his infidelities. However trivial he
might think – he was too busy trying to deceive me to have
time to look properly at his own – his own family. Perhaps if
I'd let him know how completely undeceived I was he would
have found the time. So it's my fault too – (*Suddenly crying
out*) blame, blame, blame, why do we always need to blame!
Ourselves – others! The truth is nobody did know. Nobody
did notice.

(*There is a pause.*)

RONNIE: Perhaps some people did know, friends, but he told
them not to worry you –

LOUISE: Yes, that would be like Nigel. I sometimes suspect that
Natalie – I mean, how can she sound so happy, let herself
get pregnant, when her brother – but I've never understood
what goes on between them. It's as if they have a pact to
keep their parents out of their life. At whatever cost. Even
to themselves. (*Looks at* RONNIE.) Funny, isn't it? That I
should have the kind of conversation with you that Harry
and I can't have. (*Looks around the garden, sighs.*) It *is* so
beautiful. I *do* still love it. We *were* happy here. I must hang
on to that, and – and I suppose go in and write my probably
useless letter before Harry turns up. So if I don't see you
before I go back – (*Kisses* RONNIE) dear Ronnie. Thank you
for all your listening. But I haven't even given you the

78

chance to tell me the latest about Wilemina – (*Remembering*) I mean, how her funeral went, and – and if you're late for one of your Mrs Mossop's teas or dinners, blame me.

RONNIE: (*After a little pause*) She only does my lunches, Lou. So you haven't been keeping me from anything. (*Gazes at her desperately, about to speak.*)

LOUISE: Dear Ronnie. (*Looks at him slightly puzzled. Goes in, sits down at desk, gazes at paper.*)

RONNIE: (*Stares after her, then slumping to his knees*) A few months! A few months would have saved him! And I didn't tell them, I didn't speak, why didn't I, dear God, why didn't you make me tell them? (*Presses his face to the ground in anguish.*)

HARRY: (*Enters behind him, through the gate, sees him*) Hello Ronnie, what are you up to down there, something clergical or something horticultural?

RONNIE: (*Scrambling to his feet, attempts laugh*) I thought I detected some greenfly on the – (*Gestures to nearby flower*) but it must have been merely spots before my eyes, thank heavens –

HARRY: You know, I had a feeling I'd find you here. I suppose because I can never imagine the garden without seeing you in it. (*Looks around.*) I must say, it looks in tip-top condition! (*Tests swing.*) Still sturdy. Should appeal to potential purchasers with children, eh? When did they put up the sign, did you notice?

RONNIE: The sign? Oh. About a week ago.

HARRY: Only a week! What buggers those estate agents are, eh – (*Looks at his watch.*) I still might catch them on the phone – will you excuse me, Ronnie, I've got some other calls to make as well – London, etc. – (*Gestures.*) Hang around if you like, might see you later, for an exchange of news. (*Heads towards the house.*

LOUISE *suddenly begins typing ferociously.* HARRY *takes a few more steps. Stops. Stares towards the house.*)

HARRY: Oh no, oh no, oh no.

RONNIE: What is it?

HARRY: Can't you hear it?

RONNIE: What? I can't hear anything.

HARRY: She's here though, isn't she?

RONNIE: Who, Louise? Yes. Yes, she is.

HARRY: (*Coming back*) I should have guessed she'd find out I was coming down. I told everybody at the office not to tell a soul – but she probably winkled it out of the new girl – (*Sits down on swing.*) Or she just *knew*. Her writer's instinct, she'd call it. (*Gives a little laugh, starts to swing, looks at* RONNIE.) So I suppose you already know all our news then. At any rate, her version of it.

RONNIE: I can't say how sorry I am about Nigel. It must be so distressing for you –

HARRY: Yes. Thank you. Although I expect she's given you the worst possible prognosis. It's nothing like as final as she seems determined to believe. He's got a better than even chance – the remission periods are getting longer. There are certainly grounds for hope – *more* than hope! I don't know why she – she – but that's always been her way. To worry desperately about them, to make up for neglecting them. Listen to her! (*Cocking his head.*)

RONNIE: (*Bracing himself*) Harry, I've got a confession to make. I understand that if you'd known a few months earlier – things might have been different.

HARRY: Known what?

RONNIE: Well – about Nigel's health. His head.

HARRY: Oh, yes. Well, somebody's got to be at fault, haven't they? The doctors, his friends, me – particularly me. But the truth is that the only person at fault – if that's the appropriate word – is Nigel. He told you, did he?
(RONNIE *nods.*)
He told quite a few people at Cambridge. And Natalie too, I

expect. Everybody said the same thing, 'Go and see a
doctor!' Is that what you said?
(RONNIE *nods*.)
There you are then. What more could anybody do? He's an
intelligent and responsible young man who goes about
things in his own way. (*Looks at* RONNIE.) Oh, for God's
sake, Ronnie! You don't think I didn't suspect – or Louise
didn't suspect! Of course we did. Anyway a few months
probably wouldn't have made any difference. The main
specialist isn't even convinced that there's a connection
between the tumour and his headaches – he's had the
headaches all his life, and he hasn't had the tumour all his
life. Look, there's no point – absolutely no point in going
through the 'if onlys' and the 'might have beens' – at the
moment he's alive, he's active, and there's hope – and we'll
have to settle for that this evening, won't we? Listen to her!

RONNIE: I'm sorry. I didn't mean – mean to cause more pain –

HARRY: No. Well, you've had quite enough of your own, haven't
you? I'm sorry we didn't have a chance to talk to you about,
um, your wife's death, by the way. It must have been a
complicated business for you. Your feelings about it, I
mean. But tell me – tell me – (*Cocking his head to typewriter
again*) is everything all right otherwise? Still banqueting
sumptuously off good Mrs Glossop's dinners?

RONNIE: Mossop. Betty Mossop her name was. (*Corrects
himself*.) Is. No. Was. *Was*. The truth is there's a
misunderstanding of some kind, Harry. Wilemena is alive
and well and is malevolence personified, poor sad, creature.
While Mrs Mossop, my poor, dear, Mrs Mossop, is alive
here, only here – (*Pats heart*) and will be as long as I'm –
I'm –

HARRY: (*Who has been listening to typewriter and not to* RONNIE,
vaguely) Well, good that some things never change. (*Getting
up*.) Listen to her, listen! I can't bear it! Her rattle, rattle,
rattle – rattling through my life, rattling my life away –

pretending she's too broken by Nigel, by Natalie, by me, to get on to a new novel, but all the time I knew perfectly well she'd be at it somewhere, somehow – and of course it would be down here rattle, rattle, rattle – and out will come another bloody novel.

RONNIE: Harry, it's not a novel, she's writing you a letter.

HARRY: What? Well, that's even worse. I'll have to read it. Instead of just selling it. What about? Oh, of course! About the house. She wants to keep it. Is that it?

RONNIE: She wants you *both* to keep it. To go on sharing it – your past, you see. Yours and hers and the children's –

HARRY: (*Laughs*) It's too late, far too late! But she can have it. I'll make it over to her. Yes, let's settle this once and for all. She can have this. And we'll sell the London house and get her a small place – it's much too large for just her now that I've got my own flat – and let me think. I suppose I'll have to go on representing her – well, that won't be too bad. At least from her point of view. Much better to be represented by someone who isn't your husband. If we do this properly we should be able to keep the lawyers out of it, eh? So – let's get it over with, then. (*Turns to go to the house. Stops.*) Perhaps you should do it, Ronnie.

RONNIE: Do what?

HARRY: Well, tell her, of course.

RONNIE: Tell her that your marriage is over – the terms of the settlement – ?

HARRY: Well, why not? I mean – I imagine it's a sort of pastoral duty, isn't it?

RONNIE: You're not serious, Harry. You can't be.

HARRY: Look, all I'm asking you to do as a man of God is to mediate briefly between two people you claim to care about. To lessen the all-round hurt a little. I mean, isn't hurt-lessening all you believe in – I've virtually heard you say as much. That it's the sum-total of your faith.

(RONNIE *stares at him.*)

Don't say you don't even believe that much! (*Laughs.*) So that's what it's all boiled down to! Two thousand years of Christian suffering – the virgin birth – the crucifixion – martyrdoms, crusades, inquisitions – and the result – the spiritual climax of it all – a bumbler in funny clothes who doesn't even believe he should do anything to prevent people from hurting people.

RONNIE: How dare you, how dare you, how dare you – ! (*Throws himself on* HARRY, *begins to shake him, then stops, steps away. Both then pull themselves together.*)

HARRY: I'm sorry, Ronnie – I didn't mean it. Please forgive me.

LOUISE: (*Comes out into the garden*) Oh, you're here then – I thought I heard your voice.

HARRY: I gather you've written me a letter.

LOUISE: (*Handing him letter*) Would you read it, please?

HARRY: (*Taking it*) What, here, now?

LOUISE: It won't take long.

(HARRY *begins to read letter.*)

RONNIE: Well, I'd better be – better be getting – getting –

LOUISE: Back to your Mrs Mossop.

RONNIE: Yes.

HARRY: Enjoy your dinner.

RONNIE: Thank you. (*Goes to gate, goes out, closes gate, looks at* LOUISE *and* HARRY. *Cries out*) Please! Oh, please God! (*The light in the garden changes. As it does so,* HARRY *stops reading letter, looks at* LOUISE. LOUISE *looks at* HARRY. *They begin to dance in a stately and formal manner, moving towards each other, then away from each other, etc., as over, sound of children laughing.* LOUISE *and* HARRY *end up in their former positions. Children continue laughing.* RONNIE *looks around, smiling. Laughter stops.*)

LOUISE: (*Seeing* RONNIE:) Are you all right?

RONNIE: (*As if coming out of a daze*) Yes, just a touch dizzy, that's all – a touch dizzy – but it's all back to normal now.

(*Then blurting it out*) God bless you! God bless you both!
(*Hurries off.*)
(HARRY *and* LOUISE *look at each other.* HARRY *resumes
reading the letter.* LOUISE *goes and sits on swing, as music over:
'The Paradise Duet'.*)
(*Curtain.*)

The Common Pursuit

SCENES FROM
THE LITERARY LIFE

For Ben and Lucy

The Common Pursuit: Scenes from the Literary Life was first performed on 3 July 1984 at the Lyric Theatre, Hammersmith. The cast was as follows:

STUART	Nicholas Le Provost
MARIGOLD	Nina Thomas
MARTIN	Ian Ogilvy
NICK	Robert East
PETER	Simon Williams
HUMPHRY	Clive Francis
Director	Harold Pinter
Designer	Eileen Diss
Costumes	Liz Walker
Lighting	Dave Horn

ACT ONE

Stuart's rooms, in Cambridge. Twenty years ago. It is mid-morning.
There is the door (and an oak door behind it) stage left. Stage right, a
window and window seat. A door, centre, closed, to the bedroom.
There is a table in the middle, covered with typescripts, books, etc.
There is a sofa, two armchairs, a chair for the table. Books etc., on
shelves (rather haphazardly) around the walls. There is a gramophone,
stage left. A record is playing on it. It is Bach's 'Air on a g-string.'
STUART *and* MARIGOLD *are sitting on the window seat, in the*
sunlight, holding hands, staring at each other intently. MARIGOLD
strokes STUART's *cheek. They kiss, gently, on the lips. The kiss*
becomes more passionate. They stand, kissing.

MARIGOLD: Oh you – oh you! (*They kiss again.*) Come on – come
    on! (*Pulling him, laughingly, towards the bedroom door.*)
STUART: (*Resisting*) No, we can't. They'll be here any minute.
MARIGOLD: We'll be extremely quick. Like lightning.
STUART: But I don't want to be extremely quick, like lightning.
    I want to be extremely slow. Forever, in fact.
MARIGOLD: (*After a small pause*) Forever?
STUART: (*After a little pause*) Absolutely. Forever.
MARIGOLD: And afterwards will you write a poem about it?
STUART: No, it wouldn't be good enough. But you can. And I'll
    publish it. How's that? Or I can publish your last letter.
    Instead of the usual manifesto. In fact, your letter can be
    our manifesto. (*Laughing.*)
MARIGOLD: It would be your only issue. We'd both be sent
    down on the strength of the PS alone. One of my bolder
    strokes, I thought.
STUART: Yes, you're frankly disgusting. (*He glances at his watch,*

looks out of the window.) Oh here comes one of them now, what's his name – um, Martin – Martin – oh hell, I told you! Martin – the one with the loot and the zeal for service.

MARIGOLD: (*Staring out of the window*) Isn't that our greatest living poet figure?

STUART: What?

MARIGOLD: Hubert Parkin. The man you claim is the greatest living –

STUART: Christ, it is! He must have come up for the big dinner last night – where's he going? (*He peers.*) Into one of the guest rooms. Come on. (*To* MARIGOLD.)

MARIGOLD: Where?

STUART: To see him, of course. Tell him about the magazine. Ask him if he'll contribute. Well, why not? He might. Anyway, let's try. At least I'll have met him. Come on.
(*They cross,* STUART *flings the door open.*
MARTIN *enters.*)
Oh hello, this is – um, look, there's somebody we've got to see, we won't be a minute, make yourself at home. And tell anyone else we'll be right back.

MARTIN: Oh right.

STUART: (*Gestures*) Change the record, if you want. (*He goes off with* MARIGOLD.)
(MARTIN *stands uncertainly. He crosses to the gramophone, around which is a litter of record sleeves. He picks up one. It is empty. He reads the title of the work, nods, puts the record sleeve down. He wanders over to the table, glances at the typescripts, etc.; sees a letter, glances quickly around, then picks up the letter, begins to read it, very quickly. He is clearly amazed by the contents. He puts the letter down, in exactly the same position, adjusting it slightly, and moves away from the table to the window seat. Looks out of the window, sees somebody he recognizes, and sits down on the window seat. Assumes a deeply listening posture. The record is still playing Bach's 'Air on a g-string.'*)

HUMPHRY *appears at the door.* MARTIN *is enacting too
absorbed to be aware of him.*)

HUMPHRY: (*Entering properly*) Stuart not here then?

MARTIN: (*Starting*) Oh. No, they've just dashed off somewhere.
But they'll be back in a minute. He said to wait.
(HUMPHRY *sits down. There is a pause.*)
Marvellous stuff, isn't it?
(HUMPHRY *grunts.*)
Do you like Vivaldi?

HUMPHRY: Yes. But I like Bach more. Which this is.

MARTIN: Really? Are you sure?

HUMPHRY: Yes.

MARTIN: Oh. Well, you're probably right. I had some idea it
was that Vivaldi piece in E major – which Bach is it then,
do you know?

HUMPHRY: No.
(*The record comes to an end. There is a clicking and whirring
from the gramophone.*
HUMPHRY *gets up, goes over to it. He deftly stops the
gramophone, removes the record and looks around for the
sleeve. He picks up the sleeve* MARTIN *had looked at.*)

MARTIN: What was it precisely?

HUMPHRY: (*Puts down the sleeve and glances at the record*) The
'Air on a g-string'.

MARTIN: Vivaldi, you mean?

HUMPHRY: No, Bach of course. (*He picks up another sleeve,
which is empty, checks the record against it and slips it in.*)

MARTIN: Really! You must have a terrific feeling for passages of
music. I only know them when I've heard them hundreds
of times before. And then I get them wrong. (*He laughs.*)
(HUMPHRY *sits down.*)
You're Humphry Taylor, aren't you?

HUMPHRY: That's right.

MARTIN: And you're doing history, isn't it?

HUMPHRY: Moral Sciences.

MARTIN: Oh. Well, I'm Martin Musgrove. I'm in English. I suppose you've come about the magazine too? Have you written something for it?

HUMPHRY: I sent in some poems. What about you? Have you written anything?

MARTIN: Oh no – well, actually I did submit a little thing I'd written. A sort of prose poem about well, cats, actually. (*He laughs.*) But Stuart sent it back saying I had far more grasp of cats than I did of prose or poetry, so I'd better stick to those. Quite right. It was pretty embarrassing, when I read it through. I haven't got any talent at all, you see. But I'm interested in publishing, so I want to work on the magazine from that point of view. The business side, you know, helping with subscriptions, advertising, anything of that sort. Is he going to publish your poems?

HUMPHRY: No. I've come to get them back.

MARTIN: Oh. What didn't he like about them?

HUMPHRY: He liked them. It's me. I don't like them.

MARTIN: Really, why not?

HUMPHRY: Because they make me feel sick. In fact, I've decided to give up writing. Poems, anyway.

MARTIN: But mightn't you eventually write some that don't make you feel sick?

HUMPHRY: Possibly. But it's not worth the risk. Besides I'm going to be a professional philosopher. So I'll have to concentrate on thinking until I've got my First and a job in a university.

MARTIN: That's what you want, is it?

HUMPHRY: I haven't any choice. As you can't be a professional philosopher except in a university.

MARTIN: Do you want to be in any particular university?

HUMPHRY: This one will do.

MARTIN: (*Laughs slightly*) Any particular college?

HUMPHRY: This one will do.

MARTIN: Well – that's quite a prediction, really.

HUMPHRY: It wasn't meant to be. More like an obituary, in fact. But if I'm going to institutionalize myself, I suppose I might as well do it in one of the better institutions.

MARTIN: I wish I had that sort of confidence about my own future. I only thought of publishing because I can't think of anything else.

NICK: (*Enters, coughing slightly, looks around*) Where's Stuart then?

MARTIN: He said to wait, they'd be right back.

NICK: They – oh, of course, Marigold. Well, isn't there any coffee on the go or anything? I've got a hangover.

MARTIN: Really? How did you get it?

NICK: Drank too much. In fact, look, what's that stuff, slimy, thick and yellow?

HUMPHRY: That covers a large number of revolting substances.

MARTIN: Oh, it must be avocaat, mustn't it? You know. Egg Nog.

NICK: That explains it. I'm allergic to eggs. Probably allergic to nogs too. If they're what they sound like. It was that bloody girl from Girton – Muriel what's-it?

MARTIN: Hoftstadt?

NICK: Yes, she produced it. I was perfectly all right until then. Coasting along on white wine, Martini, rum, Scotch, that sort of thing. But then that's Muriel, always there when you least want her, passing out egg nogs when you least want them, she should have been a nurse. (*He laughs and coughs slightly.*)

MARTIN: Did Muriel give the party?

NICK: Do you think I'd go to a party given by Muriel Hoftstadt? No, no, it was some prick, prickette from King's, secretary of their literary society, Jeremy – Jeremy –

MARTIN: Astle.

NICK: To meet that woman who's written a novel about her menstrual cycle, *Murdering*.

MARTIN: *Mothering*, isn't it?

NICK: What?

MARTIN: Isn't it *Mothering*, not *Murdering*?

NICK: I thought they were synonyms.

MARTIN: (*Laughs*) Angela Thark.

NICK: What?

MARTIN: That's her name. The novelist's, isn't it? Angela Thark. I wish I'd met her. I got the novel just yesterday, I haven't read it yet. What's she like?

NICK: Much sexier than her prose. Bit of a knock-out really. If you like long legs, big breasts, that sort of thing. I do. But I'm not very selective yet. I'm still a virgin. What about you two? Actually, this room reeks of passion. What were you up to before I came in? (*Laughs, coughs slightly and meets* HUMPHRY's *eye*.) Don't worry, it wouldn't show, not if Stuart and Marigold have been at it.

MARTIN: Did she have anything interesting to say?

NICK: Who?

MARTIN: Angela Thark? Did she talk about novel writing, that sort of thing?

NICK: Look, could you hold on the incisive questions, just for a moment? I'm about to do something exceptionally difficult. (*He takes out a cigarette, lights it and inhales.*) Oh God! Yes, here they come, the little buggers, bobbing from iris to pupil and back again. Now the ripples of giddiness – turning into tidal bloody waves of nausea. (*He groans.*)

MARTIN: Is it always like this when you smoke a cigarette?

NICK: Only the first.

HUMPHRY: Why have it then?

NICK: So I can get on to my next. By the third or fourth I won't even notice I'm smoking.

MARTIN: But if the first few are so ghastly, and you don't even notice the rest of them, why don't you just give up?

NICK: What for?

MARTIN: Well – I mean, for one thing you might live longer.

NICK: Oh, you don't live longer, it just seems longer. As Sam Goldwyn said. One of the poets, anyway. (*He wanders shakily to the table, picks up the typescripts, etc.*)

MARTIN: You know, sometimes I think I'm missing out on addiction. I've never been addicted to anything in my life. Not even when I was a child. I mean, I'm normal all the time, which is very boring. For everyone else as well as me. While for you I suppose normal's something you accelerate away from with drinks and cigarettes – (*He stops, aware that* HUMPHRY *is watching* NICK, *who is reading something he has extracted from an envelope.*)

NICK: Boys on their river banks, naked in the sad and dewy dawn. (*He laughs and coughs slightly.*) God, I hate queer literature. (*He reads again.*) Not for publication, at least at this stage, but glad to hear of new magazine, hope it will be noted for its critical vigour – vigour? – rigour, James Harrop, New College, Oxford, oh that explains it, probably not even queer, just Oxford, I knew a Harrop, at prep school, wonder if it's the same one, he was a creep too.

HUMPHRY: You shouldn't do that.

NICK: What? (*He picks up the letter* MARTIN *read earlier and begins to read it. He whistles.*) I say, Marigold can really turn it on. A little too well-written for my taste, though. But I suppose that's the problem with having an affair with a literary editor, keeping one's prose up to snuff.

HUMPHRY: I said don't do that.

NICK: Do what?

MARTIN: Yes, well – I must say I've never seen anyone read anyone's private letters, you know.

NICK: Of course you haven't. This is a notable breakthrough. Doing it in public, so to speak. (*He turns a page.*)

HUMPHRY: That's two warnings. You don't get a third. (*He takes a step towards* NICK.)

NICK: Actually it's from the bursar. Inviting him to pay last term's buttery bill.

MARTIN: No, it's not.

NICK: (*Grins, coughs slightly*) How do you know?

MARTIN: For one thing it's handwritten. And pages long.

NICK: Well, you know the bursar. Anything to make a conquest. Or settle an account.

HUMPHRY: (*Walks over to him*) Are you going to put it down?

NICK: Are you going to make me?

(*They stand looking at each other.* NICK *tosses the letter on the table.*)

It's time I introduced myself. I'm Nick Finchling, special agent. I've adopted this flamboyant personality as a disguise. I'm trying to find ways of persuading Stuart to accept my juvenilia but he says I haven't finished it yet. Actually, I want to do theatre criticism, as I intend to be a big-name theatre reviewer when I grow up, like Ken what's-it, only on the *Sunday Times*, would you really have hit me a moment ago?

HUMPHRY: That moment hasn't passed.

NICK: Will it, if I swear to you that I didn't read a word? You're Humphry Taylor aren't you, the philosopher-poet, I've decided we're going to be friends. It's safer. (*He laughs and coughs.*) Actually Stuart says your poems have genius. And that you're a real find. Who are you – oh, I know, the millionaire orphan, aren't you? (*To* MARTIN.)

MARTIN: Well, I'm not a millionaire.

NICK: But you're quite rich, and if you're an orphan you'll need a friend. (*He laughs.*) I'm your man. Actually I'm the opposite of an orphan, I've got six parents in all, if you include the steps and ex-steps.

PETER: (*Enters*) Sorry I'm late. Oh. (*Looking around.*)

NICK: Hello Peter. Meet the poet, philosopher and pugilist, Humphrey Taylor, and that chap who wrote the charming little piece about cats that Stuart showed us before returning it to him.

MARTIN: Martin. Martin Musgrove.

NICK: And this is Peter Whetworth. Senior scholar in history, an inevitable First, future Fellow of the college, and consequently one of my closest friends. Stuart says we've to wait for him. Why didn't you come Tharking last night?

PETER: (*Who has smiled and nodded at* HUMPHRY *and* MARTIN) Oh yes. Sorry. I met up with some people.

NICK: Female people, I suppose.

(PETER *laughs*.)

More than one female people?

PETER: There were two to begin with, but I whittled them down to one. Actually, I got the wrong one, as the one I whittled turned out to be the one who really wanted me.

NICK: Not Sonia?

PETER: Sonia?

NICK: The nurse at Addenbrooks. You met her in my room last week, when I was rounding up some hopefuls, to lose my virginity with. She wasn't interested in me at all, after you appeared.

PETER: Really? The very pretty one?

NICK: Quite pretty. Quite silly. Terribly nice. And yearns for you. In fact your usual type.

MARTIN: Are you writing for the magazine?

PETER: Not if I can help it. But I'll have some minor function – perhaps I'll be the social officer. Look after the parties, that side of things.

HUMPHRY: I heard your paper. The one you gave to the Maudsley Society.

PETER: Really?

HUMPHRY: It had one or two good things in it. And even some originality.

PETER: Thanks.

NICK: I bet he says that to all the boys. (*To* PETER.) Tell me about it. Last night. I'm anxious to acquire any information I can on this sex business, all I'm sure of at the moment is that I'm not queer. So what did you do? Did

97

you take her back? Or get her to take you to her place? Or
what? How? When? Where? And so on. With illustrations.
And I'll invite Sonia back for you, as a reward.
(PETER *laughs*.)

HUMPHRY: Can we have some music instead. (*Little pause.*) If
we're going to wait, could we at least do something
worthwhile.

NICK: I advise you not to resist him. He has a powerful
personality. (*He goes to the gramophone.*) What would you
like to hear?

HUMPHRY: Wagner would probably be the most inappropriate.
So let's have him.

NICK: I don't know if Stuart goes in for Wagner. (*Hunting.*) Or
anything musical, really. Except for reverie and romance.
Ah – here's some. (*He puts the record on the gramophone.*)
Mainly snatches from the great tunes, from the look of it. I
hope it'll do. (*He sits down.*
Wagner fills the room. NICK *lights a cigarette and coughs.*
HUMPHRY *listens.* MARTIN *assumes a listening posture.*
PETER *listens idly, smiling pleasantly.*
*They remain in that position as the set revolves off, the music
still playing, while Stuart's office revolves on,* STUART *at the
desk, for Scene Two.*)

SCENE 2

*Stuart's office in Holborn. Eleven years ago. Late morning. The
office is large, and could be handsome. But it is dingy. There is a
desk, with a telephone on it. An armchair, a sofa, a cupboard.
Books and magazines on shelves. Bottles of wine lined up on the
shelves, opened and half full, as if left over from a party.*
STUART *is at his desk, reading a typescript. He looks up, glances at
the door, checks his watch, goes resolutely back to reading. The
telephone rings.* STUART's *hand leaps out. He checks it. He lifts the
telephone and speaks in a disguised voice. Irish.*

STUART: Hello. Well, yes, I think it is. Hang on while I check.
Yes. That's right, the office of the *New Literary Review*.
Yes, well I'm the window cleaner, you see, and I'm never
sure what's on whatever floor I'm on. Who? Well, I'll have
a look, who shall I say is calling, if he's here? Right. No,
I'm afraid there's no one here by that name. There doesn't
seem to be anyone here at all, in fact. Right. Hang on, I'll
just get a pencil. (*He doesn't.*) Ready. Yes. Mappin and
Mappin, yes, got that –
(MARTIN *enters.*)
Compelled to institute legal proceedings unless – what? Oh
a cheque, right, by the end of the week. OK. I'll leave it
here where he can see it. Not at all. Goodbye. (*He hangs up
and stares at the telephone.*) I wish the post office would cut
me off. They keep threatening to, and I'm three months
overdue, after all. But I suppose they're too busy
disconnecting old age pensioners and emergency services to
get round to deserving cases like me.
MARTIN: Was it the printers again?
STUART: Yes, poor old George this time, with his wheeze and
his heart condition. They know perfectly well it's me, I
think they're quite grateful I pretend I'm not. Otherwise
they'd have to threaten me direct. There's some Nescafé
and stale milk, or last month's warm white wine.
(MARTIN *takes a bottle of wine out of his pocket and hands it
to* STUART, *who takes it and goes to look for a corkscrew.*)
MARTIN: No word from Peter yet then?
STUART: No.
MARTIN: (*Looks at his watch*) Well, I suppose it's still a bit
early.
STUART: Only just. (*Beginning to open the bottle.*)
MARTIN: Oh, by the way, who's the girl with the Welsh accent?
STUART: Mmmm? (*Struggling with the cork.*)
MARTIN: Well, I phoned you at your flat last night, and got this
girl with a Welsh accent. Very nice and talkative, but all

she seemed to know about anything was that you'd moved
out and that Marigold had had to go away.

STUART: Yes – (*Working the cork*) she's gone to Cheltenham. To
visit her parents. One of them is ill or something.

MARTIN: I thought she only had a father.

STUART: That's right. Then that must be the one that's ill. I
didn't get on with her mother either. Especially when she
was alive. Ah! (*The cork comes out.*)

MARTIN: But then who was the girl with the Welsh accent?

STUART: Marigold's flatmate.

MARTIN: I thought *you* were her flatmate. (*Slight laugh.*)

STUART: Not for a while. Last week we discovered neither of us
could afford my share of the rent. So, Marigold moved in
some new teacher from her school, who wants a place to
stay while she's looking for a flat of her own. Which means
that she's paying my share of the rent. Very nice
apparently, if slightly incomprehensible, I didn't know she
was Welsh.

MARTIN: But where are you living then?

STUART: (*Pouring wine*) Oh, here and there. (*He hands* MARTIN
a glass.)

MARTIN: Thanks. Here and there?

STUART: Well mainly here. In fact, entirely here.

MARTIN: What do you sleep on?

STUART: There's a sofa. And a sleeping bag in the cupboard.

MARTIN: But why on earth don't you come and stay with me?
You can have either of the spare rooms. Or both of them. I
can move Samantha into my bedroom. Where she longs to
be anyway, and would be, if she didn't make me sneeze.

STUART: Yes, I know. And thanks. But I had an odd feeling.
To do with territory. That it would be harder to get me out
of here if I made it into my lair. I see myself as a
threatened lion. Well, some impressive creature, with teeth
and jaws, a tattered tiger. A bankrupt rat.

MARTIN: You know, you're extraordinary.

STUART: Really, why?

MARTIN: Well, for one thing, I couldn't live like this. I'd love
to be able to. Like one of the heroes or murderers from
Russian novels. But I know I couldn't.

STUART: Oh, it's actually quite simple. All it takes is no money.
(*He looks at his watch.*) He's getting on towards being late.

MARTIN: Those meetings go on forever. Until lunch even. You
know the Arts Council.

STUART: I do.

MARTIN: Peter'll pull it off. You said yourself a man who can
hustle a full Oxford fellowship on Peter's credentials, can
hustle anything.

STUART: Yes, but on this occasion he's not hustling for himself,
he's hustling for me. Perhaps his heart isn't in it. If he
hadn't missed the last meeting he might have got our grant
doubled then. And the Hubert Parkin party wouldn't have
tipped me into bankruptcy. And I wouldn't have needed
the money so desperately now.

MARTIN: Well, of course, that was slightly unfortunate – the
Parkin party costing so much –

STUART: No, it was the right thing to do. If I hadn't thrown the
party I probably wouldn't have got his six new poems.

MARTIN: Though it does mean – (*He hesitates*) you might not
have a magazine to publish them in. I'm sorry, I only
meant – you know – anyway he probably couldn't have
done anything at that meeting. *This* is the one that counts.

STUART: What time are you seeing him?

MARTIN: What?

STUART: What time are you seeing Peter?

MARTIN: But I'm not seeing him. Except when he comes here,
of course. But he doesn't know I'll be here.

STUART: You didn't make an arrangement with him? For this
afternoon, or for lunch – ?

MARTIN: Absolutely not, I haven't spoken to him for weeks.

STUART: (*Slumps back in despair*) Oh God!

MARTIN: Why?

STUART: Because when I phoned Oxford this morning to make sure he'd at least left, I got Sonia, who said he hadn't mentioned anything about the Arts Council, only about meeting you to discuss a book you'd asked him to write. About the role of sex in nineteenth-century politics.

MARTIN: I haven't asked him to write a book.

STUART: No, of course you haven't. So he's coming to London to meet some bloody girl. He must have forgotten the Arts Council entirely, mustn't he?

MARTIN: Well, I don't quite see –

STUART: He made you his alibi. Which means he didn't remember he already had an alibi. Which was me. So he's not there. Do you know exactly how many enemies I've got on the magazine panel?

MARTIN: Well, I know your reputation for integrity –

STUART: I think I'll kill him. Yes. Kill him. The lengths I went to, to get him co-opted on the panel. And the stuff I sent him – everything. Articles, poems, the six Hubert Parkins, some of them I didn't even have time to get xeroxed – all of it stuffed into his briefcase, under some bloody girl's bed at this very minute. Or at his feet in a pub. My representative! I should have got Humphry! Why didn't I get Humphry?

MARTIN: Well, actually, because Humphry's too trenchant for the Arts Council, you thought. And you were right. They'd have hated him. You made the right choice in Peter. Apart from his not turning up. If he doesn't.

STUART: Oh, he won't. The jig's up then, isn't it? After seven years – nine years if you count the time at Cambridge – of continuous struggle, may I be presumptuous enough to call it? Struggle? The jig's up.

MARTIN: (*After slight pause*) No, it isn't. Not if you come in with me. Come in and work with me.

STUART: With you?

MARTIN: Yes.

STUART: Don't you mean Haylife and Forling's? How will that save the magazine?

MARTIN: No, I don't mean Haylife and Forling's. I mean with me, Stuart. (*Little pause.*) I've quit Haylife. And Forling too, come to that, he's far worse. (*He gives a little laugh.*) Or rather, I'm just about to quit them both. I'm going to set up on my own, which is what I always intended. I've always had the capital, and now I've got the experience. Look, Stuart, the reason I phoned you at the flat last night was that I wanted to discuss it with you. Partners, you see. You would commission and edit the fiction and the poetry. I'd do the business side and any editorial hack-work. I've learnt an enormous amount at Haylife and Forling's, I really have. I'm ready. (*Little pause.*) And the point is, we'd keep the *New Literary Review* going. As our subsidiary. (*Little pause.*) What do you think?

STUART: Subsidiary?

MARTIN: At least we'd manage without the Arts Council. And I know how much you'd like that, you've always said that they only give it out so that they have something to take away when it really matters.

(*Little pause.*)

And you could move back with Marigold. The two of you could live, well, you know, like a couple at last. As I know you've always wanted. Especially with a baby coming.

STUART: (*After a little pause*) How did you know about that?

MARTIN: Oh, well I had lunch with Marigold last week, you see. The day after she found out she was expecting, you see.

STUART: She's not expecting. She's merely pregnant. (*Little pause.*) I wonder why she didn't tell me. About your having lunch, I mean. Not about being merely pregnant.

MARTIN: Actually, because I asked her not to. You see, I wanted to know what she thought you'd feel about the prospect of coming in with me. But I didn't want to press ahead with you until I'd, well, sorted a few things out. Which I now have, actually. And was in a position to make you what they call (*Slight laugh*) a formal proposal. Which I now am. You see? (*Little laugh. Little pause.*) Stuart –

STUART: And what did she think I'd feel?

MARTIN: Well, to be honest, she refused to say. Because it had to be your decision. That's all she wanted. But Stuart, look –

STUART: I wonder why – (*He stops.*)

MARTIN: What?

STUART: Why she told you she was pregnant. We'd agreed not to make it public. Until we'd made up our minds.

MARTIN: I expect because of Samantha. She's pregnant too. Didn't I tell you?

STUART: No. Congratulations. (*Ironically.*)

MARTIN: (*Laughs*) Thank you. It's probably the only pregnancy I'll allow her poor thing, before getting her done. She should litter in about a week. And I offered Marigold a tabby, if there is one, because she adores tabbies, as you know – Marigold – I mean, not Samantha, though Samantha seems to adore them too, at least the one I hope is the father. He was hanging around at the right time. A real rogue.

(*There is a pause.*)

STUART: So you and Marigold were just swapping pregnancy gossip?

MARTIN: Oh no. Sorry. No. The point is that I started to tell Marigold about Samantha, rabbiting on in that – that boring way of mine when on cats. And she suddenly well, broke down – Marigold – and told me she was pregnant. And then asked me not to tell you she'd told me. Because of your agreement. (*Little pause.*) So I'd rather you didn't tell her.

STUART: Tell her that you've told me that she told you? But

how can I? As she only told you during a lunch you'd told
her not to tell me you were having.

MARTIN: Quite. (*He laughs.*)

(STUART *smiles.*)

So therefore – therefore – I can't tell you how passionately
she, well, seems to want to have the baby, can I?

STUART: Under the circumstances, no you can't. But then you
don't have to. As I know. These things tend to slip out,
between long-established couples.

MARTIN: (*Nods*) Sorry. (*Little pause.*) Well then. What do you
think? About our setting up as partners in publishing.
Keeping the *New Literary Review* going?

STUART: Thanks. *Really* thanks, Martin but I'm going to try
and keep it afloat and independent even if Peter and the
Arts Council let us down. I've always believed that editing
it was a full-time job. Even when it's failing to appear. I
haven't forgotten that I owe you quite a lot of money, by
the way.

MARTIN: The money was a gift to the magazine. You know how
much I want it to survive.

STUART: Yes I do. So do I. Want it to survive. But not as a
subsidiary to something else, you see.

MARTIN: Does that include Marigold and the baby? Sorry,
sorry, none of my business, but – well, it'll break her
heart –

(*The sound of footsteps, off, coming up the stairs.*)

HUMPHRY: (*Enters*) What's going on, this room reeks of passion,
in the famous phrase. What have you two been up to?

MARTIN: We're waiting for Peter.

STUART: Although we suspect he's forgotten to come.

HUMPHRY: I doubt it. Is this all there is? (*Surveying the opened
wine bottles.*)

MARTIN: No, there's some here. (*Handing him a bottle.*)

STUART: Why do you doubt it? After the way you've been
talking about him recently.

HUMPHRY: I doubt it because I saw him two days ago when I went to give a paper at Oxford. I had dinner with him. And Sonia. And their babies. He boasted that he was coming down here this morning to do what he called your street-fighting for you. Why do you think I'm here, if not to observe you in crisis and triumph. You're handling the crisis part badly, let's hope you come up to snuff in the triumph part.

STUART: And you in the disaster part. Tell him.

MARTIN: Well, there's a possibility that he's merely coming to London for his usual – um –

STUART: Fuck.

HUMPHRY: Of course he is. He'd go anywhere and do anything for a fuck. Including even attending an Arts Council meeting on your behalf.

MARTIN: Yes, but you see – he lied to Sonia about why he was coming up to London, he told her he was coming to see me to discuss a book, which isn't true, instead of saying he was going to the Arts Council meeting, which would have been true, and the obvious lie to tell, because at least it would have been true, if he remembered it. If you follow.

HUMPHRY: Of course I follow. Merely because you can't speak properly doesn't mean I can't understand you. Generally well before you're finished. I suppose you got all this from Sonia?

MARTIN: Well, not about coming for the fuck.

HUMPHRY: The reason he lied to Sonia was that it was simpler and less fatiguing than telling her the truth. Have you tried talking to that woman recently? A simple statement from you is followed by an imbecile question from her, and she doesn't stop until your statements have become as imbecile as her questions, in a ghastly parody of the Socratic dialogue. Then, as you sit drained of ideas, energy, humanity, she changes a nappy in front of you. Virtually all over you, in fact. He had absolutely no right to marry her.

Getting her pregnant was no excuse. We should have talked him out of it. It was our duty. Or talked Nick into taking his place. He's got nothing particularly important to do with his life and they'd have got on perfectly. Her pathological need to ask imbecile questions would actually give a purpose to his pathological need to tell lies. (*To* MARTIN) Do you follow?

MARTIN: I think so.

HUMPHRY: Explain it back to me, then?

MARTIN: It was easier to say he was coming to see me than to explain about the Arts Council, the magazine, grants, etc., and Stuart.

HUMPHRY: Exactly. Furthermore he won't let you down because (a) he's a good and loyal friend, (b) he actually longs to crusade on your behalf because (c) he's got nothing better to do. And he's only twenty-eight. Unlike Nick he actually had a mind, a few years back. What'll he be like when he's forty? Probably exactly the same only less so, having less energy to be it with.

MARTIN: Yes.

STUART: What?

MARTIN: I think Humpty's got it right, as usual.

STUART: Then why isn't he here? He's now actually late. Or phoned?

HUMPHRY: Wait thou child of hope. For time will give thee all things. Except a decent glass of wine ever, at least here. This is simultaneously bland and acid, is it English?

MARTIN: It's a Chablis, a vintage isn't it? That's what they said –

HUMPHRY: (*Goes to shelf, pours himself stale wine*) How's Marigold?

STUART: In Cheltenham. Visting her mother. She's ill.

MARTIN: Her father.

STUART: Yes.

HUMPHRY: Odd how Martin always seems to know more about

107

your life than you do. Perhaps it's because he takes a
greater interest. Anyway, you're all right are you, you two?

STUART: Which two?

HUMPHRY: You and Marigold.

STUART: Why?

HUMPHRY: Because I phoned you last night to say I was coming
down and got an exceptionally loquacious Indian girl, from
the sound of her, who gave me the distinct impression that
you and Marigold were no longer living together. Although
I can't be sure. Her rhythms got in the way of her sense.
(STUART *says nothing*.)

MARTIN: It's only a financial arrangement – um –

STUART: As a matter of fact she's pregnant. And we're going to
get married.
(MARTIN *looks at him*.)

HUMPHRY: (*After a little pause*) Good.

STUART: Really? You don't think we have a duty to talk me out
of it? Or get Nick to take my place?

HUMPHRY: Don't be ridiculous. I've got the greatest admiration
for Marigold, as you know.

STUART: Because she's got a fine mind?

HUMPHRY: No, she hasn't. But when it comes to the things that
matter she's got a mind of her own, which is more
important. Congratulations.
(STUART *nods*.)
And now to a vastly more passionate relationship. How's
Samantha? Kindly confine your reply to two sentences.

MARTIN: She's pregnant. But we're not going to get married.
What about you?

HUMPHRY: I'm not pregnant. And I wouldn't dream of getting
married, even if I were. But I've moved into your old
rooms at last. (*To* STUART) I've always wanted them, but
that ridiculous Scot who lived above you took them over
when he got his fellowship and so I'd given up hope. But
last month he committed suicide. Quite upsetting isn't it? I

mean, people we convert into jokes have an obligation not
to do that sort of thing. He was a mathematical genius
apparently, but his creative juices dried up suddenly. As
they tend to with mathematicians, they finish young.
Actually he must have been rather short on real
personality, in spite of his bluster. As he hasn't left the
trace of a ghost behind. Even in the bedroom, where he did
it with a razor. I haven't even bothered to have it
redecorated. The odd thing is that I feel I'm finally where I
always intended to be. At home, in other words. So much
so that this morning I rose at six, walked twice round Great
Court, and wrote the first fourteen and a half lines of my
book on Wagner. (*Little pause.*) But nothing of
consequence. At least in *your* life-enhancing terms.
(*The sound of footsteps running up the stairs.*)

MARTIN: That must be Peter.

(*There is a sudden explosive cough.*)

HUMPHRY: No, it isn't.

(STUART *groans slightly.*

NICK *enters. He stands for a moment, a cigarette between his
lips, then begins to cough again. The cough becomes explosive,
the cigarette shoots out and lands – preferably – on Stuart's
desk.*)

NICK: (*Pulling himself together*) That does it! I'm giving up taxis.
The way that shit took the corner, my bum skidding, my
stomach churning, my head pounding, God, I wish I'd
thrown up. All over the back of his neck. It was red with
ginger hair on it.

(MARTIN *hands him back his cigarette.*)

Thanks. (*He continues to smoke it.*)

MARTIN: Where were you coming from?

NICK: Don't know. Earls Court it looked like. Some girl picked
me up at the French pub last night, took me back to her
place. At least I hope it was a girl. Had her back to me
when I woke up. Had a girl's spine. Smelt like a girl. But

snoring like a man. So it was either an Australian or a hermaphrodite or both. The haunting question is whether I poked it, I keep recalling a brief spasm during the night. I hope it was just my cough. News from Peter?

MARTIN: We're waiting.

NICK: Oh, well I've only a few minutes – but don't worry. It's in the bag.

HUMPHRY: Nicholas's confidence is the first real alarm signal.

NICK: Hey, Humpty, what's all this I've been hearing? About you.

HUMPHRY: What have you been hearing?

NICK: About your lethal effect on the undergraduate sensibility, and – (*Seeing something in* HUMPHRY'*s face, changing tack*) other tittle tattle, very complimentary about you as an intellectual glamour-figure because of your lectures and stuff, from Harrop. He went up to do a poetry reading recently, he was in the French pub last night and do you know what he claims, that he's won the Cheltenham prize. For that nappy full of homosexless verse he dropped last year.

MARTIN: Well, he has, hasn't he?

NICK: How do you know, he told me he wasn't allowed to tell anyone until the announcement.

STUART: I was one of the judges. In fact I voted for him.

NICK: You didn't tell me.

STUART: No, well I'm not allowed to tell anyone either.

NICK: But how could you vote for Harrop? You know I loathe him.

STUART: I didn't vote for him. I voted for his poems. Why are you so sure it's in the bag?

NICK: What? Oh, your grant, because Peter told me.

STUART: When?

NICK: (*Being watched closely by* HUMPHRY) Last night. He phoned to say he was coming to London for the meeting, what about lunch afterwards, along with the rest of us, he

110

couldn't get hold of you, just a foreign girl at your flat, but I
can't make it because I'm having lunch with *Vogue*, to discuss
doing a series of articles on (*Faltering*) this and that, but he
said, *en passant*, the grant was in the bag. (*He coughs
violently.*)

HUMPHRY: That's aesthetically one of the least attractive ways
of killing yourself, Nicholas, why don't you stop it?

NICK: Yes. Well I will. I've got to go. Love to Peter, sorry I
missed him – oh Martin, I think I'd better not, I'm too
young to settle down, and also they turn into cats, and I'm
less soppy about those. (*He goes to the door and stops.*) Oh
God, I almost forgot – that article I sent you, reviewing the
reviewers sort of thing? I don't suppose you've had a
chance to read it yet?

STUART: No, not properly. I've looked at it of course, but I
haven't – (*He gestures.*)

NICK: No, that's all right, but can I have it back for a while!
I'm not really happy with some sections of it, especially the
couple of pages on Angela Thark, for instance, I didn't
know she was dying when I wrote it, don't forget. I'd like
to be more – more delicate. Cut out the bit about her
blood-soaked prose, etc., and get at some of the reviewers
for not admiring her more – she's got that daughter, after
all. Grieving friends. I'm one myself, in a way.

(*STUART has gone to his desk and is looking for the manuscript.*)

MARTIN: Really, I thought you couldn't stand her?

NICK: That was only when she was alive. (*He gives a little
laugh.*) Death brings its own respect, and besides I won't
have to see her again. (*Laughs again.*) All right. Of course I
couldn't stand her. Although I always maintained that she
was sexy. The point is I can't let it go as it stands. It makes
me seem a brute. Which I am, about her. But I can't afford
to seem it, can I?

STUART: I can't find it. Can you work from your own copy?
(*Still looking.*)

NICK: No, I can't. I destroyed it. I lost a bit of confidence in it, you see, when you went on failing to mention it every time I saw you. Not that I'm blaming you. I destroyed a lot of other stuff too. Although I sometimes wonder whether you realize what an influence you have, Stuart. Your approval. Doesn't he? Any luck? (*To* STUART.)

STUART: No, but it's here somewhere.

NICK: (*Conscious that* HUMPHRY *is watching him*) You know I'm beginning to wonder whether I'm really cut out for a career in literature. I find writing even more of a chore than fucking. And a lot of the people one meets are even worse. Actually, I wish I were a vicar. With a wife, a bike, a dog and some children. And a little bit of faith. And a private income, of course. Two private incomes in fact.

HUMPHRY: What I can't work out is why?

NICK: What?

HUMPHRY: Why you're lying. Nicholas. Your motive. Or are you just keeping in practice.

MARTIN: You don't think by any chance –

NICK: What?

MARTIN: Well, I mean – you wouldn't have sold it to somebody else, would you? I mean – no, I'm sorry. Of course not.

HUMPHRY: *Vogue*, of course!

NICK: What?

HUMPHRY: Nicholas has sold his article to *Vogue*. Well done. (*To* MARTIN.)

NICK: Oh come on! (*Little pause.*) Yes, well actually what happened is that I sent my copy to my agent, and she showed it to *Vogue*, without my consent, naturally, and it turned out that *Vogue* was thinking of doing a piece along my lines.

STUART: My lines, as a matter of fact. As I suggested them.

NICK: Yes, well they're hardly original, are they? It's how it's done that matters. Not that *Vogue* wants it as it stands. It's got to be spiced up, with little character-sketches and

assassinations thrown in, illustrated with cartoons and fish-
eye photographs. I've already worked out something for
Harrop. It won't be the same article at all, in the end. No
reason why they shouldn't be published in both. Eh?

HUMPHRY: Then you don't need Stuart's copy back, do you?
You can get one from *Vogue*.

NICK: Yes, well my agent says she doesn't like the thought of it
being offered to two different magazines at the same time.
She says it's unethical.

(STUART, MARTIN *and* HUMPHRY *laugh*.)

Perhaps. But bloody hell, I'm a professional literary
journalist. I live by what I sell. And you didn't bother to
acknowledge receiving it, let alone let me know what you
thought about it. And I've waited for years for you to ask
me to contribute something – and the fact is, it could lie
rotting away on your desk for ever. The magazine's failed
to come out twice running now, and there's a decent
chance it'll never come out again.

(*A pause*.)

STUART: A decent chance, is it?

NICK: According to Peter.

STUART: According to Peter when?

NICK: This morning. He stopped in for a cup of coffee on his
way to the meeting.

STUART: But you were coming from an Australian or a
hermaphrodite in Earls Court this morning.

HUMPHRY: Whom you either poked or coughed into.

NICK: Yes. Well that must have been yesterday morning. In
fact, it sounds like all my yesterday mornings recently.
Except tomorrow's. When I'll have had coffee with Peter.
Won't I? (*He attempts a laugh, coughs instead*.)

STUART: And what precisely did he say? About the grant?

NICK: Yes, well – apparently the whole Arts Council panel,
virtually, thinks you're elitist. He's going to do his best,
but he reckons you're finished. But knowing you you'll

struggle on for years, editing a magazine that never comes
out at all. And I'll have missed the chance of a deal with
Vogue. And I need it. Can I have the article please?

STUART: Actually no, you can't. I must have stuck it in with the
material I gave Peter to show the Arts Council. So it was
probably sitting in that calf-skin briefcase of his when you
had coffee with him. But don't worry, Nick, I shan't
publish it. The truth is I've been wondering how to return
it to you without hurting you. All you had to do was to say
straight out that *Vogue* wanted it, did I mind? I'd have
been delighted. It's perfect for *Vogue*. Just as it stands.
None of this need have happened.

NICK: Yes – well they're right. You *are* elitist.

STUART: Well, somebody's got to be, haven't they? Especially
at a time when nobody else wants to be.

NICK: But they don't want *you* to be, either. Do they? So
whatever you think about me the magazine's finished. And
the truth is, actually, that I'm sorry. But I think you
should face it, and not waste your life –

(MARIGOLD *enters.*)

HUMPHRY: Marigold.

MARIGOLD: Hello Humpty, I didn't know you were coming
down.

NICK: Hi, Marigold.

MARTIN: How's your mother?

MARIGOLD: Terrific. Apart from being dead, that is. It's my
father I went to see. They've discovered he's got what he
calls a bum ticker, so he'll have to give up all the things he
really lives for, Scotch, cigarettes and furtive little forays to
pornographic cinemas in London. To balance that, he's got
to give up his work too, which he's always hated.

NICK: He's a doctor, isn't he?

MARIGOLD: No a vicar.

HUMPHRY: Oh. Then Nicholas, you should meet him. Nicholas
is thinking of taking orders aren't you, Nicholas? He has

some of the right qualifications. He lies badly about things
that don't matter.

NICK: (*Attempts a laugh*) Yes, well – I'd better be – oh those
remedial students of yours – how are they doing?

MARIGOLD: Very well. By next term they should have made me
completely illiterate, what have you been up to?

NICK: What?

MARIGOLD: You look shiftier than usual, even.

HUMPHRY: Come on, Nicholas, tell her.

NICK: Oh come on – look, I've really got to go, I'm late. See
you all then. (*He exits coughing.*)

MARIGOLD: What's he done? Something uniquely disgusting?

STUART: Not really. Merely withdrawn his unwanted article on
inconsequential literary figures of our time.

MARIGOLD: But that's good, isn't it? You were agonizing over
how to tell him.

STUART: It was the way he did it, Nick being Nick.

HUMPHRY: Of course you realize he only did it that way and
sold it to *Vogue*, if he *has* sold it to *Vogue*, because he
wanted to spare himself the humiliation of your rejecting
him. Which he nevertheless still managed to achieve,
Nicholas being Nicholas. Good to hear about the baby
though, but that doesn't mean you have to marry him, you
know?

MARIGOLD: (*Laughs*) Thank you, but where's Peter – the roving
boy. I thought he was meant to be here by now?

STUART: We think he may not make it, but it doesn't matter, as
he sent a message via Nick. We're not getting our grant
doubled. On the grounds that we're elitist.

MARIGOLD: (*After a little pause*) Elitist!

STUART: Actually, let's face it, or let me face it, at last. It's
probably the right decision. The fact is that the magazine
doesn't really matter, to anyone except me. As Nick
pointed out. (*Little laugh.*) To do him credit.

MARIGOLD: Yes, it does. It matters to lots of people. Hubert

Parkin among them. Or he wouldn't have given you his six
new poems, would he?

STUART: He only gave them to me because I gave him that
bloody party, which was finally what bankrupted us, as
Martin has always refrained from pointing out, although he
came close a little while ago. Anyway, the Parkins poems
will get themselves published somewhere far more public,
and for real money, instead of promises of it.

MARIGOLD: But you're not seriously talking of giving up! Not
now! You can't. He can't, can he?

STUART: Oh, yes I can.

MARIGOLD: But – but it's not fair. (*She gives a little laugh.*) It's
actually not fair.

STUART: Being fair has nothing to do with it. The printers want
their money, and why shouldn't they have it, they've
worked for it? The landlord wants his rent, and why
shouldn't he have it, he owns the place? I can't pay the
telephone bill, the electricity bill, I can't even pay for the
issues of the magazine I fail to bring out. If fair means
anything it's not fair on them. And above all it's not fair on
you. It probably never has been. But certainly not now.
Come on, Humpty. Let's hear the truth.

HUMPHRY: But you've just spoken it. Almost. Even if you get
the grant doubled you'll be having a version of this
conversation a baby or two from now.

STUART: Yes, well trust Humpty to go the unpalatable stage
further. But he's right. In the end it won't survive.

MARTIN: It will. If you come in with me –

MARIGOLD: You don't know everything! You don't always
know everything! (*To* HUMPHRY.)

(HUMPHRY *looks at her, makes to speak, doesn't.*)

I – can I – look, do you mind if I – well I want to talk to
our editor, the literary gent, you see. Sorry. (*Little laugh.*)

HUMPHRY: Of course. (*He hesitates, takes* MARIGOLD'*s hand,
kisses it.*)

MARTIN: (*To* STUART) Look, do please think about what I said. (*To* MARIGOLD) Get him to think about it.
(*He follows* HUMPHRY *to the door, makes to speak again, then follows* HUMPHRY *out. A pause.*)

MARIGOLD: I don't want you to give it up, you see. Not now. Especially not now. Not for me, even. Not for anything. You'd be lost without it. And you'd make a nonsense of everything – I – we –

STUART: No, I wouldn't. Realizing that's a relief. The fact is, I'd be lost without you. Which, in a sense, old Martin did point out. (*Little laugh.*) I want the baby. The feeling has been growing in my bones all morning. It became an absolute certainty when I announced your pregnancy to Humpty. In a slightly rasping manner, I admit. So, in the phrase. Forget literature. Start life, eh? Old life itself.

MARIGOLD: Yes, well there's a slight irony here. Of the sort that usually only turns up in literature. There isn't a baby anymore. Actually. I stopped off on my way up to Cheltenham. In fact the reason I went up to Cheltenham was to stop off on the way up there. It went without a hitch. You'll be glad to hear.

STUART: But – but – I thought we'd agreed – that – we were going to think about it. We had time – we gave ourselves three weeks.

MARIGOLD: Yes, well, when it came to it I decided I wasn't being – fair. I want you, you see, and you and the magazine have always come together, haven't you, and I didn't really know how we could make room for anything else. Anyway it's done, the abortion. Sorry.

STUART: (*After a little pause*) My fault. I should have known what I really wanted a little earlier, shouldn't I? (*He goes to her.*) Well, we'll just have to start again. Now we both know what I really want.
(*The sound of footsteps on the stairs, very fast, door flings open.*)

PETER: (*Enters*) Christ, these stairs! Marigold! (*He goes to her, kisses her on the cheek, looks at them triumphantly*.) What it comes to is this! They'll guarantee all your costs, undertake to clear all your outstanding debts, pay your rent and provide you with a marginally above-the-dole salary, plus bona fide expenses. Such as the occasional fling for the likes of Hubert Parkin. Which is, I think, substantially more than you expected, being equivalent to a trebled rather than doubled grant, eh? And so considerably more than I thought we had a hope in hell of getting. Oh, I know it's not enough to live and breed on, but going by my own experience, who wants to do that? (*He laughs*.) And there was a lot of resistance, I told old Nick there would be, they're such shits! All some of those salaried buggers with pensions to come wanted to discuss was whether you were elitist. Thank God for old Nick, eh? His article was crucial.

STUART: Really? (*He laughs*.) How perfect.

PETER: They hadn't realized the direction you wanted to go in until I read it out, and I didn't even know I had it until I was speeding towards them in my taxi after coffee with Nick. It just happened to be the first thing I plucked out of my briefcase. All that stuff about Angela Twerk –

STUART: Thark.

PETER: Yes, had them falling about. Except for the routine po-face from Nottingham University, but they all hate her anyway, so she actually helped the cause. And those Belfast poets too, Dougan and O' – O' –

STUART: Leary. Though actually it's Leary and O'Dougan.

PETER: Yes, they liked them for their directness, their simplicity, their brutal rhymes and vocabulary, their – their – sing-song –

STUART: Lack of talent.

PETER: Yes.

STUART: (*To* MARIGOLD) They were in the wrong bundle. I thought I'd sent them back.

PETER: Well, don't. As far as the Arts Council was concerned, that one about shit exploding in our faces made up for all the Hubert Parkins, which they loathed on the grounds that they were – were –

STUART: Poems.

PETER: Yes. What were they about anyway? Has the old bugger gone permanently around the twist?

STUART: No.

PETER: You sure?

STUART: No, not any more. Most of them are about death. Four – three – no, four are great poems. In my view. Which is not to say he hasn't gone around the twist. (*With effort*) Peter, look, thanks a lot, but the thing is –

PETER: No. I enjoyed it, arguing for literature and critical standards brought back the old Cambridge days. I sometimes wonder whether Oxford isn't addling my brain, and what could be nicer than paying out large sums of taxpayers' money to one's chums, against the odds – and perverts on the Arts Council. There were nine of them, I calculated three queers, three not, three nothing. (*He laughs.*) God, you look ravishing. (*To* MARIGOLD.) But you always do. If distraught. Are you distraught?

MARIGOLD: No, perfectly um, traught, thanks.

PETER: Did Nick show up?

STUART: For a few moments.

PETER: I was worried I might have given him a too feeble impression of our chances, but I hadn't read his article. Tell him my congratulations and sorry about lunch.

STUART: Yes.

PETER: Where are Humpty and Martin, I was sure they'd be here? Especially Martin. Were they?

STUART: Yes. But they had to go.

PETER: Humpty came over to read a paper a few weeks ago, very trenchant and hateable, was the general view, on Hegel, Nietzsche and Wagner, but we had a nice dinner, scarcely ever seen him so relaxed and charming, but Sonia brings out the best in him, they seem to have a rapport, partly because she doesn't think too highly of his intellect, he likes that, can I use the phone? (*Going to it.*)

STUART: Of course.

PETER: (*Dialling*) If by any unlikely chance Sonia should take it into her head to ring – who *is* that in your flat, by the way, is she foreign or what?

MARIGOLD: Yes, she's from Surrey, Godalming in fact. A teacher from my school.

PETER: Oh, sounded Middle Eastern to me. Anyway, could you explain – (*dialling again*) that I've got an arrangement with Martin about a book, though she knows about that, and then I'm hoping to meet up with Nick for an early drink, and then Humphry for a late one, and then dinner with Stuart and Martin, and if I'm not back on the late train, I'll be spending the night in one of Martin's spare rooms, and I'll be back on one of the morning trains. Or lunch time, about? (*Little pause, grins.*) What's called tit for tat. Not that the magazine's tat, (*He laughs*) but I'm after tit. Sorry darling. (*To* MARIGOLD.)

STUART: Of course.

PETER: Is something the matter with your phone? (*Dials again.*) She's expecting me to call (*he looks at his watch*) five minutes ago, was our arrangement. We're having lunch and on. I've booked us into the Charing Cross Hotel. Views of the Strand at post-coital dawn and all that. (*He listens.*) No. Bugger. (*He slams the telephone down.*)

STUART: It's possible we've been cut off at last, I suppose. (*He catches* MARIGOLD's *eye. They laugh slightly. Lights. Curtain.*)

ACT TWO

SCENE I

Stuart's and Martin's office. Eight years ago. Late afternoon. The office is transformed, painted and orderly. STUART *still has the same desk, in the same position. Opposite is Martin's desk, slightly smaller than Stuart's, but more antique. On both desks, a telephone. There is also a desk in the corner with a typewriter on it, a vase of flowers, some photographs propped, a secretarial desk. On the walls there are some bookshelves, but now full of books, most of them evidently proofs of coffee-table style books. On the walls, covers of books on gardening, nursing, cricket, bridge, chess, various historical figures – Napoleon, Hitler, Churchill, etc., and a poster for a poetry reading, new, by Dougan and O'Leary. There is a new armchair, a new sofa, a couple of hard-backed chairs, and an elegant and antique cocktail cabinet. On Martin's desk, and on the wall above his desk are photographs, drawings, cartoons, and reproductions of paintings of cats.*

MARTIN *is sitting at the secretarial desk, typing rapidly, though not professionally. He stops. Listens.*

The sound of footsteps on the stairs.

MARTIN *increases the speed of his typing, as* HUMPHRY *enters. He is carrying an overnight bag. He looks around, has trouble locating* MARTIN *in the corner as* MARTIN *hurriedly pulls out a sheet of paper.*

MARTIN: Hi, Humpty. Won't be a second. (*Scribbling his signature at the bottom of the sheet.*)

HUMPHRY: Oh. Now you're being the secretary too, are you?

MARTIN: No, it's Michelle's evening class, so I let her go home early. She has to finish *Macbeth*. Actually (*Putting the letter on the desk*) I expect we'll have to replace her soon, she's determined to get to university.

HUMPHRY: By far the best place for her. She's not bright
    enough to be a secretary.

MARTIN: I know. So she'll probably end up as a publisher, in
    competition, I suppose. Want a drink?

HUMPHRY: A small brandy, to settle the stomach. It always
    tends to be a bit queasy after lunch with Nick.

MARTIN: (*Going to the cocktail cabinet*) I've only got a good
    French one, I'm afraid, will that do? (*Extracting the bottle,*
    pouring.) What's he up to, we haven't seen him for a few
    weeks, Nick.

HUMPHRY: You might see him later. He said he'd look in. But
    only if he gets his television job presenting some new BBC
    books programme.

MARTIN: Yes, we heard about that. Lots of competition, one
    gathers.

HUMPHRY: A half a dozen equally trivial creatures. He's
    worried about the balding, portly poet figure, the one he
    calls Nappies.

MARTIN: Oh yes, Harrop. I've never understood why he hates
    him so much.

HUMPHRY: Because they're soul mates, of course. I keep
    expecting you to move office. Aren't you getting cramped?

MARTIN: A little. But Stuart's very attached – and had a few
    financial entanglements with the landlord – so it's probably
    wiser to stay on. For the moment anyway.

HUMPHRY: Where is he? Stuart.

MARTIN: At the printers. It's his turn. He hates doing it, but he
    insists.

HUMPHRY: How's Marigold?

MARTIN: We're just waiting to hear if she's going to be made
    Assistant Headmistress. The interview's this afternoon.
    Where are you going by the way? Or are you staying
    overnight?

HUMPHRY: No, I'm passing through to Exeter to see my
    parents, so I haven't got too long.

MARTIN: They're still in decent fettle, are they?

HUMPHRY: It's his seventy-fifth birthday tomorrow, but he's OK. I've brought along a sweater I cut a hole in for my mother to darn. So she'll be OK too. I've also brought along long a book by Edwina McClusky, on Plato, which they won't understand, which is just as well, as it's mainly wrong. But it'll support my boast that she and I are having a romance. So it'll do someone some good, won't it? McClusky on Plato.

MARTIN: But Dr McClusky's in her seventies, isn't she?

HUMPHRY: Yes, but they don't know that. And I hope they don't find out or they'll think there's something wrong with me. All they know is that she's an older woman. Which worries them a little. Which is exactly the right amount, for parents of their age, with a son of my type. And that'll be balanced out by the news that I've been appointed the college's Senior Moral Tutor. Did we ever bump into one of those in our day? Apparently their job was to advise us on all our little problems, financial and especially emotional, a sort of uncle figure, with a cutting edge. I'm certainly the first one I've ever come across.

MARTIN: But you'll enjoy it won't you?

HUMPHRY: I'm afraid I probably will. Well Martin?

MARTIN: How's the brandy?

HUMPHRY: I hadn't noticed. Probably a good sign. Come on then, what do you want?

MARTIN: Why do you think I want something?

HUMPHRY: Because when you phoned to ask when I was next coming down, and I said today, you said good, please come and see us. But you didn't say Stuart wouldn't be here. You and I don't usually end up in the same room, unless Stuart's present. Do we? So it must be something you want. And probably don't want Stuart to know about. Is it?

MARTIN: I sometimes wonder whether you enjoy knowing so much. Yes. If it weren't Stuart's afternoon at the printers,

I'd have suggested meeting somewhere else. Have you –
well, have you committed your book on Wagner to a
publisher, yet?

HUMPHRY: No.

MARTIN: Would you consider committing it to us?

HUMPHRY: To make up one of your coffee table specials, a
short and breezy life padded out with photographs and
facsimiles?

MARTIN: (*Laughs. There is a small pause.*) Yes, well I expected
you'd think that. But actually I was hoping you'd do us the
honour of being our first real book. Of scholarship,
judgement and imagination. As we all know it will be. To
usher in our next phase. It can be as long as you like, and
have no illustrations at all, if you prefer. Two, three, even
four volumes. (*Slight pause.*) Three anyway. (*He laughs.*)

HUMPHRY: And you haven't talked to Stuart about it?

MARTIN: No.

HUMPHRY: Why not?

MARTIN: Because I want it to be a surprise. He'd be your
editor, you see. Would you like that?

HUMPHRY: Yes.

MARTIN: Terrific! We'll draw up a contract, then –

HUMPHRY: No, we won't. The slight catch, from all our points
of view, is that I'm not writing a book on Wagner. I
abandoned it about three weeks ago, if May the
seventeenth, at three in the morning, was about three
weeks ago.

MARTIN: But why, Humpty? The last time I was in Cambridge
I saw how much you'd done. There were what? Three
hundred pages already on your desk.

HUMPHRY: (*Looks at him, smiles slightly*) You counted them, did
you? While I was out of the room?

MARTIN: Oh come on, Humpty. I'm a publisher. I could see at
a glance how far you'd got. You mustn't give it up. You
mustn't.

HUMPHRY: Yes, I must. I've got the scholarship, and the judgement, but not the imagination to understand him. Him in relation to his music. Everything I've written about him reduces him to my own sort of size. Which makes him too small to be interesting to me. I appear to have an instinctive and ineradicable tendency to diminish what I most admire.

MARTIN: I can see you're going through some sort of – dark night of the soul, but – well, what about a monograph? If not on Wagner, somebody else. What about publishing your fellowship dissertation?

HUMPHRY: It's on Hegel, Martin. In German mostly. I stopped believing in it before I began it. I went through with it because I thought I wanted a Fellowship because it would allow me to work on the things I loved. Which I want to go on loving. Which is why I won't allow my intelligence to fix on them, ever again. I don't think I can be simpler, even for you.

MARTIN: I'm being selfish. I'm sorry.

HUMPHRY: You're being selfish for Stuart, as usual. I'm sorry. I expect it's all far harder for you than for me.

MARTIN: (*Looks at him*) No, I'm actually very happy. (*Little pause.*) Really. If that's what you mean. Although you're right, I'm sometimes not sure what you mean, being simple. (*He laughs.*)

HUMPHRY: He doesn't know, then?

MARTIN: Know what?

HUMPHRY: Don't be alarmed. (*Little pause.*) It's not my business.

MARTIN: Thank you.

HUMPHRY: Our lives aren't dissimilar. In spite of appearances on the one hand, and reality on the other. Can I give you some advice?

MARTIN: (*Thinks*) No. Really Humpty, thanks. I respect you far too much. I might listen to it, you see. And then I'd have nothing. Nothing I want, anyway.

(*The sound of footsteps on the stairs. Coughing.*)

HUMPHRY: Nick. He's got the job, then?

(*Cough, off, followed by a sneeze.*)

But do we want that sound on our screens, even though it's better than what he'll have to say, about books?

(*As other coughs and sneezes follow.*)

PETER: (*Enters*) Don't you ever get your bloody stairs swept? Humpty, how are you? It's been ages.

HUMPHRY: Peter.

PETER: Stuart not here, then?

MARTIN: No, it's his turn at the printers, I didn't know you were coming in today.

PETER: Nor did I, but I had to, as it turned out, I phoned you from Oxford station and Paddington, but of course none of the bloody boxes took my money, pumped it straight through and on to the floor. But anyway you're here. Thank God. And here's this, two weeks of exhaustion and only a month overdue. (*Slapping a typescript down on the table.*) As promised. About forty thousand words I worked it out at on the train, which is only twenty-five thousand fewer than we agreed. But I checked some of the other coffee tables at Blackwell's the other day, most of them get away with fifty-five thousand, so if we add an extra dozen pictures – who's doing the pictures by the way? I'm looking forward to seeing what she's got.

MARTIN: Well, I think you are actually, aren't you?

PETER: Am I, bugger!

MARTIN: Yes, well that's what we put in the contract. Anyway, you've done it, wonderful.

HUMPHRY: What's it on?

PETER: The great religious leaders of world history, Mohammed, Buddha, Jesus, you'll probably think I skimped on Jesus, just a few thousand words, as a matter of fact, but then let's face it, he's being over-done at the moment, he's always being over-done, in fact, but I'll pad

him out if you think it necessary, and there's a whole
chapter (*To* HUMPHRY) on Wagner, in the myth-creator
section, out of deference to you. You're in the index. And
the acknowledgements, Humpty.

HUMPHRY: Thank you. Why do you do it?

PETER: What?

HUMPHRY: Go on turning out books, like this?

PETER: Because I've got four children. Why do you think?

MARTIN: Um, even with pictures I've got a feeling that forty-
five thousand might be a trifle on the short side –

PETER: Yes, yes, well the thing is I've got to get on up to
Hampstead fairly quickly, can we go into this next time I'm
here, or you or/and Stuart are in Oxford. The really crucial
question is whether Sonia and I can have dinner with you
tonight, preferably at your place?

MARTIN: Oh, I'm sorry. Not really, I'm afraid. Not tonight.

PETER: Why not?

MARTIN: Because I'm going out to dinner.

PETER: Can't we come too?

MARTIN: Well, not really. You see, they happen to be people I
don't know. Well, I mean.

PETER: Then cancel.

MARTIN: Oh no. I couldn't do that. They've gone to a lot of
trouble. (*Little pause.*) They're an elderly couple, you see,
who've just moved into the basement flat. They're going to
be the new caretakers. They're Greeks, so it'll be all ritual
and no surprises. Like unexpected guests (*He laughs*) and
probably a ghastly evening, but I couldn't let them down,
could I?

PETER: Oh Christ! Sonia's had to make arrangements for
somebody to look after the children, on the understanding
that she'd be having dinner with you.

MARTIN: But what understanding?

HUMPHRY: He means you were his alibi and it's all gone wrong,
at last.

PETER: Exactly. I told her I was having dinner with you and
then I'd probably stay overnight in one of your extra
rooms. I always say that nowadays, when I'm coming to
London, it saves work. But just as I was leaving she took it
into her head – the first time ever. Ever! – that she wanted
to come too.
(HUMPHRY *laughs slightly*.)
Shut up, Humpty.

MARTIN: Well, tell her you got the day wrong. Or I did. Yes,
blame me, that's the easiest.

PETER: I can't.

MARTIN: Why not?

PETER: Because she made me phone you to warn her there'd be
one extra for dinner.

MARTIN: But you didn't phone me. Unless Michelle forgot –

PETER: No, of course I didn't.
(HUMPHRY *laughs again*.)
Will you shut up, Humpty! No, of course I didn't phone
you. But I had to pretend to. And pretty bloody nerve-
racking it was too, as Sonia was in the room when I did it.
I was terrified she'd grab the phone out of my hand, to
have a few words with you herself, you know what she's
like, I was phoning somebody entirely different, of course.

MARTIN: Oh, who?

HUMPHRY: The person he'd actually arranged to have dinner
with, of course.

PETER: Of course. I assumed that she'd interpret my saying
Sonia was coming to dinner to mean that my dinner with
her was off.

MARTIN: And did she?

PETER: No, because as it turned out, I wasn't talking to her at
all. I was talking to her mother-in-law. Who'd come in to
look after their two little girls. Jane had already left to do
some shopping here.

MARTIN: Good heavens! What did she make of it?

PETER: Who?

HUMPHRY: Jane's mother-in-law.

PETER: No idea, as soon as I cottoned on to who was at the other end of the line I said, so we'll *both* see you at eight, looking forward to it enormously, and hung up.

MARTIN: So the mother-in-law of the girl you're not having dinner with in London is expecting you and Sonia for dinner tonight in Cambridge, with, I suppose, the girl's husband, can that be right?

PETER: Oh, don't be ridiculous Martin, she hadn't the slightest idea who I was, so she doesn't know who to expect for dinner tonight, does she, so it doesn't matter. What matters is what am I going to do about Sonia, who expects to be having dinner with you. She was catching an afternoon train, so she's probably already here. She wanted a few hours for shopping too.

HUMPHRY: Who is Jane?

PETER: Oh, nobody. Just the wife of a friend.

MARTIN: Anyone we know?

PETER: No, no, his name's Papworth, Roland Papworth, a theologian at New College. But what –

HUMPHRY: Does he know what you're up to?

PETER: What?

HUMPHRY: With his wife Jane, does he know what you're up to?

PETER: Of course he doesn't, I wouldn't hurt Roland for the world, he and I have become extremely close, he gave me an enormous amount of help with *Great Religious Leaders*, for one thing, he's particularly strong on Buddha. (*To* MARTIN) Can't you really think of anything?

MARTIN: You don't mean he wrote it?

PETER: What?

MARTIN: This Roland Papworth, the theologian, did he write it? Your book? I need to know because of the copyright –

PETER: (*Exasperated*) No, of course he didn't write it, he merely

129

filled in a bit of the history, background, ideas, that sort of
thing, and the Buddha bits, but I did almost all the last
draft. Of course, he's probably expecting his name on the
title page, that was one of the things I wanted to discuss
with you later, and he'll want a share of the royalties, but
look –

MARTIN: There aren't any royalties. You get paid a fee.

PETER: Oh. Well, I thought –

MARTIN: Half of which you've already received, you see.

PETER: Yes, well, don't worry, I'll think up some way of
sharing something with him.

HUMPHRY: Apart from his wife, you mean?

PETER: What?

HUMPHRY: I suppose she's good in bed, is she?

PETER: Terrific. If a bit voracious. I sometimes wonder whether
old Roland's pulling his weight. But that's not the point at
the moment. The point is my marriage. It's at risk.

HUMPHRY: But does that matter?

PETER: (*Incredulously*) Does it matter? I've got four bloody
children. Do you think I want to subject them to some
quite unnecessary trauma – not to speak of Sonia. It's never
crossed her mind – she'd break down completely – do you
think I don't care?

HUMPHRY: I know you don't care. About anything that
matters.

PETER: What do you mean?

HUMPHRY: Haven't I made myself plain, even to you? That you
go on spawning children and pretending to love a fatuous
wife that you can't even be bothered to betray competently,
while writing books on subjects that you inevitably
demean.

(*There is a pause.* PETER *hits* HUMPHRY, *knocks him to the
ground*.)

PETER: What did you say that for? What did you have to say
that for?

HUMPHRY: (*Gets up, slightly shakily, smiles*) Because I've just been made a Senior Moral Tutor. It's our job to help people to see their little tangles more clearly.

PETER: But I've been a senior fucking moral what's-it for years, I don't go around insulting people and inviting them to hit me.

HUMPHRY: That's because you moved to Oxford. You've forgotten how seriously we take moral matters at Cambridge. I've got to be on my way if I'm going to just miss my train, and have an hour and a half hanging around the gents' lavatory at Paddington station waiting for the next. (*He goes to the door, turns.*) I suppose I'm sorry. (*He exits. There is a pause.*)

MARTIN: You all right?

PETER: Yes – yes – but I – I – why did he? That I should have hit Humpty, of all people. Why did he?

MARTIN: I think – well, because he's so fond of you, isn't he? Fonder than of anyone else.

PETER: But I can't spend my life being what he needs me to be, can I?

MARTIN: No. You have to make your own life. I expect your being so prolific doesn't help either.

PETER: Yes well that's a different matter. He'd be ashamed to have written what I've written, but then he hasn't got a family – (*He stops.*) I've got to get to Hampstead. Christ, what a day, and the worst part hasn't even begun yet. You've realized what's happened, haven't you?

MARTIN: You've fallen in love with um, Jane, isn't it?

PETER: (*Nods*) It's a nightmare. Because what I said to Humpty was true. I love Sonia. I wouldn't hurt her for the world. Or the children – but Jane isn't just another – another of my fucks. I've got to get her out of my system.

MARTIN: I'm sorry about dinner tonight. If I could see any way –

PETER: No, I know. I had no right to involve you, really, had

I? But you've been such a convenient fiction all these years. I must go or she'll – and there's Roland – oh Christ!
(STUART *whose steps have been sounding steadily, but not ostentatiously, through the above, enters.*)

STUART: Oh hello. I didn't know you were coming down today.

PETER: Actually, I'm on my way. I've got to be in Hampstead – oh Christ, ten minutes ago, Martin will tell you all about it.

MARTIN: The chief thing is he's delivered his book.

STUART: Oh good.

PETER: (*Wryly*) Thanks. We'll sort out the various contractual problems in due course. Don't worry. I – I – (*He looks at them both*) better go. Love to Marigold. (*He goes.*)

STUART: (*Crossing to desk*) What's been going on?

MARTIN: Oh, nothing really. He's fallen in love with somebody called Jane Papworth, wife of an Oxford theologian. And he has had the long-delayed climax with Humpty at last.

STUART: Humphry was here, was he? Pity. I'd like to have seen him. (*He sits down.*)

MARTIN: Michelle left early again, to read *Macbeth*.

STUART: Ah. And Marigold? Did she phone?

MARTIN: No, no news on the job.

STUART: Well, she said she'd come straight on here after the interview. So we'll hear, won't we?

MARTIN: Yes. You look tired. Did they give you a bad time?

STUART: Who?

MARTIN: The printers.

STUART: Actually, I didn't see them. Sorry.

MARTIN: Oh that's all right. Where did you go?

STUART: To the hospital. To see Hubert Parkin.

MARTIN: Ah. How was he?

STUART: He's written eight new poems, especially for me. He still refuses to believe the magazine doesn't exist. He's been keeping the poems under his mattress. He thinks the nurses or doctors will try to steal them.

MARTIN: Any chance we could publish them? With an introduction by you. We might make a volume of it.

STUART: They're not eight new poems, they're eight shopping lists, on eight pieces of paper. A pound of apples, a calendar, a ball of wool, knitting needles, scissors, a – I forget what, oh, a turvey-drop.

MARTIN: What's a turvey-drop?

STUART: I don't know. The last order is for eight new poems in eight different rhyme schemes including one in terza rima, good to know he's still experimenting with verse form, isn't it, he's never written anything in terza rima before.

MARTIN: What did you do?

STUART: Oh, shuffled through the papers, nodding meaningfully, until he fell asleep. Or pretended to. His eyes were shut and he was snoring. But there was a funny little grin under his beard, like a snarl. When I got up to go he was clutching at my coat, it turned out. I had trouble prising myself free. I think he's terrified. And when you think of his best poems, they're mainly all about death. So urbane, so wise. Especially on his first wife. So seeing him like this is like a – a contamination.

MARTIN: Yes. Look, I know it sounds inadequate, but let's do something different tonight. Instead of going Greek, I'll book a table at where, L'Épicure. And If Marigold's interview –

STUART: Martin, I want to quit.

MARTIN: Quit?

STUART: Yes. Sorry. I didn't mean to blurt it out like that. I was wondering how to get around to it, as a matter of fact.

MARTIN: But why?

STUART: Because I'm no use to you.

MARTIN: Oh, don't be an idiot. Of course you are. For one thing, you're the poetry and fiction editor and –

STUART: Oh come on, we put out three novels a year, which we both really know are a sort of gift from you to me, especially as nobody but me likes them much, going by the speed at which they get remaindered at least. And as for poets, a few pamphlets which nobody reads, another gift from you to me, and Dougan and O'Leary, Leary and O'Dougan, whose shit is still exploding in our faces, though at least at a profit – which you deserve because you were bright enough to predict that they had a future as sort of middle-aged stars on the poetry pub circuit. I'm not blaming you for publishing them, you're absolutely right to, but the fact is I can't face reading them, let alone editing them, and that applies to every book we've got in the works at the moment, including probably especially Peter's latest.

MARTIN: But I was going to do Peter. And I don't mind doing Dougan and O'Leary either. In fact, I quite like them, not as poets I mean, I don't know about that – but for lunch and – (*He gestures.*) The point about them is that they're useful. And so is Peter. And when we've consolidated – in a year or so I worked it out this weekend – that's all, a year! – we'll have masses of work for you to do. On books you'll be proud to edit. Humpty's on Wagner, for instance. He virtually promised it to us this afternoon. In fact, I was going to ask you to go up to Cambridge and talk to him soon – I think he's a bit stuck with it, depressed. You could offer to read it for him – you're the only person whose judgement he really respects.

STUART: Of course I'll talk to him. And there's nothing I'd rather read than a book by Humphry on Wagner. Almost. But I won't edit it. I have *got* to quit, Martin. You see, the real thing is – well, last night, just before you and Marigold got back from the concert, I was sitting in the kitchen drinking coffee and watching Martina strutting about on the counter. Then she did one of her things. You know, squatted on her haunches, arched her neck, stretched her legs. Went into a kind of trance of concentration. Aimed herself at the top of the fridge. And missed of course. No, she didn't. She caught the corner and ricochetted off, to the floor. And then she strutted away. Looking pleased with herself. And instead of finding her funny and endearing, I found myself thinking that either she was a freak – because a clumsy cat's a contradiction in terms, isn't it? Or she's a pervert. Because she *prefers* getting to the floor by way of a richochet off the fridge. And I actually found myself loathing her as a – a – oh, obviously as a symbol of my – my – anyway, I went from loathing Martina to loathing it. My life I mean. And so back to first causes, and remembering that I only came in with you – well, you know why. To have children. Comfortably. You see. At your expense. I now realize. And there's quite a lot wrong with that on any terms, but especially if there aren't any children. To justify it. Partially.

MARTIN: But there will be. Why shouldn't there be? The tests showed you were both perfectly normal, you said, and Marigold's been pregnant once –

STUART: Yes, well that was obviously something of a miracle. So what we aborted might well have been the second coming. We're not going to have them. I know it in my bones. So does Marigold. (*He sits for a moment.*) Oh hell. How shameful that a literary gent like me can be ashamed of something that's not his fault. I lied over the tests, you see. What they showed was that I'm sterile. I produce a mere million or so sperm when only a hundred million or so will do. So the only pregnancy *was* a miracle, medically speaking. And it's not going to be repeated is it? Or it ceases to be a miracle. Which is what is required. (*He laughs slightly.*) The effect of this news has been to render me almost impotent as well. But that's likely to be only a passing phase. Once I stop being worried about being sterile, I'll probably become potent again. They tell me. All of which probably explains my loathing for Martina.

Feeling at one with her, you see, a spayed freak. And that's
why I've got to change something – my life here. The reason
Marigold's so depressed, by the way, is that she blames
herself more and more for aborting our only chance. You
know what women are like – well, birth and the gods'
revenge, she's probably talked to you about it. And perhaps
she's right. Anyway things aren't too good between us just
now, as you've no doubt noticed. I know you have as you've
been more than usually terrific even by your own high
standards of delicacy and so forth. And having put almost all
my cards on the table, I might as well plonk down the last
one. *A propos* dinner tonight, really. I really should quit for
your sake too, you know. You shouldn't go on just being part
of a trio, living for other people. You really need to be your
own person at last. You do, Martin.
(MARTIN *is about to speak, turns his head suddenly towards
the door. The door opens.* MARIGOLD *enters.*)
Hello darling, we were just wondering how the interview
went. Or, in other words, did you get the job?

MARIGOLD: Not quite, I'm afraid.

MARTIN: Ah, well, in that case you'll probably need a drink.

STUART: I'll get it. I'm better at the preferred proportions, you
tend to overdo the gin and underdo the tonic, Marigold
recently confided to me. (*He goes to the drinks cabinet.*)
(MARTIN *smiles at* MARIGOLD, *squeezes her hand
comfortingly.*)
But why not? Did they offer you any but the routine
excuses, I mean having virtually insisted that you apply and
having hinted heavily that it's as good as fixed – after all,
you told them you weren't really sure you wanted it, even,
I mean what the hell are they up to, in fact? (*Fixing a
drink.*)

MARIGOLD: Oh, I suppose they decided that I wasn't Assistant
Headmistress material.

STUART: What! (*He and* MARTIN *laugh.*)

MARIGOLD: No, that's not true. I might well be Assistant
  Headmistress material for all I know, not knowing very
  much but schools for the last ten years. But I didn't get the
  job because I withdrew. No, I mean, I mean there was no
  possibility of getting it because I withdrew. I didn't even go
  to the interview.

STUART: (*Has stopped in front of her, holding her drink*) But why
  not?

MARIGOLD: Because I didn't want it. May I? Thanks. (*She takes
  the drink, takes a gulp.*) Sorry, but I do need it, as it turns
  out. I don't know how to do this, though I've spent the day
  working out different approaches. I determined to be
  simple. And comprehensive. I'm pregnant you see. And
  have been for some time. I've left it too late to choose,
  because I don't want a choice. I'm going to have the baby,
  whatever. I think that's all I worked out to say. (*She takes
  another gulp of her drink.*) Sorry, chaps. (*She gives a little
  laugh.*)

  (STUART *looks at her, turns, looks at* MARTIN. *There is a
  pause.*)

STUART: Well, congratulations. (*Pause. He turns to* MARIGOLD)
  No, don't worry. You've managed the traditional thing.
  Which is to tell the husband and father in one breath, so to
  speak.

MARTIN: I suppose I'm sorry.

STUART: No, you're not.

MARTIN: Of course I'm not. How could I be? I've never wanted
  anyone else in my life. From the moment I first saw her.
  I've never loved anyone else. Apart from you. So I'm sorry
  I hurt you, is what I meant. Of all people. If it had been
  yours I'd have loved it. But as it's mine, ours – (*He looks at
  MARIGOLD.*)

STUART: Well, I haven't got your capacity for decency, loyalty
  etc. As it's yours I want to kill it. And you. And you. (*To
  MARIGOLD.*) As a matter of fact. I'll probably get over that

in a few seconds. And then we'll have what is called a talk.
But I've no intention of letting you go. (*To* MARIGOLD.) I
love you too much. And we've spent far too many years –
(*He looks at* MARTIN, *murderously. He goes and sits down,
attempting to bring himself under control.*) – too many years.

MARTIN: You should have told me. Let me deal with it. (*To*
MARIGOLD.)

MARIGOLD: That wouldn't have been fair.

MARTIN: Yes. Well, I'm not letting you go either. How do we
proceed?

STUART: I'll tell you how we proceed! (*He gets up.
There is the sound of feet on the stairs. Explosive coughing.
Further coughing off, then the door opens.*)

NICK: (*Enters. He is smoking an enormous cigar. He coughs again*)
This is a mistake. My agent gets them free on Concorde, she
dishes them out as school prizes when we've done well. So
you'll gather that the answer is yes, I am about to be a
television star. You shall have the first kiss from a celebrity-
soon, (*He kisses* MARIGOLD) being my all time favourite lady
and my first real love, I your chevalier. Before I break the bad
news. Nappies Harrop has got the job too. We're going to be
co-bloody presenting. Can you believe it! Apparently the
Boring Buggers Corporation thinks Nappies and I
complement each other, my brio striking off his lumpishness,
I assume, so it'll be over to Nappies for Angus Wilson, back
to me for Kingsley Amis sort of stuff, but once they go over to
me they won't be going over to him very often, I'll see to that,
in fact I intend to make this my chance to wipe Nappies out of
public life and back to wanking poesy, where he belongs, and
I'll tell you something else, his agent told my agent – (*He
stops.*) Is something the matter? A death been announced, or
something? (*Looking around.*)

MARTIN: Nick, do you think you could go?

NICK: You want me to go?

STUART: Yes, Nick, please.

NICK: (*After a pause*) Right. Well – (*He exits.*
The sound of NICK *going downstairs, coughing. A door slams.*
Silence.)
MARTIN: (*To* STUART) Well?
(*The telephone on Stuart's desk rings.*)
STUART: (*Lets it ring, then answers it*) Yes. Oh, hello. I see. Yes, I
will. No, no, don't worry, I'll tell him. Right. Well – I'm in
the middle of an important meeting right now, with one of
our authors, you see. Right. See you soon, I trust. Bye. (*He
puts the telephone down. Pause.*) That was Sonia. Her
babysitter's let her down, she's still in Oxford, so she won't
be able to make dinner after all, she's sorry if she's caused
any problems.
MARTIN: Oh. (*Little pause.*) Right. (*Pause.*
Lights.)

SCENE 2

*Martin's office. A few years later. Late autumn. About 6.30 in the
evening. Thin sunshine through the windows. The office door is open.
Martin's jacket is over the back of his desk chair. Stuart's old desk is
still there, but at a different angle, no longer directly facing Martin's.
There is a bottle of whisky on Martin's desk, and a glass with some
whisky in it.*
NICK *is in the armchair, a drink in his hand. He is pale and gaunt.*
PETER *is lolling in the sofa, a drink in his hand.*

NICK: (*After a pause*) What about 'Fear no more –'
PETER: Fear no more what?
NICK: The heat of the sun/ Nor the furious winter's rages,/ Thou
thy worldly task hast done/ Home art gone and ta'en thy
wages/ Golden lads and girls all must/ As chimney sweepers,
come to – (*He wheezes uncontrollably, starts to cough violently.
Sits breathing heavily, clearly shaken.*)
PETER: I thought you'd been ordered to stop.

NICK: (*Faintly*) Yes.

PETER: Emphysema, and you chain smoke.

NICK: Well, I still hold to my life's single principle. You don't live longer, it just seems – (*He coughs again rackingly. The sound of footsteps, coming up the stairs.*)

PETER: But you'll never know, will you, how long it might have been. If you go on like this.

NICK: No. That's an extra perk.

MARTIN: (*Enters, in his shirt sleeves*) I know I heard footsteps. And there was an odd smell at the bottom of the stairs. Of alcohol and hospitals. Probably some old wino staggered in for a moment.

PETER: Or the ghost of Hubert Parkin. Came on ahead.

MARTIN: Well, I've risked leaving the door on the latch – so if he still turns up. He probably didn't get the message on his answering machine. He might not even be back. What train (*To* PETER) are you catching?

PETER: The seven forty. Sonia's dumping my lot on us for the weekend. It's sheer malice, as she's got nothing to do but look after the kids, which is all she's ever been up to anyway. So what with Jane's lot, there are going to be seven kids and the baby, and so with all the catering, the bed-making, the quarrels over sleeping-bags etc., she expects me back on the seven forty. Can't say I blame her, poor love.

NICK: I was just saying, what about 'Fear no more'?

MARTIN: What?

PETER: The dirge. From *Cymbeline*. Nick's idea is to recite the first few lines, and then cough himself to death, he's got emphysema. And then we could have a double funeral.

MARTIN: Emphysema. (*He looks at* NICK.)

PETER: He's losing his lungs, day by day, inch by inch. And every cigarette he smokes –

MARTIN: You're an idiot, Nick.

PETER: How do you control your cough on your dreadful

programme? Or is that when they cut to Nappies, I've
noticed his appearances have been getting longer.

NICK: Actually, Nappies is leaving. He's going to be theatre
critic on the *Sunday Times*, apparently they're impressed by
his lack of qualifications. But he's under the impression I'll
allow him back now and then as my guest, to read out
some of his wankings. We're having dinner (*he looks at his
watch*) to celebrate. Five minutes ago.

MARTIN: Nappies is coming over to me, did I tell you? We're
publishing his next collection of poems.

NICK: Really, well he's not a bad poet, a bit derivative, but
that's what he should stick to. As a matter of fact I'll miss
him. One needs someone one hates meshed into the texture
of one's life.

PETER: Look, we're not really getting anywhere, and we
haven't much time.

(*The sound of footsteps on the stairs.*)

NICK: The thing is to be personal, dignified, simple and – (*He
coughs, looks towards the door.*

STUART *enters.*)

STUART: Sorry. I only got in an hour ago. And your message
came at the very end, and was cut off. The tape ran out I
think. So all I really grasped was that you'd be here for a
bit, but not for long.

(*There is a pause.*)

MARTIN: You got the bit about Humphry, did you?

STUART: Only that he was dead. (*He sits down.*) Was it suicide?

PETER: Sort of.

MARTIN: Though in fact he was murdered. Somebody he
picked up in the Cambridge market-place. At the tea-stall
actually. Humpty took him back and – (*He gestures.*)

NICK: Apparently he didn't put up much of a fight. Just let
himself be beaten to death.

MARTIN: He was naked, apparently.

PETER: Except for a sock.

MARTIN: We'd heard what he was getting up to. The risks he was taking. I think we all tried to warn him.

STUART: Yes, I did too. We had lunch just before I left.

MARTIN: Have a drink?

STUART: Thanks.

(*He gets a glass.* MARTIN *pours him a drink.*)

Thanks.

PETER: He anticipated it. For one thing he left some stuff in an envelope. A letter to me. Which I won't go into because it was characteristically scathing.

MARTIN: And some poems. About a dozen. With a note saying that they were for you. He'd started writing poetry again about six months before. But the reason we're meeting is that his father is in a state of shock. The mother died last year and he's, what, nearly eighty. Anyway he asked me to organize the funeral. He wants to do the right thing you see. And he wants to have something characteristic of Humphry, whom he obviously didn't know very well. We've pretty well got to decide tonight. I have to phone Trinity tomorrow, and let the Master know what we've proposed. He hopes it won't be anything too bizarre, as he'll be there himself, of course.

PETER: I should think so. For one of their Senior Moral Tutors.

MARTIN: So far we've had proposals of a brief reading of those poems he wouldn't let you publish when he was an undergraduate – I know you've always kept copies. And the new poems, if you think they're appropriate. And the introduction to the Wagner book he never wrote.

NICK: And 'Fear no more'. (*He coughs badly.*)

STUART: I thought you'd given up.

(NICK *sits wheezing, gestures.*)

I can't see that that's appropriate. Golden lads and girls all must – Humphry was scarcely a golden lad. And thou thy worldly task hast done – what partly killed him was that he couldn't perform his worldly task. At least to his standards.

And as for Wagner and having his own poems read, well –
he'd have viewed it with his usual contempt.

PETER: Well then what? He always respected you most. You
decide. (*He glances at his watch.*)

STUART: I'd have thought the traditional Church of England
service, in the traditional version. He'd have wanted to
please his father, wouldn't he, he always took such care of
him.

(*A pause.*)

MARTIN: I agree.

(NICK *coughs, nods.*)

PETER: Sure.

MARTIN: And one of us can make a short and telling speech. In
the Humpty style, but sweeter, naturally. (*To* STUART)
Will you do it?

STUART: Of course. But actually, from Humpty's point of view,
I think Peter should. As he's the one of us Humpty loved.
Most, anyway.

PETER: Yes, I had an idea it would come out like that. All
right.

NICK: (*Getting up*) So that's settled then? I mustn't keep
Nappies waiting more than half an hour, he might take
offence and stay on the programme. Oh, Stuart, have you
seen that stuff from your agent yet? About appearing for
us. Me.

STUART: Well, I only glanced at it. But thanks Nick. I'd like to.

NICK: We'll get together. But the thing is to keep it anecdotal.
Your own experience of Parkin, that sort of thing. People
still don't know much about his poems. But we'll plug the
book, don't worry.

STUART: Thanks.

PETER: (*To* NICK, *who has also got up*) I'll come with you. You
can drop me. It's a good book, Stuart. I wish I could write
something like it. You didn't care for him very much, did
you?

STUART: Not as much as I hoped when I began.
Congratulations on Leeds, by the way. I meant to write you a note.
PETER: It's a dump with a chair in it. The only one I'll ever be offered, so I've got no choice. Jane sends her love by the way. Next time you're in Oxford – or Leeds, from next term –
NICK: Peter, if you're coming –
PETER: Right.
(NICK *and* PETER *go. There is a pause.*)
MARTIN: So how was New York?
STUART: OK. A lot of lectures, interviews, all that. Like Nick, they're not much interested in Parkin's poetry. Only his life. Especially in its brutal beginning and its spectacular degeneration.
MARTIN: Do you mind if we do a different cover? We're not keen on the American one. We'll show you some ideas – we've got a very bright girl.
STUART: Right.
MARTIN: (*Putting on his jacket*) Oh. Here's Humpty's stuff. (*Taking a packet out of his pocket, handing it to* STUART.) And if you think they should be published, perhaps you'd do the introduction?
STUART: Yes. If they're any good.
MARTIN: Right. Look, I've got to go. I'm meeting (*Slight hesitation*) Marigold for dinner, our once-a-week outing. Our babysitter – Michelle, by the way, re-doing her A levels fulltime – doesn't allow us out late. So if you want to stay and have a drink – and lock up after. You don't need a key – but you know the procedure. I haven't made copies of the poems yet, you see, so we'd better not risk –
STUART: No, right. I'll look at them here. How is Marigold?
MARTIN: She's fine.
STUART: And the twins.
MARTIN: They're fine.

STUART: Good. And Martina?

MARTIN: Martina? Oh! I'm afraid we had to have her put down.
All mine as well. Including Samantha. The twins are
asthmatic, you see, and the cats were too old to find a new
home for. We'd have offered you Martina back, of course,
but you're away so much these days –
(STUART *nods*.)
We're moving out of here. We're looking for premises on
two floors.

STUART: I'm sure that's the right thing to do.

MARTIN: Might you come and see Marigold and the twins one
day? She'd like that.

STUART: Oh, one day I'm sure I will.
(*They look at each other.* MARTIN *smiles.* STUART *smiles
back.* MARTIN *goes to his glass, picks it up, holds it out to*
STUART.)

MARTIN: Humpty, eh?

STUART: Yes. Humpty. (*He lifts his glass.*)

MARTIN: (*Little pause*) Do you think Humpty was the best of
us? I've been wondering that since it happened.

STUART: Well, he didn't mess up any lives except his own. I
suppose. Except – I suppose the wretched creature he
probably provoked into murdering him. Have they caught
him?

MARTIN: Oh yes. Trying to flog his hi-fi and a whole stack of
records. He didn't give himself a chance. (*He drains off the
glass.*) Well then, if not the best, then the first to go. If
Nick doesn't look out he'll be next.

STUART: That doesn't follow. What you mean is that he
deserves to be next.

MARTIN: (*Laughs*) Yes. Stuart – (*He stops.*) Please come and see
us. She misses you dreadfully, of course.
(*He turns and goes out quickly.*
STUART *sits for a moment, then gets up, goes to Martin's desk,
looks at it then crosses to his old desk. He turns on the desk*

*light, sits down, takes the poems out of the envelope. He begins
to read, as:*
*Strains of Wagner, in full and majestic flow, towards the end
side of the record from Act One, Scene One.*
STUART *takes his spectacles out of his pocket, puts them on,
settles to read as Wagner continues. He remains in his position
as the set revolves off, while the Cambridge room revolves on,
the music coming from the gramophone, for the Epilogue.*)

EPILOGUE

*Stuart's rooms in Cambridge. Twenty years ago and about fifteen
minutes on from Act One, Scene One. Wagner is in full and majestic
flow.* MARTIN *is still in his intensely-listening posture.* PETER *is
sitting, casually, looking through a pocket diary.* HUMPHRY *is
watching* NICK, *who is standing in the centre of the room,
conducting and humming along with Wagner.*
HUMPHRY, *not noticed by* NICK, *gets up, goes over, turns off the
record in mid-bar.* NICK *hums and conducts a second longer. He
stops.* HUMPHRY *puts the record away.*

NICK: I was just getting into it, what did you do that for?
HUMPHRY: Because I don't enjoy having Wagner trivialized.
NICK: But I'm deeply fond of Wagner. (*To* PETER) Aren't I?
PETER: (*Laughs*) Yes, you are, quite.
HUMPHRY: (*Looks at* PETER, *then to* NICK) I wasn't talking
    about you, I was talking about the performance. In fact,
    your conducting was probably marginally better than the
    conductor's.
NICK: Thank you. (*He bows, as if on a podium.*
    STUART *and* MARIGOLD *enter,* STUART *in a state of controlled
    excitement.*)
STUART: Oh, hello everybody, I'm very sorry.
MARIGOLD: Yes.
PETER: Where have you been?

146

STUART: Talking to Hubert Parkin.

NICK: Hubert Parkin!

STUART: Yes, the thing is we saw him crossing the court to one of the guest rooms, he was at the feast last night. So I nobbled him.

NICK: You mean to say that while we've been seething passionately away in here, close to violence from time to time, you two have been calmly having it off with Hubert Parkin! And you didn't come and tell us!

STUART: I wanted to talk to him about the magazine. He was very interested. He might even contribute a poem.

MARIGOLD: Actually, he virtually promised.

STUART: Although it'll depend on what our first issue looks like, I imagine. The point is that meeting him today seemed like a sort of omen. Anyway, let's get started. Oh, Marigold, this is Humphry Taylor, who sent in the poems I told you about, Marigold Watson.

MARIGOLD: Hello.

STUART: And this is um, um, I'm terribly sorry.

MARTIN: Martin Musgrove.

STUART: Who's offered to take over the advertising, business, etc.

MARTIN: All the really boring stuff, in fact, is my level. (*To* MARIGOLD, *smiles.*)

STUART: Well then, um – let's –

HUMPHRY: As a matter of fact, I just wanted to pick up my poems.

STUART: Why?

HUMPHRY: I'm not really happy with them. You see –

STUART: Well, there's lots of time for revisions. They're not into proof yet, after all. (*Little laugh.*) I mean – you still want to be associated with the magazine, don't you? (*In sudden alarm.*) All we want to talk about is what we think it should stand for. Whether we should issue a manifesto. What should be in it. And the financial stuff, of course.

(HUMPHRY *makes to speak*.)
Although I'll be titular editor, as the founding father, so to speak, and anyway somebody has to be, but I want us to be a nucleus. A creative nucleus. Feeding off each other.

NICK: Yes, but is there going to be a theatre column?

STUART: Come on, Nick. We'll get to that in due course. Let's begin by being absolutely clear about what we want to happen. What it is precisely we want to offer the world.
(NICK *goes into a coughing spasm, which he turns into a theatrical event, culminating in a collapse backwards into a chair*.)

NICK: Whoops! Sorry. If this goes on, I'm going to have to think seriously about taking up another sort of cigarette. Or replacing smoking with sex. Hey, if we don't have a theatre page, can we have a sex page? Marigold and I can do it together, can't we Marigold? Or Peter and Sonia? If I choose to bring them together. *And* Marigold and I? Well?
(STUART *and* MARIGOLD *laugh*. HUMPHRY *lets out a little laugh*.)

MARIGOLD: Shut up, Nick.
(MARTIN *grins*.)

STUART: Yes, shut up Nick. Now where were we?
(*A slight pause*.)

MARTIN: Um. What we're we about to give the world. Wasn't it?
(*Lights. Curtain*.)

The Holy Terror

MELON REVISED

For Victoria

The Holy Terror: Melon Revised was first broadcast on BBC Radio 3 in October 1989. The cast included:

MARK MELON	James Laurenson
GLADSTONE	Robin Bailey
SAMANTHA	Susie Brann
MICHAEL	Sylvester Morand
JACOB	Brian Miller
RUPERT	Struan Rodger
GRAEME	Joe Dunlop
JOSH MELON	Samuel West
GLADYS POWERS	Joan Walker
KATE MELON	Marcia King
SHRINK	Geoffrey Whitehead

The Holy Terror: Melon Revised was first performed on 15 February 1991 at the Temple [of Arts] Theatre, Tucson, Arizona. The cast was as follows:

MARK MELON	Daniel Gerroll
GLADSTONE	George Hall
SAMANTHA	Tracy Sallows
MICHAEL	Anthony Fusco
JACOB	Anthony Fusco
RUPERT	Anthony Fusco
GRAEME	Anthony Fusco
JOSH MELON	Noel Derecki
GLADYS POWERS	Julie Boyd
KATE MELON	Rebecca Nelson
SHRINK 1	George Hall
SHRINK 2	George Hall

Director	Simon Gray
Set design	David Jenkins
Costume design	David Murin
Lighting	Dennis Parichy
Sound	Brian Jerome Peterson
Production Stage Manager	Cheryl Mintz

The action of the play takes place in the Cheltenham Women's Institute where Mark Melon is giving a talk; and in his memory, as he gives it. Two chairs face each other downstage; behind them is a window in which, from time to time, characters appear and disappear.

ACT ONE

MELON: Ms. Um, chairperson, ladies and – well, ladies, eh?
First I am under instruction to tell you not to worry. When
your delightful Mrs Macdonald told me of the tradition of
your tea-break, a tradition far more honoured in the
observing than in the breach, as Mrs Macdonald wittily put
it, I decided to play absolutely safe by bringing along this
rather natty little alarm clock – a recent birthday present
from someone – someone very dear to me – and I've set it
to go off at four fifteen precisely. So don't be alarmed by
the alarm, eh, it's rather loud and piercing, and rush for
the exits thinking there's a fire or some such. Rush to the
exits by all means, but only for your tea and sandwiches.
There. We've got almost the most important thing out of
the way haven't we? But I hope that the rest of what I say
won't be just a way of filling time until the tea and
sandwiches, oh, and cakes, too, I know, as Mrs Macdonald
allowed me a little peep at them on the way in, what a
scrumptious selection – but even so, with those in prospect,
I hope I'll be able to say something interesting about my
life and times as a publisher. A little warning here, though,
ladies. I'm not one for formal addresses carefully structured
and skilfully organized and meticulously rehearsed. All I've
got to keep me on the straight and narrow, so to speak, are
few notes on a few cards, so that when I'm in danger of
getting lost, or even worse, losing you, I can furnish myself
with a little signpost and so point my nose back towards
you, here in Chichester. Cheltenham, that is. So sorry,
ladies. If I sometimes confuse them in my mind, it's only
because they sound the same, and they share a tranquillity,
a charm, a peacefulness that is balm to the turbulent soul –

153

so indeed I felt this morning, when I got off the train and
treated myself to a little stroll along the leafy avenues. Such
a relief from the broil and moil, the lunacy –
(KATE *appears in the window right.*)
um, chaos (*Faltering, upset*) of London life. As Kate, my
wife, Kate, always used to say . . .
(KATE *disappears from the window.*)
Time for a card methinks, eh? But where are they? I had
them here. In my hand. I know I did. Ah yes. Here we
are. Card number one. 'Say sorry.' Say sorry? But what
for? I haven't said anything to say sorry for yet, have I?
Oh, it must be to apologize in advance for some of the
things I might suddenly find myself saying. Yes. Indeed.
That's it – it must be. Because I've discovered from
recent experience that one of the dangers of a free-
wheeling style is that certain matters tend to bob up by
association so to speak, that may be quite relevant – so
I'm not talking about getting lost here – quite relevant,
in fact of the utmost relevance but nevertheless be a
trifle – a trifle unexpected. By being rather personal. So
if I should find myself suddenly describing myself as
behaving like a Hashemite widow, as I've been known to
do when speaking publicly – known to describe myself, I
mean, not actually – *behave* like a Hashemite widow –
good heavens, I hope not, no, no, that sort of thing is all
very much in the past – I'm not actually sure, now that
I've spoken the words, that I know what a Hashemite is,
by the way. Do any of you ladies know what a
Hashemite is? Oh, well, never mind. I'm sure we can all
imagine how his widow would behave, can't we? Gosh, I
feel comfortable! Here in this room with so many kind
and interested ladies – at least you look interested, thank
you for that – there was a time, you know, and not so
long ago either, when I would have laughed out loud at
the thought of standing here in front of you today. Yes,

I would not only have thrown an invitation to address
the Chichester – Cheltenham Women's Institute straight
into the wastepaper basket, but I'd have made a bawdy
joke or two into the bargain. You can guess the sort of
thing. Well, I can tell you ladies, not any more. Things
have changed. It's not my habit these days to make jokes
about women, or indeed about sex. There seems to me
nothing funny to be found in either, so never fear,
ladies, you won't be getting any bawdiness from me! But
now you're probably saying to yourself, 'Oh, I do wish
the silly fellow would stop telling us what he's not going
to tell us, and just get on with it and tell us what he is
going to tell us.' And if you're not, it's only because
you're too kind and patient. So why don't I just leap in
and – and – now where did I intend to start? Oh yes.
'Conquering all before me.' Perhaps I shouldn't have
read that out, it does sound so immodest, doesn't it –
But the truth is, it's the truth. I began my career in
publishing with a company I'm sure you'll all have heard
of, called Dominicus, Dominicus Publishing, and – I
began as an assistant editor, then I became an editor,
and then I became a senior editor and was quite
successful as a senior editor and then I became a
managing editor and – and so I conquered all before me.
(GLADSTONE *enters to sit on chair, left.*)
Well, no – no, those weren't my great days, my halcyon
days, no, they came later when I took over Haylife and
Gladstone. (*To* GLADSTONE) Well, Edward, you play your
cards and I'll play mine.

GLADSTONE: Well, as I'm sure you understand, Mark, what we
  want above all is to maintain our reputation as a great
  publishing house with great traditions.

MELON: Presumably you also wish to remain solvent.

GLADSTONE: Our economic difficulties won't, I hope, lead us
  into pursuing current trends and fads –

MELON: In other words, you'd prefer not to move with the times.

GLADSTONE: With the times, yes. Certainly with the times. But the values that made us what we are –

MELON: Were.

GLADSTONE: Mmmmm?

MELON: What you were, Edward. You aren't any longer what you were. What you are is nearly bankrupt. Or you wouldn't have sent for me, would you?

GLADSTONE: We have the greatest respect for what you've done at Dominicus Publishing. Who were, though of course in a less distinguished way, having a less distinguished list –

MELON: In less of a pickle than you are.

GLADSTONE: Some of our finest literary adornments are still alive and kicking.

MELON: Cut the crap, Edward. You're going to go under in two years – possibly eighteen months – unless you do something very quickly. And the quickest thing you can do is to take me on as a full partner. In order to do that, you have to give me editorial control. I shan't mind the board meeting regularly to hear, approve and endorse my decisions, as long as it doesn't take up too much of my time.

GLADSTONE: My only wish, you know, speaking personally, is to relinquish the reins, retire completely to my little attic and get on with collating my memoirs. You haven't any idea what I've got up there! Letters from Ezra Pound, Tom Eliot, even Yeats – yes, even Yeats –

MELON: I'd like to begin recruiting immediately. My own editors. Right down to secretaries and so forth.

GLADSTONE: What?

MELON: Editors.

GLADSTONE: Editors. Oh, don't worry about editors, Mark, we've got some very fine ones, as I'm sure you know. With your experience –

MELON: They've got to go, Edward!

GLADSTONE: Go? Go where?

MELON: Go where they like once I've fired them.

GLADSTONE: Fired them? But – I can't be party – not after all these years –

MELON: You're not party to anything, Edward. If I'm running the show I'll do all the important work, including the dirty work. Now tell me about your personal secretary.

GLADSTONE: My personal secretary?

MELON: Yes. Tell me about her.

GLADSTONE: That's my dear Mrs Muncie. She's been with us – oh, for many, many years. An absolutely devoted, conscientious self-sacrificing – a treasure, really. A complete treasure. I couldn't manage without her.

MELON: Well, you'll have to, won't you, Edward? Once you've relinquished the reins you won't be needing a personal secretary any more – your treasure will be coming over to me – but don't worry, only for a few minutes, Edward. Then she'll be on her bike.

GLADSTONE: Her bike?

MELON: Unless, of course, you're prepared to pay for her out of your own pocket. Then you can keep her on. Well, Edward. What do I say to Muncie? On her bike or out of your pocket?

GLADSTONE: Oh, my poor Charlotte, my poor, poor Charlotte. Tell her.

MELON: Oh. what a brute! Oh, what a beast! Oh, what a brute and a beast to ride roughshod over that dignified old gentleman, that's what you're thinking, aren't you, ladies? But – and yes, there's a but! Funny how there's always a but, isn't there? Whether you want to kiss it or kick it, the but's always there. Excuse my little play on words, turning the conjunction but into the part of the body *butt*, which is of course an Americanism for – for – I think it's the Americans who are always – um – kissing or – um – kicking their – their – but – but – um the truth is I can't –

I can't quite – (*Looks at his cards in panic, then remembers.*)
Oh, yes! That's it! The truth. The truth about Edward
Ewart Gladstone, yes, you were quite right, ladies, quite
right in thinking of him as an old bore and an old nuisance,
that's how I've always thought of him myself, but where
you're wrong. Absolutely wrong! Is in thinking that he's
also an old fool. (*Standing behind him, caressing him.*) He
may not have heard a word I said, but he knew he was
getting exactly what he wanted. Someone who knew not
only whom to fire, which was virtually everybody, but
how, which was quickly, from top to bottom I went –
senior editors, editors, assistant editors, junior editors,
right down to the last clucking, maternal antique of a Mrs
Muncie. (*'Shoots' Mrs Muncie as* GLADSTONE *exits.*) Right,
Miss Eggerley, let's see what you can do. On your marks –
get set – go!
(SAMANTHA *enters to right of centre.*)
Dear Mr Sudsbury comma re my plan to move our
distribution centre from Hull to Watford stop It is
important that you do everything to facilitate this highly
cost effective decision stop Further excuse for delay will
not be accepted stop Therefore kindly exclude from future
professional correspondence all references to the difficulties
of your domestic situation stop Your problems with your
wife are not the concern of your employers stop
Furthermore your visits with her to the police station,
social worker, psychiatric wards etcetera must be confined
to your leisure hours stop Sincerely Mark Melon. Now read
it back to me.

SAMANTHA: Dear Mr Sudsbury, re my plan to move our
distribution centre from Hull to Watford. It is important
that you do everything to facilitate –

MELON: Spell facilitate.

SAMANTHA: F-a-c-i-l-i-t-a-t-e.

MELON: Well, Miss Eggerley, you've learnt two things from

that letter, haven't you? That I demand speed and
efficiency and I don't put up with any nonsense. Do you
still want to work for me?

SAMANTHA: Yes.

MELON: Why?

SAMANTHA: Well – because – because I want to be in
publishing, Mr Melon.

MELON: Why?

SAMANTHA: Well, I've always been interested in books.

MELON: Books?

SAMANTHA: Well – literature. English literature. I'm working
for my O levels now. I left school early, you see. And then
I decided to go back. In the evenings.

MELON: You're planning to go to university.

SAMANTHA: Oh no.

MELON: Not ambitious then?

SAMANTHA: Well – yes. But I like reading, you see. Studying
helps me read. Makes me. I don't care whether I pass the
exams, really.

MELON: You're ambitious. You want to go to university. Until
you do you'd like to knock about in publishing. But we're
just something on your way to somewhere else. Which
means we'd have to replace you about the time we'd got
you properly trained and useful. Right?

SAMANTHA: It's not altogether like that. Really.

MELON: No. Well, I'm sorry to hear that, Miss Eggerley.
Because I want everybody here to be ambitious about
something. As far as I'm concerned it's the only completely
necessary qualification.

SAMANTHA: I'd like to work here very much. I'd do my best. I
really do want to be in an atmosphere of books –

MELON: So you keep saying. But now I come to think of it
publishers aren't likely to provide it. At least this
publishers. What I want here is an atmosphere of success,
with no time wasted on idle reading and other forms of self

abuse. That's meant to be a joke, Miss Eggerley. With a germ of truth in it, of course. If you come to work here you'll have to get used to my jokes, and learn how to respond to them. They're not very good jokes, sometimes almost impossible to identify as jokes, but I generally help people to detect them by laughing at them myself. Rather loudly. Sometimes I even slap my knee. Is that your letter of application, Miss Eggerley?

SAMANTHA: Yes, yes it is.

MELON: I see that your first name is Samantha, Miss Eggerley. What do your friends call you? Sam or Sammy?

SAMANTHA: Well, Samantha, actually.

MELON: Pity, I'd have put my money on Sammy. I've always wanted to know a girl called Sammy. One last thing, Miss Eggerley. If you come to work here, I don't want any office romances or girlish gossip in the lavatories. Or flouncing about or tears or pouting because you get the occasional sharp word from me. You'll be here to do a job, and if you don't do it with charm and obedience you'll be out on your bum in no time, is that understood?

SAMANTHA: I've changed my mind, Mr Melon. I don't want the job after all.

MELON: Why not?

SAMANTHA: I don't like the way you just spoke to me.

MELON: In that case I shall have to try not to do it again, shan't I. You're hired as from Monday.

(SAMANTHA *exits. Stands framed in window, right.*)

Well, there you – there you – But where was I – *why* was I – with Sammy – hiring her, yes, that was it, wasn't it, ladies, hiring her at the very bottom. And then I – I think I need a little help again, eh. 'Say sorry.'

(SAMANTHA *exits from window.*)

No no, we've had that – and that – and card number three we're up to, aren't we? 'Don't boast.' Oh no that's a general note to myself – I do hope I haven't, if I have my apologies, ladies. No boasting from this time forth – yes, here we are, card number three, 'my genius for unexpected recruiting at the higher levels, too, start with Ruff.' Ruff? Michael Ruff. 'Quote old publisher's axiom made up by self: Those that can, write. Those that can't, edit!' (MICHAEL *has entered* – MELON *speaks to him*.) Michael.

MICHAEL: Mark!

MELON: Is it confirmed that you're pregnant? No, I mean that you are going to have a baby, the two of you. That Melissa's pregnant in other words. Is it confirmed, Michael?

MICHAEL: Yes, it is confirmed, Mark. She's pregnant.

MELON: Congratulations.

MICHAEL: Thank you.

MELON: What are you going to call it?

MICHAEL: We thought we'd call it Jocasta if it's a girl.

MELON: Jocasta?

MICHAEL: Yes. And Marcus if it's a boy. Not exactly after you. But somewhere behind you, Mark, with you in mind.

MELON: What do you intend to do about accommodation? Battle it out in that one room, the three of you?

MICHAEL: Well, we can't really do that, of course, not the three of us in the one small room, it isn't big enough for the two of us –

MELON: Haylife and Gladstone need an editor. Responsible mainly for poetry and fiction. We can pay ten thousand a year. I can wangle you three mornings off a week for your writing. Well, what do you say, Michael?

MICHAEL: Well, it's generous, very generous of you, Mark – you're always such a good friend, unexpectedly good if I may – when it really counts – but I don't think – you see, I don't think – I'd have to talk it over with Melissa of course but she's already worried that I'm going to abandon what she calls my art – and she feels strongly that . . .

MELON: (*Interrupting*) I'm not asking you to join just any

publishing company, Michael, but to join Haylife and
Gladstone. It has the most distinguished poetry and fiction
list in the country. Just think of the great names.

MICHAEL: I know. I know. Yeats, Eliot, Pound –

MELON: Your responsibility would be to add to them. And to
add yourself to them.

MICHAEL: So you'd be publishing me then?

MELON: Well, Haylife and Gladstone would be. In other words,
I hope you'd be publishing yourself.

MICHAEL: I see.

MELON: We'd want first refusal on anything you wrote – you'd
have to give us that, of course, in return for the time off
we'd be giving you to write it in. Now tell me about your
play – how far have you gone with it? When can you take a
look at it as our editor?

MICHAEL: Well, I've only roughed in a few scenes as yet. But
it's essentially going to be a comedy of contemporary
manners. Infidelity, greed, political corruption. Set in a
country house. But written in heroic couplets.

MELON: Heroic couplets?

MICHAEL: Yes, heroic couplets. Oh, I know it isn't a
fashionable form at the moment, but, then, no form is
fashionable until somebody sets the fashion.

MELON: (*Turning to audience/ladies*) Heroic couplets, need I say
more? I bet most of you ladies have forgotten what they are,
think they're famous twins from the age of chivalry or
something, eh, it's such a long time since I've come across
them that I'm not sure I can quote any to give you a feel, but
the first line goes tee-tum tee-tum tee-tum tee-tum tee-tum,
the last tee-tum being a word you can rhyme with easily, and
the second line goes tee-tum tee-tum tee-tum tee-tum tee-
tum, the last tee-tum rhyming with the word you can rhyme
easily with from the first line. Got it, ladies? So what old
Michael would need for a play written in heroic couplets
would be a heroic audience, eh? Actually, it would be like

being at a tennis match, except that instead of your head going back and forth, it would go up and down – tee-tum tee-tum tee-tum – so needless to say, ladies, I'd as soon publish Melissa's pregnancy diary, with all medical notes attached, than Michael's play. Not that I had to worry about that. After all, old Michael has too much integrity as an editor ever to accept anything written by himself as an author. In fact, that was one of the minor reasons for employing him, to make sure that nothing of his was ever published. Now I'm sure you know as well as I do, ladies, and if you don't, your husbands will have told you, that all the great achievements, in publishing just as in poetry, music, architecture, plumbing, require one, luck, two, hard work, three, dedication, four, cunning, five, cunning and six cunning. Right up to ten, cunning.

GLADSTONE: (*Entering*) Mark, a word if you please . . .

MICHAEL: (*Entering*) Hello, Edward.

GLADSTONE: Oh, hello, young man, hello.

MICHAEL: I've been meaning to ask – how are your memoirs coming along? I just happen to have glanced into the attic –

GLADSTONE: What?

MICHAEL: Glanced into the attic.

GLADSTONE: Danced into the attic?

MICHAEL: No. Glanced into the attic. I've been thinking – would you like me to help you sort through –

GLADSTONE: Excuse me. Do excuse me, please. I'm frightfully busy. I'll leave you to Mark –

MICHAEL: Well, if you do need any help –

(GLADSTONE *exits*.)

Have you noticed that he always leaves the room the moment I come in?

MELON: Yes, and I'm very grateful. He's a dear old dog, but he does rather use up valuable time.

MICHAEL: Perhaps. But he never leaves the room when other people come in, in fact they usually complain that they

can't get him out. And this morning, the way he kept
scowling at me during the board meeting. I just can't
imagine what I said!

MELON: You really mustn't get paranoid, Michael. The truth is
he admires you enormously, but he finds your intellect
rather formidable.

MICHAEL: Oh, I see.

MELON: You make him a bit nervous. And he wasn't scowling
at you this morning. He was thinking very seriously about
your proposal for sex manuals. He was just telling me he
believes it could be a winner. As so do I.

MICHAEL: My – my proposal! But that was a joke.

MELON: A joke?

MICHAEL: Yes. I said that if we go on doing some of the things
on our present list, we'd end up putting out sex instruction
manuals –

MELON: Really? Well, I wouldn't tell Edward that. It might
make him feel a bit of a fool.

MICHAEL: But surely, Mark, *you* realized it was a joke.

MELON: To tell you the truth, Michael, I thought it was such a
humdinger of an idea that I didn't care whether it came in
joke form or not.

MICHAEL: But you're not seriously thinking – you're not
seriously thinking that Haylife and Gladstone of all people
should put out sex instruction manuals.

MELON: Why not? Haylife and Gladstone have an obligation
to take care of ordinary folk, too, Michael. And what
group in our society – many of them very ordinary folk
indeed – gets least attention when it comes to sexual
matters. The lonely, the neurotically shy, the desperate
bachelors and spinsters.

MICHAEL: Well, granted but – but –

MELON: So, following your idea through, we won't go in for any
old sex manuals, but thorough, well-written,
compassionately unembarrassed ones. We'd be using the

name of Haylife and Gladstone to a really important social
end. Just as you've always wanted, Michael.

MICHAEL: Well – I must remember to try out a few more jokes
at board meetings, eh?

MELON: Absolutely. Keep them coming. I'd like you to take
charge of it, Michael. To guarantee good taste. We'll call it
'Masturbation Without Shame'. Start with a prospectus.
Circulate it with your name on it so that people know we're
serious. And for God's sake, make sure Edward gets a
copy.

MICHAEL: Right. Right. 'Masturbation Without Shame'. And a
copy for Edward. I'll start right away. And it'll make an
exciting change from writing all those letters of rejection.
(*Exits.*)

GLADSTONE: (*Entering*) Mark, a word, if you please, about that
young man you just brought in as poetry and fiction editor.

MELON: If you mean Michael, Edward, he's been with us for
nearly five years.

GLADSTONE: What?

MELON: He's been with us *five years*, Edward!

GLADSTONE: Really? That long! Well, it's evident he's still very
raw to our ways. Naturally we all understand he wants to
cut a dash, but nevertheless I have to tell you, Mark, that I
find his manners at our editorial boards quite alarming.
Must he debate quite so ferociously, while remaining
completely inaudible? You will please correct me on this,
Mark, but the only thing of his I heard distinctly, or
distinctly thought I heard this morning, was his suggestion
that we should launch sex instruction manuals. You know
I've always endorsed everything you've committed us to,
but then your common sense and energy are always
accompanied by an innate good taste, Mark –

MELON: I hope and believe that that's not true, Edward.

GLADSTONE: Not at all. You deserve every tribute. But it's
quite clear that that young man has yet to come to terms

with what our house has always represented, and I am dismayed, yes I admit *dismayed* that it should even pass through his mind that we should give our imprimature to such a project.

MELON: It's just that he passionately believes we should think less about literature and more about the needs of everyday folk.

GLADSTONE: What?

MELON: Needs. Of everyday folk.

GLADSTONE: A joke! A joke you say! But surely – surely he doesn't think our monthly board meetings – conducted at the famous long table, the table that Ezra Pound himself helped us to choose – are occasions for frivolity and obscenity.

MELON: I don't know what else they're occasions for.

GLADSTONE: Exactly. Exactly. And I'll leave you to put him in his place. (*Exits.*)

MICHAEL: (*Entering*) Mark, Mark, I forgot to mention – one of my reject author's transcripts has gone missing. I was sure it was on my desk yesterday evening. An absolutely ghastly novel by a woman called Gladys something. Gladys Powers. All about what she calls the self-bondage tendencies of women. You can imagine the sort of thing. I read some of it out to Melissa. It made her absolutely livid. So I was wondering if it had come your way –

MELON: How *is* Melissa?

MICHAEL: Oh . . . well . . . you know . . . dreadfully worried about Marcus. As I am. They're threatening to expel him from his nursery school. He's been beating up the other children, you see. The little girls, to be precise. Just runs up to them and boots away at them until the teachers drag him off.

MELON: Sounds perfectly natural to me.

MICHAEL: Yes, but the trouble is . . .

MELON: Good God, I've got an author due any moment!

MICHAEL: Oh, then I'd better clear off. I'll start in on
'Masturbation Without Shame' right away.
(*As* MICHAEL *starts to exit* MELON *calls out.*)

MELON: Oh, Michael, throw in a few diagrams, I think.

MICHAEL: Right, Mark, I'll do that. Diagrams. Right. Thank
you. (*Exits.*)

MELON: See ladies, how I turned a potentially lethal situation
into an office sport and a profit-making one? Furthermore,
I had a gift for detecting talent in some of the most
unexpected people. No one could accuse me of wanting to
stamp out the creative urge. On the contrary. I looked for
potential. I encouraged it. I had a feeling for it – a great
feeling for it – take what I still regard as my greatest coup –
Jacob Isaacson, my little friend Jacob, so reticent, so
remote, so full of pain and doubt . . . (JACOB *has entered
and sat in chair, left.* MELON *turns and speaks to* JACOB.)
Jacob. Did you bring it with you?

JACOB: Bring what?

MELON: Your diary of your trip to Israel. What it's really like to
live on a kibbutz. What I want from you is kibbutz life as
observed by a sensitive, Cambridge-educated, middle-class
Jew. I hope you haven't made it sound like summer camp
with the fear of death thrown in.

JACOB: I'm afraid I didn't stay on a kibbutz, Mark. As a matter
of fact, I didn't even go to Israel.

MELON: What? Where have you been these last few months
then?

JACOB: Here, in London, in the East End. Working in my
uncle's practice. I've been desperately busy – that's why I
haven't been in touch.

MELON: What the hell do you want to go down to the East End
for, surely you can do better than that? Anyway, I thought
you wanted to be a psychiatrist –

JACOB: Yes, well you see, I have an idea that a lot of mental
illness could be detected much earlier. And an ordinary

practice in the East End might be just the place to do it. A
lot of those patients who come in demanding nosedrops are
really looking for a way of talking about their nightmares,
their erratic behaviour – I want the truth of other lives.
Now that I've decided to live out the truth of my own life.
You see, Mark – you see – I'm a homosexual. And I've
decided to come out of the cupboard at last.

MELON: Now, Jake, do try to get our idioms right. We keep
our skeletons in the cupboard, and our queens in the
closet.

JACOB: You're not surprised then?

MELON: Oh come on, Jake, the only thing I don't understand is
why you've pussy-footed around your own inclinations for
so long. Being homosexual has been legal for years now.
Not only legal, but in some quarters mandatory. Try
buying a theatre ticket, for instance – That's our book!

JACOB: What?

MELON: Well, think about it, Jake. What it's like for a
sensitive, Cambridge-educated Jewish queer to work with
the shop-soiled psyches and moral disorders you're bound
to come across down there in the East End. That's our
diary! And that's our title – *The Shop-Soiled Psyche*.

JACOB: *The Shop-Soiled Psyche*. Oh. Well, really, Mark, I
couldn't do that, you know. I mean, let people talk to me
thinking I was their friend and confidante, and then
afterwards go back and write them up –

MELON: Oh, don't write them up, Jake. Far too inaccurate. Use
a concealed tape-recorder.

JACOB: Really, Mark!

MELON: A joke, Jake, a joke! (*To audience/ladies*) Oh, aren't they
coy, these little writers of ours? But I knew he had a book in
him and I knew that he knew. And that in the end he'd want
it out – I mean, what's the point of working devotedly and
modestly away in self-inflicted obscurity if nobody knows
about it, eh? He wanted to be famously devoted, famously

modest, famously obscure. (*Caressing* JAKE.) And why
shouldn't he? So, you see, if I could make a household name
out of the likes of little Jake, (JAKE *exits*.) you can imagine
how easy my task was with those who were swollen with fame
but ever greedy for more. Take any celebrity – even the great
Rupert Rupertson – it wasn't enough that he was seen five
times a week on television. He wanted us to see him on the
back of a book, too. A large photograph of . . .
(RUPERT *has entered* – MELON, *continuing, speaks to him*.)
Rupert! Saw your programme the other night, by the way.
Talking to the Russian ballerina. God, isn't she a stunner.
Even Kate thought she was gorgeous. What happened
afterwards?

RUPERT: After what?

MELON: After the interview. Did you continue your
investigation? Do report.

RUPERT: To the best of my knowledge, the BBC had her driven
back to the Ritz, in a taxi.

MELON: And you didn't go with her?

RUPERT: Look Mark, I wish to Christ you'd understand. For
some reason nature made me a one-woman man, and I've
had mine. Since Gwen's death I've never wanted to make
love to anybody else. I'm still in love with her, you see.
Physically in love.

MELON: Look, I *do* understand something of what you feel about
Kate. I feel like that, up to a point, about Gwen. But –

RUPERT: The other way around, Mark.

MELON: What?

RUPERT: Gwen was my wife. Kate's yours.

MELON: Yes, a slip of the tongue, but on to what really matters.
Had a chance to think it over yet? That little project I
mentioned to you?

RUPERT: Yes. Yes, I have. But really I don't think an
autobiography at my age. I'd never get away with it. After
all, I'm only thirty-eight –

MELON: Forty, isn't it? We're exactly the same age –

RUPERT: Yes, yes, yes, you're probably right, I don't keep close tally, you know, but whatever age I actually am, it's too young for an autobiography. Besides, they'd want details of my personal life, and since Gwen's death, I haven't had one. It's been work, work, work – But if I'm going to do a book, it's got to be the right one. Like some kind of tie-in on a documentary that I wouldn't just be fronting, but editing and writing.

MELON: You know what we should do a book about? Death.

RUPERT: Death?

MELON: Or more specifically – grief. Your grief. The Public and Private Faces of Grief – with lots of pictures of funerals, State funerals, family funerals, and running through it all, your face in close-up, your mouth, your eyes, full of the realization of loss – the memories – I'd go with that, I really would. Think about it. Be in touch. Love to Kate, as always, eh! (*Turns to address the ladies.*) There your are, what did I tell you, easy as pie! The only problem with the Ruperts of the world is marketing them to their full potential. The only other problem is to trust them to, to . . .

(MELON *has been holding* RUPERT's *face with his hand, squeezing hard.* RUPERT *takes Melon's hand away and exits.* MELON *reads another card.*)

– 'tell them a little anecdote against yourself psychopath.' What! Who put – ? Who put? Oh – A full stop after yourself. So it must mean tell them – that's you, ladies – a little anecdote against yourself. Then full stop. Then psychopath. So a little anecdote *about* a psychopath. But what psychopath? Which of my friends that I tried to get to write a book turned out to be a psycho –

(GRAEME *has entered and sat in left chair* – MELON *continues.*)

Oh, of course! Graeme!

GRAEME: Mark!

MELON: Long time no see.

GRAEME: Yes, I'm sorry I gave you such a short notice, Mark. It's not easy to get away from Edinburgh at the moment what with the various family problems, and the children, of course, but I decided I had to come and talk to you face to face. You remember when I first told you I was going to become a prison education officer, I felt I had a vocation for it, and you asked me to keep an eye out for a possible book?

MELON: I think I said I'd be particularly interested in sex offenders. Particularly middle-class married ones.

GRAEME: Well, Angus Tait is not only a sex offender, but an all round hard case. In fact, they don't come much harder. Which is why he's so remarkable. Angus Tait is almost certainly a psychopath, in my view. All his numerous acts of violence have been directed at obvious authority figures. Teachers, policemen, social workers needless to say, doctors, even clergymen.

MELON: What did he do to them?

GRAEME: Well, for one thing he – I'd rather not go into the details, if you don't mind.

MELON: Well, Graeme, details are of the essence. That would be the whole point of your book, wouldn't it?

GRAEME: Ah, there's a slight misunderstanding here. I'm not writing the book. He is. In fact, he's already done it. I've got it here with me, Mark. All three hundred pages, Mark.

MELON: Good God – this could be even better – no offence, Graeme, but if it's any good – than a book for you!

GRAEME: Any good? Why do you think I'm here. It's a work of genius, Mark. Sheer genius! Here. Let me show you! Just take a glance – any page will give you the flavour – I couldn't write anything like this! Never!

MELON: (*Looks at the manuscript*) It – it seems to be a poem.

GRAEME: Exactly. But not just a poem, Mark. An epic poem.

MELON: But it's in an odd sort of language. Not English –

GRAEME: No, it's a kind of patois. A mixture of Glaswegian –
Gorbals – but mainly he's invented it. It only takes a line or
two to get familiar with it, then you're away – there's a
glossary at the back. Along with a map I drew up myself –
so you can actually trace with your finger the whole saga of
McBlone's journey.

MELON: Here's the glossary, is it?

GRAEME: Why, what don't you understand?

MELON: Well, only the title so far, actually.

GRAEME: No, no – as I said, just let yourself rip and it'll all
make sense. Here – (*Takes the manuscript from* MELON.)
here. Any section – ah, yes, a great passage. A great, great
passage. (*Begins to read.*) Ya wadna wee haach, on doon a
bra/ bae al yon totsle fra fern awa/ Macsleek and Macblone
– Macsleek's the hero. Macblone is the lord of the
trumpets, half god and half darkness.

MELON: Right.

GRAEME: (*Reading*) Macsleek and Macblone tagaether wee had/
An together thae made ta reight an the bad/ Och the mad
and tha bad/ Tha bad and tha mad/ But com awa bad/ An
don head wit mad/ Fra Macsleek and Macblone –

MELON: (*Holds up his hand to stop* GRAEME *reading;* GRAEME
stops.) His own stuff, of course. I realized that the moment
I looked at the manuscript. You see, he hoped I'd agree to
publish it because it was the work of a psychopathic
jailbird, and then he'd be able to say –

GRAEME: Well, I'm glad you like it, Mark, very glad. The truth
is, I wrote it myself, you see.

MELON: No! (MELON *walks* GRAEME *out as he continues*.) Oh, if
you knew these authors as I do, ladies, deceitful in their
deceptions, even, the stories I could tell you – but what
they all show is that I was a great publisher who never,
ever missed an opportunity, not a single opportunity,
however remote and improbable – not a single *whiff* of an
opportunity did I ever once miss –

172

(JOSH *has entered and sits on chair right. He is eating a yogurt.*)

JOSH: Hello, Dad.

MELON: Ah hello, Josh, where's Mum?

JOSH: She phoned. Said she had an examiner's meeting. And can we make do with something from the fridge.

MELON: Well, I can see you already have. Been in all evening?

JOSH: No, I went around to a friend for a bit.

MELON: Ah. Which one?

JOSH: Oh, just someone from school. His name's Howard.

MELON: And what did you do?

JOSH: Well, nothing really.

MELON: I've often wondered how one does that. I've never managed it myself. It must require some special skill.

JOSH: Well, Howard – well, he wants to be a writer. And he's been keeping this diary, you see – Putting down day-to-day stuff about his mum and his new step-dad. He read it out to me, you see – and I thought that it should . . .

MELON: (*Interrupting*) Good. Did you manage to squeeze in a little work on your A levels before you went to Harold's?

JOSH: Well, a little. His name's Howard, Howard Skart, and I wondered if . . .

MELON: (*Interrupting*) Just because that school is expensive doesn't mean they'll get you into university unaided. You have to do a bit yourself, you know.

JOSH: I know, Dad. I did some. And I'll do some later. I really enjoyed it, Howard's diary. I thought some of it was really funny. In fact, I think it should be published.

MELON: You know, that yoghurt carton must be a miracle of packaging.

(JOSH *looks at* MELON *questioningly.*)

You've already spooned down yourself three times as much as it looks as if it could contain.

JOSH: It's banana flavoured.

MELON: Ah, that explains it. Now, I'd better get on with some work. When are you going to do yours, exactly?

JOSH: After I get back from Howard's. He wants me to help pick out the best passages.

MELON: You're not by any chance on drugs, are you, Josh?

JOSH: Drugs? No, why?

MELON: Well, I'm beginning to think that such a complete lack of concern about your future can only be artificially induced.

JOSH: I'm not on drugs, Dad. I never have more than three or four joints a week. You know that. The thing about Howard's diary is . . .

MELON: (*Interrupting*) I believe you. I know you never lie to me. I mean, how can you? You don't use enough words to tell lies, eh? Just a joke, Josh.

JOSH: Oh. I told Howard you were a publisher, by the way. Hope you don't mind.

MELON: You know, Josh – the brute fact is you won't get into university without two decent A levels. And then where will you be?

JOSH: Well, not in university, I suppose. (*Laughs then continues.*) That was a joke, Dad. Sorry.

MELON: A joke! A joke! (MELON *turns to audience.*) For a week or two I was the biggest bloody joke in London publishing. The dynamic, aggressive, never-miss-a-chance Mark Melon missing out on the best-seller of the year – *The Confessions of a Pubescent, The Diaries of Howard Skart, Age 16* – that – that his son, yes, his own son had actually tried to interest him in. But remember this, ladies, remember this, you ladies, you understand, don't you, you know what it's like trying to get through to your offspring. Especially when you're a man, and your offspring is a son! We're so busy trying to do our best by our hostages to fortune, so busy worrying about them, fretting for them, coaxing them, bullying, nagging them for their own good, for their *own* good, that when they do now and then break their silence what we listen for is the slur of drugs, the whine of the

ambulance, the policeman's knock on the door. True?
True? Of course it's true! But still I blame myself – *there*,
sorry, at last I'm saying *sorry* – *sorry* that Harold – Howard,
Howard Skart and his damned diaries had nine months at
the top of the best-seller list! *Sorry* when the theatre version
opened in the West End! *Sorry*, *sorry*, by God I was sorry
when the television series went out, everywhere I looked –
there was his face, *Howard* Skart's face, with his ridiculous
glasses, those pubescent tufts on his upper lip and chin,
and that smirk, above all that smirk – there it was in the
newspaper advertisements, on posters in the underground,
on the sides of buses, everywhere I looked –
(JOSH *wearing a T-shirt with the likeness of Howard Skart on
it is eating as* MELON *speaks.*)
What's that?
JOSH: Oh, gorp, dried fruit, nuts . . .
MELON: No, no, not what you're eating, what you're wearing.
JOSH: Oh, it's a Skart T-shirt. Howard gave me a dozen.
MELON: Well, that's lucky, isn't it, as you seem to have spilled
gorp all over the face on that one.
JOSH: Oh, no. Those are meant to be his spots and blackheads.
MELON: Ah. Oh, by the way, Josh – I've been meaning to
ask. Why did you pass him on to Dominicus of all
publishers?
JOSH: Well, because you used to work for them.
MELON: And so?
JOSH: And so they're the only other publishers I'd ever heard
of. Why? Aren't they any good?
MELON: Well, they seem to be doing quite well at the moment.
Thanks to Hector Skart and you.
JOSH: Yes, Howard says his agent says they've given him a
really good deal on his next.
MELON: Good, good. Well, um, I hope you're going to buckle
down to it this evening, eh?
JOSH: Mmmm?

MELON: To your A levels. After all, it's not your diary that's
the top of the best-seller list, is it?

JOSH: Well, I'll just go and . . . just . . . (*Exits right.*)

MELON: Oh, I know what you're thinking, ladies, you're
thinking 'Oh, I do wish he'd stop punishing himself – and
us – by going on and on about his one teeny-weeny
mistake, good heavens, he's a famously successful
publisher, let's have some upbeat, some lift off, let's hear
about his almost legendary feats of alchemy, how he took
hold of a lump of pure gold and transformed it in a jiffy
into a lump of base metal'
(*JOSH appears in window right.*)
– that's what you're – No, no, a lump of base metal and
transformed it into pure gold. *That's* alchemy. The other
way around it what we do most of the time. With our lives,
eh? Josh . . . Josh! (*Makes to go to* JOSH *who disappears.*
MELON *stops, stares out, looks down at cards.*) On to the
next. On to the next. 'Modes of distribution. Transport
cost efficiency. Illustrate comparative percentages,
Swanage, Huddersfield. Keep lively.' Now ladies, if you
consider the location of our two warehouses when I arrived
at Haylife and Gladstone, the one in Swanage and the one
in Huddersfield, and then consider them in their
relationship to our major market, which was, of course,
London, soon to include New York, Boston, Sydney,
Melbourne, Toronto, Montreal, and so forth, so forth, so
forth – you'll understand – understand why I – I – I
insisted. To. The. Powers. That. Be. Powers. That. Be. In
accounts, that is.
(*GLADYS has entered and stands at* MELON's *left. He turns to
her and offers his hand.*)
Miss Powers! Thank you so much for coming to see me.

GLADYS: No, no, thank you for – for – actually the name is
Wiggins. Mrs Wiggins. But I though Powers would make
a – a –

MELON: Good *nom de plume*. Or *nom de guerre* even. And so it
   does. Well, please sit down Mrs – no, I'll stick with Powers
   and Miss. So please sit down, Miss Powers.

GLADYS: Thank you. (*She sits on chair left,* MELON *chair right.*)

MELON: Look, let's pass on the preliminary courtesies, shall we,
   Miss Powers? Let's get straight to the point. As we both
   know what it is I've asked you here to talk about. *The
   Madonna in Chains*. Interesting title.

GLADYS: I've made up a list of six or seven others – *Phyllis
   Unleashed* is one, and *Uncuff Me, Sir*! – that's with an
   exclamation mark, and *Gladys in* – I mean *Phyllis in
   Bondage*, and several more, most of them with her name in,
   perhaps it's better just to call it Phyllis, straight out.

MELON: Phyllis Straight Out?

GLADYS: No, come straight out with it and call it Phyllis, as
   she's what my novel's about, after all.

MELON: Look, Miss Powers – can I call you Gladys?

GLADYS: Yes. Yes, please do. Yes.

MELON: I'm Mark.

GLADYS: Mark. Yes.

MELON: Listen, Gladys, we won't get anywhere unless we're
   absolutely honest with each other.

GLADYS: I agree. Go on, Mark.

MELON: Who else has seen it?

GLADYS: Well, almost every publisher I could find out about.

MELON: What did they say?

GLADYS: The ones who bothered to say anything said it's
   terrible. The dialogue's feeble, there isn't a proper plot,
   and I have an eye for the sort of detail that doesn't count.

MELON: And what do you think?

GLADYS: I think I have an important talent.

MELON: So do I, Gladys.

GLADYS: Go on, Mark, please.

MELON: We've had an amazing stroke of luck, Gladys, you and
   I. I just happened to see it on my fiction editor's desk when

he wasn't there. I glanced into it and then made off with it because I'd opened it at the right page, as it turned out. I couldn't stop reading. I was aroused – frankly aroused. Had an erection. Never came across anything like it. Simultaneously erotic and ill-natured. Self-righteous pornography, that's what it is.

GLADYS: Thank you, Mark.

MELON: Of course, when I went back and read the beginning, and then forward to read the end, I realized he was right, our fiction editor, as were all the other publishers. It's hopeless as a novel. Quite hopeless. A penis-shriveller.

GLADYS: Go on, Mark.

MELON: If we stuck to the middle section, from where you write as yourself about what a woman experiences when she lusts for a man, what happens to you physically, what happens in your imagination – your sense of humiliation, Phyllis –

GLADYS: Gladys, don't you mean, Mark?

MELON: Yes, of course. Gladys, I mean, Phyllis. I mean Gladys, I mean Gladys.

GLADYS: I wrote that whole bit when I'd had too much sherry. The rest of it I thought about.

MELON: Then give up thinking and stick to the sherry.

GLADYS: I will. Yes, I will, Mark.

MELON: I'll do it in hardback and paperback simultaneously and I'll get them on the market six months sooner than is humanly possible. We'll keep agents out of it, and speak to each other direct. When you know more about these things, you'll understand that that's a very good deal. But you don't have to give me your decision right away. Take your time to think about it, Phyllis.

GLADYS: Very well, Mark, I will. It's Gladys.

MELON: Gladys. And what does your husband, Mr Wiggins, think of your book.

GLADYS: He says it all stinks except for the middle bit. It gave him an erection, too.

178

MELON: What does he do?

GLADYS: He's a policeman.

MELON: I'll bet he's a damn good one.

GLADYS: Well, he's very good at arresting people but very bad at giving evidence against them. He doesn't know how to make things up, you see. However hard he tries, the juries always know he's lying, poor dear. He's my ex-husband, by the way.

MELON: Is he, indeed? We'll have lunch, then, shall we? One day next week? You can give me your decision.

GLADYS: I'd like that, Mark. Thank you. But you probably already know my decision. → p. 189

MELON: The lunch will be to celebrate it. Next week, then.

GLADYS: Next week, Mark. (*Exits.*)

MELON: So what did I do, what did I do to relieve myself of the throbbing, almost sobbing – my lust for Gladys – my excitement at the deal I knew I was going to pull off – because I knew, yes knew in my publisher's bones, my publisher's loins – what did I do? Oh, *of course*! (*Begins to undress.*) What every man does – given that any man could look at a lump of dross called *Madonna in Chains* and convert it into a best-selling nugget of pure gold called *Gladys Unbound* – the usual thing – the quite routine thing whatever state I was in. Sammy, love, come in and take a memo. (SAMANTHA *enters.*) Ah, poppet, there you are at last, what kept you?

SAMANTHA: In one of your excitements, are you?

MELON: Yes, yes, take a memo, poppet. Take lots of memos. No, don't take any memos. We're about to have a celebration. I'm giving you a forty-five-minute tea break.

SAMANTHA: Tea break from what? I finish work in five minutes.

MELON: Then I'm giving you a five-minute tea break.

SAMANTHA: Five minutes!

MELON: And forty minutes of overtime. An hour if you want. I'm in the mood for whatever you like this evening, poppet.

179

SAMANTHA: What I'd like is for you to go through my essay on *Twelfth Night* with me.

MELON: Then I shall. We'll fit in an extra twenty minutes when we're done. (*He begins to undress her.*)

SAMANTHA: But you've got to be at the Savoy in an hour exactly.

MELON: The Savoy? Why do I have to be at the Savoy?

SAMANTHA: To meet Mr McKinley, the Canadian sales representative.

MELON: Oh yes. Of course. To fire him. This is for reminding me – (*He kisses her.*) God, what a treasure you are, Sammy poppet. (*Continues undressing her.*)

SAMANTHA: But I've got to hand *Twelfth Night* in this evening. And I only got a B-minus for the *Macbeth* we did last week.

MELON: Probably my fault. Never could work out those bloody witches. But what's the point of my getting you into university, Sammy, what will happen to me, tell me that?

SAMANTHA: Oh, you'll always find someone for your office pokes. That new tea-girl wouldn't mind a go, for instance.

MELON: Really? How do you know?

SAMANTHA: Because the other day I heard her saying she fancied somebody absolutely rotten. And who could that be but you? (*He has removed almost all of her clothing.*) Aren't you going to take the rest off? I hate standing around looking like something from a dirty magazine.

MELON: First we kiss poppet's lovely shoulder – (*Does so.*) Then we kiss poppet's pretty breasts – (*Does so.*) And then poppet's delicious navel – (*Does so.*) And then poppet's delicious memo pad – (*Does so.*) Ah, poppet, ah, love. (*They lower to the floor.*)

SAMANTHA: Oh, my Mark!

MELON: Oh poppet, oh, love, oh, poppet!

SAMANTHA: Oh, Mark, Mark, my Mark!

(*During this love-making,* KATE *has entered and sat in chair right.* MELON *looks up, sees her, gets to his feet as he speaks.*)

MELON: Hello, Kate, love. I like that dress, when did you get it?

(SAMANTHA *lies still for a moment, then slowly sits up, beginning to gather her things.*)

KATE: Oh – about two years ago, I think. I decided to keep on wearing it until you noticed it.

MELON: Then your patience has paid off. God, what a day!

KATE: Oh, bad then was it?

MELON: No, great! A great day, Kate, love. A bit of the usual arsing about with old-bore-and-old-nuisance and young beaten-down-by-life and then on to Gladys Powers.

KATE: What happened? Did you sign her up?

MELON: Sign her up? I hog-tied her. Then I . . .

(*Momentarily,* MELON *and* SAMANTHA *look at each other. He continues speaking as she continues to gather her things, then exits.*)

went on to the Savoy. Dinner with McKinley. The Canadian rep. Sacked him. And what about you, what sort of day did you have, my love? What sort of day?

KATE: You really must calm down, darling. *Calm down.* You look as if you're going to explode.

MELON: You're right, love, you're right. Adrenalin's been flowing ever since I lassoed Gladys, slung her over my horse, and galloped her off to the best-seller list.

KATE: Now sit down. Sit down. Ask me again.

MELON: (*Sits on* KATE's *knee*) Ask you what?

KATE: What sort of day I've had.

MELON: Tell me, love, what sort of day have you had?

KATE: You won't want to hear about it. Too dull.

MELON: Thank you.

KATE: Oh! Except for the examiner's meeting. That got nasty. So I thought of you.

MELON: Of me. Thank you, love. Why?

KATE: The question was whether we should set up a course on misogyny and the English male.

MELON: And what did you decide?

KATE: Well, as I say, I thought of you. And explained to my English colleagues that as their males were already misogynists, they didn't need a course.

MELON: (*Begins to undo buttons on* KATE's *dress*) Tell me, my love, did you put this on for him too?

KATE: Mmmmm?

MELON: For your lover, love. Which of us did you wear it for?

KATE: Oh, not for you as you've never noticed it. And not for him, because he noticed it the first time I wore it, so I could never wear it again, could I, for him?

MELON: So what do you wear for him?

KATE: What I wear for you. Until he notices. Which is almost at once.

MELON: So you have to wear a new outfit every time you see him?

KATE: That's right. That's why you and I have to work so hard. To keep me in new clothes.

MELON: So he likes you to look sexy for him, does he?

KATE: Of course he does. Don't you?

MELON: What, like you to look sexy for him?

KATE: No. For you.

MELON: But how can I tell that when you're looking sexy you're looking sexy for me? Perhaps you're thinking about him.

KATE: Or it could be the other way around. When I'm with him, looking sexy, I'm thinking about you. Come on, you can finish me off in the bedroom, I've got an examiner's meeting at nine tomorrow –

MELON: Do you love him more?

KATE: More?

MELON: More than you love me.

KATE: I could never love any man more than I love you. He doesn't exist, my lover, darling, thank God. He's just a game we play. Now don't forget. So come to bed.

MELON: Just one more question.

KATE: Only one then.

MELON: Does he dare do all that becomes a man?

KATE: Who dares do more is none. So come to bed my man and be a husband.

(*They exit up centre. Recorded voice of* MELON: *Oh, my love – my darling, Kate. Followed by recorded voice of* KATE: *Oh, oh my sweet – my darling, darling darling – Followed by recorded sounds of love-making followed by snores.* MELON *speaks to the silence.*)

So he's real then, is he, love? Your lover, eh, love. I know he is – I know he is, love – because he's here now all right – making love to you. I can see him, I can hear him, I can smell him – in here – (*Tapping his head*) – in here . . . (*The alarm clock goes off –* MELON *finds it turns it off and speaks to the ladies.*) I warned them I wasn't ready, said I'd get caught up and certain things would tumble out – but no, they said, no those bloody doctors said go on, just a pack of old ladies in Cheltenham, Chelmsford, Chippendale, Chislehurst, wherever, so look them straight in the eye and stick to your cards, but there you are, aren't you, making your judgements, despising me, well, well, go ahead, go ahead, judge and despise, but remember – I'm telling you – no, you tell me, you – you ladies out there, what harm did I do, what harm did we do, however often I did it, with however many – just because I had a perfectly easy, relaxed, healthy liking – yes, that's the word, *healthy* liking. And relaxed. And good. And so forth. And so forth. And so forth. What harm. I didn't. None. No harm at all. I merely let the emotions rip *and* brought into play all kinds of muscles you don't use on the tennis courts, even some – certainly one – you don't use in swimming. Hey, where are you going? You, the plump lady there waddling towards the exit, hey there, fattie, where are you off to, back home to your dreary, faithless hubby, do you think he's any different, do you think he hasn't had his poppet,

his poppet – and you – you spindle-shanks, oh, and look,
flounce, flounce, flounce, look at them – the one with the
carrier bag! See her – do you know what they can't bear?
That my Kate and I were happy! That's what they can't
bear. That on top of everything else I had a happy
marriage. No – no – *you* there, how dare you push your
way through like that, you bloody sit down, sit down you
old cow, do you hear me! Sit down and get it into your
skulls that whatever you might think, I was that rare thing,
a happy man. A happy, happy, happy man. Oh God, I was
happy! (*Stares at the ladies then looks down and sees that he is
not clothed.*) But where are my trousers, why am I
undressed, where are my clothes? Oh God, I'm sorry, I'm
so sorry. Please forgive me, ladies, please, please forgive
me. (*Begins to sob.*)

ACT TWO

MELON: Thank you, thank you, the lady in the blue hat, such a charming hat, for the kleenex. But first I mustn't forget this – (*Takes out and re-sets alarm clock.*) It did splendid service the first round, didn't it, beloved old thing – present, you know, a present from a beloved – so we can trust it to bring me to heel in the second round. I mustn't overstep the mark, must I, ladies, and keep you from all your duties. You have husbands to get home to, meals to prepare – oh, and there's this – (*Takes a piece of paper from his pocket*) which Mrs Macdonald asked me to read out. News – and very exciting news, it seems too – about next week's talk. Perhaps I should keep that for the end so that we can close on a note of anticipation. Now. Perhaps you'd like to move forward and fill all those now empty chairs at the front. I shan't be shouting at you any more, shall I, as you've asked me not to and – and – to be quite frank my voice – I think I'm having trouble making myself heard. (*Blows his nose and surveys them.*) There. That's better, isn't it? Now I feel I'm just sitting among friends. In a cosy little group. And I can talk at last intimately and naturally and – as you'd like me to talk to you. As you told me you would. No boasting. No shouting. No lying. No, no. Just the truth. But you see, ladies, please believe me, you must believe me, please when I say. That I still don't know what the truth is. No, I don't. That's still my problem. That I've had the experience, you see. But as the poet, some poet, famous poet said, had the experience but missed the meaning. No. He'd had the meaning but missed the experience. So it was – in my case it was – exactly the opposite of what some famous poet said. If he was famous.

185

Was a poet even. Not that it matters. What matters for me,
even now, is that for me, experience, no meaning. Now I
know – yes, I know, from what one or two of you were
kind enough to whisper to me at tea-time, Miss – Miss –
and the lady there, and you, too, madame, that you'd
become rather intrigued by – by the nature of my marriage.
Wanted to hear more about it. What went on behind the
bedroom door, eh? No, no, please don't be embarrassed,
after all there's no doubt that in the end my – my – what
word would you like me to use, ladies? Bonking? May I try
bonking to see if I can catch the – the proper note for what
I did? Thank you. Well, there's no doubt that my tendency
to bonk whomever whenever wherever I could played – no,
became somehow involved in what eventually befell me,
and it would be satisfying, wouldn't it, you'd be satisfied, a
lot of people would be satisfied, why even I, yes I would,
ladies, would be satisfied if I felt that my – fate, I suppose
it was, was the consequence of a bonk bonk here, a bonk
bonk there, here a bonk, there a bonk, everywhere a bonk
bonk – Again – sorry. And sorry for the sorry. Perhaps the
word bonk leads one into a certain onomatopoeic – which
means, I should just explain, a word that sounds like or
enacts the action it describes if I recall correctly, as with
say – say, yes whipping, *whip*, whip! Whip!ing – you hear
it, hear the noise through the air, don't you, ladies, eh?
Well, with bonking – bonking.
(KATE *enters from up centre and very slowly makes her way to
the chair right to sit. She does up the front of her dress.*)
No, It's not really the same, is it? Not onomatopoeic at all.
I mean bonk isn't like – like – doesn't enact the action. I
must say, I do rather miss those little cards, that I
discarded, even though there almost certainly wouldn't
have been one that would have helped me get away from
bonking and on to – on to what I was trying to explain
about my – my (*To* KATE.) But what's the matter with you,

love? Is there something you've been up to, have you been up to something again with your lover, love? But you look so sad, love, and frightened. What's been going on? Have you and he done something that's frightened you? Tell me, you can tell me, I won't mind knowing. Nothing you could do could ever – no, love, not ever – even with him. So tell me . . . tell me . . . tell me . . .

(MICHAEL *enters carrying an envelope.*)

MICHAEL: Mark, a word if you please about this package – this package of pornography you sent to me. To my home. For *Further Masturbation Without Shame*. I thought you'd like to know – like to know – that Melissa opened it – and as poor little Marcus was in one of his tantrums he knocked it out of her hand – and there they were – scattered all over the floor, picture after picture of homosexual men and women doing vile – unspeakable – *unspeakable* things to each other! And then poor little Marcus actually – actually picked them up, grabbed them up before we could stop him and – and –

MELON: Oh, don't tell me, Michael! Got his sticky little fingers all over them! But don't worry – don't worry – I shan't say a word to Edward about it.

MICHAEL: Edward?

MELON: Well, they were from him, you see, and as he went to a lot of trouble finding them, he'd be a bit upset if he found out they'd been messed up even though it was obviously an accident.

MICHAEL: And did Edward explain what *use* he thought I'd make of this filth? Did he?

MELON: Well, I *think* he's got it into his head that you're not being serious enough about *Further Masturbation Without Shame*.

MICHAEL: Shame, shame, yes, that's the word, shame – has he lost all sense of it, all sense of shame that this house – this house – his house – the great names that he boasts of – Yeats, Eliot, Ezra Pound should – should roll about in the gutter – in the gutter – I don't think I have anything to offer to *this* house any longer.

MELON: Now calm down, Michael – let's not be hasty, let's not be rash. Let's think this through logically. You're asking what you have to offer this house? Haylife and Gladstone needs a man who can take conventional wisdom and turn it on its head, a creator of the unorthodox, the bold, the daring – a genius, in other words. And thank God we have that – the necessary genius – in me.

MICHAEL: I thought we were talking about what I have to offer.

MELON: I'm coming to that. What you have to offer is a very rare quality indeed, Michael. Blind obedience to your true master.

MICHAEL: Master?! My true master?

MELON: That's what I pay you such generous – over-generous I sometimes think – wages for. But I realize you need them, if you're going to send little Marcus to the kind of school that'll keep him out of your way and leave you with a clear conscience, rather than having him forcibly removed to a State-run correctional institution – and then perhaps you could get rid of Melissa, too.

MICHAEL: What? What are you saying?

MELON: I've got great plans, Michael – and you're included in them. We're going to diversify. We're going into ice-skating shows. Restaurants. Chinese, Indian, Greek. Dry-cleaning. At the moment I'm keeping a close eye on brickles.

MICHAEL: Brickles, brickles, brickles – and what the hell – what the bloody hell are brickles? True master!

MELON: Up three per cent on last week. Otherwise don't worry your faithful little head about what brickles are.

MICHAEL: You're mad! You've gone completely mad. I have no choice but to offer my resignation.

GLADSTONE: (*Enters, sees* MICHAEL) Oh, I'll come back when you're free, Mark.

MICHAEL: (*To* GLADSTONE *as he hands him the envelope*) Just a

moment, Edward. These belong to you, I believe. You
filthy old man.

GLADSTONE: (*Taking envelope*) Oh, thank you very much,
young man. I'm frightfully busy right now. I'll read them
later. (*Exits.*)

MICHAEL: (*To* MELON) My resignation will be on your desk in
ten minutes.

MELON: Oh Michael, no, please make it five . . .
(MICHAEL *exits*.)
(*Calling*) Poppet . . . poppet . . . come and take a memo!
(GLADYS *enters and sits on chair left*.)

GLADYS: I've just dropped in to tell you, Mark, that I've got
myself an agent after all. He tells me that you actually
swindled me on our original contract. He's sending my new
book, *Phyllis* . . . I mean *Gladys, Part Two: The Chastity
Belt* to another publisher.

MELON: Congratulations. So you've come of age at last, Gladys,
thank God. Now I can collect.

GLADYS: Collect? What is there left for you to collect?

MELON: What I collect from all my lady authors in the end. A
fuck, Gladys, because I've earned it. You see, I'm your
alchemist. Yes, your alchemist. I took your dross and
turned it into gold. And all I ask in return is a fuck
whenever I need it. Look, we'll have lunch followed by a
session at the Charing Cross Hotel. We'll dance together
naked in our little bedroom before you slip into something
indecent and we begin our games – oh, what games we'll
have, Gladys! I'll spank your bare bottom and tie you to
the bedpost – your wrists – your ankles –

GLADYS: Thank you very much, Mark, but you see, I've never
had the slightest interest in sex except as a literary topic.
(*Exits.*)

MELON: That's why I want to fuck you, fuck you, fuck you . . .
Sammy, poppet, I need my memo. (SAMANTHA *enters*.)
There you are. What kept you? (*Lowers his trousers.*)

SAMANTHA: What are you doing?

MELON: What do you mean, what am I doing? You know perfectly well what I'm doing. What I always do.

SAMANTHA: But you've just done it.

MELON: You mean – you mean we've already –

SAMANTHA: You really don't remember? But how could you – even you? Either you're lying, Mark, or there's something wrong with you and you ought to see someone. A doctor even.

MELON: Oh come on, Sammy, you mustn't be upset. We do it so often that I probably didn't even notice. Like having a cup of coffee, eh, Love? And now I fancy another one.

SAMANTHA: Don't you touch me, don't you dare touch me! I don't want it ever again – sex like a cup of coffee, Mark – sex that you don't remember. With your poppet – your poppet.

(SAMANTHA *exits as* MELON *follows, trousers around his ankles.*)

MELON: Oh come on, Sammy – just a quick dip. One for the road to see me home. (*Pulls up his trousers while speaking.*) Oh, women, women, bloody women! You're all the same. (JACOB *enters.*)
A bit of fun in the afternoon and you turn it into some sort of sacred ritual, eh ladies? (*Turns to see* JACOB.) Oh hello, Jake. How's your sex life? Young Donald still giving you decent service?

JACOB: Who's Donald?

MELON: Who is it then, works in a Turkish bath, moved into your place a few weeks ago.

JACOB: David. He works at the box office at the National Theatre. Interesting.

MELON: What?

JACOB: Your contempt for homosexuals, Mark.

MELON: Contempt! What do you mean, contempt? Even if you do put the part of the body I most admire into the part for which I have the least respect! No, no, your problem isn't that you're a queer but that you're a Jew. However much you may want the sex, all you let yourself think about is love. And when it's not love, it's shame and retribution. Face it, Jake, your cock is still under orders from the Old Testament.

JACOB: You're evidently on the way to becoming very sick, Mark. And that's a professional opinion. I can't treat you myself of course, but I can give you the names of some very good people . . .

MELON: Fuck off, Jake.

JACOB: Very well, Mark, if that's what you want.

MELON: Yes it is what I want so fuck off fuck off fuck off fuck off . . .

(JACOB *exits left.*)

Professional opinion – professional opinion – I made him a household name but all he's really good for is aspirin-peddling and looney-coddling down in the East End, dishing out nosedrops to people with colds while they whine on about their jobs, their lack of jobs, their illegitimate babies, their legitimate babies, their wife-battering husbands, their incompetent sex-denying wives. He's never known what it's like to encounter a sane, robustly healthy, cheerful, fun-loving prankster of an Englishman, isn't that right, ladies?

(GRAEME *has entered right.*)

Oh, hello, Graeme, what do you want?

GRAEME: What do I want? But you asked me here.

MELON: What?

GRAEME: But don't you remember? You phoned me in Edinburgh last night. After midnight. Woke the whole household up. You said it was absolutely urgent, Mark! A matter of life and death.

MELON: Good God, yes, of course. And I was right. It is!

GRAEME: Well, here I am at your disposal, Mark.

MELON: I've written something especially for you. In fact, I'm
going to dedicate it to you, my favourite epic poet. It's
called 'The Ballad of McTit and McTwat.' (*In Scottish
accent*.) Oh here is a tale of McTit and McTwat, T'wan
small and firrum/ T'other long an' fat/ Nah McTit and
McTwat tgathurr they/ Ta whoole of a wahman/ Reet doon
to ta pee. (MELON *chases* GRAEME *off the stage*.) Oh, I can
see what you're thinking, ladies, you're thinking 'what a
very silly, very naughty boy'! What he needs is a good slap
on the bottom, then off to bed with him, eh. No, no of
course you're not. You're not thinking that at all, are you?
You're thinking that I must have gone bonkers, aren't you?
Bonkers. Did we decide – did we decide that I mustn't use
that word any more? No, No, it was the verb we turned
against, wasn't it? No more bonk*ing*. But bonk*ers*
acceptable. As a word, that is. Not as a condition, of
course. Bonking, the verb, out. Bonkers, the adjective, in.
Odd, though, isn't it, I can't think of any other adjectives
that end in ers. Can you? Ers – ers – bonkers – Crackers.
There's another one. Bonkers and crackers. Now isn't that
a coincidence, because that's exactly what I was, wasn't I,
two adjectives ending in ers, absolutely bonkers.
Completely crackers. And how much further could I go
then to be absolutely and completely ers, bonk and crack,
eh, ladies. And so forth. So forth and so forth and so forth
and so forth and – and. Now where were we? You know if
things had been different I'd be pulling out one of those
little cards about now again, wouldn't I? Preferably the one
about Swanage and London, Huddersfield and London,
ratio of distance to cost-efficiency factors, and how I – I – I
single-handedly managed – to merge our Huddersfield and
Swanage depots into one depot at Watford, branching in
south to London, branching out north to – to
Huddersfield. Can that be right? But what would have been
the point of that? That wouldn't have been cost effective,

that would have been – would have been – both
economically unfeasible and unviable economically, so what
exactly did I do that transformed the whole transport
structure – that saved us three quarters of a million, put us
in the black, what did I do, love (*To* KATE) that turned the
whole thing around, transformed us in the course of an
evening from a playful, cheerful, happy, happy – yes,
above all we were happy, weren't we, love, until he
suddenly popped up between us. And turned everything
around. And ruined everything. What did I do? Where did
he come from? Your lover, love. He was just a game, a
fiction, a pretence, a little itch we created for ourselves to
scratch when we wanted, foreplay – our little bit of
foreplay. For years and years. So why suddenly did he –
without explanation – how did he – get into our lives? Out
of our game and into my brain. And out of my brain into
our lives? What was his trick? How did he manage it, your
lover, that's what we all need to know. So tell me, tell me,
tell me. I need to know. Tell me. Tell me, love, tell me,
Kate love, who he is and why you let him, love! That's all I
need to know, love, eh love?
(JOSH *has entered left and sat in left chair, noisily eating*
cornflakes. MELON *turns to* JOSH *and speaks to him.*)
What's that you're eating?

JOSH: Cornflakes.

MELON: I thought cornflakes were for breakfast.
(JOSH *mumbles something inaudible.*)
What? What did you say?

JOSH: I said, well, yes.

MELON: To what?

JOSH: To cornflakes being for breakfast.

MELON: But it's nearly seven o'clock. In the evening. What we
have outside this house is twilight. Not dawn. They're
different things. Almost opposites, in some respects. So
why are you eating cornflakes at twilight when according to

your own statement you take them for breakfast, which everybody knows follows on after the dawn. Eh? Eh?

JOSH: I only just got up.

MELON: Why?

JOSH: Didn't get to sleep all night.

MELON: Why? I'm waiting.

JOSH: Lot of noise.

MELON: Indeed? What sort of noise?

JOSH: From your bedroom. You and Mum talking, I suppose.

MELON: Suppose? What do you mean suppose? Who else would you expect to hear in our bedroom all night but me and Mum. Eh?

JOSH: Well, nobody.

MELON: Have you ever heard anybody but me talking with Mum in our bedroom?

JOSH: Well – only the cleaning woman.

MELON: The cleaning woman? Has it ever crossed your mind that she might be – lesbian?

JOSH: Who?

MELON: The cleaning woman.

JOSH: Lesbian?

MELON: Why not? Stranger things.

JOSH: Well, she's a granny, isn't she?

MELON: Nonsense. She's young and black, pretty and enlightened. One knows the type. Active. Radical. Gay rights. Possibly a dyke. Why not?

JOSH: That was the one before last. The student. Filling in.

MELON: Where are you going?

JOSH: Nowhere. To get an apple.

MELON: Oh, you think that's where they come from, do you, just like the food in the fridge, the clothes on your back, the money in your pocket, a modern youth's version of it all growing on trees, eh, nowhere – appropriate, as it's even stupider and vaguely nasty and justifies taking as much as you want whenever you want it, well, grasp this, grasp this, it comes from *me*, I provide it, I work to provide it, I'm a great worker that's why I'm a great provider, I provide evening cornflakes for my son, and apples at dawn for my son, and friends for my wife and my wife for my friends, so sit down – sit down! – and you bloody well answer my question.

JOSH: What question?

MELON: Who is it? Who is it? Who is it, who is it, who is it. . .
(MELON *grabs at* JOSH *who tries to escape as* MELON *chases after him.* JOSH *exits left. At up-left centre,* MELON *speaks.*)
It's one of my friends, isn't it, love?

KATE: Now listen, darling, listen. It isn't one of your friends, it isn't anyone. I've never had a lover. He's a fiction. You made him up. You.

MELON: But why would I do that, love?

KATE: I don't know, my darling. For fun. It was – it was part of your foreplay. For ages. It's in your head that he existed. Nowhere else.

MELON: Then how has he got out of it and into our lives? How did he manage it, love, if he didn't really exist? Because he's there now all right. Here now all right. I can see him, I can hear him, I can smell him making love to you.

KATE: You're very ill, my darling. Everybody knows it – Jacob, Graeme, Michael, Rupert – even Gladys. They all know you're ill. And that's how he got out of your head. Because of your illness. That's who he is, my lover. He's your illness.

MELON: That's not true, Kate. We both know that isn't true. Are you afraid I'll be angry again? I won't be angry any more, I promise. Just tell me which of my friends it is, that's all. That's all, Kate.

KATE: Oh, God, Oh God.

MELON: What?

KATE: I've got a job to do, work to do, a life to get on with. Can't you see – can't you see what's happened to you?

MELON: Yes – yes, something, something. But if you just tell me I'd be all right. Tell me. Tell me which of my friends it is. It's him, isn't it?

KATE: Oh, him. Yes. A very likely candidate. A perfectly reasonable choice. Him. Congratulations.

MELON: So it's him.

KATE: And if I said no?

MELON: You'd by lying, Kate, my love, now I know it's him, I *know* it's him. He is your bloke as – as I'm your husband. As surely as that.

KATE: And there's nothing surer than that, Mark. Is there?

MELON: Just say it then. Then we'll be finished. It's all I've ever wanted. Just to know. That's all.

KATE: But you say you do know.

MELON: I still need you to say it, love. Then we can all rest. Just say it's him, just say it please.

KATE: Very well, I'll say it. It's him.

MELON: Oh, thank you. Thank you, love. Already I feel much better. So much better.

KATE: Good. Then I'll just go and – and rest at last. Such a hard day tomorrow. Such a hard day.

MELON: One thing, love. Just one thing. How often did you do it, you and he?

KATE: We agreed that once I said it – you said that once I'd said it was him, we'd rest.

MELON: But we are resting, love. Look at us. I just want to know whether you love him, that's all. No harm in that, surely?

KATE: I have never loved anybody but you. Is there any point in my saying that I have never slept with anybody but you?

MELON: It's too late, Kate. You can't go back now. You've already confessed.

KATE: I've confessed nothing. Nothing. There's nothing to confess! You're mad, don't you see, you're mad! You need help. You must get help.

MELON: I'm not mad, love. Not any longer. I just want to get to the bottom of this. Why did you and he become lovers? Was it because of my little adventures? Because I had them you wanted them too?

KATE: Your little adventures? What do you mean?

MELON: My little flings. With secretaries and Gladys and ladies here and there in publishing.

KATE: Your little flings? Secretaries and Gladys – Gladys! You mean you've been unfaithful to me? All this! And *you've* been unfaithful to me? And with Gladys!

MELON: Actually not Gladys, come to think of it. She turned me down. But it doesn't matter because they didn't mean anything to me. Not any of them. Not even my poppet. That's the difference. While you and he for ages, you said – you said yourself, for ages – that's something else entirely. That's a kind of love you see. Yours and his. His and yours.

KATE: Little flings, little adventures, your poppet, and Gladys, who turned you down.

MELON: It's not funny, love! Oh, it's not funny! You've got to tell me. You've got to tell me.

KATE: Tell you what? What is there left to tell? Now we both know everything.

MELON: Did you love him more? That's what I need to know. Did you love him more? What sort of things did you do together. In his bed? In our bed? Did you go to restaurants? Hotels? In the afternoon? How many people saw you? How many people know? Who have you told? Who has he told? Does everybody know? Am I the only one – am I the last – the last – am I? Am I? Just answer that one question. That's all I ask. Do you love him more? More? Oh God, Oh God – Kate . . . Kate . . . Kate . . . Do you love him more? . . . Do you love him more? . . .

GLADSTONE: (*Entering*) Mark, Mark, I just remembered – I keep forgetting to tell you that wonderful story about Ezra

197

Pound. He spent a week staying with the Duke of Sussex, you see, and when he left, getting into the train, he leaned out of the window and said to the Duke, 'You know, it's been a wonderful week – good food, the relaxed company, the country air. And – furthermore I just want you to know that your wife is the greatest fuck in England.' And the train pulled out and an elderly gentleman said, 'Did you really just say, sir – did you really just say that about his wife?' and Ezra said, 'I know, I know, she's a dreadful fuck, but he's such a sweet, kind old chap that I wanted to be sweet and kind back.' (*Laughs.*)

MELON: Do you really think it's funny? A man betraying his host, taking his wife, you think that's funny – oh, you old – you old . . .

(MELON *chases* GLADSTONE *out, off left.* RUPERT *enters from right to* KATE *then crosses up stage to meet* MELON *at left. They walk downstage to just right of centre.*)

You've seen her today, haven't you, Rupert?

RUPERT: Yes. I have.

MELON: You know how I know. I saw you in here. (*Tapping his head.*) Whispering and kissing.

RUPERT: We were talking about you. She asked me to meet her to talk about you.

MELON: Did she?

RUPERT: Yes. She wants me to assure you that we're not having and have never had an affair. Well, that's really it.

MELON: Really what?

RUPERT: Kate and I have never had an affair. That's it. The whole story. There isn't one, Mark. Alas!

MELON: Alas? What do you mean alas, Rupert?

RUPERT: Nothing – only that I've always admired Kate enormously. But as you know better than anyone, I'm a one-woman man and I've had mine. But this is no place for Gwen. Look, Mark, we all of us, all your friends, Kate, all of us, Jacob especially who knows about these things – we

all know that what's happened to you is not your fault,
Mark, but you've really got to get help. For Kate's sake as
much as for your own –

MELON: God, how you must have loved it, weeping about your
dead wife while all the time you were fucking mine! (*He
grabs* RUPERT's *face hard.*) Oh you sod, you sod, you
treacherous, pious, hypocritical . . .
(MELON *releases his grip and falls to the floor, on all fours as*
RUPERT *exits.* MELON *turns to the audience.*)
Really ladies, I do promise you, there's not much more of
this to go. A few more skirmishes, a tussle here and there –
restaurants were bad places for me at this period, by the
way, I always seemed to end the evening just after the main
course, rolling about the floor, yelping, thus giving the
impression that the fault was in the kitchens. Very unfair
on the chefs – I was banned, actually, from quite a few –
but what impresses me now I can say it, ladies, without
fear or favour, now that I've been so honest and direct and
truthful and so forth and so forth and so forth, just as I
promised after tea, and so forth was – was – (*To* KATE) you
must help me. Please.

KATE: Get up. You mustn't be down there on your hands and
knees like a dog. It's not – becoming, Mark.

MELON: Love me, please. That's all I ask. Love me.

KATE: I will, I will, oh I will! If only you'll help me.

MELON: Oh yes, yes. Anything. Just tell me what it is. I'll do
anything to help you.

KATE: Then see someone who can help you. And then you'll be
helping me, you see.

MELON: Who? Who is this someone?

KATE: If you do, then I'll be able to love you again. I know I
will.

MELON: I love you, I love you.

KATE: Then come with me.

MELON: I can't. I want to be with you. I have to be with you.

KATE: I'm always with you, darling. You know that. (*Gets*
MELON *to his feet.*) Come, my darling, come. And
everything will be all right, you'll see.
(*She has walked* MELON *upstage – as they get to centre opening
she snatches her hand away and disappears off right.*)

MELON: Kate! Kate! Kate!
(MELON *falls to the floor and begins to crawl downstage as*
SHRINK 1 *enters from left to sit in left chair as* SHRINK 2
enters from right and sits right.)

SHRINK 1: And then I said, What do you think this is? A lay-by
for layabouts? Last week you didn't exist for me. Last
week you were failing somewhere else with some other
psychiatrist. You're a bit of a gadabout when it comes to
failure, Mr Melon. You like to fail all over the place. And
of course, he said, but I said, Health isn't a gift. It has to
be earned. You must work to be cured, Mr Melon. I can't
remember how long it took to hose down the Augean
stables, but by general consent, your psyche is in a fouler
state than they were. We'll do our best. Even if you're not
good enough. That's all for today. Time's up. Bill's in the
post. Let's hope that tomorrow the cheque will be, eh?

SHRINK 2: And I said, Tell me, Mr Melon, how many do you
smoke? So of course he said, so I said but you've smoked
ten while we've been talking. You've smoked ten. That's
eleven. So you're deluding yourself, aren't you? About the
amount you smoke. And a gross delusion at that, Mr
Melon. Why? Why lie about it? Why say you smoke three
or four when you evidently smoke – what? Fifty? Sixty?
And of course he said, and then I said, Did you? Or did
you leave packets unsaid as a way of deceiving me? Your
smoking could have something to do with the breakdown.
Its effect over the years on the nervous system – and of
course he said and then I said Indeed? How interesting. So
the breakdown has flushed you out as a smoker. Until then
you were a latent smoker. I consider that to be important

progress. The next step is to get you to stop again. Then at least you'll be able to afford my fees.

SHRINK 1: And I said, I've just grasped something rather interesting about your case Mr Melon. There are one or two classic symptoms. They're of the kind we usually associate with sibling rivalry. And of course he said and I said, Not in the slightest. In fact quite the contrary. Not having an actual sibling to rival meant you had to make one up. Having made him up you had to assault him for not existing. Which is precisely what you did to that famous television friend of yours who was *not* having an affair with your wife. His not having an affair was the treachery of the brother who didn't exist. If he had existed he would have affirmed the rivalry and thus his siblingness by actually having an affair with your wife and would have eventually required psychiatric help himself. As it is you've had to come in his place. In other words, *you* are your non-existent brother.

SHRINK 2: Non-existent brother.

SHRINK 1: See how it all fits together, Mr Melon.

SHRINK 2: And I said, You're feeling better, and of course he said and I said, Well, look at you, man. For one thing, we've stopped you smoking. I've never seen anyone not smoke as much as you're not smoking – you must be up to the two-hundred, three-hundred a day mark, Mark. Well done, Melon.

SHRINK 1: And I said You really must start trying to pull yourself together. Anyway, I suppose we'd better try you out on some new drugs. If those don't work we'll try some newer drugs. By the time we've discovered what effect they have on you, there'll be even newer drugs, and of course he said . . .

SHRINK 2: And I said, Now we start reducing the dosage of whatever it is you're on at the moment. Don't worry. We'll give you others to counter the effect of taking you off them.

We might even try the same ones. That often works. The truth is, Mr Melon – the truth is you're a nuisance. And a bore. And of course he said, and I said – There. You've turned the corner. You've started to bore yourself.

SHRINK I: Bore yourself.

SHRINK 2: Haven't you? A sure sign of returning health. I don't know who will be given credit for your recovery.

SHRINK I: You've been treated to a great variety of treatments.

SHRINK 2: Many of them completely contradictory. One day we may know more about what we did to cure you.

SHRINK I: And then perhaps we shall discover more about what made you ill.

SHRINK 2: But for the moment,

SHRINK I: All we can do . . .

SHRINK 2: Is to congratulate ourselves. But don't you congratulate yourself, Mr Melon.

SHRINK I: We've seen enough of cases like yours to know that even when you're cured, you're not actually well.

SHRINK 2: In fact you'll never be actually well again.

SHRINK I: But then you don't deserve to be, do you, after all the trouble you've given everyone.

SHRINK 2: I'm sure you understand that, Mr Lemon.

SHRINK I: You're an educated man.

SHRINK 2: Now go on your way, my son and sin no more.

SHRINK I: You heard me. On your bike, and no more fucking about.

SHRINK 2: You've got bills to pay, before you sleep.

SHRINK I: Bills to pay before you sleep. (SHRINKS *exit from where they entered.*)

MELON: And so forth, and so forth, and so forth. You see, ladies, how it was done! It may seem arbitrary, unthought out, a hop from one brutality to the other, to the mere layman, the yous and mes who never think of the need for experts in matters of this kind until we have a need for them – but – but – whatever your doubts, ladies, look at me, by God, look at me! Oh, I know what you're thinking! Why didn't someone just take the beggar by the scruff of the neck, shake him about a bit, paddle his bottom, tell him to pull his socks up, say your prayers, gentle Jesus meek and mild, look upon your little child, pity him his simply sitting, teach him, Lord, to come to Thee and so forth. Forth. Forth and forth.

(KATE *enters to sit on chair right.*)

KATE: It's time to come home.

MELON: Is it, love? Oh good.

KATE: Come along then.

MELON: Right. But – but what about us, love? Are we going to be all right?

KATE: We're going to do our best. Aren't we?

MELON: But what frightens me, love, is – whether you'll be able to forgive me. That's the question. That's what's been frightening me, love. Whether you'll be able to forgive me.

KATE: You were ill. So what is there to forgive?

(MELON *reaches out his hand to* KATE. *She moves to take it but before their hands join,* JOSH *enters from right.*)

MELON: Ah, Josh. That looks good, what is it?

JOSH: Well, um, cottage cheese. It's got carrots in it. And raisins.

MELON: Well, I hope it tastes even more delicious than it sounds, eh?

JOSH: I'm glad you're back, Dad.

MELON: Thank you.

JOSH: I'd better tell you now. I probably won't be going to university. I didn't do too well in my A levels, you see.

MELON: A levels? Oh, who cares. Look at me. Ten O levels, five A levels, first-class honours degree from Cambridge, and what did it lead to? Electric shocks in a mental institution, that's what it led to. No, all I want from you, Josh, all your mother and I want from you is that you should be – be – you know. Be. Old Chap.

(MELON *moves to embrace* JOSH, *but before he can, something stops him and he walks away to sit on chair left. When* MELON *is seated,* MICHAEL *enters from left.*)

MICHAEL: Mark. I had some idea you weren't coming in 'til Monday. At the top of the week.

MELON: Really? Is that what we – ? Well, can't do any harm to put the toe in the water, test the temperature. Can it?

MICHAEL: Still it would have given us a chance to get your office ready for you.

MELON: Oh, well it looks – it really looks –

MICHAEL: I mean your new office.

MELON: Oh. Oh I – yes. I should have thought. That we might be exchanging offices –

MICHAEL: Well, not so much exchanging. Edward's in my office. You'll be in Edward's attic – as he and I both need more space. If I'm going to continue as General Managing Editor. And Edward's going to continue as fiction and poetry editor. When he retires – again – we'll reconsider the situation, of course. So I'm in . . .

MELON: Oh of course. And – until then – what will I be doing, Michael?

MICHAEL: What Edward was doing. Sorting out his memoirs. We both feel there's a very valuable book there, and that you're just the chap to find it. As Edward doesn't have the time at the moment. I don't quite know what else there is for you here, at Haylife and Gladstone, Mark. At the moment.

MELON: No, no. That's fine. Just to be in the building and to be doing something connected with the great tradition. Helping keep it alive, it'll be a privilege, Michael to work on Edward's memoirs, etc., etc. How's little Rufus? Marcus, Marcus. Sorry.

MICHAEL: We've found him a very good all-the-year-round boarding school. In Canada. We gather that he's showing signs of settling down.

(SAMANTHA *enters from right and stops at centre when she sees* MELON.)

SAMANTHA: Oh. Oh, sorry. I didn't know . . .

MICHAEL: That's all right, love, I didn't either. Say hello.

SAMANTHA: Hello, Mr Melon.

MELON: Hello, Sammy. Um – how's the – Shakespeare going, Sammy?

SAMANTHA: Um, well . . .

MICHAEL: Sammy and I had a little talk. She's decided to stay here and make a career in publishing.

MELON: Quite right, quite right, as you've always liked books, after all –

SAMANTHA: Well, they're better than other forms of self-abuse, I suppose, Mr Melon.

MELON: What?

MICHAEL: Quoting *Macbeth*, weren't you? 'This strange and self-abuse.' But the thing is we've got rather a lot to do – and I've got an author coming in any minute.

MELON: Oh. Oh yes. Of course, Michael. Then I'll just –
(GLADSTONE *enters*.)

GLADSTONE: Michael, Michael, she's terribly late. I've been waiting on the pavement. I do hope that lunatic Melon hasn't been in touch with . . .
(MICHAEL *points out* MELON *to* GLADSTONE, *who then backs away*.)

MELON: It's only me, Edward!

MICHAEL: That's all right, Edward. Mark's much better now. And we must all be kind to him. As we agreed.

GLADYS: (*Entering*) Hello, darlings! Sorry I'm late.

MICHAEL: And how's our favorite author?

GLADSTONE: Ah, Gladys, my dear. We were just celebrating the arrival of *The Chastity Belt*.

MICHAEL: A great title, great title for a follow-up. Sammy adored it. Didn't you, Sammy?

SAMANTHA: I thought it was the most . . .

KATE: Darling, I'd rather you didn't.

JOSH: But Mum, I'll be back before midnight, I swear.

(*The alarm goes off and* MELON *stops it.*)

MELON: Well, there we are, ladies. We seem to have got to the end, haven't we? May I thank you for inviting me to share my – my experiences with you. I feel oddly better for the occasion and hope that you are – none of you – any the worse for it. After all, what has happened when it comes to it? Nothing so terrible, really. Nothing so very terrible when you think about it. I mean, there I was going about my life – my happy, happy life – and then one day the earth opened at my feet and I hurtled into the – the – but on the other hand here I am back again. And where's the damage, eh, ladies? Just because I don't understand, you don't understand, and they don't understand, none of us understands why the earth opened doesn't make it any sort of disaster, or mystery even. And there is, as lots of people always say, a funny side, isn't there, ladies? I mean – well, for instance, if what had happened to me hadn't happened to me I would still be married to my Kate. And she would never, would she, have left me for Rupert, would she? It was all their worry, all their intimate conversations about me and my behaviour that brought them together. So there's a – well, if it isn't funny it's a bit of an irony at least, isn't it? I often think about that. That's one of the things I often think about. Perhaps that's what was intended all the time. That she and he, he and she – and I was just their instrument. Or God's of course. Because we all know God moves in a mysterious way. Especially as she, my Kate, is going to have another baby at last. Perhaps that's why I had to take a little punishment, so that a new life could be brought into the world – I mean, that's one way of looking at it, isn't it? On the other hand, it's also possible that they really had been having an affair all the time. Just as I suspected. Little pieces of evidence seem to

pop up now and then. But naturally I ignore them. After all, who am I to say? Who am I to know? The important thing is that though she's happy at last – deservedly happy – she's never really gone from me. In here (*Tapping his head*) or here (*Touching his heart*) I can still feel her sometimes. And I try to make the best of things, the best of things as they really are. As I understand them. Oh, one last thing. I've nearly finished Edward's memoirs which are to be published by Haylife and Gladstone – sometime in the – we hope – in the autumn. So you see my life goes on. And ladies, on that, I trust, upward beating note I take my – oh, good heavens. I'd nearly forgotten. Your delightful Mrs Macdonald would never have forgiven me – except I suspect that she forgives everyone everything – here we are – (*Takes paper out of his pocket; reads*) 'Next week's talk in the series "Why me?" will be given by Mr Maxwell Dodsworth, general manager of Floy's Brewery. The title he has chosen is: *One morning I bent to pick a tulip*. In it he'll describe how the resultant back injury and his anxiety to return to work as quickly as possible led him to undergo a miracle cure that caused hallucination, blindness, incontinence, obesity and finally carried him to the very brink of death.' Obviously another story with a comparatively happy outcome, eh, ladies? Otherwise he wouldn't be able to come here and tell it to you, would he? And I must say, it sounds so tempting that I might well find myself back in Chichester – Cheltenham next week. Especially if in the interim I let my tummy's memory stray to your sandwiches and cakes. Thank you for them again. And for your kind attention. Thank you, ladies and ladies, Mrs Macdonald.
(*Curtain.*)

After Pilkington

After Pilkington was first broadcast by BBC Television on 11 November 1986. The cast was as follows:

JAMES	Bob Peck
PENNY	Miranda Richardson
DEREK	Barry Foster
BORIS	Gary Waldhorn
DEIRDRE	Mary Miller
AMANDA	Reina James
WILKINS	Richard Brenner
POTTS	John Gill
DOCTOR	Nigel Nevinson
YOUNG PENNY	Sarah Butler
YOUNG JAMES	Richard Grant
PILKINGTON	Derek Ware

Director	Christopher Morahan
Producer	Ken Trodd
Costume Designer	Catriona Tomalin
Film Cameraman	Andrew Dunn
Sound Recordist	Graham Roff

1. EXT. THE HIGH. OXFORD. DAY

*From Carfax Tower a panning shot of Oxford spires to see cyclists
in The High. They pass The Mitre.
In the Turl.* JAMES *stops at a bookshop. He picks out a book, a
collection of poems by Herrick. He opens it, looks through it rapidly
and puts the book back.
As he looks up, see* PENNY *from his point of view and glimpsed
through the traffic. She is on a bicycle on the far side of The High.
Her face is only momentarily visible under a straw hat. See her go
out with the traffic and out of sight.
Cut from* JAMES *to little glimpses of* PENNY *as music over of
Schubert's 'The Trout' begins. It is as if this is a continuation of the
previous scene:*

2. INT. OXFORD CONCERT HALL. DAY

'The Trout' continues. See PENNY *in the front row from* JAMES'S
*point of view, far back in the hall.
Cut from* JAMES *to little glimpses of* PENNY *as she occasionally
turns her head, listening to the music which is nearing its end.
Take in* JAMES'S *hand, a woman's hand on it. He turns his head
and see from his point of view,* AMANDA. *She smiles at him. He
smiles back, then looks again towards* PENNY. *We have a glimpse
of her as the music reaches its climax, and on that glimpse:*

3. INT. OXFORD PSYCHOLOGICAL LABORATORY. DAY

JAMES *pushes the door of a laboratory open. There is an aisle of
cages made of glass and wire which evidently contain a variety of
animals judging from the sounds they emit; they are not seen during
the scene.*
BORIS, *in shirt-sleeves, is bent at a cage at the end of the aisle,*

jotting something into a notebook. He is about five years older than
JAMES *with the slighest hint of a middle-European accent.*

BORIS: You're late.

JAMES: Untrue. It's exactly five.

BORIS: (*Looks at his watch*) Yes. I must have decided you were
going to funk it.

(BORIS *goes into his office at the end of the aisle, on which 'Dr
Boris Heinz' is inscribed. He takes off his white coat and puts
on a jacket.*

JAMES, *meanwhile, is peering into a cage. He shudders, passes
on and looks into another cage.*)

JAMES: Why should I funk it?

BORIS: Because you're going to hate this guy.

(JAMES, *with an expression of slight disgust, passes on to the
next cage.*)

JAMES: I thought you said he was your oldest friend.

(BORIS, *emerging from his office, is adjusting various
temperature controls etc. by the office.*)

BORIS: Oldest *living* friend.

JAMES: And you said he was a bit of a charmer.

BORIS: No, charmless. I said completely charmless.

JAMES: (*Not really listening*) What's this?

BORIS: A rabbit.

JAMES: Yes, I can see it's a rabbit. But what's it eating?

BORIS: (*Looking*) Pigs' kidneys, they look like. Yes, pigs'
kidneys. One of my research students is trying to induce a
primitive form of schizophrenia. Probably all she'll get in
the end is a carnivorous rabbit. Just another of our freaks.
Still, she's a bright girl.

(*He raps on the window affectionately, turns, and goes up the aisle.*)
By the way, I'll drive.

JAMES: (*Follows*) No, you won't.

BORIS: Yes, I will. I know the way, and besides I need the
relaxation.

JAMES: You're not driving, Boris.

    (BORIS, *stops at the door, looking back.*)

BORIS: I'm sure I've forgotten to do something important.

JAMES: You're absolutely not driving, Boris.

BORIS: (*Shakes his head*) Ah well. It'll probably come back to me.

    (*He turns off the overhead lights. Individual lights continue to shine from some of the cages.*)

4. EXT. MAIN ROAD, OUTSIDE OXFORD. DAY

See the car externally first. It is going very fast, then begins to slow.

5. INT. CAR. MAIN ROAD OUTSIDE OXFORD. DAY

JAMES: (*Watching speedometer*) More.

BORIS: Oh really, James.

    (*He slows a little more.*)

JAMES: And keep it there, please. I really don't know why you gave up your own car.

BORIS: Probably because driving other chaps' is my version of making love to their wives. Only better. As they have to sit beside me while I do it. No, the truth is, the sods took away my licence.

JAMES: (*Stares at him*) You – you bloody fool! Stop the car!

BORIS: Joke, James, joke. I told you at the time why I was giving it up. For ecological reasons. Now that I've discovered I can't do without it, for sexual reasons, I've ordered a new one. A Jap job. It does a hundred and forty. And arrives next week. If the bastards keep their promise.

JAMES: Well, you won't be driving me in it.

BORIS: I hope not. I hope I shall be driving something prettier. And more exciting. Why are you so tetchy?

JAMES: I'm not tetchy.

BORIS: How's it going with that new girlie of yours, Samantha, isn't it?

JAMES: Amanda her name is, actually.

BORIS: Samantha, Amanda, they're all the same, surely.

JAMES: No doubt to you. But not to me. As a matter of fact
she's a bit fraught at the moment, she's giving her first
lecture tomorrow.

BORIS: Why don't you marry her, James?

JAMES: Marry her? But I scarcely know her.

BORIS: All the better. Then there'll be a strong element of risk
and it's time you took a risk. You need to shake up your
pattern, James. I mean, my dear fellow, just look at you!
The least sound startles you, the slightest burst of speed
frightens you. In fact, I see little difference between your
life and the life of one of the reconditioned rats in my lab.
Cheese, fuck, treadmill, sleep, cheese, fuck, treadmill –
except in your case, there isn't much of a treadmill. Merely
a leisurely ramble around a few poems. So for you it's
cheese, fuck, leisurely ramble, sleep, cheese, fuck – which
is why the rats are quite trim, and you're distinctly
overweight, I suppose.

JAMES: I'm not in the slightest bit overweight. I've kept at
thirteen one for the last two years.

BORIS: But you agree with the rest of it?

JAMES: Certainly.

BORIS: And so?

JAMES: And so nothing. What's wrong with it?

BORIS: But you're in danger of becoming a bit of a crashing
bore, old chap. Look at that stupid sod!
(*Honks angrily. A car overtaking on the inside. For a moment
the two cars are running parallel. The other car honks derisively
back, then goes in front.*)
I'll show the bugger!
(*He puts his foot down on the accelerator and swings his car out
to overtake.*
JAMES *sees a juggernaut through the window bearing down on
them. He screams.*

BORIS, *who has been honking at the other car, also sees.*)
Oh Christ!
(*Their position looks pretty hopeless, until at the last second*
BORIS *manages to get into a gap behind the car, which has
spurted away.* BORIS *drives on for a second or two.*)
JAMES: (*Quietly*) Pull over.
(BORIS *pulls over to the side of the road.* JAMES *sits blinking in
shock.* BORIS *is grinning rigidly.*
In a whisper) You nearly got us killed.
BORIS: Nonsense. My reflexes –
(JAMES *leans across* BORIS *and opens the driving-seat door.*)
JAMES: Out.
(BORIS *looks at him. He sees something in* JAMES's *face, gets
out, and walks round to the passenger side, as* JAMES *gets out
and walks round to the driver's side. They get in.*)
JAMES: (*Buckling himself*) Never never never never again, Boris.
BORIS: It's not my fault you possess a car that –
(JAMES *looks at* BORIS. BORIS *stops.*)
JAMES: And do up your safety-belt.
(BORIS *does so.* JAMES *drives off sedately.*)
BORIS: Nevertheless James, I must ask you to hurry a little.
The excitement seems to have loosened my bowels.
Excellent, as I've been somewhat constipated recently.
(*Little pause.*) Nevertheless, the need is urgent. (*Grins.*
JAMES *continues to drive sedately.* BORIS *gives him an anxious
look. Cut to:*)

6. EXT. DEREK'S COTTAGE. DAY

*There is a drive up to the cottage and on the other side, a lawn. A
vintage sports car is parked on the drive. On the lawn are a trestle
table, wine in an ice bucket and scattered deck-chairs.*
DEREK, *a man of about Boris's age, is sitting in a deck-chair,
writing. He glances up as* JAMES *parks behind the sports car, then
goes quickly back to his writing.*

BORIS: (*Unbuckling*) For God's sake, James, hurry.

(*He gets out of the car.* JAMES *follows. We see* JAMES *and* BORIS *who is now going towards* DEREK. DEREK *continues writing until the last minute, then puts down his board and rises.*)

Hello Derek. This is James Westgate. Fellow of Hertford, delivered as asked. James, this is Derek Newhouse, newly-elected Fellow of Magdalen.

(JAMES *and* DEREK *nod at each other.*)

But before we proceed further, I must beg the use of your lavatory. Where is it located?

DEREK: In the house. (*He gives a small, barking laugh.*) Ask Penny, she's in the kitchen, she'll show you.

(BORIS *hurries of.*)

He looks as if he's going to throw up. Is he all right?

JAMES: I think so. We had a nearish thing on the way. He's still a bit shaken, probably.

DEREK: And it scared the shit out of him, did it? (*He gives a barking laugh.*) What happened to his MG?

JAMES: He sold it.

DEREK: Thinks it's more exciting going about in a wheelchair does he? (*Indicating James's car.*)

JAMES: No, actually that's mine. My wheelchair.

DEREK: (*Barks laughter*) Wine?

JAMES: Lovely. Thank you.

(DEREK *goes to the table and pours out the wine.*)

DEREK: So you're at Hertford are you? What's your line?

(*He gives* JAMES *a glass of wine.*)

JAMES: English. Thank you. (*Taking the glass.*) Yours?

DEREK: Classics.

JAMES: (*Checking surprise*) Ah. And where were you before Magdalen?

DEREK: London. Queen Mary College. A dump down in the East End. You won't have heard of it.

JAMES: Oh, I've heard of it.

DEREK: (*Sits*) Really? What context?

JAMES: My father used to be one of the governors. He had a
great affection for the place.

(*He sits down himself. The deck-chair collapses under him. He
spills his wine.* DEREK *gives a little bark of laughter.*)

DEREK: Sorry about that. My wife set them up. She's a bit
cack-handed. You all right?

(JAMES, *struggling up, wipes at his shirt.*)

Don't worry. Only white wine. Won't stain. Although this
lot tastes as if it should. Don't know where the hell she gets
it from, probably the post office down the village – try that
one, it looks safe.

(JAMES *lowers himself gingerly.* DEREK *gets up with the wine
bottle and brings it over.*)

Here.

(*He pours in more wine.*)

JAMES: No, it's –

(*He moves his glass away. Wine goes over his trousers.*)

DEREK: Oh, sorry. It'll dry out in a second. Or eat its way
through your trousers.

(*He barks with laughter and stands looming over* JAMES.)

It's Perks at Hertford, isn't it?

JAMES: Mmmm? (*Confused.*)

DEREK: Your Principal. Perks.

JAMES: Oh. Pottsy, yes.

DEREK: (*Laughs*) Pottsy, is that what he's called?

JAMES: It's what I call him.

DEREK: What's he like? A bit of a prick, from what I can
gather.

JAMES: I suppose he is really. But quite a – a decent one.

DEREK: Well, I've only come across him professionally. In book
form. You know him well, do you?

JAMES: Yes. He's my uncle.

DEREK: (*After a little pause*) Uncle? (*He gives a small bark of
laughter.*) Sorry.

JAMES: (*Continues*) Pottsy is a family nickname. After Beatrix
Potter. He used to give me one of her tales every
Christmas. He still does now and then, as a matter of fact.

DEREK: Well, as I say I've never met him. In fact, I'd very
much like to.

JAMES: I'm sure that won't be a problem. He's quite an
accessible prick. (*He smiles.*)

DEREK: Yes, well you see, I have a slight problem over that.

JAMES: Really?

(*The sound of* BORIS's *voice with a woman's laughter coming
over it.* DEREK *turns his head,* JAMES *follows his look, and
from* JAMES's *point of view see* PENNY *and* BORIS *coming
towards them. Both are carrying trays of sandwiches, coffee,
another bottle of wine, strawberries, etc.*)

DEREK: Oh Christ. I'll leave it until later.

(*Cut to* JAMES *who is still looking at* PENNY *and* BORIS. *He is
in some way clearly astonished by* PENNY. *There is an odd
smile on his lips as he half-rises from his chair.*)

BORIS: (*Meanwhile*) Yes, yes, Derek, it really is a charming
little place; one expects gingerbread on the roof, and the
plants to be growing chocolate buttons and other goodies.
(*Putting the tray down*) How much did you pay for it?

DEREK: Christ, Boris, you are a Wog.

BORIS: Penny, Penny (*Taking her in his arms*), have I
complimented you on your looks, your health, your
sparkling eyes, the bloom on your cheeks –

DEREK: Oh, do take your hands off her, Boris, it doesn't fool
anyone.

BORIS: Penny my dear, this is James Westgate, from Hertford
College; James, the ravishing Penelope, who has the
misfortune to be Derek's wife.

(BORIS *is leading her to* JAMES *by the hand.* JAMES *struggles
out of his chair. He is smiling intently. Cut to* PENNY's *face
from* JAMES's *point of view. She is taking in his expression,
and looking slightly puzzled by it.*)

JAMES: (*Holding out his hand*) How do you do?
PENNY: How do you do?

7. EXT. DEREK'S COTTAGE. DAY

Later. JAMES, DEREK *and* BORIS *are in deck-chairs. The sandwiches etc. have been eaten. Plates, coffee cups etc. are spread about.*
PENNY *is sitting, being observed by* JAMES. *Now and then she glances at him, as if disturbed by his scrutiny.*

PENNY: So the Marquis of whatever it was made her his mistress and bought her this house. He was absolutely bonkers about her, at least until he got her set up here, completely cut off from everybody else.
(*See* DEREK *from* JAMES's *point of view, grunting without much interest.*)
Then of course, after a time he simply stopped coming here, staying on up in London and forgot about her entirely. So then *she* went absolutely bonkers –
DEREK: (*Interrupting*) Started screwing stable-boys, farm-hands, the bulls in the fields, anything that moved.
BORIS: Why is that bonkers? It seems an acceptable rural occupation for an out-of-work actress. For most people in fact.
PENNY: Oh, it wasn't like that at all, not at all. She merely – merely dallied with the occasional passing gentleman –
DEREK: You know who gave us all this information? Pilkington.
PENNY: No, it wasn't, darling surely. It was the people who sold it – the Merryweathers –
DEREK: No, it was Pilkington.
(PENNY, *seeing* JAMES's *eyes on her, gets up.*)
PENNY: Was it? Oh, well, would anyone like another sandwich? Or strawberries or wine?
BORIS: How come Pilkington?

DEREK: Oh, he was always hanging around here. Looking for some Anglo-Saxon burial mound. In the woods at the back. Drove us mad popping in and out of the kitchen for cups of tea, prosing on about sites and measurements – Christ what a bore. And we had to go to dinner –

PENNY: (*Interrupting*) If everybody's finished do you mind if I clear away?

(PENNY *looks towards* JAMES, *meets his eyes, looks away, and then begins to clear away plates.* JAMES *keeps his attention on her during the following, while she is obviously avoiding his look.*)

DEREK: And as for his wife, what was her name, Daphne –

PENNY: Deirdre, darling. Deirdre. Actually she's been very kind to me. Showing me all the shops –

(*She comes to* JAMES *who has picked up some plates. He hands them to her.*)

Thank you.

(*She gives a quick smile, but avoids his glance.*)

DEREK: Anyway, what's *your* theory?

BORIS: About what?

DEREK: About where he's vanished to, of course.

BORIS: Oh, it's perfectly obvious. It's just the usual mid-life crisis.

DEREK: Oh, balls, Boris!

PENNY: Thank you.

(*She takes the cups, etc. from* JAMES. JAMES *smiles at her. She gives him a quick, nervous smile, then turns away.*)

DEREK: You only had to spend ten minutes in Pilkington's company to know he wasn't going through any sort of crisis, he wouldn't know what a crisis was, would he, Pen?

(PENNY *has picked up a wine bottle and is pouring the last of it into some glasses. See her from* JAMES's *point of view, still watching her from the table.*)

He loves everything about his life, from being a Medieval historian to being short and bald with a wart on his nose.

He probably even likes his lisp. And he not only dotes on his Daphne, he positively worships his two sons, he's also a children bore, isn't he, Pen?

PENNY: Actually they're daughters, darling.

DEREK: What? Yes, well the point is, he adores them, whatever they are.

BORIS: James, you know him, don't you?

JAMES: Mmmm?

BORIS: Pilkington, our vanishing don.

JAMES: Oh, Pilkington, yes. Well, only slightly. I gave a paper to that history society he runs. And went back afterwards to dinner –

BORIS: So what's your explanation?

JAMES: I haven't got one.

BORIS: Penny, some woman's wisdom please. What's happened to Pilkington?

PENNY: I really don't know, all I know is (*Picking up tray*) that Deirdre and the girls miss him dreadfully, I just hope it's nothing ghastly, would anyone like some more coffee?

BORIS: There you are, Derek, as always your wife's heart has gone straight to the heart of the matter.

(PENNY *turns to go.* JAMES *is offering to take the tray.*)

JAMES: Let me.

PENNY: No, it's all right, thanks.

DEREK: Yes, but the question we were discussing is not what people feel about what's happened but what's happened, and I'll tell you what's happened. He's been murdered. Oh, nothing exotic, knowing Pilkington.

JAMES: Please. I insist. (*He tries again to take the tray.*)

PENNY: No, I'm all right, thank you.

DEREK: Probably picked up a hitch-hiker who bashed him over the head. Or got himself done over by a gang of hell's angels.

PENNY: (*Hissing*) I said I'm all right. And would you please, please, please stop staring at me, it's exceptionally rude. (*She turns with the tray and goes off with it.*)

DEREK: Eventually his body'll turn up, crammed into the boot of his car, in some wasteland somewhere. Or a squad of boys scouts will tread on him in a ditch.

(PENNY, *seen from* JAMES's *point of view is carrying the tray; still within earshot she stumbles and almost drops the tray.* JAMES *starts, and makes to go after her but stops himself as:*) And now that that's settled, on your feet, Wog. It's time I gave you your thrashing.

(PENNY, *seen from* JAMES's *point of view, enters the house. Cut from* PENNY *closing the door to* DEREK's *face in close-up, followed by a thwack and a grunt.* BORIS's *face in close-up is followed by a grunt and a thwack.* DEREK's *face in close-up is followed by a grunt and thwack.* BORIS's *face in close-up is followed by a thwack and grunt. Cut to them both as seen by* JAMES *who is sitting in a deck-chair. They are playing badminton.* JAMES *turns his head and looks towards the house.*)

DEREK: (*Voice over*) Bloody hell, Boris. You smashed that straight at my face.

BORIS: (*Voice over*) A perfectly legitimate tactic, I believe.

DEREK: (*Voice over*) At the body. Not at the face.

BORIS: (*Voice over*) James, ruling please.

JAMES: (*Turning back*) I can't remember a rule against it.

(DEREK *immediately serves.* BORIS *is not ready.*)

BORIS: (*Retrieving*) Hah!

(JAMES *turns his head and looks towards the house again.*)

DEREK: (*Voice over*) What's the score?

BORIS: (*Voice over*) Yes, score, James, please.

JAMES: Um – three – one.

DEREK: Three – one! How can it be –

BORIS: Umpire's word is final, Derek.

JAMES: You'll have to get on without me for a bit, I'm afraid. I'm going in for a pee. (*Getting up.*)

BORIS: Well, hurry back. Unless you want to see blood on the lawn.

(JAMES *goes towards the cottage. See him in long shot*

approaching the house with the game in vicious progress behind him.)

8. INT. THE COTTAGE: HALL. DAY

JAMES *enters the hall. A small passage leading to a door at the end which is closed. Some stairs ahead lead to a half-landing. To the left is a door, slightly ajar.* JAMES *hesitates, clears his throat and pushes open the door. The room is empty. It is clearly a combined sitting-room and study. There are armchairs, a sofa and bookcases with books half arranged on shelves. There is a box of books half unpacked, a desk with a typewriter on it. Books lie open on the desk along with a typescript.* JAMES *is about to shut the door, then stops himself. He looks towards the desk, looks up the stairs and along the passageway, then slips into the room.*

9. INT. THE COTTAGE: STUDY. DAY

JAMES *hurries over to the desk. He looks at the telephone, which has a pad and pencil beside it and writes the telephone's number on to the pad, rips off the page and puts it into his pocket. He hurries across the room and slips out.*

10. INT. THE COTTAGE: HALL. DAY

JAMES *looks towards the door at the end of the hall. He goes towards it, clears his throat again and listens. There is the sound of voices, low, almost muttering – a man's and a woman's. He opens the door. It is the kitchen.*

11. INT. THE COTTAGE: KITCHEN. DAY

On the kitchen table is the tray from the garden. On the side of the table, a radio is on. A man and woman are discussing a piece of music. Behind the table is a door with windows. It is shut.

JAMES *goes to the door and looks out. From his point of view we see a kitchen garden and behind it, a wood. There is a flash of movement from the wood, not distinct.* JAMES *frowns. Peers harder. He sees nothing. He turns and goes back into the hallway, to the bottom of the stairs.*

12. INT. THE COTTAGE: HALL AND STAIRS. DAY

JAMES *looks up, clears his throat, then walks up to the half-landing. The door is closed. He enters and closes the door. There is the sound of a lavatory flushing, a tap running etc.* JAMES *re-emerges and stands on the half-landing. He glances down then looks up the stairs. There is a door on the landing above, half-open.* JAMES *hesitates, then goes up the stairs.*

JAMES: Hello. (*He hesitates at the door.*) Hello. (*He pushes the door open.*)

13. INT. THE COTTAGE: BEDROOM. DAY

The bedroom. This is quite large, two rooms having been made into one, with a double bed. There are two windows, one quite large in the corner of the room, the other smaller adjacent to it, so that there are views of the front and side of the house. Underneath the windows is a desk and on it, envelopes, writing paper, etc. On either side of the bed are tables, one with an alarm clock and books, the other with books and photographs.
JAMES *goes over to the table with the photographs. He picks them up and looks at them. There is one of an elderly couple, arms around each other.* JAMES *looks at it, registers something, and puts it down. He picks up the other photographs. He sees* DEREK *and* PENNY *in swimming-clothes seated at a table on a beach,* PENNY *with her hand on* DEREK'S. JAMES *looks at it with an expression of distaste. Puts it down.*
He goes over to the window. On the table underneath is a framed

study of DEREK *looking dramatic and handsome.* JAMES *glances at it, then down at the desk. On the desk is an envelope not yet sealed, addressed to: Mrs Emily Postlethwaite, 4 The Cedars, Deal, Kent.* JAMES *nods and smiles, as if confirming something to himself.* JAMES *glances out of the window and from his point of view see* DEREK *and* BORIS *having a heated altercation over the badminton net.*
JAMES *turns, looks out of the other window casually and see from his point of view the figure of* PENNY, *walking quickly between the trees.* JAMES *watches for a second, then puts the letter back in the envelope and places it on the desk. He hurries out of the room.*

14. INT. THE COTTAGE: HALL AND STAIRS. DAY

JAMES *goes downstairs to the lower passage. He stops and looks towards the front door, then goes into the kitchen.*

15. INT. THE COTTAGE: KITCHEN. DAY

A radio is now playing the piece of music previously discussed. JAMES *goes to the door, opens it and hurries outside.*

16. EXT. THE COTTAGE: KITCHEN GARDEN. DAY

JAMES *is hurrying through the kitchen garden, then hurrying towards the wood.*

17. EXT. WOOD BEHIND COTTAGE. DAY

JAMES *sees a flash of* PENNY'S *dress through the trees. He hurries after her. A twig snaps underfoot.* PENNY *turns quickly, looks startled, then recognizes* JAMES.

JAMES: I'm sorry I didn't mean to – to alarm you.
PENNY: You were following me!

JAMES: No, no, I wasn't. I was merely wandering in this
    direction –

PENNY: You were following me! Just as you were staring at me
    before – why?

JAMES: But I assure you, I really – (*Stops*) – you're quite right
    of course. I was following you. And I was staring at you.

PENNY: But why? Why were you? You've made me feel quite –
    quite horrid. As if you were – were after me in some way.

JAMES: Well – because – to renew our acquaintance. We've met
    before, you see.

PENNY: Where?

JAMES: In Cornwall. In the village of Clogmellish, in the
    summer of (*Thinks*) – 1961, it must have been, when I was
    ten and you were eight. You don't remember?
    (PENNY *shakes her head.*)
    I've never forgotten. Especially the first time I saw you. I
    was sitting in my room. Wondering how to get through
    another sunny day. And you appeared. Beneath my
    window. I'd never seen you before, and you shouted up,
    'Well are you coming out or aren't you?' Just like that. 'Are
    you coming out or aren't you?' And I went straight out –
    rather as if I'd just been sitting there waiting for you to
    turn up. And presented myself to you. As ordered. You
    looked me up and down, and you said, 'You're not up to
    much, from what I can see. But they say you're all there is.
    So you'll have to do. I suppose.' I was a bit chubby, you
    see. Fat, actually. And of course my glasses – anyway, off
    we went – on that very first day you made me do the most
    appalling things. Do you really not remember? When I let
    you down, some failure of nerve or clumsiness that messed
    up one of your plans, you'd assault me. Really rather
    violently. I've never come across such a temper. And –
    well, once or twice, if you were particularly tired you made
    me, well, put you to bed. Undress you and – tuck you up.
    You're the first lady I ever saw naked – and the last, for

quite a few years. (*Laughs.*) And once when I was having a
bath when *they* were out – actually you insisted on my
having a bath, you said I smelt, you soaped me and dried
me – surely you remember that?
(PENNY *frowns as if in concentration.*)
Look, I'm really not making this up, your real name is
Prudence isn't it? Though they seem to call you Penny and
Pen – ah, of course! Penelope was your second name.
Right? Prudence Penelope Postlethwaite. Only you weren't
Prudence or Penelope to me. Because sometimes you wore
a patch over your eye – to make you look more piratical.
And I had to call you Captain Patch or Patch. And you
called me –

PENNY: Piglet! I remember! Of course! It's Piglet, isn't it?

JAMES: Well, Porker actually. You called me Porker.

PENNY: Of course! Porker! But I can't believe – I can't believe
– but how on earth – how on earth did you recognize me? I
can't possibly look the same –

JAMES: Well, that's the extraordinary thing. It wasn't you I
recognized. It was the sensation. When I saw you coming
across your lawn my stomach dipped. Just as it always did
when I saw you coming then. In anticipation, I suppose.
And a kind of – of terror. At what you had in store. That's
what I recognized. The dip of my stomach. Nobody else
has ever made my stomach do that. And then I recognized
you – the nose. The eyes of course. Your um, well beauty
actually. If I may say. (*Little laugh.*) The same beauty in a
different form. And – the other day – about a week ago, I
caught a glimpse of you – just a glimpse – on the other side
of the High. And you went to a concert – at Hollywell –
that would be what – two weeks ago, I suppose, wasn't it?

PENNY: Do you mind if I – if I touch you? I want to make sure
you're not a – a ghost – (*Takes his hand*) – no, no, you're
flesh and you're blood, all right.

JAMES: Oh yes.

PENNY: Not a trick or a joke.

JAMES: Well, perhaps a bit of a joke. But not a trick, I don't think.

PENNY: No, you were the one person I always trusted, weren't you? That's virtually what you've been saying isn't it? You did these – these things for me – isn't that right?

JAMES: Well, I did always try –

PENNY: No, but when things were wrong. Or difficult. You see, I've been, I've been – oh, I must be careful, but I've been praying, praying frantically, just as I used to pray as a child, you know the one, Oh God, please help me, please save me, oh if you do I'll never not believe in you again – (*Stops*) – and here you are. Piglet.

JAMES: Porker. Well, I'm not sure that I'm the answer to a prayer exactly – but – if you need help and there's anything I can do – well, I'm yours. (*Little laugh.*) Up to a point of course.

PENNY: Up to a point?

JAMES: Well, within the usual limits.

PENNY: What limits, what are the usual limits?

JAMES: Well, of me being me. That's all I mean. I'm probably not any braver – though I'm quite a bit stronger –

PENNY: Oh, don't worry about being brave. Leave that to me. It's your help I want. That's what I need.
(*They look at each other.*)

JAMES: Oh good Lord, Patch. Of course I'll help you. How could I not?
(PENNY *looks past him.* JAMES *turns. See from his point of view,* DEREK *coming towards them.*)

PENNY: Not fair, not fair, not bloody fair – hello, Darling, are you looking for me then?

DEREK: No, for him. (*Nodding at* JAMES.) It's all right, Boris, I've found them.

PENNY: (Sotto voce *to* JAMES) You've got to get in touch with me, you can't leave me in the lurch – (*To* DEREK) – but darling, you're absolutely soaking!

DEREK: Of course I'm soaking. I've been running around in the sun trying to thrash a Wog. Then running around the countryside because he's got himself into a woggish panic.

PENNY: Panic? Why's he in a panic, Darling?

DEREK: He says he's got to go back.

(BORIS *appears from further down.*)

BORIS: Yes, James, sorry, I remembered what it was in the lab – it was the cat. I forgot to disconnect the bloody cat. I'll have to go straight back or I'll have the animal rights lot ripping the place apart again.

DEREK: Oh Christ, Boris did you have to tell Penny? You know what she's like about animals.

(*Both* BORIS *and* DEREK *are hot and sweaty from running.*)

BORIS: (*Goes to her*) Ah! Sorry, Penny, my love, but anyway it's not what it sounds like. (*He puts his arm around her waist, leading her off.*) The cat was to all intents and purposes dead when it was brought to us. A very acute brain condition – not dissimilar to what is known as Alzheimer's syndrome . . .

(*They are now ahead of* JAMES *and* DEREK. BORIS *is gesticulating and expostulating.* JAMES *and* DEREK *walk together.*)

JAMES: (*After a pause*) Your wife was showing me the woods. Very lucky to have them so close.

DEREK: Oh yes, aren't we. Apropos that conversation we were having. As our time's been cut short, I'll come straight out with it. I need a bit of help in something.

JAMES: Oh.

DEREK: Yes, with your uncle, the Principal of Hertford. Old Pottsy, as you call him. (*He gives a little bark of laughter.*)

JAMES: Oh. Well, what can I do?

DEREK: This major series he's been appointed to edit. With a Channel-4 link-up. It's going to be called *Mundus Antiquorum*. The point is, I need to be a part of it. At least get in on the Greek philosophers' section.

JAMES: Ah. Well, why don't you drop him a note? He really is very amenable.

DEREK: Yes, well, a few years ago, I wrote an article dumping all over his book on Greek tragedy. So I've got a bit of brown-nosing to do. The best thing would be to ricochet off him in a social context. Oh, look out around here, by the way, Penny says she's seen an adder.

JAMES: Really? Well, they're very sensitive little creatures. As long as you don't positively step on them.

DEREK: Dinner in Hall would be best. And then back to your rooms for a quiet drink. Do you think you could arrange that?

JAMES: I'll see what I can do. Oops – (*He gives a little jump.*) No, no, only a twig.

18. EXT. THE COTTAGE: DRIVE. DAY

BORIS *and* PENNY *are standing beside the car,* BORIS *is talking extravagantly.* JAMES *and* DEREK *are approaching.*

BORIS: (*Breaking off*) Come on, James. Get a move on.
(*He kisses* PENNY's *hand and gets into the car on the driving side.*)

JAMES: Other side, Boris.

BORIS: If you drive we won't arrive until tomorrow.

JAMES: At least we'll arrive.

BORIS: (*Gets out*) Oh, thank you, Derek, for letting me give you a beating yet again.

DEREK: I don't believe all this stuff about the cat. You were beginning to fold, I'd have won the third set.
(BORIS *gets in the other side,* DEREK *following him and talking through the window.* JAMES, *during this, has gone up to* PENNY.)

JAMES: Thank you for a lovely afternoon.

PENNY: Not at all.

JAMES: The next time you're in Oxford – drop in for a cup of
    tea or coffee. I'm in Hertford New Court. E Staircase.
    (*Bursts of laughter from* BORIS *and* DEREK.)
PENNY: (*Obviously not quite hearing*) Where?
JAMES: (*Quickly*) New Court. E Staircase.
BORIS: Come on, James!
PENNY: I'll come tomorrow morning.
JAMES: When?
PENNY: Don't know. In the morning.
BORIS: James!

19. INT. CAR. MAIN ROAD OUTSIDE OXFORD. DAY

BORIS *and* JAMES *are travelling back to Oxford.*

BORIS: In London he was known as the ram. His real
    preference is for the barmaid type. By the way, he seems to
    have got it into his head that you're one of my lovers. Or
    one of my ex-lovers, possibly. He referred to you as my
    friend, the portly pansy.
JAMES: Did he? (*Little pause.*) Tell me, does she know?
BORIS: That he thinks you're a portly pansy?
JAMES: No, about him and his barmaids.
BORIS: Well I imagine he hopes she doesn't. After all, that must
    be part of the fun. Deceiving Mummy. But could we get a
    move on please, James?
    (JAMES *puts his foot down very slightly on the accelerator.*)

20. INT. JAMES'S ROOM. NIGHT

JAMES *is sitting on the window-seat, looking out. On the
gramophone we hear over, 'The Trout'. Cut from* JAMES, *in the
context of the room as a whole, looking out of the window, to*
JAMES'S *face in a trance of memory. He is smiling.*

21. FADE INTO MONTAGE

Concert. *Day*

A glimpse of PENNY *at the concert. Not properly seen.*

Cottage. *Day*

PENNY *on the lawn at the cottage, smiling.*

Concert. *Day*

PENNY's *face intent at the concert, listening.*

Barn. *Day*

PENNY, *as a child of ten, patch over one eye, her face turned up, intent. This seen from* JAMES's *point of view on a barn roof, as he looks down. He has an elderly camera in his hands. His position is precarious. Cut to* JAMES *staring down at* PENNY, *in a state of just-controlled panic. Cut back to* PENNY *seen from* JAMES's *point of view. She makes an imperious gesture to* JAMES *indicating: get on with it.* JAMES *nods, scrambles further up the barn, stops, peers down through a crack in the rafters.*

Barn. *Day*

From JAMES's *point of view are seen a young man and woman, both in stages of undress, the girl sighing, the man heaving himself on top of her. This seen through a crack in the rafters.*

Barn. *Day*

Cut to JAMES *staring down at them as if hypnotized. He glances down towards* PENNY. *Cut to* PENNY, *seen from* JAMES's *point of view, staring up, as before.* JAMES *nods, lifts the camera, makes to aim it through the crack in the rafters. Cut to:*

Barn. *Day*

Young woman's face under young man, seeming to stare straight up at JAMES.

Barn. Day

JAMES *losing his nerve, panicking, half turns. Camera slips from his grasp and rolls down the roof towards* PENNY.

Barn. Day

JAMES *looking down towards* PENNY. *Her face staring up. Then through the crack, the young woman's face staring up at him in a ferocious ecstasy.*

Barn. Day

JAMES, *now terrified, turns, slips and skids, finally topples off the barn to the ground.* PENNY *is standing over him looking down, holding the shattered camera, and cut to:*
JAMES's *and* PENNY's *point of view, both turning at a noise. Standing at the barn door is the young man, hiking up his trousers, and cut to:*

Wood near barn. Day

JAMES *and* PENNY *running,* JAMES *limping, trailing;* PENNY *gracefully sprinting, and cut to:*

Clearing in wood near barn. Day

JAMES *and* PENNY. JAMES *standing abjectly, sweating, spectacles dangling off his nose, chest heaving.* PENNY *standing, glaring at him.*

PENNY: Can't you do anything right? *Anything.* Anything at all! Can't you?
   (*She shakes the camera at him.*)
JAMES: But I didn't mean to. Honestly I didn't.
PENNY: What does it matter whether you didn't mean to if you did. Oh, you're such a fool, such a fool, such a great, fat fool, Porker!
   (*She throws the camera at him, runs at him, pushes him to the ground aiming blows and kicks until* JAMES *is scrambling about blindly, spectacles broken, and cut to:*

Bathroom. Day

JAMES *is in the bath,* PENNY *is soaping his back, and cut to:*

Bedroom. Day

JAMES *bathed, towel around him, is undressing* PENNY. *Helping her into her pyjamas.* JAMES *is sitting on the edge of a bed, looking down.* PENNY *is asleep.* JAMES *takes off his spectacles, polishes the lens with the sheet as he stares down at* PENNY. *He bends over, takes the eye patch off her, bends forward and kisses her on the forehead.* PENNY *murmurs, opens her eyes drowsily, smiles slightly, and sinks back to sleep.*

Cut from her face, serene, to JAMES *in college room.*

22. INT. JAMES'S ROOM. NIGHT

Cut back to JAMES *in his college room, smiling as over, the sound of a telephone ringing.* JAMES *starts, stares at the telephone uncomprehendingly, goes over to the gramophone and turns off music reluctantly. He answers the telephone.*

JAMES: (*On telephone*) Hello? Oh, hello my dear, um – how are you? Good, good. What – no, no, I can't right now, my – um, the thing is I'm right in the middle of marking some essays, I've got to give them back tomorrow morning, you see, and I've spent rather a – a fruitless afternoon out visiting some of Boris's friends – oh, ghastly, quite ghastly, and now I'm running behind so – what? What lecture? Oh, yours, *of course* I remember, for a moment I thought you were telling me *I* was giving a lecture – (*Laughs*) – yes, yes, no, no, I hadn't forgotten, how could I forget, your first lecture – (*Then, remembering in sudden alarm*) but – just a minute, what time is it exactly? Oh, yes, that's fine, that's fine, I'd had some idea it was in the morning, which I couldn't have managed – my own teaching, you know. Certainly I'll be there at three thirty on the dot, don't

worry – um – (*He writes on a pad:* AMANDA. *Lecture. 3.30*)
– goodnight then. Goodnight.
(*He puts the telephone down, goes over to the gramophone, puts on 'The Trout', goes back to the window-seat, sits down and looks out. A smile returns to his face.*)

23. INT. JAMES'S ROOM. DAY

JAMES *is standing at the window, looking out impatiently for* PENNY. *He turns into the room.*

JAMES: Um, yes. Well, we really can't go on – (*He gives a little laugh*) – meeting like this, can we Edmund?
(*Cut to* WILKINS *sitting in an armchair, a large, lumpish, intense student. His hands are folded tensely in his lap.*)
After all, this is the third week running you've failed to produce an essay. Isn't it? Third week Edmund?
(WILKINS *nods.* JAMES *looks out of the window and see, from his point of view, the college courtyard. He looks back at* WILKINS.)
Well, what do you say?
WILKINS: (*After a strangulated silence*) I don't know, sir.
JAMES: Well, look Edmund –
WILKINS: (*With a ghastly grin*) Actually, it's Edward, sir.
JAMES: Mmmm?
WILKINS: Not Edmund, sir. Edward Wilkins, Edward Wilkins. Not Edmund.
JAMES: Sorry. Edward. Yes, Well – have you got a reason? For not writing me essays?
(*Cut to* WILKINS *looking down at his hands, as if struggling to say something.* JAMES *glances at him impatiently. Then looks out of the window. See the courtyard from his point of view. A young woman wearing a straw hat is coming along the side of the court, not entirely visible but seems to be* PENNY. JAMES *peers towards her expectantly.* WILKINS, *over, makes*

an odd embarrassed noise, a kind of cough. JAMES *turns towards him.*)
Yes, well what it comes to is this. You'd better either produce an essay or at least a plausible excuse for not doing them within the next day or so, all right?
(JAMES *turns back to the window. The young woman is approaching the staircase below* JAMES. *She lifts her face up and points, it seems, straight at* JAMES. *An elderly American tourist joins her with a camera. He points it at* JAMES.
Cut to JAMES's *face, disappointed. He turns away and discovers* WILKINS *staring at him intensely, as if on the point of saying something urgent.* JAMES *looks at him, slightly puzzled, lifts his hand in a farewell gesture, and turns back to the window. Over, the sound of a door shutting.*
Fade into JAMES *standing at the window. Bells are tolling midday.*
Fade into a shot of the court, JAMES *staring out. Bells tolling one.*
JAMES *is sitting at the window-seat, looking out. Bells are tolling two.*
See the telephone from JAMES's *point of view. Cut to the telephone and beside it a piece of paper with* PENNY's *number on it.* JAMES *evidently makes a decision. He goes over to the telephone and starts to dial. His eye catches the piece of paper on which is written:* AMANDA. *Lecture. 3.30. He hangs up. Looks at his watch. It is 3.20 p.m. He looks towards the window in despair, then turns, and goes out.*)

24. INT. LECTURE HALL. DAY

JAMES *goes through the main door, to the hall.*
See AMANDA *through the window of the door opposite. She is standing on a podium, reading something from a book. She is in her mid-thirties, rather plain. Other books are spread out on the lectern in front of her.*

Cut to JAMES *looking in, then back to* AMANDA. *Students, not many, are scattered about the hall. Two of them get up and go through the door.* AMANDA *glances desperately after them, then goes back to reading.*

FIRST STUDENT: (*Coming through door*) I rate that as the second most demeaning lecture I've heard this term.
SECOND STUDENT: What does she do with her voice – I mean, she can't think that's how Baudelaire's meant to sound? (*The* TWO STUDENTS *pass through the main door.* JAMES *stares after them as they go out on to the street, and has a quick glimpse of* PENNY (*it certainly looks like her*) *cycling past. She is wearing her hat, which mostly conceals her face. (This shot is reminiscent of the shot of* PENNY *on a bicycle at the beginning of the film.) In the bicycle basket are assorted flowers, freshly cut.* JAMES *hesitates, looks at* AMANDA *lecturing, then hurries into the street in time to see* PENNY *cycling around the corner.*)

25. EXT. STREETS OF OXFORD. DAY

JAMES *hurries along, catching occasional glimpses of* PENNY's *hat, before she turns up another street. He runs to its corner and runs along it.* PENNY *is not in sight. Suddenly he sees the bicycle, with the basket and flowers and now the hat, leaning against the wall outside a tea-room.* JAMES *looks through the window. The shop is fairly crowded. He eventually distinguishes* PENNY, *sitting at a table by herself.*
Cut to his face, sweaty. He is breathing heavily from running. He enters the tea-room.

26. INT. TEA-ROOM. DAY

In the queue for buying cakes and bread to take out, is a middle-aged woman with long, grey hair. She is not noticed by JAMES. JAMES *goes to* PENNY, *wiping sweat from his face with a handkerchief. Still slightly breathless. He stands looking down at* *her.*

JAMES: I've been waiting for you. All morning. What are you doing here?

PENNY: You gave me the wrong address. There isn't any E Staircase New Court at Magdalen.

JAMES: But I'm not at Magdalen. I'm at Hertford. Your husband's at Magdalen. And Boris is at Magdalen. I'm at Hertford.

PENNY: Oh. I suppose I just assumed – we can't talk now. I'm meant to be meeting somebody here, that's how I got away, you see, and all for nothing, all wasted. Oh God!
    (*She looks at him desperately.*)

JAMES: I'm meant to be meeting somebody too. But afterwards –

PENNY: No, I've got to go back. Almost immediately. Derek needs the car, you see. I can't be late.

JAMES: Oh. (*Then realizing*) The car? But you haven't got the car – you're on a bicycle.

PENNY: Bicycle?
    (*She looks beyond* JAMES, *sees someone and smiles.* JAMES *turns, as a distraught woman in her middle thirties appears and sits down, unaware of* JAMES.)

DEIRDRE: (*To* PENNY) I'm sorry I'm late. Especially after summoning you out like this. But I desperately needed – need – to talk. I – I –
    (*She fumbles in her bag and takes out a cigarette. Hand trembling, she lights it and puffs on it.*) – I'd given them up. But this last week –
    (DEIRDRE *gives a little laugh, fraught, she suddenly takes in* JAMES)
    – sorry, I interrupted you.

PENNY: No, no, we just bumped into each other –
    (*She looks at* DEIRDRE *with concern.*)

DEIRDRE: But we've met, haven't we? You're James Westgate. You came to dinner once. About a year ago.

JAMES: Oh – um – (*Not placing her.*)

DEIRDRE: After you'd given a paper for my husband's history thing – I'm Deirdre Pilkington.

JAMES: Oh. Oh yes. Yes.

DEIRDRE: I don't know what your views are – everybody has a view, I know, including, I gather, that he was on the verge of being unmasked as an embezzler, and there are even a couple of scatty – no, not scatty, *vicious* girls going around claiming – although why they think that's a reason for him to run away from his home and his work – I mean, if they were telling the truth he could scarcely be better off, could he, with lots of nubile students and a completely unsuspecting wife – (*She gives a little laugh*) – but the fact is, whatever your particular view, he's dead. Murdered. (*This said defiantly.*)

PENNY: Oh Deirdre! (*Upset*) Don't –

DEIRDRE: Now all they've got to do is find a shred of evidence. His body, for instance. But to do that, they'll have to start looking seriously for him, won't they?

(*All this is said to* JAMES. *He stands, smiling meaninglessly.*) Sorry, sorry, my dear. (*To* PENNY.) But I've just come from the police, you see. I told myself I wasn't going to go today, but I had to pass the station to get here, and found myself dropping in – and the dreadful man behind the desk, just like that one who used to be on television years back, the 'hello, hello, hello' one, pretending to be so avuncular but all the time I could tell what *his* real view was, his particular view, that I'm a sad but tiresome middle-aged woman who can't accept the obvious, that her husband's abandoned her from boredom or run off with his floozie, and it's really all my own fault for not knowing how to keep him at home. Nobody – nobody in the world – except me and his children seems to understand that he was

a nice man – a good man. Who loves us actually. And
would never – never just abandon us. (*To* PENNY) Of
course you understand, Penny. I do know that. Sorry, my
dear.

(DEIRDRE *puts her hand on* PENNY's. *Both women are upset.*)

JAMES: I – I can't say how sorry, how very sorry um – well, I'd
better leave you – oh, may I just ask, what time is Derek
leaving, I mean if I went out now would I catch him –
excuse me? (*To* DEIRDRE.)

PENNY: He's going at four thirty promptly, I'm terribly sorry,
Deirdre, that's when I've got to get back – because of the
car, you see.

DEIRDRE: It's my own fault, for being late.

PENNY: So if you're after four thirty you'll miss him completely.
But he probably won't be gone too long – probably not more
than an hour or so. And then he'll be back.

JAMES: Right. I've got that.

(JAMES *looks at* DEIRDRE *blankly*.)

Well, nice to have met you.

(*With a smile, he turns and goes. Turns as he leaves and nods
to* PENNY *then goes out into the street*.)

27. EXT. THE TEA-ROOM. DAY

Through the window, from JAMES's *point of view see* PENNY *still
leaning forward and* DEIRDRE *wiping her eyes with a handkerchief.*
JAMES *stands for a moment, then turns as the middle-aged woman
with long, grey hair from the queue comes out of the shop. She has
rather a ravaged face. She is holding a box of cakes. She goes to the
bicycle, puts the box in the basket beside the flowers, pushes her hair
on her head, puts on her hat, and cycles off. As she recedes, the
image becomes like* PENNY *again.*
JAMES *stares after her, then turns and walks slowly down the street.
He suddenly stops in realization, looks at his watch and hurries off,
almost running.*

28. INT. LECTURE ROOM. DAY

JAMES *hurries in, panting and sweating. He goes to the lecture room. Looks through the window. It appears to be empty. He looks around, then looks through the window of the lecture room again. He sees* AMANDA *sitting, hunched in a corner, smoking. He enters the lecture room.*

29. INT. LECTURE ROOM. DAY

AMANDA *looks up at* JAMES *and attempts a smile. He goes over to her.*

JAMES: Sorry I'm late, the thing is – (*Checks himself*) – how did it go?

AMANDA: Oh James, it was awful. They left in droves and then when I started reading Baudelaire something happened to my throat, nerves I suppose, I sounded just like Donald Duck. At least from the inside, I expect I did from the outside too. (*She looks at him. Her mouth trembles. She is clearly on the verge of tears.*) Well, let's be off to somewhere I can feel invisible for a time. (*Gets up.*)

JAMES: Yes, well the awful thing is I've got to go.

AMANDA: Oh.

JAMES: You see, it's my father. I've just heard he's very ill, very ill indeed, so I've got to go to London, he's in hospital.

AMANDA: Oh James, I am so sorry and here I've been whingeing on about a silly lecture.

JAMES: Look, we'll have dinner. I'll take you to the French place.

AMANDA: You won't be back in time. Come straight to me and I'll cook us something.

JAMES: Right. Thank you.

(*He bends forward and kisses her.* AMANDA *puts her arms around him.*)

AMANDA: Oh, James, I am sorry.
JAMES: Well, um, see you later then.
>(*He hurries to the door and glances through the window. See* AMANDA *from his point of view. He gives her a little wave.*)

30. INT./EXT. CAR. END OF DEREK'S DRIVE. DAY

JAMES *is sitting in his car parked by the side of the road off* DEREK's *drive. He looks at his watch. It is 4.35. There is the sound of the sports car coming up the drive.*
JAMES *ducks his head as* DEREK *comes up the drive and turns towards the main road. He watches it as it gets to the turning. It is coughing slightly but goes around the corner.* JAMES *drives his car down the drive.*

31. EXT. DEREK'S COTTAGE. DAY

As JAMES *approaches the cottage, the door opens.* PENNY *comes out, walking very quickly, almost running towards him. He gets out of the car.*

PENNY: (*Anxiously*) Did Derek see you?
JAMES: No, no, it's all right. I waited around the corner. He went past me without a glance.
>(*There is a roaring sound from the drive.* JAMES *and* PENNY *turn towards the noise and from their point of view, see* DEREK *coming back down the drive. Just before he gets to the house, the car jumps a bit, then stalls.* DEREK *gets out, furious.*)
DEREK: You forgot to get the petrol. I asked you to fill her up in Oxford. I reminded you just before you left. If I hadn't noticed, I'd have been stuck on the bloody bypass.
PENNY: Oh darling, I'm so sorry. So sorry. It went straight out of my mind. Because of Deirdre being so upset and –
DEREK: Bugger Deirdre, you were late getting back anyway.

What am I going to do, I've got a seminar in twenty
minutes' time, post-graduates –

PENNY: I'll phone for a taxi.

DEREK: You know how I hate wasting money on taxis. Besides,
it'll take them half an hour to get here –
(*He sees* JAMES.)

32. INT. JAMES'S CAR. MAIN ROAD OUTSIDE OXFORD. DAY

DEREK *and* JAMES *are in the car.* JAMES *is driving,* DEREK *beside
him. There is silence between them. During the course of the journey*
DEREK *is only just suppressing irritation with* JAMES'S *careful
driving.*

DEREK: (*After a moment*) Very good of you.

JAMES: Not at all. I was on my way back anyway.

DEREK: Where from?

JAMES: Mmmm?

DEREK: Where were you on your way back from?

JAMES: Oh. Visiting my father. He's in hospital.

DEREK: He lives around here, does he?

JAMES: No. In London, as a matter of fact.

DEREK: Rather a long way around.

JAMES: Mmmm?

DEREK: Coming from London.

JAMES: Yes. I like to go by the side-roads. A whiff of the
country –
(DEREK, *paying no attention, glances at the speedometer.*)

DEREK: Anything serious?

JAMES: Mmmm?

DEREK: Your father.

JAMES: Oh, it is rather, I'm afraid. Yes. What's the seminar on?

DEREK: Plato. *The Symposium.*

JAMES: Ah. The Greek ideal of love, eh?

DEREK: That's the ticket. (*Looking at his watch.*)

JAMES: I re-read it often. The school chaplain introduced me to
 it. He was a great teacher, and an exceptionally sensitive
 and feeling man. Especially with boys of my age.
 (DEREK *glances sardonically at* JAMES *and grunts.*)
 I mean boys of my age the age I was then. (*Little laugh.*)
 Sixteen. He'd have little seminars – well, symposiums, he
 actually called them – with the two or three lads in whom
 he took a special interest.
 (DEREK *throws him a contemptuous glance.*)
 Really, it was because of him, and through him because of
 Plato . . .

33. EXT. MAGDALEN COLLEGE. DAY

JAMES *pulls up beside it.*

JAMES: There you are, and not even late.
DEREK: Thanks. You saved my bacon. Now the question is how
 the hell am I going to get back? Look, what are you up to
 this evening?
JAMES: (*Stares at* DEREK) Well, um, nothing. (JAMES *gives a
 little laugh.*)
DEREK: Good. Then why don't you pick me up here at seven
 thirty.
JAMES: Oh, right.
DEREK: You can come and have a bite of supper with us or
 something.
JAMES: Thank you.
 (DEREK *wags his hand as he turns to go.* JAMES *wags his
 hand.*)

34. EXT. MAIN ROAD OUTSIDE OXFORD. DAY

JAMES *is driving his car back to the cottage.*

35. EXT. END OF DEREK'S DRIVE. DAY

JAMES *goes down the drive.*

36. INT. DEREK'S COTTAGE: HALL: FRONT DOOR. DAY

The door is ajar. JAMES *pushes it open and see from his point of view down the length of the corridor into the kitchen.*
PENNY *is sitting at the kitchen table, her cheek resting on her hand. The radio is on. Mozart playing. She is softly lit by light from the kitchen windows. The effect is almost religious.* JAMES *stands looking, in wonder.* PENNY *looks up.*

37. INT. THE COTTAGE: KITCHEN. DAY

From PENNY's *point of view* JAMES's *figure is indistinct. She stares for a second, then screams hysterically, getting up. She continues to scream, close to hysteria.* JAMES *runs to her, grabs her as she continues to scream, and puts his arms around her.*

JAMES: It's only me, it's only me.
(PENNY *collapses within his arms.* JAMES *strokes her hair with an expression of tender concern on his face.*)
Only me, Patch, only me, only me.

38. INT. THE COTTAGE: KITCHEN. DAY

JAMES *and* PENNY *sit at the kitchen table in silence.* JAMES *has his hand on hers.*

PENNY: Can I really trust you? Really?
JAMES: You lead, I'll follow – that's what you used to say, when we were setting out on one of your escapades.
PENNY: But this isn't an escapade, you see. It's a nightmare. And today you've been part of it, turning up when I was

245

meeting Deirdre, of all people, then driving up, and
driving straight off with Derek, then Derek phoning up
saying you were coming back with him, then standing at
the door looking just like – like – with your glasses
glinting – just more out of the nightmare.

JAMES: Here, feel – (*He squeezes her hand and raises it to his
cheek*) – still flesh and blood, just as I was yesterday. And
I'm here in spite of everything. Now tell me what the
matter is, Patch. Is it – (*Hesitates*) – is it Derek?
(PENNY *looks at him.*)
Something wrong between you and Derek?

PENNY: No, no, it isn't him. Well, of course it is in a way.
Because he's the whole point. Whatever happens he musn't
know, you see. Musn't.

JAMES: I've already promised I won't tell a soul. (*Then
swallowing*) It's another man then, perhaps, is it?

PENNY: You might put it that way, yes. Another man.

39. EXT. DITCH IN WOODS. DAY

See PILKINGTON'*s face, glasses down over his nose, eyes open,
scissors sticking through his neck. See this from* JAMES'*s point of
view, then the camera travels along to take in the whole body, bits of
leaves and twigs scattered over it.*
Cut to JAMES'*s face, looking down.* PENNY, *beside him, watches
him. After a long pause:*

PENNY: Look at his glasses. See how they glint!
JAMES: Yes. Who is it exactly?
PENNY: Horace.
JAMES: Horace. Um, Horace who?
PENNY: Pilkington.
JAMES: Ah. What – what exactly happened to him, then?
PENNY: I killed him, you see. So there you are, Piglet. Your
little chum Patch has grown up into a murderess.

JAMES: (*Nods*) Do you mind if we go and sit somewhere, I feel a trifle –

40. EXT. A WALL NEAR THE WOODS. DAY

JAMES *and* PENNY *sit on the wall.* JAMES *stares straight ahead.* PENNY *watches him anxiously.*

PENNY: You're not going to let me down now, are you? After all you've promised?

JAMES: Um – well how did it happen precisely?

PENNY: I told you. I killed him.

JAMES: Yes, but it must have been a sort of – sort of accident, mustn't it? I mean you didn't just – just stick those things into him on a whim, I take it. (*Little laugh.*) Did you?

PENNY: No, no, of course not. I stuck them into him on purpose.

JAMES: What was the purpose, Patch?

PENNY: To stop him, of course. You see, he came over – when Derek was in London, seeing his publisher – and was messing about in the woods, looking for his precious burial mound or whatever it was he was always looking for. And I was reading on the lawn and he suddenly came gambolling up – saying he'd found it, he was sure he'd found it at last, come and look, please Penny. So I went – I – I'd much rather not go through it all again, Piglet.

JAMES: I think I really need to know, Patch.
    (JAMES *looks at her.*)

PENNY: (*After a pause*) Oh, all right then. Well, where was I?

JAMES: He was showing you the burial mound.

PENNY: Yes. (*Pause.*) And then he began. That's when it happened, you see.

JAMES: Began what?

PENNY: To touch me. He was everywhere. His hands, I mean, they were everywhere. Under my skirt and on my breasts

247

and his spectacles – and his spectacles were butting against
my face, and then I saw his scissors. I picked them up and
just – just stuck them in him.

JAMES: What did you do then, Patch?

PENNY: Went in and had a bath, of course. I was covered with
blood.

JAMES: And then?

PENNY: I sat in the kitchen, waiting for Derek. Thinking about
how to tell him. Tell him what I'd done to Horace.

JAMES: Why didn't you?

PENNY: Oh, I tried to once or twice but it was impossible. Quite
impossible. When he got home he was in such a state because
his book had been turned down by the publishers, you see.
On Socrates, Man and something – myth – myth. So of
course that's what he wanted to talk about and I had to keep
saying how disgusting, how disgraceful, how shameful and
shocking as he went over and over what they'd said to him
and he'd said to them. Then I heated up some soup, we went
through it all again and then we went to bed.
(*She looks at* JAMES.)
That's all, really. So what should we do, Piglet?

41. INT. THE COTTAGE: KITCHEN. DAY

JAMES *pours himself a large Scotch. His hand trembles.* PENNY
watches him anxiously.

JAMES: (*After a long pause*) But surely, if you told it to them just
as you've told it to me . . .

PENNY: Yes, but you see, think of the publicity. The trial.
There'd certainly have to be a trial, wouldn't there?
(JAMES *nods.*)
I might even go to jail, mightn't I?

JAMES: Oh, I don't think – I'm sure that – after all, he assaulted
you.

PENNY: Oh, it's not my going to jail, but what it would do to
    Derek, even if I didn't. He's only just come to Oxford, it
    would be talked about in the College, among his students,
    everywhere. He couldn't endure that. He'd hate me for it.
JAMES: Yes. I see. (*Clears his throat.*) I take you point but – I
    can't help feeling that the proper course, in the long run –
    (PENNY *looks at* JAMES *and smiles bitterly.*)
PENNY: You're going to tell them, aren't you? Derek and the
    Police.
JAMES: No. No, of course not. (*Pause.*) But if you – we – *we*
    don't do the normal thing – *proper* thing – legal thing, that
    is – you can't leave him where he is, can you?
PENNY: Of course not. That's what I want you to help me with.
JAMES: (*After a slight pause*) Yes.
    (DEREK *enters.*)
PENNY: Darling! You're back. How lovely!
    (JAMES *assumes beaming nonchalance.*)
JAMES: Oh, hello there. Um. Derek –
    (DEREK *gives a little bark of angry laughter as he stares at*
    JAMES.)
DEREK: What happened to you then?
JAMES: Mmmm?
DEREK: You were going to pick me up at half-past seven.
JAMES: Oh Lord! (*Slaps his forehead.*) Derek, I'm terribly sorry,
    I suppose – I suppose that with one thing and another you
    completely slipped my mind.
    (DEREK *gives a short bark of incredulous laughter.*)
    You see, I had to chair the wine committee, and it ran over
    a bit. Because of the port. I am sorry. How did you get
    back?
DEREK: By bloody taxi. (*He attempts a slightly more jocular tone.*)
    I slipped your mind too, did I?
PENNY: What?
DEREK: Well, I did phone and tell you he'd be picking me up.
    Didn't you notice I wasn't here?

PENNY: But he's only just arrived, darling. I thought you were together. Or just behind him, rather. What you need is a drink. (*She sees the Scotch bottle and glass on the table, and picks them up smoothly.*) I was just about to pour one for Piglet.

DEREK: Piglet?

JAMES: Actually it's Porker, my – my friends call me Porker, as I was just in the middle of explaining to – um – Pa – Patch – (*Checking himself*) – Prudence. Thank you. (*Receiving drink.*)

DEREK: Prudence? (*Looks at* PENNY.)

PENNY: Yes, well I was explaining that my real name was Prudence, though my friends call me Penny or Pen.

DEREK: In my case we'll settle for Derek, can we?

(JAMES *and* PENNY *laugh.*)

JAMES: Well, I'll drink to that. (*Catches* PENNY'*s eye.*) How did the seminar go?

42. INT. THE COTTAGE: KITCHEN. NIGHT

DEREK, JAMES *and* PENNY *sit around the kitchen table.* DEREK *is at the head,* JAMES *and* PENNY *opposite each other. They eat dinner.* PENNY *is talking with too much animation to* DEREK.

PENNY: . . . when I told him he'd actually taken the measurements down himself, because I remembered his name, it was Parker, (*Small hesitation*) he said, do you know what he said, darling, he said, 'Oh well, I must have mislaid them!'

JAMES: How infuriating! But there's another place, you know, just around the corner from Hubblewickes called Fabrics and Frolics, I think it is. Some such name anyway. I went there with a friend's wife when she was doing up their flat, and they really do have some very charming patterns. (DEREK *glances at* JAMES *contemptuously.*)

PENNY: Just around the corner from Hubblewickes, you say,
    oh, I must go and have a look.
DEREK: Did you remember to call the garage?
PENNY: The garage?
DEREK: Yes, the garage. To get them to bring some petrol over.
    To save me hiking up there in the morning.
PENNY: Oh darling, I'm terribly sorry. I can't think why –
DEREK: It probably just slipped your mind, eh?
PENNY: Sorry.
    (*They eat in silence for a moment.*)
    (*Desperately*) Oh, that reminds me, somebody phoned.
    Now, who did she say she was – oh, oh – oh, that's right,
    Liz Maybrick.
DEREK: Who?
PENNY: Liz Maybrick, one of your research students from
    London, she said she was.
DEREK: Oh. Oh yes. What did she want?
PENNY: Only to tell you that they've taken away her grant and
    could you phone her back.
DEREK: Grant? (*A moment's pause.*) Taken it away, eh? I'm not
    surprised. Utterly chaotic little mind. I warned her they would.
PENNY: Actually, I did say you'd call her back as soon as you
    got in. She said you had her number.
DEREK: I expect I have, somewhere at College. So she'll have to
    wait until tomorrow. (*A pause.*) Oh, by the way, I was right
    about Pilkington, he's been murdered.
    (*A silence.*)
JAMES: Indeed? How do you know?
DEREK: College porter told me. Police found his car. Just up the
    road in Little Mitford. Some woman's been complaining all
    week about its having been parked outside her house, in
    her spot, so this morning they got around to having a look
    at it. (*Bark of laughter.*) So much for Boris and the mid-life
    crisis. But it's bad news for you, Pen. (*To* PENNY) You can
    expect them around any time.

(PENNY *is frozen.*)

JAMES: How exciting – this is delicious, by the way.

PENNY: Thank you, I'm sorry it's only frozen. (*Then somewhat restored*) Why do you think they'll come here, darling?

DEREK: Because Pilkington used to hang about here, of course, and Little Mitford's walking distance. So they're bound to come trampling over the lawn, thundering through the woods, and dragging through the ditches.

JAMES: (*Seeing* PENNY's *face*) But tell me why exactly, exactly why finding the car means he was murdered, Derek. Doesn't altogether follow surely, I'm speaking on behalf of Boris, of course, and the mid-life theory. (*Little laugh.*)

DEREK: Because the keys were in the ignition. So either somebody drove it there and left it in a panic, or Pilkington got out with every intention of coming back. So what would your Boris have to say to that little lot?

JAMES: Well, well I suppose he might say –

(*The telephone rings.*)

DEREK: (*Quickly*) I'll get it.

(*He goes out. Pause.*)

JAMES: You didn't tell me about the car.

PENNY: He used to park it at the top of the drive. I couldn't just leave it there, could I?

JAMES: Yes, but – um – why did you leave it so close? Within walking distance he said.

PENNY: Because I had to walk back.

JAMES: Ah. And you left the keys in the ignition.

PENNY: Because I hoped someone would steal it. There's no point in telling me I've done everything wrong, I know I have, I know it. The question is what are we going to do now?

JAMES: Yes, well it's obvious that whatever it is, we're going to have to do it straight away.

PENNY: Tomorrow. You've got to do it tomorrow.

JAMES: What time does Derek go out?

PENNY: He doesn't. He works at home on Thursdays.

JAMES: Can you get him out? In the evening? Or at night,
would be best. More conventional, too, I'd think. For
burying bodies on the quiet. (*Little laugh*.)

(PENNY *gives him a look*.)

Sorry.

(*Sound of* DEREK *returning*.)

PENNY: And for God's sake, stop him talking about it.

(DEREK *enters, trying to look casual*.)

DEREK: Sorry, wrong number. But the fool wouldn't believe
me. Seemed to think I was a pub or something. (*Sitting
down*) Yes, now you were just about to give us the Boris
line on Pilkington, I believe.

JAMES: Was I? Well I don't know what it would be, even Boris
would be a bit floored by the car business. A pub, eh?
That's unusual. To be mistaken for a pub. Which one did
he think you were?

DEREK: Oh, (*Desperately*) The Cat's Whiskers, I think it was,
yes. The Cat's Whiskers. Oh, and another thing about
Pilkington's car –

JAMES: I don't believe I've ever come across a pub called The
Cat's Whiskers before, have you? (*To* PENNY.)

PENNY: Not The Cat's Whiskers, no. Never.

JAMES: Was it a man or a woman?

DEREK: Man, why, what's that got to do with it?

JAMES: Oh I was just sort of curious. What sort of accent?

DEREK: Accent?

JAMES: Yes. Did he sound like a local chap or –

DEREK: No idea, I suppose he sounded a bit – bit North
Country, anyway, it doesn't matter, what I'd like to ask the
police –

JAMES: North Country! Now that *is* interesting. Because of
these new dialling codes, you see. They're so complicated
that if someone wanted, say a pub called The Cat's
Whiskers in Leeds he'd only have to get one digit wrong to

find himself asking if you were The Cat's Whiskers here in Oxford. Although I admit that doesn't settle the question as to whether you'd be likely to be The Cat's Whiskers anywhere, in fact, the Cat's anything . . . I mean, not only have I never come across The Cat's Whiskers . . . The Cat's Pyjamas, for instance, I don't believe I've ever come across The Cat's Cradle, The Cat on the Mat, The Cat and Dog – The Cat –

DEREK: (*Interrupting*) Well, I assure you that's what she said. The Cat's Pyjamas. (*Slight pause.*) Cat's Whiskers, that is.

JAMES: She said?

DEREK: What?

JAMES: You said she said. But before you said –

DEREK: I meant he. He said. I must say – I must say – I'd really like to get back to the topic of the moment, if you don't mind. Which happens to be the scissors.

JAMES: Scissors?

DEREK: Pilkington's scissors. The ones he used to cut up his tape with. Now what I'd ask the police, if I could be bothered, was whether the scissors were in the car. Because if they *weren't* in the car –

(PENNY *lets out a moan.*)

Something the matter?

PENNY: Just – just a headache.

DEREK: What, another one? (*Gets up.*) I'll get you an aspirin. That makes one almost every evening for the last week or so, if it keeps up you'll *have* to see a doctor, Pen.

(*He goes to the tap and pours a glass of water.*

PENNY *grabs* JAMES's *hand, clutches at it, then relinquishes it as* DEREK *turns.* PENNY *takes the aspirin and drinks the water.*)

PENNY: I think – if you don't mind – I think I'd better go and lie down.

(*She gets up.*)

DEREK: Won't do you much good unless you turn the lights off. She's taken to trying to sleep with the light on.

PENNY: (*To* JAMES) I'm sorry to abandon you –

JAMES: Not at all. You get some rest.

(PENNY *smiles, then nods. As she goes out she turns and stares at* JAMES, *pleadingly.* JAMES *gives her a little nod of encouragement.* PENNY *closes the door.*)

DEREK: Never used to have them in London. Must be the country air. (*He hesitates, and attempts a smile.*) By the way, all that stuff about the cat's what's it and pubs, what was that all about?

JAMES: Sorry?

DEREK: Well, you gave the impression you were trying to tell me something. Or Penny something. Or something.

JAMES: Really? What sort of something?

DEREK: I don't know. That's what I'm asking you.

JAMES: No, I assure you – I've always had a great interest in the derivation of things like pubs' names, in fact I once wrote a little paper –

DEREK: Oh, I see. That's all right then. I just don't want Penny to be worried about anything, you see. What with all these headaches and bad nights she's been having. So I don't want her worried, that's all.

JAMES: Of course, I'll be very careful.

DEREK: Right. That's understood then.

(*A pause.*)

JAMES: Well, er, I'd better be off then. Leave you to look after my wife – (*Little laugh*) – your wife, I mean.

DEREK: Well, perhaps I'd better make sure she's put herself to bed.

(*They go into the hall.*)

43. INT. THE COTTAGE: HALL. NIGHT

JAMES: Thank her for dinner for me. (*Turning to go*) I hope her head clears up – um – oh – (*As he opens the front door*) oh, something, *yes of course!* (*Slaps his forehead.*) How could I

255

have forgotten – old Pottsy, I saw him this evening – at the wine comittee. Now the thing is, he's off to the States for a couple of months, leaves on Saturday. To recruit contributors for the series.

DEREK: Well, that cuts me out, doesn't it? Bugger! Bugger the Americans!

JAMES: Ah, well all isn't quite lost. He's going to be in Hall tomorrow night, why don't you come to dinner and I'll find some way of bringing you two together?

DEREK: Right. That's very good of you. Thanks.

JAMES: Good. I'm in New Court. The porter will show you where, so see you in my rooms at seven thirty.

DEREK: I'll be there.

(JAMES *turns to go, then turns back.*)

JAMES: Look, why don't you stay the night in College?

DEREK: Why?

JAMES: Well, um, you know what it's like, one tends to drink rather a lot in Hall on these occasions. And you see a few years ago some chap I invited, well, rather a tragedy, he didn't make it home. I'm afraid. In fact he's virtually a vegetable.

DEREK: (*Little laugh*) Really, Well don't worry about me, I can keep an eye on myself, thanks.

JAMES: Oh. Right. Well, do you mind if I reserve a guest room just in case you change your mind?

DEREK: If you want to (*Little laugh*) but I doubt if I'll be using it.

JAMES: See you tomorrow then.

(JAMES *wags his hand, and goes out.*)

44. EXT. THE COTTAGE: DRIVE. NIGHT

DEREK *wags his hand.* JAMES *goes to his car and gets in.* DEREK *wags his hand again.* JAMES *wags his back as he drives off. See* DEREK *from* JAMES'S *point of view, closing the door. Stay with*

JAMES *going up the drive. He stops the car. Gets out, and comes quietly back down the drive. He sees* DEREK *framed at the sitting-room window, as he draws the curtains.* JAMES *steals closer and looks through a slight gap in the curtains.* DEREK *is standing in a state of indecision. He looks up at the ceiling, looks at his watch, then goes to the telephone and dials.* JAMES *bends down, picks up a handful of gravel and throws it against the window above. Silence.*

JAMES: (*Urgently, in a low voice*) Patch! Patch! Patch!
(*Silence. He looks through the curtain again.* DEREK *is talking on the telephone.* JAMES *picks up more gravel and throws it against the window. From inside* PENNY's *room comes a shriek of terror.*
Cut to JAMES's *face, appalled. He glances through the curtains.* DEREK *glances, puzzled, up at the ceiling, waits for a second, then goes on talking on the telephone.* JAMES *looks up at the window above.* PENNY *opens the curtains and stares down at him, terrified.* JAMES *steps back a bit so she can see him properly. She recognizes him, pushes the window open wider and leans out.*)

PENNY: What are you doing? You frightened me nearly to death.

JAMES: Sorry.
(*He glances through the window to make sure* DEREK *is still on the telephone.*)
Listen, we'll do it tomorrow. I'll be coming out around midnight. I'll phone you just before I leave.

PENNY: What about Derek?

JAMES: Don't worry, I'm working that out, but he's coming to dinner tomorrow with me. You try and persuade him to spend the night at my College. Because of drinking and driving and so forth. Have you got that?
(*He glances through the window again. He sees* DEREK *still on the telephone.*)

PENNY: He won't.

JAMES: Well try anyway. But don't worry, I'll find a way of keeping him there. Everything's going to be all right.

PENNY: Do you promise?

JAMES: I promise.

(JAMES *glances through the window, and sees* DEREK *has left the room.*)

Don't forget I'll phone you.

DEREK: (*Voice over*) What are you doing? You're meant to be in bed.

PENNY: (*Withdrawing from window*) Oh, just getting – getting some fresh air.

(DEREK *comes to the window. We have just a glimpse of him standing beside* PENNY *as she draws the curtains. The sound of their voices is no longer audible as* JAMES *looks once at the window, then turns.*)

46. INT. JAMES'S ROOMS. MORNING

The camera comes straight in on a writing pad. 'Hall' and 'Guestroom' have been ticked off. Cut to JAMES *on the telephone.*

JAMES: (*On telephone*) Master, please. Oh hello, Potts. Nutkin. Just wondering whether you're going to be in Hall tonight. Oh, good, because there's somebody who's frantically keen to meet you. Oh, his name is – um Derek Newhouse, actually. Yes, that's right, Derek Newhouse. (*Little pause.*) Oh, I see. I'd no idea. Wrote what! Good Lord! I'd have thought that's libellous. Oh dear, well listen Potts, I promise I won't inflict him on you for more than a few minutes, over the port, would you mind, be as rude to him as you like, you see I did promise and perhaps he wants to apologize, eh? Oh come on Potts, just a very little nut for Nutkin. Thanks. (*Hangs up.*)

(*He ticks off 'Potts' on the list, then hesitates a moment before starting to dial once more.*)

(*Dials*) Hello. I wonder if I could speak to Doctor Ramsay.
(*Pause.*) James Westgate of Hertford College, I'm one of
her patients. (*Little pause.*) Well it's just that I need a
prescription for sleeping pills. I see. Well could she give me
a ring the moment she's free?
(*There is a knock at the door.*)
(*Abstractedly*) Come in.
(WILKINS *walks in, knotted with feeling.*)
Right, thank you. (*Puts down phone. Looks at him.*) Yes?

WILKINS: You told me to come and see you.

JAMES: Did I? About what?

WILKINS: Well – um – to give you an essay or my excuse.
(*He comes into the room a bit more.*)
And I've – um – come to give you my excuse.

JAMES: Oh right. Fire away.

WILKINS: The thing is I'm in love. Hopelessly in love. That's
my excuse – er – James.

JAMES: Really? Well, don't worry about it. It happens to all of
us, so –

WILKINS: But it's a question – of who – who I'm in love with.

JAMES: Well, I suppose it does make a difference but the thing
is – look – Ed – um – Ed – um – I've got rather a busy day.
Perhaps this isn't the time – for one thing I'm waiting for
the doctor to –

WILKINS: (*Blurts out*) It's you James.

JAMES: What?

WILKINS: It's you I'm in love with.

JAMES: Ah.

WILKINS: I have been since our first supervision. It's paralysed
me. That's why I haven't been able to do a shred of work.
I'm terrified of your judgement on me.

JAMES: Well, that explains everything, Ed – um.

WILKINS: What do you mean, James?

JAMES: I mean – well, excuse accepted. Quite all right. I
understand. You can go.

WILKINS: Go?

AMANDA: (*Appears at the door*) Oh, sorry. I didn't realize. (*She is clearly in an emotional state.*)

(WILKINS *stares yearningly at* JAMES, *smoulderingly at* AMANDA, *turns, and goes out.*)

(*Looking after* WILKINS) Have I come at a bad time?

JAMES: Well – (*Gives a little laugh.*)

AMANDA: I just wanted to know how he was.

JAMES: Who?

AMANDA: Your father.

JAMES: Oh – um – much better, much better than everyone seemed to think.

AMANDA: Good. I was a bit worried, you see, as you were going to come straight to me from the hospital. So of course I assumed something rather serious must have happened.

JAMES: Oh, God, I'm terribly sorry, I completely forgot. You see, I suddenly remembered I had a wine committee meeting last night. I got back just in time for it.

AMANDA: A wine committee meeting?

JAMES: Yes, it was interminable. A question of whether to buy some port or wait until a better year came up for auction. It all got rather fractious, you know how these things go, and by the time we'd finished it would have been far too late to – er – disturb you anyway.

AMANDA: Well, did you or didn't you?

JAMES: What?

AMANDA: Buy the port.

JAMES: Ah, no. Final vote went against. Twelve ten, I think it was.

AMANDA: You mean there were twenty-two people on the wine committee?

(JAMES, *in spite of himself, lets out a little laugh.*)

There wasn't a wine committee, was there?

(JAMES, *about to protest, decides against.*)

JAMES: No.

AMANDA: In other words, you just didn't want to see me, did
you?
(JAMES *looks at her. The telephone rings.*)
JAMES: (*Picking up telephone*) Hello? Yes, that's right, speaking.
Doctor who? (*Pause.*) No, it was Doctor Ramsay I wanted
to speak to. (*Pause.*) What? Oh, oh I see. I see. Yes, of
course. I'll come straight away.
(*He puts the telephone down and looks at* AMANDA.)
Sorry, I can't – I can't – that was a doctor. I've got to dash
you see. Up to London.
(*Cut to* AMANDA's *face, then back to* JAMES.)
Apparently it's my father.

47. INT. HOSPITAL: CORRIDOR OUTSIDE PRIVATE ROOM. DAY

From JAMES's *point of view, with a doctor standing beside him, we
look through a window in a door. A robust, elderly man sits up in
bed, and writes furiously on a typewriter on a board across the bed.
He throws back his head and laughs.*

JAMES: That's not my father.
DOCTOR: Isn't it? No, you're quite right. It isn't. (*The* DOCTOR
moves a door down and consults the list in his hand.) Here he is.
(JAMES *looks through the window and from his point of view
we see an elderly man lying in bed, eyes and mouth open,
staring blankly, clearly the victim of a stroke.* JAMES *pushes the
door and goes in.*)

48. INT. HOSPITAL: PRIVATE ROOM. DAY

JAMES *sits down and stares at his father blankly. Cut to his face,
then from his* FATHER's *face back to* JAMES's *face, staring at his*
FATHER, *appalled.*
*Cut to a shot of the two of them and hold on to this, suggesting time
passing.*

Cut to JAMES's *face. Suddenly remembering, he looks down at his watch, rises quickly, and goes out. He glances in through the window at his* FATHER, *then hurries along the corridor.*

49. INT. HOSPITAL: DOCTOR'S OFFICE. DAY

JAMES *enters. The doctor sits behind a desk.*

DOCTOR: Are you all right?

JAMES: Well, it's all been – been something of a shock. Last thing I expected.

DOCTOR: Yes, well that's the thing with strokes. They strike without – without, um – (*Gestures. Pause.*) We'll let you know when there's any, um, dramatic change. It shouldn't be too long.

JAMES: (*Nods*) Well I'd better be getting back. (*He makes for the door, and turns.*) Oh by the way, perhaps you could help me. I had an appointment with my own doctor – today, as a matter of fact to get a prescription but of course I've – um – I've missed it.

DOCTOR: What was the prescription for?

JAMES: Sleeping pills. I've had some rather bad nights recently and – and now of course, with this.

DOCTOR: Ah. Well I really think the best thing is for you to see your own doctor, you know, first thing tomorrow. You see, I make it a principle never to prescribe except for my own patients.

JAMES: But what about tonight – my getting to sleep?

DOCTOR: Well why don't you try a cup of camomile tea and a good book. It always works for me.

(JAMES *is about to say something, but hurries out.*)

50. INT. OXFORD PSYCHOLOGICAL LABORATORY. DAY

Animal noises as before and come in on BORIS *in a lab coat. He holds down a frenzied creature with one hand and with the other injects it with a syringe. We cannot see the creature.*

BORIS: (*Injecting*) We've driven the poor brute completely mad. It's got a vicious bite . . . but we'll soon have you out of it, won't we. What do you want them for?
  (*Cut to* JAMES.)
JAMES: Well, to get some sleep, obviously.
BORIS: But you never have any trouble with sleep. You don't even have dreams. You boast about it.
JAMES: Yes, well I'm having trouble now.
  (*The creature is rigid but still not seen.* BORIS *picks it up and takes it over to the fridge. He puts the animal into the fridge and closes the door.*)
BORIS: Of course you realize, James, that what you're asking is quite illegal.

51. INT. COLLEGE: STAIRS. DAY

JAMES *runs up the stairs to his room. He glances at his watch. It is 7.15 p.m. He opens the door.*

52. INT. JAMES'S BATHROOM. DAY

JAMES *hurries into the bathroom, grabs a glass from the drinks table outside, hesitates, grabs another, then goes back into the bathroom. He takes two pills out of his pocket and looks up. He sees his face in the cabinet mirror, stares at it in surprise, then opens the cabinet door to avoid his reflection. He opens one of the capsules and shakes the contents into one of the glasses.*

DEREK: (*Voice over*) Oh, you're in there.
  (*As* JAMES *freezes.*)

I knocked but you weren't there. So I thought I'd have a quick pee.

JAMES: I won't be a minute. Right out. Just going to have a gargle. Raw throat.

(DEREK *enters the bathroom.* JAMES *attempts to block the glasses from* DEREK'*s view. He opens the cabinet door and takes out a bottle.*)

DEREK: (*Undoing trousers*) What sort of gargle do you use?

JAMES: This one.

(*He pours the bottle into a glass from the cabinet.* DEREK *begins to pee. We hear the sound of* JAMES *gargling and* DEREK *peeing.* DEREK *finishes peeing and comes over to the sink.*)

DEREK: Excuse me.

(JAMES *continues desperately to gargle as* DEREK *shoves his fingers under the tap.*)

Old nursery habit. Can't break it. Do you mind if I use your telephone?

(JAMES *gargles and shakes his head.* DEREK *withdraws.* JAMES *speeds up the gargling, picks up the other capsule, hand shaking, and empties it into the other glass. He takes both glasses into the sitting room.*)

53. INT. JAMES'S SITTING-ROOM. DAY

DEREK *speaks urgently in a low, inaudible voice into the telephone, his back half-turned towards* JAMES. JAMES *saunters past him, puts the two glasses behind other glasses and moves away as* DEREK *hangs up.* DEREK, *though obviously tense, tries for a smile.*

JAMES: (*Smiling back*) Everything all right?

DEREK: Yes, fine.

JAMES: Right, I'll pour us a drink, what would you like?

DEREK: A Scotch if you've got one.

JAMES: Yes, I have. A malt?

DEREK: Perfect.
  (JAMES *picks up one of the two glasses and pours in some malt.*
  Granules of powder are visible. He whirls the whisky around
  frantically. The whisky becomes clouded. He pours in more
  whisky and desperately continues to whisk the drink.)
JAMES: And how is – Penny?
DEREK: (*Voice over*) Oh, seems a bit on edge. Had another bad
  night. Nightmares – that sort of thing.
  (*Cut to the whisky, still cloudy, a few specks of powder still*
  visible. JAMES *continues to whisk.*)
JAMES: I'm sorry to hear it.
DEREK: Yes. Consequently I had a pretty bad night myself.
  Didn't get much sleep either.
JAMES: Oh.
  (*He gives the whisky to* DEREK.)
  Well, let's hope this evening's a success, eh?
  (DEREK *lifts his glass and looks down into it. He frowns.*)
  (*Quickly*) I'll be very interested to hear your views on that,
  by the way. It's a Glenmuldoon, the distillers only do a
  thousand bottles, and three hundred come to this college,
  one of my little coups on the wine committee.
DEREK: (*Sips*) Rather odd.
JAMES: Isn't it? And have you thought out your strategy?
DEREK: Mmmm?
JAMES: With my uncle.

54. INT. SENIOR COMMON ROOM. NIGHT

Various dons stand around talking, holding glasses of port, brandy
etc. Among them, see POTTS *and* DEREK *from* JAMES's *point of*
view. POTTS *tells off points on the fingers of one hand.* DEREK
stares at POTTS's *fingers. Suddenly, unable to control himself, his*
mouth gapes in an enormous yawn. DEREK *forces his mouth shut,*
makes a Herculean effort to concentrate, then suddenly yawns again
and shakes his head.

265

POTTS *says something polite, turns and leaves* DEREK. *See* DEREK *shake his head muzzily and watch, as* POTTS *goes over to* JAMES.

POTTS: Amazing. Even more ill-mannered in the flesh than in his prose.
JAMES: Yes, terribly sorry, Potts. And thanks.
    (POTTS *squeezes his arm.*)
POTTS: By the way, any news from me baby brother-in-law.
JAMES: Mmmm?
POTTS: Your father. How is he, do you know?
JAMES: Oh, still clinging on as far as I know.
POTTS: (*Puzzled*) Clinging on?
JAMES: (*Gives a little laugh*) Yes, well – um – you know what he's like.
    (*During this* POTTS *looks with distaste towards* DEREK *who stumbles dozily towards them.*)
POTTS: Well I've been meaning to give him a ring . . .
    (*He squeezes* JAMES's *arm as* DEREK, *yawning, is almost upon them.*)

55. INT. JAMES'S SITTING-ROOM. NIGHT

The camera comes in on DEREK *in an armchair, yawning. It then includes* JAMES *in the shot. He stands by the drinks table.*

DEREK: I don't know what the hell's the matter with me, must be last night catching up.
JAMES: Oh, don't worry. He thinks you're charming. He told me so when he left. What'll you have? There's brandy, port, malt of course –
DEREK: Nothing for me, thanks. I already feel as if I'm in the middle of a hangover.
JAMES: Ah. Then I've got just the thing.
    (*With his back to* DEREK, *he pours a large amount of vodka into a glass.*)

DEREK: (*Voice over*) But I'm sure he said something about going to Cambridge next week.

(JAMES *picks up a bottle of Fernibranca*.)

JAMES: Really?

DEREK: But I thought the point of all this was his going to the States –

(JAMES, *about to pour in Fernibranca, falters slightly*.)

JAMES: Yes, he is. But he's terrified of flying. So he tells everybody he's going somewhere he doesn't have to fly to. But he usually ends up on the plane, here you are.

DEREK: (*Taking it automatically*) What is it?

JAMES: It's called a Witch's Nipple in Argentina, where I'm told they drink it all the time. Became particularly popular after the Falklands' war, when they had a lot of hangovers to deal with. Filthy taste, but it works. You have to take it down in one gulp virtually –

DEREK: Right. Thanks. I certainly need something to clear my head because I've got a hell of a night ahead of me.

JAMES: What?

DEREK: That guest room. I've got a use for it after all.

JAMES: Oh, you're going to stay the night then! Terrific.

DEREK: No, I'm not. I'm going to London. Look, I'll have to trust you. There's someone that's turning awkward. Bloody awkward as a matter of fact, leaving messages at College, phoning me at home, making threats. Last night, for instance – just as you suspected. Anyway, if I don't go down there tonight she'll be up here doing her worst first thing tomorrow. So you're going to have to lie for me. I told Penny I'm spending the night here – she wants me to anyway. Needless to say if she ever found out – even got the slightest whiff –

JAMES: I wouldn't dream of saying a word.

DEREK: Right. Thanks. If she phones at all, and knowing her she probably will –

JAMES: I'll say you're safely tucked up in the guest room, there's no phone there.

DEREK: Right. And I'll look in on my way back in the morning. To see if she's left any message I should know about.

JAMES: And if I'm out I'll leave it there. On the desk.

DEREK: Right. Well, I'd better get moving. Thank God my head's beginning to clear. I hope this stuff finishes the job. (*He throws his head back and swallows the drink.* JAMES, *realizing too late, makes a small move to check him.*) (*Shudders*) Anything that tastes this vile can only be good for you. (*He puts the glass down.*) Thanks for your help. I appreciate it. (*He leaves.*)

(JAMES *stands for a moment. We see* DEREK *emerge into the court. He walks quickly. Takes a sudden lurching step to one side, straightens himself and goes on resolutely.* JAMES *gets up and goes over to the telephone. He dials.*)

JAMES: Hello, it's um Porker. He's just gone – to bed, of course. I filled him full of booze and – so forth, so I'm sure he'll go out like a light. We're safe until the morning. (*Little pause.*) Yes, I'm on my way right now. Oh, we'll need shovels, and – and a torch and – anything else you can think of. Something to wrap him in.

56. EXT./INT. CAR. COTTAGE DRIVE. NIGHT

JAMES *drives carefully down the drive. The front door is open and* PENNY *stands at it.* JAMES *gets out of the car and walks to the front door.* PENNY *wears a raincoat and waterproof hat. There are two spades by the door and some sheets.*

JAMES: Well – we'd better get to it. You – you don't have to come.

PENNY: Oh yes I do. I've got to see him gone. See for myself.

JAMES: All right. Well then. We sally forth, eh? (*He picks up the two shovels.*) Why are you wearing all that?

PENNY: It might rain.

JAMES: What are those?

PENNY: (*Has picked up sheets*) Sheets. For wrapping him in.
    You said –
JAMES: But won't they be identifiable? If he's found –
PENNY: But they're only sheets. Ordinary sheets. The sort you
    can get –
JAMES: What's that?
    (*He points to embroidery on the corner.*)
PENNY: What – oh, our initials. It must be the pair Derek's
    mother gave us. I'll get some others.
JAMES: No sheets.
PENNY: But I haven't got anything else.
JAMES: Nothing is better than sheets.
PENNY: It's only that you said –
JAMES: Let's go.

57. EXT. THE COTTAGE: LAWN. NIGHT

JAMES *and* PENNY *walk across the lawn in the moonlight.*

PENNY: Where shall we put him?
JAMES: If we move him somewhere the other side of the ditch –
    there's some ground there, isn't there?
PENNY: Oh no. No no. I can't have him on our property.
JAMES: But Patch –
PENNY: He shouldn't have been there in the first place. That's
    why the whole thing started. If he's going to be lying under
    our ground, rotting away – poisoning me –
JAMES: But we can't move him far. I'm not going to move him
    far. It's too dangerous.
PENNY: In that case, why bother to do it at all? If you can't
    help me *properly* – (*She stops.*)
    (JAMES *stares at her.*)

58. EXT. THE WOODS: UNDERGROWTH. NIGHT

Shot of PILKINGTON's *body being dragged through the undergrowth. Cut to* JAMES's *face, straining.*

JAMES: Is this far enough?
PENNY: (*Shines torch ahead*) Just a bit more. Another few yards, or so.

59. EXT. THE WOODS: SMALL CLEARING. NIGHT

PENNY *shines the torch around.*

PENNY: Here. A very nice spot.
(JAMES *sweating, nods.*)
I probably wouldn't be able to find it, even in daytime.
(JAMES *nods. Cut to* JAMES *digging.* PENNY *shines the torch on him. She sits quite comfortably under a tree. It is raining.*)
Yes, it said on the radio it was going to. I expect it's making the ground softer. Is it?
(JAMES *continues to dig. He is soaked, dirty. Cut to later. A shot of the deep grave. Cut to* PILKINGTON, *then to* JAMES. *He pulls* PILKINGTON *to the lip of the grave, makes a supreme effort, and rolls him in.* JAMES *looks down and from his point of view we see for the first time that* PILKINGTON's *body is covered in cuts.* JAMES *frowns, as though he realizes something, then puts the thought away. He bends and throws the scissors down. Cut to* JAMES *who sits beside* PENNY *under a tree, exhausted.*)
It's stopped raining, at least.
JAMES: Yes.
PENNY: They said it would only be a shower. (*After a moment*) Hadn't we better get on with the last bit. Then we're done.
(*Cut to* PILKINGTON's *body, the scissors on his face. A spadeful of earth covers it. Cut to* JAMES. *He packs down the grave then stands heaving, resting on his shovel.*

Flashes light over it) It looks very fresh.

JAMES: It is fresh.

PENNY: Well, we'd better put something over it.

(JAMES *is pulling up briars, then digging them up and sticking them on the grave, illuminated by* PENNY's *torch.*)

What do you think?

(JAMES, *near collapse, leans on his shovel.*)

JAMES: Fine. Fine. Just fine.

PENNY: Yes.

(JAMES *throws her a glance of relief.*)

There you are, Horace. At rest at last. No more lying about in a ditch. Thou thy worldly task hast done, home art gone, and taken thy wages.

(*She looks at* JAMES.)

JAMES: It's ta'en. Not taken. Ta'en thy wages. Not taken thy –

(*He gestures, exhaustedly.*)

60. EXT. THE COTTAGE: LAWN. DAWN

JAMES *and* PENNY *walk across the lawn.* JAMES *is dragging the two shovels,* PENNY *is carrying the torch.*

61. EXT. THE COTTAGE. DAWN

PENNY *puts the spades against the cottage wall and opens the front door.* JAMES *makes as if to follow.*

PENNY: (*Turning, stops him*) No, just a minute. (*Looks at him.*)

You're a terrible mess. You should have worn something over. You'd better get undressed here, otherwise you'll be tramping mud all over the house. I'll go and run you a bath – unless you'd rather have a bath at your own place?

JAMES: No.

(PENNY *takes off her raincoat, hat, wellingtons, etc. and goes upstairs as* JAMES *begins to undress.*)

62. INT. THE COTTAGE: STAIRS. DAWN

JAMES, *in his underwear, climbs the stairs, seen from below. He is wet to the skin.*

63. INT. THE COTTAGE: BATHROOM. DAWN

JAMES *enters.* PENNY *is there, putting out a towel. The bath is run. Foamy.*

PENNY: There's your towel. And I've put in lots of bath
 bubbles. Why are you still in your knickers? Give them to
 me.
 (JAMES *hesitates, then steps out of his underpants and hands
 them to* PENNY.)
 Right, in you get. I'll find you some clothes.
 (*Cut to* JAMES, *almost asleep in the bath. The water is filthy.*
 PENNY *appears at the door. She is seen blearily, from* JAMES's
 point of view.
 Looks at bath) Run it out, shower it down, run yourself
 another one. Here. (*Hands him a mug.*) You should have
 showered first. It's a rum toddy. (*Withdraws, reappears.*)
 Clothes are in the bedroom.

64. INT. THE COTTAGE: STAIRS TO BEDROOM. DAY

JAMES, *a towel around his waist, goes up the stairs, seen from
below. He enters the bedroom.*

65. INT. THE COTTAGE: BEDROOM. DAY

PENNY *sits on the bed, cross-legged. She sews, a work-basket beside
her.* JAMES *stands at the door gazing at her.*

JAMES: What – what are you doing?
PENNY: Sewing a button on Derek's shirt.

JAMES: Oh.

(PENNY *looks up at him and smiles.*)

PENNY: It's for you. I can't give you one of his good ones, he always knows exactly about his clothes, but there are some he's thrown out for Help the Aged, but I took all the buttons off them, now I'm having to put some back on. Serves me right for being so mean – (*She looks up at him and grins*) – you can put on the rest of them – there.

(PENNY *indicates a pile of clothes on the bed with* JAMES's *wallet, keys, etc. beside them.*)

I've put your belt through the trousers, they're a bit ragged but they'll get you home – and there are your dirty ones – (*She indicates a plastic dustbin liner.*

JAMES *stands.*)

Well, go on, get dressed, I won't be a minute. I've given you his flip flops –

(*As* JAMES *begins to get dressed*)

– he won't miss those, I think they're Turkish – there we are! (*Cutting thread.*) How are you doing? (*Looks at him. Cut to a few minutes later.* JAMES *is togged out in* DEREK's *clothes. He puts the wallet, keys etc. in the pockets. The clothes are too big for him. He looks preposterous. The shirt has only one button.*)

That's all right. Well, they'll do to get you back.

JAMES: Can I really walk across New Court like this?

PENNY: Of course you can. You look perfectly – (*She shrieks with laughter.*) Sorry. Sorry. It's just that I can scarcely believe – I still really haven't taken in – my head feels so – I mean, he's actually gone. For good. Gone. Gone. Gone. Gone. Gone. We did it, didn't we?

(*She looks at him with glowing eyes.*)

JAMES: (*Grins*) Yes, we did. Just like the old – old days. You lead. I follow. But not to any corpses next time, please Patch.

PENNY: Porker, I think you're wonderful.

JAMES: Do you?

PENNY: Yes, I do. Quite wonderful. And adorable with it.
(*She kisses him on the cheek.* JAMES *puts his arms around her. He strokes her hair.*)

JAMES: Oh, my Patch! My Patch! Do you know – do you know what you mean to me? Have always meant to me? I think ever since that summer – all these years I've been locked in some little cell, hunched in some little cell – I must have been waiting for you to come back, and let me out – I love you. (*Kisses her.*) Love you.

PENNY: What are you doing?

JAMES: (*Kisses her again*) I'm not going to let you go again – ever. You're mine. (*Kisses her again.*)

PENNY: (*Steps away*) You can't. (*Little laugh.*) You can't.

JAMES: Why not?

PENNY: Well, for one thing, you're homosexual.

JAMES: What! (*Laughs.*) Don't be ridiculous.

PENNY: But you are. Derek told me. He said you were Boris's boyfriend, sort of, as far as he could make out. And anyway, he said you admitted it yourself, he said you were quite open about it. He said – (*Looks at him.*)

JAMES: How could you of all people – you of all people. I only let Derek believe it for – for your sake.

PENNY: For my sake!

JAMES: So he wouldn't mind my – our – seeing each other. But you can't – you can't ever have thought – no. You didn't. Not in your heart, you didn't. (*Steps forward.*)

PENNY: But I haven't thought about you in my heart. I never think about anyone in my heart except Derek. I thought you understood that, Piglet.

JAMES: Porker. It's Porker. There was someone called Piglet wasn't there? Someone else. It's not just the names you keep confusing.

PENNY: Well, there might have been – I think there was – another boy the summer before or after. He wasn't

274

anything as nice as you, though. (*Smiles.*) I remember you
far better. But now I really think you'd better go, you
know. It's getting late – early, I mean. We've both got to
get some rest and Derek might come back early and –

JAMES: No, I'm not going. I can't. You don't love him. You
can't. I've seen the way he talks to you, the way he looks at
you – or doesn't look at you. His indifference, his
rudeness. And you say yourself you're frightened of him.
What has he done to deserve you?

PENNY: Oh, Porker, you don't know anything about it.
(*Laughs.*) He loves me. We have a happy, happy marriage.

JAMES: A happy marriage? (*Laughs.*) Oh Patch, you know what
sort of man he is.

PENNY: Yes I do. And I don't want you to say another – not
another –

JAMES: Do you know where he is now? He's not asleep in my
College, he's gone down to London to see one of his
barmaids, that girl who called last night, Liz . . . she's
been making trouble. He sat in my room telling me all
about her because he wanted me to lie to you.

PENNY: (*Shaking her head*) It's not true, it's not true. (*Turns
away.*)

JAMES: Yes it is. Why, even Boris knows all about him. In
London he was known as the ram. I know it isn't in the
rules to tell on husbands, but I'm not playing by the rules.
I'd do anything for you, Patch. Anything but let you go. I
wasn't just sent to you to help you. You were sent to me
because I need you. So I can start my life at last. I have
always needed you. (*Moves towards her.*
PENNY *turns around. On her face, a grimace of loathing.*
JAMES *stands in shock.*)

PENNY: You're worse than Pilkington, worse, you should have
buried yourself with him, buried yourself, he just put his
hands on me, but you – lie and lie and lie about everything,
everything –

(*She runs at him and attacks him with her fingers, scratching and punching*)
hate you, hate you, hate you –
(JAMES *tries desperately to get away.* PENNY *continues to assault him.* JAMES, *back against the bed, falls on to it.* PENNY *scrambles after him on her hands and knees and as she does so, sees the scissors from her work-basket knocked over by* JAMES. *She grabs them.*)
JAMES: No – no – no – no –
(*As* PENNY *pursues him, stabbing viciously but only making contact with his clothes, not his body.*)

66. INT. THE COTTAGE: STAIRS AND HALL. DAY

JAMES, *impeded by flip-flops and baggy trousers, tumbles downstairs, pursued by* PENNY. *He scrambles to his feet, through the door.*

67. EXT. THE COTTAGE: DRIVE. DAY

JAMES *scrambles to his car and manages to get in. He shuts the door and locks it, just before* PENNY *reaches him. She runs around the car to the other door.* JAMES *leans across and locks it in the nick of time, then, as she runs around and around the car, snarling in at him, seemingly everywhere, he fumbles his keys out of his pocket and gets the car started.*
From his point of view, as the car leaps down the drive, see PENNY *running after it, jabbing the scissors up and down. She throws back her head and gives a hideous scream.*

68. INT. BORIS'S ROOMS: COLLEGE. DAY

Come in first on BORIS *in his pyjamas, at his door. He is just aroused from sleep. Cut to* JAMES *staring at him.*

69. INT. OXFORD PSYCHOLOGY LAB. DAY

BORIS *has dressed as if hastily.*

JAMES: And another thing. When I was burying Pilkington – I suddenly noticed there were gashes all over him – not just in his neck. So she slaughtered him just as she tried to slaughter me.

BORIS: Yes, well she's quite evidently gone mad. Far madder than you've gone, even.

JAMES: Look, what precisely are we going to do?

BORIS: First obviously calm her down. Then phone a shrink of my acquaintance, give him a highly edited version of the facts and get her hospitalized immediately. Then we'll have to work out how to save you from jail and Penny from a lifetime in an institute for the criminally insane. Also how much we tell Derek. If he's survived the night, that is.
(Grins at JAMES.

BORIS *has been packing his briefcase. He checks a syringe professionally.)*

JAMES: What's that?

BORIS: A sedative.

*(*BORIS *packs a bottle and pad.)*

JAMES: What's that?

BORIS: Chloroform.

JAMES: But if you've got a sedative –

BORIS: Yes, but I may have to subdue her first. Especially if she comes at me with her scissors –
(He turns off the lights.)

70. EXT. THE COTTAGE: DRIVE. DAY

A car goes slowly down the drive. It is past dawn. Birds are twittering and so forth.

71. INT./EXT. CAR. THE COTTAGE DRIVE. DAY

BORIS *parks the car. They look towards the house. See the house from their point of view. The front door is closed.*

JAMES: You will be careful, won't you?

BORIS: My dear James, I have to deal with frenzied monkeys all the time.

JAMES: No, I meant – be careful with her.

(BORIS *looks at* JAMES *and laughs slightly.*)

BORIS: Good God, James!

JAMES: I wish you weren't enjoying it all so much.

(*He looks at* BORIS. BORIS *looks towards the house. We see it from their point of view. The door is now slightly ajar.*)

BORIS: Is the door open?

JAMES: Yes.

BORIS: Was it a minute ago?

JAMES: I don't know. I think so, yes.

BORIS: Good. Then I might take her unawares.

(*He makes a move to get out of the car.* JAMES *does also.*)

No, you stay here.

JAMES: I'm coming with you.

BORIS: You're not James. It's you she wants to kill, don't forget. I'll call you when I'm ready.

(*He gets out and walks briskly to the door, pushes it open carefully, and slides smoothly into the house. Pause. See the house from* JAMES's *point of view. The front door opens and* BORIS *reappears. The door slams behind him.* BORIS *walks back to the car, grinning, and leans against* JAMES's *window which* JAMES *lowers.*)

She was waiting for me behind the door. Must have been the car. Thought I was you – (*Grins*) – help me, please, eh? Help me.

(*He falls to the ground.* JAMES *opens the door with difficulty.* BORIS, *hideously gashed, has a pair of scissors sticking from his neck. He is dying.* JAMES *gets out of the car and walks slowly towards the house. He stands at the door, hesitates, then tries the knob. The door opens.*)

72. INT. COTTAGE: HALL AND STAIRS. DAY

JAMES *goes in cautiously, looking behind the door. No one there.* BORIS's *case is on the floor.* JAMES *closes his eyes in terror as a faint sound is heard above. He looks up the stairs, hesitates, then goes up quietly. He approaches the bedroom door. It is half open. He pushes it open more fully.* PENNY *is sitting on the edge of the bed, hands folded in her lap. She stares at* JAMES *for a moment.*

73. INT. COTTAGE: BEDROOM. DAY

JAMES: Hello, Patch.

PENNY: Oh, hello Piglet. I knew you were all right, really. I knew I could never hurt you, could I?

JAMES: No Patch, you couldn't.

PENNY: I was just going to go downstairs to make sure. And then here you are. So I don't have to now, do I?

JAMES: No, Patch, you don't.

(*He goes over and sits down beside her.*)

PENNY: Oh, it's so good to see you, Piglet, alive and well. I'm awfully tired. I've had such a strange time recently. Shall I go to bed now?

JAMES: Yes, I think you should.

PENNY: Would you help me, please? Such a long night it's been, you see. Up to all kinds of things, haven't we?

JAMES: Yes, we have. Here. Stand up, Patch. And let's get you tucked in, shall we?

(PENNY *stands up.* JAMES *helps* PENNY *to get undressed, beginning with her shoes.*)

JAMES: (*Undoing shoes*) Lift up, there's a good girl. Now the other one. There. And now your dress. (*Unbuttons it.*) Just slip your arms – (*Puts dress over chair*) – keep it neatly so it doesn't crease.

(*He goes behind her, unclips her bra and puts it over a chair.*)
And now just –

(*He pulls down her pants. She steps out of them. He looks at her and we see her from his point of view.*)
Where are your night things, under the pillow?

PENNY: Under the pillow, yes.

(JAMES *lifts up the pillow.* DEREK's *pyjamas. He lifts up the other pillow.* PENNY's *nightdress.*)

JAMES: Lift your arms then, Patch.

(PENNY *does.*)
Now (*Turning back covers*) In you get.

PENNY: (*Crosses to bed. Stops*) Oh, but I haven't brushed my teeth. Do you think it matters?

JAMES: No, not this once, Patch, it doesn't.

PENNY: No, once won't hurt.

(*She gets into bed.* JAMES *comes and sits on the edge of the bed. After a pause*) I don't want to go through any of that again, Piglet. Not ever. I'm too old now.

JAMES: Yes. (*Takes her hand.*) So am I.

PENNY: You won't let it happen again then?

JAMES: No.

PENNY: Do you promise?

JAMES: I promise, Patch.

PENNY: Goodnight then, Piglet.

JAMES: (*Gently*) It's Porker.

PENNY: Yes. Sorry. Goodnight Porker.

JAMES: Goodnight Patch.

(*Cut to the two, hands enfolded. Then cut to* PENNY's *face. She is asleep, but restless, murmuring. Cut to* JAMES's *face, looking down on hers.* JAMES *releases her hand and gets up.*)

74. INT. COTTAGE: STAIRS. DAY

JAMES *goes down the stairs. He opens* BORIS's *case and takes out the chloroform and the pad.*

75. INT. COTTAGE: BEDROOM. DAY

JAMES *sits down on the edge of the bed and pours some chloroform on to the pad. He puts the pad to* PENNY's *nose. She is still sleeping restlessly. She inhales several times then goes into a deeper sleep. Her face is calm and untroubled.*
JAMES *screws the cap back on the bottle then puts the pad and bottle in his pocket. See* PENNY's *face from his point of view. He picks up* DEREK's *pillow and puts it over* PENNY's *face, holding it firmly but gently.*
Cut to JAMES's *face looking down at* PENNY, *then to* PENNY *dead.* JAMES *kisses her on the forehead and turns to go. As he does so, his eye catches the dustbin liner with his clothes inside. He picks it up.*

76. EXT. THE COTTAGE. DAY

JAMES *bends to examine* BORIS *beside the car. He is clearly dead.* JAMES *walks round the other side of the car, gets in and drives off, being careful to avoid* BORIS's *body.*

77. EXT. HERTFORD COLLEGE: NEW COURT. DAY

It is about nine in the morning. JAMES *is walking across the court, carrying the bag of clothes. He cuts a bizarre figure, still in* DEREK's *togs. He is noticed by various people as they pass him. He turns into his stairway.*

78. INT. JAMES'S ROOMS. DAY

JAMES *enters, drops the bag on the floor and goes towards the bedroom/bathroom. As he makes to open the door there is a sound from the armchair.*
He turns and from his point of view we see a figure heaving himself out of the armchair. It is DEREK, *eyes bloodshot, unshaven. He stands looking at* JAMES, *swaying slightly.*

DEREK: (*Dully*) Just checked in to see if she phoned. Nothing on the desk.

JAMES: No.

DEREK: Then made the mistake of sitting down for a minute. I had a sort of – of black-out on the motorway. Felt myself going so I pulled into a layby. Out for hours. By the time I got to her place she had left. Just hope to God she hasn't come up here. To make trouble on my doorstep. Well, at least no messages, eh?

JAMES: No, no messages.

(DEREK *goes to the door, turns, and looks at* JAMES, *clearly noticing something odd about his appearance. He frowns. He turns to go out, turns back, looks at* JAMES *once more and again frowns slightly at his appearance.*
JAMES *goes to the window and looks down. From his point of view we see* DEREK *walking doggedly across the court.*)

Old Flames

Old Flames was broadcast by BBC Television on 14 January 1990. The cast was included:

DANIEL	Stephen Fry
QUASS	Simon Callow
JACKABOY	Clive Francis
NELLIE	Miriam Margolyes
SOPHIE	Hettie Baynes
CAROLINE	Zoe Rutland
Director	Christopher Morahan
Producer	Kenith Trodd
Lighting Cameraman	David Feig
Designer	Don Taylor
Sound	Terry Elms
Costumes	Anna Buruma

EXT. CRICKET GROUND. DAY

A game of cricket is in progress. The game is taking place on a large ground between the Amplesides Old Boys and the Metropolitan Police. We see the match in long shot, the Police fielding, two middle-aged men batting, as if from DANIEL's *point of view. Then cut to* DANIEL *at the crease. A montage of his batting with great panache. A series of hooks, cuts, drives, against a fast bowler, a spin bowler, etc. All this observed from the point of view of* QUASS, *in his late thirties, seated on a bench.* QUASS *is plump, unhealthy-looking, and has trouble with his breathing, having to use now and then an asthmatic's inhaler. He is dressed in flannels, a silk shirt, a striped blazer, and a boater on top of what is obviously a wig. Cutting between him and* DANIEL, DANIEL *hitting, running, obviously enjoying himself immensely,* QUASS *watching him impassively, once having to use his inhaler, until* DANIEL *is caught on the boundary. Cut to:*

JACKABOY: Nice knock, Daniel. Nice *little* knock.

> (JACKABOY, *the Old Boys' Captain, is padded up. He is an intense man, with spectacles and a commanding manner that is slightly odd and clearly has trouble restraining himself.*)

Pity you didn't hold yourself in check a bit. If you had, we might have won.

> (DANIEL *is at a bench unbuckling his pads. During this, we see from the corner of the camera's eye* QUASS *getting up, beginning to wander, purposively, over to* DANIEL *and* JACKABOY.)

DANIEL: (*Barely suppressing indignation*) Well, I'm very sorry, Jack, but I've always believed one ought to play one's natural game. Especially at this level. I mean, after all, we're merely the Amplesides Old Boys playing one of the Metropolitan Police's worst elevens –

JACKABOY: (*Breaking in*) I know who we're playing and I have

personal reasons for wanting to beat the hell out of them! I
don't care which eleven they field – their wives, for all I care
– anything to do with the buggers –

(*Over this shouts of triumph from the field.*)

DANIEL: You're in, Jack, I believe.

JACKABOY: What?

(*He turns, glares at the pitch. We see from their point of view the
various massive police fielders looking in their direction.
In a mutter*) All right, you sods. Try and get me!

(JACKABOY *braces himself, stalks towards the pitch.* DANIEL
stares after him in disgust.)

QUASS: (*From the side of the bench*) Excuse me, wasn't that
Jackaboy?

DANIEL: What? (*Seeing* QUASS) Oh, yes. Jackaboy.

QUASS: (*Sitting down*) Odd, isn't it, how one goes on recognizing
people, even people one hasn't seen for what, over twenty-
five years.

(*During this we see* JACKABOY *arrive at the crease, take guard,
and completely miss the first ball, which just misses the wicket.*)
It's not really the looks, is it? It's something in the manner –
(*Has a slight wheezing attack*) – or I suppose the nature. The
something unchangeable that's in all our – um – (*Wheezes
again.*) And you're Davenport. Daniel Davenport, aren't
you?

DANIEL: That's right.

QUASS: Quass. Nathaniel Quass. I was at Amplesides. We were
in the same house.

DANIEL: (*Clearly not remembering* QUASS) Oh. I'm afraid I
don't –

QUASS: You were a prefect. And Jackaboy was Head of House. I
don't expect he'd remember me either, though he did beat
me once or twice. So perhaps he'd recognize my rear end.
Especially if it was naked and had stripes on it, eh? (*He
laughs.* DANIEL, *finding this image unattractive, attempts to
smile politely.*)

But you only had cause to speak to me once, I believe.

DANIEL: Really? And what did I say?

QUASS: Well, actually you said, 'Oh dear. Well, one does have to conform. Or try to. As they say.' And you smiled and sort of winked. Your life is going well, I imagine, isn't it? (DANIEL *makes to speak, doesn't.*)
I mean, no little stutters or stammers, embarrassing hiccoughs, wayward mishaps, eh?

DANIEL: You're not by any chance attempting to sell me something, are you?

QUASS: What? (*Laughs.*) Against stutters and hiccoughs and mishaps? Oh, I wish I were! I mean, do I look like the kind of chap who'd have dung delivered to a neighbour's doorstep? (*He stares at* DANIEL *intently. Sudden sound of clapping, and we see from* DANIEL's *point of view* JACKABOY, *his stumps spreadeagled, walking furiously towards the pavilion ahead of the other batsman, fielders leaving.*)

DANIEL: (*Rising*) The game's over. And I must get back to the pavilion.

QUASS: Oh. (*Clearly disappointed*) There was so much I wanted to – to – but look. I say –
(*Getting up, staring at him almost pleadingly, he reaches into his pocket, hands* DANIEL *a card*)
– if ever you want – or need to – well, make contact –

DANIEL: Thank you.

QUASS: I haven't done anything wrong, you know. I've done my best to – to conform.

DANIEL: Well, that's all any of us can do, really. (*Firmly*) Goodbye, Mr – um – um – (*Glances down at card*) Quass. (*He walks off, slipping the card into his pocket. As he does so, heading towards the pavilion, he glances back once, and sees, from his point of view,* QUASS *staring after him, forlornly.*)

INT. CHANGING ROOM. DAY

DANIEL *undressing, along with others, glancing towards* JACKABOY *as he does so.* JACKABOY *is sitting by himself, jaw set, staring furiously down at the floor. The other cricketers are clearly giving him a wide berth.*

CRICKETER: (*In a mutter to* DANIEL) It was bad enough last
    season, when he was just bad-tempered, rude and blustery.
    Actually some of us were wondering if you'd have a word
    Daniel.
    (JACKABOY *suddenly smashes his bat against the ground, gets
    up, starts to get undressed.* DANIEL *raises his eyebrows, goes
    over. Other cricketers in and out of shower during this.*)
DANIEL: Everything all right, Jack?
    (JACKABOY *looks at him witheringly.*)
JACKABOY: It was a bloody long hop! I was out to a bloody long
    hop! But it was off a short run. Did you notice that? I think
    the swine was chucking. But with a fellow cop doing the
    umpiring – what do you expect, eh?
    (*He's now undressed, glaring at* DANIEL.)
DANIEL: Jack, some of the chaps have asked me to have a word
    with you. They've become rather concerned.
JACKABOY: (*Ignoring him*) Could you hurry with the showers
    there! (*Going towards the showers*) I've got to get off!

INT. SHOWER ROOM. DAY

A cricketer comes out of the shower; JACKABOY *steps in. We see*
JACKABOY *from* DANIEL's *point of view under the shower. A second
shower is vacated, and as* DANIEL *makes for it the water in both
showers dwindles to a trickle, then gutters out.*

JACKABOY: (*Twisting with increasing savagery at the tap*) What the
    hell – what the hell! (*To* DANIEL, *intensely*) You know what
    they've done!

DANIEL: Who?

JACKABOY: The bloody fuzz! They've turned it off at the mains. They've had their showers next door, they're on their way to the pub to swill beer into their bellies – so screw the rest of you, eh?

DANIEL: Well, I don't really think that's likely to be . . .

JACKABOY: I'm meant to be having dinner with Caroline and her parents-in-law. *My* parents-in-law, I mean. Appalling couple.

DANIEL: Can't you have a bath there?

JACKABOY: At the Savoy Grill? (*Throws his towel across the room.*) Oh, those buggers, those buggers!
(*They both begin to get dressed.*
Furiously) Every time I turn around I find one of them at my elbow – warnings for this, warnings for that, my car clamped, towed away, I even got a wigging for looking up a girl's skirt on the tube – that's what they *claimed* I was doing – I merely happened to glance at her knees – turned out she was a woman cop and the man with her – a brute of a fellow – 'lewd and insulting behaviour' they called it and when I said I'm a gynaecologist, rather a well-established gynaecologist it may interest you to know, she said, 'Well, keep your eyes to yourself when you're not on the job.' Can you believe? And the next day, the very next morning, I got a summons for – where the hell are they? They were here! (*Looking furiously around*) I left them here – *and* my jacket!

EXT. CAR PARK. DAY

DANIEL *and* JACKABOY *are walking rapidly through the car park.*

JACKABOY: What I don't understand is why steal my trousers and jacket, but leave my bag with my wallet and keys. (*Goes to car, looks at watch, stops.*) Do you really think they'll let me in at the Savoy like this?

(*Pull back to take him in cricketing flannels and tatty, garish blazer and matching stringy tie.*)

I mean – this blazer, what is it anyway? And tie –

DANIEL: I suppose it must be their colours. The police. As we found it in their dressing room.

JACKABOY: (*Gives a bitter laugh*) Pretentious sods! *And* I stink.

DANIEL: Listen, Jack, I'll give you a call during the week. We'll thrash a few things out about the chaps' feelings –

(JACKABOY, *clearly not paying attention, is putting his key in the car door, forcing it.*)

JACKABOY: (*Holding up the key*) It won't bloody turn! (*Looks at the key.*) It's mine all right. These are mine.

(*He turns, tries again, then straightens, stands smouldering, then lashes out with his foot at the car door, kicks it in a kind of frenzy.*

Shouting in a rage) Enough, enough, I've had enough, enough –

(*A* BURLY MAN *appears carrying cricketing gear, watches this in amazement, then begins to run towards* JACKABOY.)

BURLY MAN: (*Shouting*) Hey – you – hey – stop that, you bloody stop that!

JACKABOY: (*Beside himself*) Bugger off! Mind your own bloody business!

BURLY MAN: I saw you. I saw you kicking the door!

JACKABOY: I'll kick the bloody door any time I want. It's my bloody foot and my bloody door.

BURLY MAN: It may be your bloody foot but that's *my* bloody door!

(*All this is seen from* DANIEL's *point of view. First hesitating, then he begins to sidle away to where his car, a new BMW, is parked.*)

JACKABOY: What?

(*He stares at the car, then looks at the licence plate, then looks further down, spots an identical car.*)

Oh. Right. You're right. Look, I'm sorry. Mine's over there
– identical – but I'm in a rush –
BURLY MAN: Oh, are you? In a rush, eh? Look at that door, just
look at it – that's malicious damage.
JACKABOY: Malicious damage, what are you talking about? A
slight scratch, a dent, all right a dent –
(DANIEL *is now hurrying towards his own car, glancing back
occasionally to take in the scene between* JACKABOY *and the*
BURLY MAN.)
BURLY MAN: I want a few details. Name, address –
(JACKABOY *takes a wad of money out of his wallet.*)
JACKABOY: Here you are.
(JACKABOY *shoves money at the* BURLY MAN.)
BURLY MAN: What's this?
JACKABOY: What's this? It's money, that's what it is.
BURLY MAN: Are you trying to bribe me?
JACKABOY: Bribe you? I'm giving you some money to pay for the
scratch on your door. Don't you understand I'm in a rush,
you imbecile?
BURLY MAN: Imbecile. (*Looks at him.*) I should advise you that
you're talking to a police officer.
(DANIEL *slides into his car.*)
JACKABOY: A police – oh, of course. Yes. Of course. Hah! Well
– (*Trying desperately to bring himself under control*) – that's
only to be expected, isn't it?
BURLY MAN: (*Taking* JACKABOY *in carefully*) What's that you're
wearing?
JACKABOY: Eh?
BURLY MAN: That blazer. That tie.
(DANIEL *starts the engine gently as:*)
Where did you get them?
(DANIEL *glides the car out, drives off. As he goes we see*
JACKABOY *expostulating furiously as the* BURLY MAN *takes his
arm, then struggling, and the* BURLY MAN *fixing him in an
armlock, shouting. Two other cops in blazers come running, and*

we cut to DANIEL, *his face, his expression shifty but relieved.*
He opens the glove compartment, and we see from his point of
view an assortment of packages of sweets. He takes a sweet out
of a package, pops it into his mouth. Last image of JACKABOY
being frogmarched to car.)

INT. DANIEL'S HOUSE: LIVING ROOM. NIGHT

We come in on SOPHIE's *face pressed against the sofa, eyes closed,*
breathing heavily with pleasure, her head moving rhythmically up
and down. She is wearing a nightdress which is rumpled up around
her shoulders. Mozart from the radio.

DANIEL: (*Out of shot*) But of course in my position I have to be
    careful about getting involved with the police. Anyway, I
    don't really see what I could have done, do you?
SOPHIE: Lovely, lovely, Popsie. 'S all I want. Does for me.
    (*Cut to* DANIEL, *his dressing gown open, seeming to be sitting*
    astride SOPHIE, *his hands on her naked back. He smiles in*
    affectionate reproof.)
DANIEL: You haven't heard a word I've said, have you, Bootsie?
SOPHIE: Mmmm? Yes, I have. You scored nearly fifty.
    (DANIEL *bends over and kisses the top of her head, then gets*
    up.)
DANIEL: (*Pulling down her nightdress and helping her to sit up*)
    Come on, let's get you all to bye-byes.
    (*Cut to* SOPHIE *blinking, slightly dazed.*)
SOPHIE: Oh, you don't mean you're going to do some work!
DANIEL: *Got* to do some work, Bootsie. So that I'm properly
    prepared for the morning.
    (SOPHIE *nods.* DANIEL *begins to help her to her feet.*)
SOPHIE: (*Then remembering*) Oh, it's on your desk. The letter.
DANIEL: What letter?
SOPHIE: Don't know. One of those special-delivery chaps
    brought it round. Jolly frightening actually in those great

goggles and gauntlets, standing there thrusting an envelope out at you. And you can't hear a word they say.

(DANIEL *is going towards his study.*)

Oh, and I heard your telephone ring a couple of times so there're probably some messages on the machine.

INT. DANIEL'S HOUSE: STUDY. NIGHT

Legal books, etc., on shelves, a desk on which there is an answering machine, telephone and papers, neatly stacked. There is a large white envelope on the desk. Sound of Mozart continuing over. DANIEL *picks up the envelope, begins to open it, and as he does so opens a drawer of the desk in which there is again an assortment of sweets. He pops one into his mouth, then notices two messages signalled on his answering machine, winds them back, plays them, continues opening envelope as:*

FIRST MESSAGE: (CARPER's *voice over*) Remember, Daniel, it's not how we played the game, but whether we won or lost. You've lost.

(DANIEL *looks puzzled.*)

SECOND MESSAGE: (WOMAN PHOTOGRAPHER's *voice over, cheerful, lively*) Hello, Daniel Davenport. Congratters on a terrific little innings. But the umpire's finger is up and you're out! Hit wicket.

(DANIEL *stands for a moment, then looks up to see* SOPHIE *at the door to his study.*)

SOPHIE: (*Yawning*) Who was it?

DANIEL: Just some fools messing about on the answering machine. That's the trouble with those things. (*Finishes opening the envelope.*) People can't resist being childish – (*He pulls a ticket out of the envelope, studies it, perplexed.*)

SOPHIE: Is that an airline ticket?

DANIEL: It does seem to be, yes.

SOPHIE: Where to?

DANIEL: (*Looks.*) Rio de Janeiro.

SOPHIE: (*Suddenly becoming alert*) Rio de Janeiro?

DANIEL: Yes. (*Studying it*) A one way ticket to Rio de Janeiro, economy class. The flight leaves at midnight. Tonight. (*Staring at ticket*) Obviously some dolt of a travel agent has . . .

SOPHIE: (*Smiling but slightly tremulously*) Well, as long as you're not running out on me.

(*Cut to* DANIEL *smiling at her dotingly.*)

DANIEL: How could I, Bootsie, when I need you so much?

(*Cut to* SOPHIE *standing, resplendently pregnant.*)

(*Out of shot*) All of you.

SOPHIE: You know something, you look so beautiful, Popsie.

INT. COURTROOM. DAY

We come straight in on DANIEL *in his barrister's wig.*

DANIEL: My client, Mr Herman, who as you know stands here accused of a very serious charge indeed – (*He gestures. Cut to* HERMAN, *a man in his mid-fifties, prosperous, respectable-looking, in dock.*

Out of shot) – Mr Herman, about whom you knew absolutely nothing, rings you up out of the blue, arranges to meet you in a pub in Paddington, and without much ado offers you a large sum of money, ten thousand pounds, if you'll burn down a warehouse in Ilford for him. That is your account, isn't it, Mr Parkes?

(*Cut to* PARKES *in the witness box.*)

PARKES: (*As if himself bewildered*) Yes.

DANIEL: Why, do you think?

PARKES: He said because he needed the insurance –

DANIEL: No, I mean why *you*, do you think, Mr Parkes? Why entrust his reputation, his liberty, his whole future, to you? When he'd never even met you before.

PARKES: I don't know. I suppose he made a mistake.
DANIEL: To have entrusted his future to you?
    (PARKES *is for a moment at a loss for words.*)

INT. WINE BAR. DAY

We come in on DANIEL, *eating, while glancing at notes on the table.*

CARPER: (*Over*) He's lying, of course.
    (DANIEL *looks up and we see from his point of view* CARPER, *a man in his mid-forties, well dressed, but with an air of indefinable sleaziness about him. He sits down at Daniel's table.*)
Ask him about Estapona.
    (DANIEL *stares at him.*)
Ask Parkes how he managed to have a conversation in Paddington with your client when he and his mum were registered in a hotel in Estapona.
DANIEL: (*After a second*) What hotel?
    (*And cut to* QUASS, *watching from across the wine bar. We see from his point of view* DANIEL *and* CARPER, CARPER *talking, then we see, also from his point of view a* MAN *and a* WOMAN *at a nearby table. The* WOMAN *is laughing, taking photographs of the* MAN, *as if practising with the camera. She suddenly swings the camera around, takes several quick photographs of* DANIEL *and* CARPER *talking. Then cut back to* DANIEL's *face.*)
And you don't want anything for this?
CARPER: Course I do. I want twenty-five thousand pounds. But if you can't manage that, I'll just have to be satisfied with seeing justice done, eh? At least for now.
    (DANIEL *hesitates, studies* CARPER *again, gets up, gathers his notes together, goes towards the door.*)
QUASS: (*Agitated, approaching* DANIEL) Mr Davenport – Mr Davenport – please –

(DANIEL *turns to him.*)
(*Urgently*) Nathaniel Quass. We met at the Amplesides Old
Boys' cricket match –
DANIEL: Oh, yes. I'm sorry, Mr Quass, I'm due in court.
(*He hurries out.* QUASS *turns, looks towards* CARPER, *who has
gone over to the table with the* MAN *and the* WOMAN
PHOTOGRAPHER. *The* WOMAN *swings camera up, takes a
picture of* CARPER, *who laughs, sits down beside them.*)

INT. COURTROOM. DAY

We come in on DANIEL.

DANIEL: Now, Mr Parkes. Does the name Estapona mean
anything to you?
(*Cut to* PARKES *looking shifty.*)
PARKES: No, I don't think so.
DANIEL: (*Out of shot, silkily*) It's the name of a seaside resort on
the Costa del Sol, Mr Parkes.

INT. COURT CORRIDOR. DAY

DANIEL, ZELDA (*Daniel's junior*), STRAUSS (*a solicitor*), *coming out
of court into a corridor.*

ZELDA: How did you know?
STRAUSS: Yes, how *did* you know?
DANIEL: Let's just say I found out. Acting on information
received.
STRAUSS: You mean somebody just came up to you and gave you
the name of the village, the name of the hotel, the exact
dates?
DANIEL: Yes.
STRAUSS: Why?
DANIEL: He said he wanted to see justice done.

STRAUSS: A likely story.

    (HERMAN *approaches, radiant.*)

HERMAN: Mr Davenport, Mr Davenport –

    (*Then, on impulse, he embraces* DANIEL. *And we see from* DANIEL's *point of view over* HERMAN's *shoulder* PARKES *talking to someone.* PARKES *glances at* DANIEL, *gives him an odd smirking look. The man he is talking to becomes fleetingly visible. It is* CARPER.)

ZELDA: (*Out of shot*) You're expected in Court Three, Mr Davenport.

DANIEL: Mmmm?

ZELDA: (*Handing him a brief*) Butley. Receiving stolen goods.

DANIEL: Ah, yes, our Mr Butley.

    (*He looks once more quickly at* PARKES *and* CARPER, *then away.*)

INT. LUIGI'S RESTAURANT. NIGHT

SOPHIE *and* DANIEL *have eaten their meal. On the table are coffee and* petits fours.

SOPHIE: (*Slightly befuddled*) I didn't know you were allowed to do that sort of thing.

DANIEL: My dear Bootsie, it's nothing to do with me if our Mr Herman fixed it with our Mr Parkes and our Johnnie in the wine bar so nothing our Mr Parkes said would be believed, as long as nobody tells me about it. (*Smiles, lifts up* SOPHIE's *hand, kisses it.*) I am merely speculating idly over my birthday dinner – (*Looks lovingly into her eyes*) – with my dear, dear –

    (*Piped music begins loudly.* DANIEL *winces, gives an exclamation of disgust.*)

Oh, really, I thought I'd trained him not to.

    (DANIEL *turns, looks around as* LUIGI *approaches.*)

Ah, Luigi. (*Smiles reprovingly.*) You put the music on.

LUIGI: Music? Oh, sorry, Signor Davenport, I didn't notice it –

DANIEL: (*Interrupting*) Exactly my point, Luigi. It irritates some of your clients and the others don't even notice.

LUIGI: (*Obsequiously*) I turn it off immediately, Signor Davenport. But I just want to tell you you are wanted on the telephone. A Miss Wright. She say it is urgent.

DANIEL: (*Just suppressing shock*) Miss Wright?

SOPHIE: Who's Miss Wright?

DANIEL: (*Casually, as* LUIGI *turns the music off*) I haven't the slightest idea.

(*He gets up, goes across the restaurant to the telephone, picks it up. We see him keeping an eye on* SOPHIE, *also seeing* SOPHIE *from his point of view sipping coffee, vaguely watching him, beginning to yawn.*)

Hello?

(*Silence on the line, not dead.*)

Davina – (*In a low voice, turning away*) Davina, is that you? (*There is the sound of someone hanging up.* DANIEL *glances towards* SOPHIE, *and we see from his point of view* LUIGI *going to their table, handing* SOPHIE *something – all of which* DANIEL *doesn't really take in. He dials rapidly. There is a disconnected sound the other end. He hangs up, clearly worried, goes back to the table.*

Hurriedly sitting down) It wasn't for me at all. Well, how could it be as nobody knew we were here? (*Seeing envelope*) What's this?

SOPHIE: Luigi brought it over. It arrived by taxi –

(DANIEL *is ripping it open as sounds of 'Happy Birthday to You' get stronger.* DANIEL *glances down at the note. Cut to the note, rapidly seen list of names, some in boxes, some crossed out, then home in on close-up of sentence:*

  What is the difference between Miss Wright and Wrong?
  Happy birthday, Davenport.

'Happy Birthday' now very loud. DANIEL *looks up in*

298

bewilderment as LUIGI, *leading a gang of waiters, and bearing
a cake with candles on it, is now at the table. They group
around it singing, 'Happy birthday, dear Daniel.'* DANIEL,
*cramming the letter back into the envelope, clearly completely
unfocused, attempts joviality.*)

DANIEL: Good heavens – well, well. Thank you, Bootsie.

SOPHIE: (*Bewildered*) But it isn't me.

(DANIEL *stares at her, then at* LUIGI.)

LUIGI: The cake, it came from the taxi driver with the note. He
tell us to surprise you.

SOPHIE: Well, what's in the note?

DANIEL: Nothing. I mean, it just says, 'Happy birthday.' No
name, no signature, nothing. Probably (*Shoving the note into
his pocket*) the girls from chambers – Zelda, Barbara, that
lot. I rather wish they hadn't.

SOPHIE: (*Proudly*) But it shows how fond of you they are,
Popsie.

(LUIGI *gestures towards the candles.* DANIEL, *attempting a
cheerful manner, sucks in his breath, blows at the candles. They
all seem to go out, to applause from waiters,* LUIGI *and*
SOPHIE.)

LUIGI, SOPHIE *and* WAITERS: (*Together*) Bravo, Signor
Davenport, darling, bravissimo, *etc.*

(*And take in, at a distant table, the* CAMERA WOMAN *and her*
COMPANION *from the wine bar, looking grinningly towards*
DANIEL, SOPHIE, LUIGI, *waiters, grinning and cut to cake.
The candles flaming back into life. They are trick candles. And
over the shot of candles flickering:*)

ZELDA: (*Voice over, on answering machine*) Hello. A message for
Mr Davenport from Zelda Tate. Just to let you know that
I've got the Cookson brief. I'll bring it in with me in the
morning so you can look at it –

INT. DANIEL'S HOUSE: STUDY. NIGHT

DANIEL *winding forward the answering machine. Take in the sweet drawer, his hand unconsciously taking a sweet and putting it into his mouth. He winds the machine back a little to adjust to:*

MESSAGE: (WOMAN PHOTOGRAPHER's *voice over*) Hello, Daniel. Dangerous Daniel. I'm calling on behalf of Miss Davina Wright. Or should it be Misdemeanour Wright? (*Slight laugh.*) Happy Birthday.
(*Click.* DANIEL *stops the answering machine, looks up at the ceiling, listening for sounds, then takes out of his pocket the letter he opened in the restaurant. We see it properly:*

> *Coveney*
> *Billington*
> *Cropper*
> *Wardle*
> *Jackaboy*
> *Shulman*
> *Quass*
> *Davenport*
> *What is the difference between Miss Wright and Wrong?*
> *Happy birthday, Davenport.*

DANIEL *studies the list of names. He focuses on* JACKABOY. *He flicks through his address book to Jackaboy, Jack, dials. It is answered almost at once.*)

CAROLINE: (*Voice over, fraught*) Hello.

DANIEL: Oh, Caroline, it's Daniel, Daniel Davenport. I do apologize for – phoning so late, but I have to talk to Jack about something rather important, is he there?

CAROLINE: (*Voice over*) Yes, he's here. But he can't talk now. (*A strange sound, almost like a laugh.*)
Could you come over, please? He needs your help.
(SOPHIE, *in nightdress, appears at door.*)

DANIEL: (*Registering* SOPHIE) My help?
CAROLINE: (*Voice over*) Please hurry.
 (*Click.*)

EXT. JACKABOY'S HOUSE. NIGHT

The front door opens. JACKABOY, *handcuffed, kicking and shouting, is being hustled out by police.* CAROLINE *behind, following. Indecipherable expression on her face as she watches* JACKABOY *being bundled into a police van, driven screechingly off, followed by police car.*
All this seen from DANIEL'S *point of view as he sits in his car, clearly having just arrived.* DANIEL *begins to start his car, stops when he sees that* CAROLINE *has seen him.* DANIEL *hesitates, gets out of the car, goes towards her.*

INT. DANIEL'S HOUSE: STUDY. NIGHT

DANIEL *goes to his desk, picks up the list, studies it. Homes in on* QUASS'S *name. Not quite able to make it out because of crosses on letters.*

DANIEL: Ass. Ass. Uass. Quass. Quass!
 (*He stands, thinking, trying to remember, then remembers, turns, hurries out of the study.*)

INT. DANIEL'S HOUSE: LAUNDRY ROOM. NIGHT

DANIEL *goes to the laundry basket, begins to fumble through it, extracts his cricket trousers, digs into the pocket, and is just pulling out a card when he hears a noise at the door. He turns.* SOPHIE *is staring at him, sleepy but astonished.*

DANIEL: No, no – (*Inspecting his cricket trousers*) – they don't
 really need washing for Sunday.
 (*He surreptitiously pulls the card out of cricket-bags pocket.*)

SOPHIE: Surely Jack didn't call you over just to make sure your cricket flannels –

DANIEL: No, no, of course not. No, I'm afraid Jack is in a spot of trouble. Serious trouble.

(*He slips the card into his trouser pocket.*)

INT. DANIEL'S HOUSE: BEDROOM. NIGHT

SOPHIE *sitting on the bed*, DANIEL *getting undressed.*

DANIEL: (*Continuing undressing*) Caroline says it's – persecution mania – anyway, he's been filing all kinds of complaints and this evening an inspector came around to warn him against wasting police time. An official warning. He had a rather overbearing manner, I expect – but then, of course, Jack's own manner – anyway, he told Jack he was either crazy or a malicious liar. Jack told him he was a liar and a fool. The detective inspector poked him in the chest with his finger. Jack poked him back with a knife. They were in the kitchen. The worst place ever to have a confrontation. Because there are so many to hand. Knives, I mean. And cut him badly in the arm. Pity he didn't try to patch it up.

SOPHIE: Patch it up! After attacking him with a knife!

DANIEL: No, no, patch up the arm, I mean. After all he's a gynaecologist, he can probably put a bandage on, or whatever. Instead he ended up sitting on the detective inspector's face. That's when little Lucas phoned the police – he'd watched the whole thing through the keyhole. Then Caroline came back from her class. Primal-scream class. Then the police arrived. Then I turned up. I suppose the question is whether they'll charge him with attempted murder or GBH. I gave her Quass's name.

SOPHIE: Quass?

DANIEL: Strauss, I mean, the solicitor. Very good chap. Told her I couldn't take the case myself, of course.

(*Cut to* SOPHIE, *sitting, looking worried.*)

SOPHIE: I don't understand, Popsie.

DANIEL: Yes, I know, it's all – all – very unexpected. Jack of all people –

SOPHIE: No, I mean you, Popsie. After all that, how could you then come straight home and check on the state of your cricket flannels?

DANIEL: Yes, I know, Bootsie, but not as odd as it seems. (*Goes into the bathroom.*) I hear that sort of thing every day from the witness box – people who do something – something mundane or routine when in a state of shock.
(*Sound of running water.*)

SOPHIE: Yes, I suppose – when Daddy died Mummy went straight to the henhouse. (*Yawns. Suddenly seeing the telephone*) Oh. Somebody phoned for you. Not on your study number, on our number. Just as I was comfortable at last and beginning to fall asleep –

DANIEL: (*Out of shot, interrupting*) Who was it?

SOPHIE: He had one of those names – Papgood.

DANIEL: (*After a slight pause*) Not, um. Hopjoy by any chance?

SOPHIE: Yes. To say that he might get caught in the traffic in the Mile End Road, but don't worry, he was certain to turn up.
(*Silence from the bathroom.*)
Have I got that right, Popsie? Hopjoy in the traffic.

DANIEL: (*Coming to the bathroom door, not yet seen, trying for nonchalance*) Yes, yes, not that important – not worth phoning late and on the house number –
(SOPHIE *looks at him properly.*)

SOPHIE: What are you doing?
(*Cut to* DANIEL. *He is in his pyjama bottoms, his face covered with shaving cream, holding a razor.*)

DANIEL: Mmmm?

SOPHIE: You're shaving.

DANIEL: Oh, good heavens! My mind was so full of Jack, the

poor devil – I mean that I must have thought I was getting up, eh? (*Gesturing and attempting a laugh*) Instead of –

EXT. ELGIN CRESCENT. NIGHT

A girl, DAVINA WRIGHT, *at a window, waving. Cut to* DAVINA *at the window, an expression of horror, not waving but gesturing.*

INT. CAR. NIGHT

Cut to a YOUNGER DANIEL's *face, also horrified as sound over of soft bump. Stay on his face as we hear again and again the soft bump,* DANIEL's *face lifting on every bump. Over sound of telephone ringing.*

INT. DANIEL'S HOUSE: BEDROOM. NIGHT

Cut to DANIEL's *face in bed. The telephone ringing continues. Cut to* DANIEL *sitting up in bed, telephone still ringing.* SOPHIE *beside him, snoring.*

DANIEL: (*Picking up the telephone*) Yes?
CARPER: (*Voice over*) Daniel Davenport?
DANIEL: Yes.
CARPER: (*Voice over*) Happy birthday, Daniel. But we mustn't forget absent friends, must we? Like Davina and Geoffrey Hopjoy.
(*Click.*)
SOPHIE: (*In a slurred voice*) Who is it?
DANIEL: Oh, no one, just some fool. Wrong number.
(*He lies down, his eyes open, staring.*)

EXT. ELGIN CRESCENT. DAY

Eight in the morning. DANIEL *parking his car. He gets out, hurries up the steps of a house, looks at the row of names under the row of*

*bells. The one he is looking for clearly isn't there. He turns away,
perplexed and anxious, and we see coming down the steps of the
identical house next door,* DAVINA WRIGHT. *He hurries down the
steps so they meet between the two houses.* DAVINA *is in her early
forties, pretty, composed-looking, something slightly odd about the
composure.* DAVINA *stares at him.*

DANIEL: (*Sickly smile*) Wrong house. (*Gestures backwards.*) I was
    sure it was fifty-two. But of course it was fifty-four, wasn't it?
DAVINA: (*Smiles brightly*) Yes, fifty-four. That's where I live.
    Fifty-four.
DANIEL: I couldn't get you by phone. The number's
    disconnected –
DAVINA: Oh, yes. I had it disconnected.
DANIEL: Very wise. Given the kind of people who phone one up
    these days. Was somebody phoning you up?
DAVINA: Oh, no. Nobody at all. That's why I had it taken away.
    It was so silly waiting for it to ring if nobody was going to
    ring me.
    (*They are walking along the pavement,* DAVINA *rather briskly.*)
DANIEL: I see. But – but it did make it very difficult to return
    your calls, you see?
DAVINA: Calls? What calls? I haven't made any calls since they
    took it away. How could I?
DANIEL: You didn't phone me at the restaurant last night or
    leave a message on my answering machine or have
    somebody else phone my wife –
DAVINA: Your wife?
    (DANIEL *nods.*)
    What's her name?
DANIEL: Um – Sophie.
DAVINA: Is she a good wife to you?
DANIEL: Yes.
DAVINA: Yes, she would be. You'd find yourself a good wife,
    Daniel. And children, have you any children?

DANIEL: No.

DAVINA: I expect you will in due course, won't you? You'll be a good father, Daniel, and your wife Sophie will be a good mother.

DANIEL: Thank you. Um, you haven't phoned her then? Or me?

DAVINA: (*Brightly*) Why should I?

DANIEL: Well, I thought that perhaps you wanted to be in touch.

DAVINA: Our arrangement was that we shouldn't see each other or speak to each other. You shouldn't be here now, Daniel. You shouldn't.

DANIEL: I know. But it is – is an emergency. And nobody has come around asking questions about Geoff?

(DAVINA *looks at him in a sort of shock.*

Gently) I'm sorry. But I have to know. It's important.

DAVINA: (*Lips trembling*) Nobody's come around asking questions about anything.

DANIEL: And you've never – never told anybody?

DAVINA: You know who I've told, Daniel. Who I have to tell. I tell Him all the time.

DANIEL: (*Thinks, nods*) But nobody else?

DAVINA: Nobody else. Nobody. Ever. How could I? There isn't anybody else to tell.

DANIEL: (*Nods again*) Where are you going?

DAVINA: I'm going to Bartholomew's school to watch the children arrive. I do that every morning in term time. Afterwards I go to St Ignatius and sweep the aisles and polish – yes, this morning I shall polish the candlesticks. Then I shall go over to St Mary's, where Father Thomas will find me something to do, I'm sure.

DANIEL: You can't – Davina, you can't live your life in – in a state of – of continual repentance.

DAVINA: I must try.

(*The school is now in sight, with parents and children going in.*)

DANIEL: It wasn't your fault. You had nothing to do with it.

(DAVINA *looks at him brightly.*)

DAVINA: He was my husband. Married in church. A holy
    service.

DANIEL: Yes. But it wasn't your fault.

DAVINA: (*As if comprehension breaking*) Oh – oh – *that's* why
    you've come back. To tempt me. Oh, you devil! You *devil!*
    (*Slaps him viciously.*) Go away, devil! Go away!
    (*She slaps him again, turns, walks briskly towards the school.*
    DANIEL *stares after her, stroking his cheek.* DAVINA *turns,*
    stares at him, screams:)
    Go away, devil! Stop following me, go away!

EXT. DANIEL'S CHAMBERS. DAY

Long shot. DANIEL *hurrying up the steps to his chambers.*

INT. CHAMBERS: LOBBY. DAY

DANIEL *hurrying across the main office, past the receptionist*
(BARBARA), *who has an enormous bouquet of flowers which she is*
unwrapping. We see also peripherally STRAUSS, COOKSON *and*
ZELDA.

BARBARA: (*As* DANIEL *speeds past her desk*) Oh, Mr Davenport,
    Mr Davenport –

INT. DANIEL'S OFFICE. DAY

DANIEL *pays no attention, goes straight into his office, strides to his*
desk, takes the card out of his pocket, picks up the telephone and is
about to dial when there is a knock on the door. ZELDA *comes in,*
holding the door open.

DANIEL: (*Sharply*) Yes, Zelda?

ZELDA: Um, Mr Strauss is here with Mr Cookson.

DANIEL: Well then, tell them to wait a moment, will you, I've
    got to make a –

(STRAUSS *enters with a middle-aged, rather desperate and slightly shifty-looking man* – COOKSON.)

STRAUSS: Good morning, Daniel. This is Mr Cookson. Mr Cookson, this is Daniel Davenport who is going to be your counsel.

(COOKSON *and* DANIEL *shake hands.*)

DANIEL: Please sit down. Will you – will you excuse me a moment? I'll be right back.

(*He is about to leave. His eye catches the file on his desk. He surreptitiously picks it up, goes out of the office.*)

INT. CHAMBERS. DAY

As DANIEL *does so,* BARBARA *is coming towards Daniel's office, carrying an enormous bowl of flowers, and makes to say something to* DANIEL. DANIEL *hurries into another office, obviously* ZELDA'S.

INT. ZELDA'S OFFICE. DAY

DANIEL *takes the card out of his pocket, dials.*

QUASS: (*Voice over, cautiously*) Hello, yes.

DANIEL: Can I speak to Nathaniel Quass, please?

QUASS: (*Voice over*) Who is it, please?

DANIEL: Davenport. Daniel Davenport.

QUASS: (*Voice over*) Ah. They've started on you then, have they?

DANIEL: Can we meet this evening? The Garrick Club. Seven o'clock.

QUASS: (*Voice over*) Is it safe?

DANIEL: Of course it is.

(DANIEL *slams down the telephone. He looks at the file in his hand, runs through it quickly, turning pages, muttering to himself, braces himself, goes back to main lobby.*)

INT. CHAMBERS: LOBBY. DAY

We see from DANIEL's *point of view* STRAUSS *and* ZELDA *looking concerned. Then take in* COOKSON *sitting on a chair, sniffing, dabbing at his eyes with a handkerchief, tears in evidence.* DANIEL *goes over to* COOKSON, *who gets up, dabbing at his eyes.*

DANIEL: Come, come, Mr Henshaw, I can assure you the matter's really not that serious, you know. Even if it comes to the worst you're only technically a bigamist.
    (COOKSON *looks up at him in bewilderment.*)
STRAUSS: Perhaps I could just have a quick word, Daniel?
DANIEL: Mmmm?
    (STRAUSS *leads him away. The following is conducted in urgent whispers.*)
STRAUSS: That's Cookson.
ZELDA: You've got (*Indicating Daniel's file*) the wrong file. Henshaw's coming in this afternoon. I've got the Cookson file here –
STRAUSS: (*Interrupting*) Cookson's charged with demanding money with menaces. Particularly from old ladies living alone. They haven't got anything, really, apart from some shaky identification. And a confession. Without the confession the whole thing would collapse. He claims it was beaten out of him.
    (*Cut to, during this,* COOKSON *snivelling.*)
ZELDA: (*Out of shot*) He was interrogated for fifteen hours without a break. Pushed around and slapped. One of them, Cooper, pulled his hair, and the other – Sowerboy – squeezed his testicles.
STRAUSS: Unfortunately the doctor's report isn't as helpful as we would like. They were careful not to bruise him.
ZELDA: But there were some scratches around the scrotum.
STRAUSS: Yes, but not incompatible with rough sex, apparently. He was on his way back from his girlfriend's when they picked him up.

DANIEL: (*Attempting dignity*) Yes, thank you, thank you. But I think I'll hear the rest from Mr Dawson direct, if you don't mind. (*He steps forward.*)

STRAUSS: (*Muttering*) Cookson. The name's Cookson.

DANIEL: (*To* COOKSON) Mr Cookson, I'm sorry about the earlier confusion. But look, we really can't afford to allow our – um – emotions to get in the way of our thinking, can we? (*He guides* COOKSON *into his office.*)

INT. DANIEL'S OFFICE. DAY

DANIEL: (*Suppressing irritation, as* COOKSON *continues to sniff*) Do please try and –

STRAUSS: (*From the door*) No, it's the pollen. He has an allergy. (DANIEL *stares at him blankly, then sees the bowl of flowers with a card protruding.*
Out of shot) That's why we came out.
(DANIEL *looks at the card and we see from his point of view:* 'Davina and Geoffrey Hopjoy. In memoriam.')

EXT. GARRICK CLUB. NIGHT

DANIEL *going up steps. He stops at the porter's lodge.*

DANIEL: I've got a guest arriving in (*he looks at his watch*) half an hour or so. A Mr Quass.

PORTER: He's already here, sir. He's been here for some time. He's waiting in the Long Lounge.
(*There is something slightly odd in the porter's manner.*)

DANIEL: Ah. Thank you.

INT. GARRICK CLUB: STAIRS AND LANDING. NIGHT

We follow DANIEL *up through various rooms, men sedately dressed in sombre-ish suits, one or two in dinner jackets, etc. We see from his point of view* QUASS *on his hands and knees, groping under an armchair. An* ELDERLY MEMBER *comes over in front of* QUASS. QUASS *gets up in disarray. He is wearing a dinner-jacket of exotic design, too big for him, and is in a different wig that fits badly.*

ELDERLY MEMBER: (*Not quite concealing surprise at the spectacle of* QUASS) Is this what you're looking for?
QUASS: Oh yes, how kind. How very kind. Thank you, sir.
ELDERLY MEMBER: Not at all.
    (*He withdraws.*)

INT. GARRICK CLUB: LONG LOUNGE. NIGHT

DANIEL *steps forward.* QUASS *sees him.*

QUASS: I arrived a bit early. I hope that's all right.
DANIEL: Oh. And what were you – (*He gestures towards a chair.*)
QUASS: My inhaler. (*Shows it to* DANIEL.) I thought I was going to have an attack, you see. And dropped it.
    (*He looks at* DANIEL, *wheezes slightly.*)
DANIEL: But you're all right now, are you?
QUASS: Yes, yes. If I just sit down. May I?
    (DANIEL *gestures to the chair, conscious that they are the centre of surreptitious attention.*
    Sitting) Thank you.
    (DANIEL *sits.*)
    You know what they did today? They sent a whole roast pig to Rabbi Goldman. For his nephew's bar mitzvah. And said it came from me. Is that the kind of thing they've started doing to you?
DANIEL: Along those lines, yes. Did they send you a list?
    (QUASS *nods.*)
    Did you bring it with you?
    (QUASS *takes a list out of his pocket, hands it to* DANIEL. DANIEL *studies it.*)

QUASS: Um – can I see yours, do you think?

(DANIEL *looks at him, then hands over his list.*)

Thank you, Davenport.

DANIEL: They're almost identical – except there are fewer lines and crosses on yours. But the same names in boxes –

QUASS: And on both we're bracketed. As if whatever they're going to do they're going to do to us together.

DANIEL: There's no message on yours.

QUASS: No.

(DANIEL *looks at* QUASS, *then takes his list back from* QUASS, *compares the two sheets.*)

DANIEL: Mine is longer. (*Little pause.*) You've cut your message off.

(QUASS *after a second nods.*)

You may have to tell me.

QUASS: Yes, well if I have to I will. As long as you tell me what yours means.

DANIEL: (*Nods*) Now the first thing to find out is who the others are. What connects us –

QUASS: You mean you haven't realized?

DANIEL: The only name I recognize is Jackaboy's – and now yours.

QUASS: Of course, of course. The rest of us would have been too insignificant, wouldn't we?

(DANIEL *stares at him impatiently.*)

We were all at Amplesides in the same house. I mean I understood that much immediately. In fact it was part of it for me – the nightmare – their names and Jackaboy's particularly. But I suppose we'll have to talk to him, won't we?

DANIEL: Who?

QUASS: Jackaboots. (*Little pause.*) Jackaboy, I mean. Jackaboots is what we used to call him –

DANIEL: We can't talk to him. Not at the moment.

QUASS: Why not?

DANIEL: Because he's gone mad. He's going to be out of circulation for quite a time, I suspect, in gaol or . . .
(QUASS *stares at him apprehensively*.)

QUASS: Oh, dear God!

DANIEL: Have you talked to the others?

QUASS: I've tried to. All of them except Jackab–ab – I didn't have the nerve to phone him. But all the rest. But I only got the wives or mothers or children in one case – Wardle's, I think – and for some reason they were all hostile. I'm not at my best on the telephone – tell me, tell me why do you think it's crosses for Shulman and me, and lines and boxes for the rest of you. I've got a feeling crosses are worse – (*getting slightly shrill*) unless the boxes are tombs –

DANIEL: (*Looking around*) Ssssh.

QUASS: Sorry, Davenport.
(QUASS *wheezes. There is a pause*.)
What's going on then, do you think?

DANIEL: Somebody's trying to mess up my life. That's what's going on.

QUASS: Well, what do we plan to do about it?

DANIEL: Find out who they are and stop them.

SERVANT: (*Approaching*) Mr Davenport.

DANIEL: Yes.

SERVANT: Is your guest Mr Quass?

DANIEL: (*After a pause*) Yes.

SERVANT: He's wanted on the phone, sir. (*To* QUASS) I'll show you where it is, sir.

QUASS: (*Getting up*) I didn't tell anybody I'd be here. Did you?
(DANIEL *shakes his head*.)
Then we were followed.
(*Cut to* SERVANT *and* QUASS *walking off together, watched by* DANIEL. *Cut to* QUASS, *returning, wheezing, agitated. He sits down*.)
(*Nods*.) Them all right. I know the voice. The gruff one.

DANIEL: What did he say?

313

QUASS: She. It was one of the shes.

DANIEL: Well, what did she say? Come on, Quass.

QUASS: (*Controls wheezing.*) That we're expected at Luigi's. And that you'd know where to go.

DANIEL: Luigi's?

QUASS: Who's Luigi?

EXT. GARRICK: STEPS. NIGHT

QUASS *and* DANIEL *going down the steps.*

QUASS: I told you they find out everything. (*Stops.*) How can you be sure it isn't a trap?

DANIEL: I *know* Luigi. He's almost a friend. And it's a very quiet place.
(*As they talk a pack of Japanese come up the steps, chatting excitedly. They surge around* DANIEL *and* QUASS. DANIEL *takes them in, slightly puzzled.*)

QUASS: But he might not know it's a trap.

DANIEL: (*Looking at the Japanese, smiling to their bows*) Look, Quass, if you're too frightened to come, just say so. I'll go by myself.
(*Cut to* QUASS's *face, torn by indecision as* DANIEL *strides off.* QUASS *and the last of the Japanese do a kind of dance, attempting to get past each other, then* QUASS *hurries to catch up with* DANIEL.)

INT. LUIGI'S RESTAURANT. NIGHT

The restaurant is completely empty apart from LUIGI *and the* WAITERS *hanging listlessly about, seen from* DANIEL's *and* QUASS's *point of view as they enter.* LUIGI *and* WAITERS *straighten hopefully.*

LUIGI: (*Inclining from the hips to* DANIEL) Ah, Signor Davenport, *buona sera* –

DANIEL: (*Tensely, looking around*) Evening, Luigi, I gather you're expecting me.

LUIGI: (*Slightly surprised*) Well, you did book, Signor Davenport.

DANIEL: Right. Good.

LUIGI: (*Glancing towards the door*) And how many will you be altogether?

DANIEL: Don't know really, Luigi, there's a chance somebody else might turn up. If so, you know where I am, bring them over, eh?

LUIGI: Might?

DANIEL: Mmmm?

LUIGI: Somebody might turn up?

DANIEL: Yes. If they do, bring them over.

LUIGI: But you're not sure?

DANIEL: (*Testily*) No, but if they do, bring them over, there seems to be plenty of room.
(*He corrects this with a taut smile, goes over to a table, followed by* QUASS.)

QUASS: (*Looking around*) I see what you mean by quiet.
(*Sudden blast of music.*)

DANIEL: (*Jumps.*) Luigi, Luigi – music!
(LUIGI *adjusts the music until it's even louder, then struts away.*)
What the hell – Luigi – Luigi –

QUASS: (*Terrified*) To cover the noise.

DANIEL: What noise?

QUASS: (*Screeching*) Pistol shots. Screams. It's a trap, I tell you, Davenport.

DANIEL: (*Bellowing*) Luigi!
(LUIGI *comes towards him, smiling.*)

LUIGI: Signor Davenport?

DANIEL: The music, Luigi. You know how I feel –

LUIGI: If I want music in my restaurant, I have music in my restaurant. You don't like it, go eat somewhere else, eh? (DANIEL *stares at him in disbelief.*

Losing control) Who do you think you are! You reserve my whole restaurant – my whole restaurant – for the whole evening from seven o'clock, I turn people away, old customers, I cancel reservations and then you come in at nearly nine o'clock and you say, just the two of us, Luigi, somebody might turn up, and you sit down and you tell me, Luigi, off with the music, well, out, get out my restaurant, never again I want to see your face here – eh? Eh? Out, out! Roberto, Angelo, Guiseppe, show these gentlemen the street, show the street –

(*He struts angrily off.*)

INT. DANIEL'S CAR. NIGHT

DANIEL *is driving with just controlled fury with one hand, while from the other he is extracting a sweet from the glove compartment.*

DANIEL: My wife and I have been going there since it opened! We were virtually their first customers! So whatever he was told – however he was tricked – there was no justification – absolutely no justification – for that tone.

QUASS: I know. (*Indignantly*) As if he'd *always* disliked you! (DANIEL *shoots him a sharp look.*

Hurriedly) Where shall we go? Shall we go to your place, then?

DANIEL: Of course not. I told my wife I was going out with an important client. How could I possibly explain *you*?

QUASS: (*Shyly*) Well, it'd better be my place, then, hadn't it?

OLD FLAMES

EXT. QUASS'S HOUSE. NIGHT

Daniel's car is parked in the drive. They are standing at the door,
QUASS *groping for his keys nervously, conscious of* DANIEL's *eye
impatiently on him.*

QUASS: They're here – I know they're here – always in my right-
hand pocket – (*Suddenly slaps his forehead*) – of course!
(*He presses the button.*)

NELLIE: (*Voice over, entry phone*) Who?

QUASS: Nathaniel, Nellie.

NELLIE: (*Voice over, entry phone*) Where are your keys?

QUASS: I forgot to take them out of my trouser pocket.

NELLIE: (*Voice over, entry phone*) Well, remember now and take
them out. Or aren't you wearing trousers?

QUASS: No, no, I mean when I put on one of father's dinner-
jackets, remember. The keys are in my ordinary trousers.

NELLIE: (*Voice over, entry phone*) Just a minute.

QUASS: Nellie, Nellie, where are you going?

NELLIE: (*Voice over, entry phone*) To look in your ordinary
trousers.

QUASS: But you don't need my keys. Just press the button I
showed you and open the door.

NELLIE: (*Voice over, entry phone*) But how do I know it's you
unless I check? You tell me that I have to be careful every
time I open the door these days. You'll be furious with me if
I let you in and it's not you after all –

QUASS: (*Shouting*) Nellie!

NELLIE: (*Voice over, entry phone*) You wait, Nathaniel, don't be
so impatient!
(QUASS *looks at* DANIEL, *whose expression is incredulous, takes
him away from entry phone.*)

QUASS: (*Whispering*) I know. She still thinks of me as a child, she
likes to play games – you see, she's a bit, a bit of a child
herself and – and – Of course I haven't told her anything

about all this. She wouldn't understand that people can be
so cruel and I wouldn't want her to understand –
(NELLIE *opens the door, hands* QUASS *the keys.*)

NELLIE: Now you let yourself in properly like a grown-up
householder –
(*She makes to close the door, sees* DANIEL.)
Oh, my goodness!

QUASS: Yes, Nellie, this is Davenport. Davenport, my sister,
Nellie.

DANIEL: (*Frigidly*) How do you do?

NELLIE: Davenport! This is Davenport! Oh, come in,
Davenport, please.

INT. QUASS'S HOUSE: HALL AND STAIRS. NIGHT

NELLIE: He's talked about you so often, you know, especially
recently, how he's longed to get hold of you again. Come
this way –
(*She leads them through the house, which is opulently furnished,
upstairs, with every so often visible pictures of violin players.*)
So how was the Mozart, did you bump into each other at the
Mozart?

DANIEL: Yes, that's right. The interval.

INT. QUASS'S HOUSE: LIVING ROOM. NIGHT

*A music stand, expensive hi-fi equipment, television and video,
cassettes, etc.*

NELLIE: (*Opening the door*) Here. Sit. What would you like to
drink, Davenport?

DANIEL: Well – what have you got?

NELLIE: Every cordial under the sun. Made by myself.

QUASS: Nellie, Nellie, offer a proper drink, please. There's malt
whisky, gin, vodka –

NELLIE: Where?

QUASS: In the cupboard in my study.

NELLIE: Since when?

QUASS: I got it in last week.

NELLIE: Why?

QUASS: Well, um – (*Embarrassed*) in case we had visitors.

NELLIE: Well, none for you. Cordial for you.

QUASS: (*To* DANIEL) What would you like, Davenport?

DANIEL: Well, actually, a cordial for me too, please.

QUASS: What? Not a Glenfiddich or – Martini, I could make you a Martini. Or a bloody Mary? (*Pleadingly*) Something with rum?

NELLIE: You heard him, Nathaniel. There's strawberry, raspberry, apricot –

DANIEL: Raspberry, please.

NELLIE: (*Triumphantly*) Good choice. For you too, Nathaniel. (*Goes to the drinks.*) And so you're the famous Davenport then, such terrible pranks the two of you got up to. My favourite is the time the two of you climbed through the house master's window and –
(DANIEL *glances at* QUASS, *who is sitting in acute embarrassment, half meeting and half avoiding his eye.*)
Ice, Davenport?

DANIEL: Yes, please.

NELLIE: – put glue on his seat so there he stuck – (*Handing* DANIEL *the drink*) Here, wait, a straw. It's best with a straw.
(*She hands him a straw.*)

DANIEL: Oh. Thank you.

NELLIE: – and then Nathaniel writing all those poems, the rhyming ones, to the senior boys, Jackaboots, he was so happy under your wing. He talks about you in his sleep – (*Handing* QUASS *his drink*) – you know, Davenport. Only the other night I heard him shout out –
(*She turns back to* DANIEL.)

QUASS: (*Cutting across*) Nellie, I think Davenport must be a mite peckish.

NELLIE: (*To* DANIEL) Good. What would you like?

DANIEL: Oh, anything. Anything really.

NELLIE: Then what about sardines in chocolate sauce with whipped cream on top, eh?

DANIEL: Well –

NELLIE: So why say 'anything', Davenport? Give me an order.

DANIEL: Well, if there were some scrambled eggs, for instance.

NELLIE: With smoked salmon.

DANIEL: Thank you.

NELLIE: For you too, Nathaniel. Only no salt. And, of course, no smoked salmon.
(*She exits. There is a pause.*)

QUASS: Of course you were much on my mind.
(NELLIE *puts her head around the door.*)

NELLIE: Oh, a lot of messages for you, Nathaniel. Mr Rosenblum from the Synagogue Commission very angry, he didn't say why, some people in Lewisham who say thank you for the hundred goat's cheeses, what are they for and can they send them back. And Rabbi Harwood – and the wife of the Yiddish playwright about some turkeys you sent for his first night. Why upset with turkeys – the ones they don't want they can freeze or give away –

QUASS: Please, Nellie, please. Davenport's hungry.

NELLIE: Yes, yes, poor Davenport –
(*She exits.*)

QUASS: Rabbi Harwood! Oh, God, he's a monster! (*Sits trembling.*)
What am I going to do, what am I going to do?

DANIEL: Those phone numbers you said you'd got. Of the others on the list. Where are they?

INT. QUASS'S HOUSE: STUDY. NIGHT

Rather dark, the study gives the impression of mustiness and much use. There is a desk, a telephone (antique) on it, a diary open, with not many entries visible ('Phone Jewish Youth Centre, Lambeth re grant', and 'Phone Shoreditch Jewish Amateur Theatricals: re purchase props', etc.) Otherwise clear. On the wall there is an oil painting of the infant Quass playing a violin. DANIEL is sitting at the desk, a page of telephone numbers in one hand, the telephone held to his ear by the other. His eye goes to the diary, takes in the entries.

DANIEL: What do you do?

QUASS: Mmmm?

DANIEL: For a living.

QUASS: Oh, nothing really. Administer a few trusts, charities, Jewish this and that. I've retired, you see.

DANIEL: Retired? At what age?

QUASS: Well, when I left school. Most of this (*Indicating files around the room*) is from my father. He left me certain responsibilities, you see.

(MRS BILLINGTON, *voice over, answers the telephone and gives her number.*)

DANIEL: (*Into telephone*) Oh, hello, can I speak to (*Looks down at sheet*) Mr Billington, please?

MRS BILLINGTON: (*Voice over, telephone*) This is Mrs Billington.

DANIEL: (*Into telephone*) Oh, hello, Mrs Billington. (*Smoothly and confidently*) I'm an old school friend of your husband's, and I was just wondering –

MRS BILLINGTON: (*Voice over, telephone*) He's not here.

DANIEL: (*Into telephone*) Oh, when will he be back, do you know?

MRS BILLINGTON: (*Voice over, telephone*) I've no idea.

DANIEL: (*Into telephone*) I see. Well, thank you very much. (*Hangs up.*) She doesn't know.
(*He dials again.*)

QUASS: Well, at least she was civil with you. When I phoned –
(ROGER COVENEY, *voice over, answers the telephone and gives his number.*)

DANIEL: (*Into telephone*) Is that Mr Coveney?

ROGER COVENEY: (*Voice over, telephone*) No, his son.

DANIEL: (*Into telephone*) Oh, sorry, your voice sounded like your father's. Is he in?
(*Little pause.*)

ROGER COVENEY: (*Voice over, telephone*) Who is it, please?

DANIEL: (*Into telephone*) Just a friend from the old school –

ROGER COVENEY: (*Voice over, telephone*) He's gone away.

DANIEL: (*Into telephone*) Oh, I see. You don't have his number, do you?

ROGER COVENEY: (*Voice over, telephone*) No, goodbye.

DANIEL: (*Into telephone*) Oh. Right, well, thank you – (*Stares at telephone, clearly having been hung up on.*) Apparently his father has left home. No number.

QUASS: But he told you that much. He refused to speak to me.
(DANIEL *telephones again. Hangs up.*)

DANIEL: Number disconnected.

QUASS: Who?

DANIEL: Wardle.
(*He dials again.*)

QUASS: They were connected last week. Abusive but connected. Who are you dialling?

DANIEL: (*Dialling*) Shulman.

QUASS: Oh, she was the worst –
(MRS SHULMAN, *voice over, answers the telephone and gives her number.*)

DANIEL: (*Into telephone*) Oh, hello, can I speak to Mr Shulman, please?
(*Little pause.*)

MRS SHULMAN: (*Voice over, telephone*) Oh, God.

DANIEL: (*Into telephone*) Is that Mrs Shulman? Well, the thing is I'm only in London a few days, *en route* from Dubai to New

322

York, and I suddenly had the urge to look up all my old
school friends, and of course old Shully was top of my list.
We had such times together at Amplesides, we were known
as the Terror Twins, Dangerous Davenport and – and
Suicide Shulman –
(*He laughs.* MRS SHULMAN, *voice over, shrieks.*)
Mrs Shulman, Mrs Shulman, are you there? (*Hangs up.*
Looks at QUASS.) She just let out a sort of shriek and hung up.
(NELLIE *puts her head in through the door.*)
NELLIE: Scrambled eggs and smoked salmon on the table, boys!

INT. QUASS'S HOUSE: KITCHEN. NIGHT

QUASS *picking at food,* NELLIE *not eating,* DANIEL *gobbling down
his food, a jug of orange squash in front of him to which he helps
himself. He swills, guzzles, swills, guzzles.* DANIEL *is suddenly
aware of their gaze upon him,* NELLIE *nodding proudly.*

DANIEL: I – I hadn't realized quite how hungry I was.
NELLIE: But look at Nathaniel, everything on his plate
    untouched. It's like nursing a sparrow, what a joy it is to
    have a real forksman in the house at last, so tell me, what is
    your second name, Davenport?
DANIEL: Um, well, Davenport as a matter of fact.
NELLIE: What! So you're Davenport Davenport? My heavens!
DANIEL: No, I'm Daniel Davenport.
NELLIE: You're Daniel! How come then you always call him
    Davenport? Just Davenport?
QUASS: Well, at school that's how we called each other, Nellie. I
    was Quass, he was Davenport –
NELLIE: But now you're grown-ups, call each other Mr Quass,
    Mr Davenport, or Daniel Nathaniel, why not?
    (QUASS *looks at* DANIEL *shyly.*)
    I mean, to think I've been going around calling you
    Davenport –

(*She lets out a scream of laughter.* DANIEL, *almost against his will, lets out a little laugh.* QUASS *laughs with pleasure, but shyly.*)

Now, Daniel, have you finished, what more would you like, plum pie?

DANIEL: Well – well, er – (*Little laugh.*) Thank you.

NELLIE: With a scoop of ice-cream.

(*Cut to* DANIEL *putting in the last spoonful of pudding.*)

DANIEL: That was delicious. Thank you.

(NELLIE *plonks a cup of coffee in front of him, and a bowl with lumps of chocolate in it.* DANIEL *looks at it.*)

NELLIE: Chocolate. Don't be put off by its shape, it's homemade. And now Nathaniel will give you your spiritual pudding. Won't you, Nathaniel?

QUASS: Oh, no. Nellie, really –

NELLIE: Feed the stomach. Then the soul. Would you send him on his way with an empty soul, Nathaniel?

QUASS: (*Seriously*) Nellie, I'm not sure I can.

NELLIE: (*Gently, understandingly*) I think you must try, Nathaniel. I think you must try. (*To* DANIEL, *seriously*) You're a married man, aren't you, Daniel?

DANIEL: Yes.

NELLIE: There, I could tell. And children, have you children?

DANIEL: No – well, yes, my wife is pregnant.

NELLIE: And do you want a boy or a girl?

DANIEL: Well, both actually. She's going to have twins.

NELLIE: Twins! (*Claps her hands.*) So for Daniel's wife and her twins, Nathaniel, you must.

(*Cut to* QUASS'*s face as, over, violin music. Then take in* QUASS, *seen full-length from* DANIEL'*s point of view, playing the violin, exquisitely. Then take in* NELLIE, *her face aglow with love, watching him, and then take in* DANIEL, *concealing impatience initially, then seduced by the music, popping chocolate into his mouth as he listens.* QUASS, *in a tricky, lyrical passage, eyes closed in concentration. Suddenly his face shows*

324

*distress. He is clearly having trouble breathing, doesn't quite get
to the end of the passage, stops suddenly in despair, goes to chair
and sits down, wheezing, fumbles out his inhaler, recovers his
breath before he needs to use it.*)
QUASS: I'm sorry. (*Desolated*) Sorry, Davenport.
(NELLIE *goes to* QUASS, *kneels beside him, pats his hand.*)
NELLIE: No, I'm sorry, my love. Sorry I made you. I was sure it
would be all right – (*Turns to* DANIEL.) He would have been
a great concert player! A great one! But before an audience
it always happens. I hoped that, with such an old friend, it
would leave him alone for once. For me every night he plays
like an angel.
DANIEL: (*Awkwardly*) Yes, well, um, for me tonight you
certainly played – (*Gestures. Glances at his watch.*) Now I
really ought to be – um –
(*He looks pointedly at* QUASS.)

INT. QUASS'S HOUSE: STAIRS. NIGHT

QUASS: (*Whispering urgently*) What are we going to do, Daniel?
(*As they get to the front door,* DANIEL *turns.*)

EXT. QUASS'S HOUSE: FRONT DOOR. NIGHT

DANIEL: Something very obvious. Get a private detective, of
course. Ask him to check on the names, find out where they
are, what's happened to them. It shouldn't take a good one
long.
(*Above, the sound of the telephone ringing.* QUASS *glances up
apprehensively.*)
QUASS: When will you do that?
DANIEL: You'll have to do it. I'm in court tomorrow.
QUASS: But a private detective – how do I know a private
detective?
NELLIE: (*Voice over, entry phone*) Nathaniel, Nathaniel, you still

down there, Mrs Mossberg is on the phone. To thank you
for your present. She sounds very angry.

QUASS: Oh, God, what did I send her!

DANIEL: There's one called Jackson. Frank Jackson. He does a
lot of work for solicitors. They say he's very efficient. But of
course he'll know my name so don't mention me.

QUASS: How do I get hold of him?

DANIEL: He'll be in the phone book. The moment you find out
anything – anything at all – let me know.

NELLIE: (*Voice over, entry phone*) Nathaniel, come now for Mrs
Mossberg. Also for your chest. Daniel, send him up straight
away.

QUASS: Just coming, Nellie, just coming.

DANIEL: Here's the number of my chamber. (*Scribbling it down
on a piece of paper, handing it to* QUASS) They'll know which
court I'm in.

NELLIE: (*Voice over, entry phone*) I count to ten, then I come and
get you.

DANIEL: Have you got that? The moment you find out anything,
get in touch.

(QUASS *nods.*)

Right.

(*He turns, hurries off.*)

QUASS: Good night, Daniel.

INT. DANIEL'S HOUSE: STUDY. NIGHT

DANIEL *enters quietly, turns on desk light, checks for messages on the
answering machine. There is one. He opens the sweet drawer, takes
out a sweet, and is about to play back the message when he hears a
noise from the shadows.* DANIEL *freezes, then very carefully swivels
the desk light towards the corner. There is a little cry and
simultaneously we take in that the light has hit* SOPHIE, *who has
clearly been asleep, full in the face. She is wearing her nightdress,
dressing gown, slippers.*

DANIEL: What are you doing in here, Bootsie?

SOPHIE: (*Drowsy, in a baby voice.*) I always come and sit here when you're away and I miss you, Popsie. Because it's so full of you. Do you mind me doing that?

DANIEL: (*Taking her hand*) No, no, of course not, my love.

SOPHIE: And I've been so worried. Where have you been, Popsie?

DANIEL: Why – with that Turk I told you about, the one who wants me to defend him on a currency charge. I phoned you about him, don't you remember me saying I'd be late?

SOPHIE: Of course, I remember. I thought you said he was a Greek.

DANIEL: Well, yes – but resident in Turkey.

SOPHIE: And you said you were going to have dinner in the Garrick.

DANIEL: Well, we met at the Garrick. Then decided to go off somewhere else for dinner. But why, Bootsie, I mean how did you know that we didn't stay at the Garrick?

SOPHIE: Because they phoned to say you'd left.

DANIEL: The Garrick phoned to say I'd left? Why on earth would they do that?

SOPHIE: Because they wanted to know where you were. Apparently there was a little herd of Japanese lawyers milling about in the entrance hall saying that you'd invited them to dinner. They even had invitation cards with your name on it. Apparently it was all a terrible fuss. The man who spoke to me was really quite angry. Quite rude even, Popsie.

DANIEL: How – how preposterous! (*Attempts a laugh.*) Obviously some mistake. Probably confused me with another Davenport. There're several Davenports at the Garrick. I'll phone tomorrow and put it right. And I'll certainly have a word with them about the way they spoke to you. I won't put up with that sort of thing. But come, Bootsie, let's get you upstairs to bed.

(*He assists her up.*)

SOPHIE: No, no, play your message.

DANIEL: It can wait.

SOPHIE: No, do it now so you won't have to come down again. Then you can give me a backy rub.

(DANIEL *hesitates, then winds back the tape, plays the message.*)

WOMAN PHOTOGRAPHER: (*Voice over*) Oh, Daniel dear, what is that mess that looks like strawberry jam? Hush, hush, my love, it's poor Hopjoy run over by a – (DANIEL *switches the machine off. Cut to* SOPHIE, *looking bewildered.*)

DANIEL: I told you it was nothing important.

SOPHIE: But who was it?

DANIEL: Just Hopjoy. His way of apologizing for missing our meeting. Got stuck in the traffic, you see.

INT/EXT. CAR. NIGHT

Cut to MAN *lying dead, neck broken, on rear seat. Cut to* DAVINA *in front passenger seat, eyes transfixed. Cut to* DANIEL *behind the wheel, driving in a state of panic,* DAVINA *beside him in a state of shock. He glances into the mirror and we see from his point of view another car in the mirror.*

EXT. MILE END ROAD. NIGHT

Cut to corpse spread out on Mile End Road. Completely silent. Cut to DANIEL *and* DAVINA *in the car, staring towards the corpse. Over the sound of a juggernaut approaching. Cut to the juggernaut driving towards the corpse. Cut to* DAVINA, *mouth opening in a scream.*

INT. DANIEL'S HOUSE: BEDROOM. NIGHT

Cut to DANIEL *sitting up in bed, blinking. He puts his hands to his eyes as we hear slight noise over and see* SOPHIE, *snoring slightly, which is rather like the noise of a juggernaut approaching in the distance.*

INT. COURT CORRIDOR. DAY

STRAUSS, DANIEL, ZELDA *coming out of court, but we come straight in on* DANIEL *in his wig, looking slightly unfocused.*

STRAUSS: (*Out of shot*) Are you all right?

DANIEL: (*Blinks*) Yes, yes, just rather a bad night, thank you. Why?
    (*Cut to* STRAUSS *stopping in the corridor.*)

STRAUSS: Well, I was just wondering if it was a ploy or you really did get his name wrong.

DANIEL: Whose?

STRAUSS: Detective Sergeant Cooper's.
    (DANIEL *stares at him blankly, and we see beyond other people coming out of court, among them* COOKSON.)

ZELDA: (*Apologetically*) You kept calling him Detective Inspector Copper.

DANIEL: Merely a slip of the tongue.

STRAUSS: And Cropper. You also called him Cropper.

ZELDA: Some of the jury thought it was funny, anyway. Copper and Cropper for Cooper.

STRAUSS: (*Upset*) The judge didn't. There's Cookson, we better go and talk to him. Let him know our strategy. He looks a bit – um – concerned.
    (*As* STRAUSS *speaks, an usher comes up to* DANIEL.)

USHER: Mr Davenport? Telephone.

DANIEL: (*To* STRAUSS) I'll be right back.
    (*He hurries to the telephone, picks it up.*)
    Hello, Davenport here.
    (*Little pause.*)

QUASS: (*Voice over, telephone*) It's awful, Davenport. Awful.

DANIEL: Well, go on, tell me.

QUASS: (*Voice over, telephone*) I can't on the phone. It's a call box and I've only got one 10p and there's somebody else waiting.

DANIEL: Well, where are you then?

QUASS: (*Voice over, telephone*) A pub. The Rising Sun, Euston Road.

DANIEL: Euston Road! (*Looking at his watch*) All right. Stay there, I'll be right over.

(*He hangs up, comes out of the kiosk, makes to go, then sees* STRAUSS, ZELDA *and* COOKSON *staring at him.* DANIEL *goes over.*)

Look, something's come up. (*Hurrying to the door*) But don't worry, I'll be there in time to cook Cookson's goose.

STRAUSS: *Mr* Cookson is our client.

EXT. STREET NEAR LAWCOURT. DAY

DANIEL *trying to get a taxi, gown and wig over his arm. He carries them throughout the next sequence.*

EXT. THE RISING SUN. DAY

DANIEL *getting out of the taxi, entering the pub.*

INT. THE RISING SUN. DAY

It is crowded, as for lunchtime. QUASS *is not immediately visible.* DANIEL *stares around. The door to the gents opens.* QUASS's *head appears. He beckons to* DANIEL. DANIEL *goes to lavatory urinal, etc. It appears to be empty. Then* QUASS *opens the lavatory door.*

QUASS: In here.

(DANIEL *goes to the entrance.*)

INT. THE RISING SUN: LAVATORY. DAY

QUASS *is sitting on the lavatory, seat down.*

DANIEL: What the hell are you doing?

QUASS: The smoke. Nearly killed me. The news is terrible,
Davenport, terrible!
(*As he fumbles sheets out of his pocket.*)

DANIEL: Yes, you've already told me that, get on with it. I've
only got a few minutes.
(*The sound of the door opening, footsteps.* DANIEL *closes the
door, locks it. The following conversation is conducted in
whispers.*)
Well, go on, go on!
(*He attempts to take the sheet from* QUASS's *hand.*)

QUASS: Coveney, Billington, Cropper, Wardle are in gaol. Just
like Jackaboots.

DANIEL: Gaol!

QUASS: That's how your Mr Jackson found out so quickly.
Phoned the school for their initials (*Talking slightly
hysterically*) then phoned a friend of his on a newspaper just
on the offchance, and they all came up on the computer.
One after the other.

DANIEL: But – but what did they do?

QUASS: Billington tried to smuggle drugs into Turkey. Cropper's
doing five years for misappropriation. He was a solicitor.
Coveney and Wardle are doing five and three years
respectively. Wardle was party to a swindle connected with
a children's charity. Coveney was a hit-and-run case. Wiped
out a couple of pensioners and a social worker.
(*Cut to* DANIEL, *deeply disturbed.*)
And look – I've worked it out – the lines and blocks – that's
what the blocks mean. Gaol. And three lines for Jackaboy
on his way to gaol. A line for you on your way to gaol. And
Shulman – the crosses for me and Shulman – (*Voice shaking*)

are for death. Shulman flung himself under a train at Archway tube station. So now we know why Mrs Shulman sobbed when she hung up on you. Suicide Shulman committed suicide. (*Whinnies with terrified laughter.*) So either they drove him mad –

DANIEL: (*Dully*) Like Jackaboots.

QUASS: Or they pushed him under the train. And that's what they've got in mind for me. Cross cross cross cross Quass.

DANIEL: (*Looks at watch*) I've got to get back.

(*He turns towards the door. There is a terrible wheezing sound from* QUASS. DANIEL *turns.* QUASS *clutches his chest, collapses back, fumbles out his inhaler, drops it, is gasping so much that he can't grope for it.* DANIEL, *momentarily torn between leaving and helping, picks up spray.* QUASS's *arms are hanging limp, his mouth agape. His wheeze is frightening.* DANIEL *bends over him and squirts spray into his mouth.* QUASS *recovers slowly. Cut from* QUASS's *face to* DANIEL's, *impatient.*)

Are you all right?

(*He looks at him.* QUASS *nods, clearly enfeebled.*)

Can you get up?

QUASS: Yes, yes. You go. (*He gestures weakly.*)

DANIEL: (*Hesitates*) Come on, I'll get you into a taxi.

(*He helps* QUASS *up. His wig is completely askew.* DANIEL *opens the door just as a* MAN *passing, unzipping his flies, stares in.* DANIEL *half supports* QUASS *out of lavatory.*)

QUASS: It's very kind of you, Davenport.

(*A couple of* OTHER MEN, *peeing, watch.*)

EXT. THE RISING SUN. DAY

It is now raining. Several occupied taxis go by, although DANIEL *still gestures at them desperately. One comes along with the 'for hire' sign on.* DANIEL *signals to it, all the time supporting* QUASS. *The* TAXI DRIVER *slows down, sees* QUASS, *speeds off.*

DANIEL: What the – he must have thought you were drunk. Can't you stand up properly, man? And put your – (*gestures to his head*) – your – back.

(QUASS *adjusts his wig, tries to stand up. Another taxi appears, stops.* DANIEL *helps* QUASS *into it.* QUASS *gets into it shakily.*)

QUASS: (*As he does so, tremulously*) But what are we going to do?

DANIEL: (*Seeing another taxi approach*) I'll come round – I'll come round this evening.

(*He shuts the door, signals to the taxi which goes on past him. Cut to shot of* DANIEL *on pavement, shaking his fist at retreating taxi, then shaking his wig and gown despairingly towards another, occupied, taxi.*)

INT. CORRIDOR/COURT. DAY

The doors of the courtroom, seen from DANIEL's *point of view, as he races towards them, struggling into his barrister's togs which are now wet, his wig bedraggled, and take in from his point of view* STRAUSS *turning, staring in suppressed anger, while* ZELDA *is rising to her feet.* ZELDA *turns.* DANIEL, *advancing to the defence table, takes the papers from her hand.*

DANIEL: Beg the court's um – sorry I'm late, m'lud. Um – may I proceed with the witness? (*Going straight on*) Now, Detector Inspective – Detective Inspector (*Then carefully*) Cooper –

JUDGE: (*Out of shot, courteously*) Detective Inspector Cooper has left the stand. This is Detective Inspector Sowerboy.

DANIEL: Indeed, m'lud.

(*He looks down at papers in his hand in evident bewilderment, then desperately fakes a cough.*)

Excuse me, m'lud, a touch of – a touch of – (*coughs slightly again*) – some water, please.

(*He turns to* ZELDA *and* STRAUSS.)

333

INT. COURT CORRIDOR. DAY

DANIEL, ZELDA, STRAUSS *walking along the corridor in silence.*

ZELDA: I thought you had him backing away at the end. (*To* STRAUSS) Didn't you?

STRAUSS: Yes. (*As they approach room*) Perhaps he thought the cough was contagious.

DANIEL: Look – I – I don't think I should speak any more this evening.

STRAUSS: You mean, not to Cookson?

DANIEL: Cookson?

STRAUSS: Our client!

DANIEL: Not to anyone.

STRAUSS: But he needs to hear your view.

DANIEL: Oh, for God's sake, Strauss, if a chap's losing his voice, he's losing his voice. Surely he'll understand that. Just tell him I can't speak, for God's sake! (*Bellowing*) My voice has gone, damn it!

(DANIEL *goes to the telephone booth. He picks up the telephone, dials.* SOPHIE, *voice over, answers, giving her telephone number.*)

How are you all?

SOPHIE: (*Voice over, telephone*) I've got a backy and cramps in the tum.

DANIEL: Oh, cramps, really? Well, the thing is, my lovey, to lie on the floor and lift your –

SOPHIE: (*Voice over, telephone*) Do you think it's started? Come home soon.

DANIEL: What? No, no, it can't be, not for another three weeks at least, eh? But, um, but that Greek I met last night –

SOPHIE: (*Voice over, telephone*) I thought he was Turkish.

DANIEL: Well, yes, Turk but resident in Greece, if you remember. (*Pauses as if not quite sure he's got it right.*) Anyway, Greek or Turk or whatever he is, Greek resident in Turkey or Turkey resident in Greek –

(*He catches sight of* COOKSON, STRAUSS, *and* ZELDA *coming down the corridor.* COOKSON, STRAUSS *and* ZELDA *approach the telephone booth,* COOKSON *indignant. As they pass,* DANIEL *is mouthing kisses down the telephone.*)

INT. QUASS'S HOUSE: LIVING ROOM. NIGHT

We come in on newspaper clippings spread out on the desk, DANIEL's *hand pushing them around and we see from clipping to clipping with headlines:* GRANTHAM SOLICITOR GAOLED; KIDDIES' HEARTACHE AS CHARITY CON MAN GOES TO GAOL; ARCHWAY STOCKBROKER INQUEST. WIFE DENIES SUICIDE; ACCOUNTANT HELD IN TURKISH HELL-HOLE; *and then* DARBY, JOAN, MISS DUTIFUL — MASSACRE AT THE CROSSROADS.

DANIEL: (*Out of shot*) I can't tell anything from these. Just the usual journalist's nonsense. 'Remained unmoved'; 'Broke down and wept', etc.

QUASS: (*Out of shot*) But five boys out of one house from one school. All gaoled over the last six months for different offences. And Shulman's suicide.

DANIEL: (*Out of shot*) Yes.
(DANIEL *lays aside the newspaper cuttings, and helps himself to a piece of fudge in the bowl beside him.*)

QUASS: (*Tentatively*) That Miss Wright in your message? Is that something you could go to gaol for?
(DANIEL, *after a pause, nods.*)

DANIEL: The bit missing from your message. Is it something you might commit suicide because of?
(QUASS, *after a pause, nods. There is a long pause. They stare at each other.*)

QUASS: I tell, you tell. That was the agreement.

DANIEL: What did your message say, Nathaniel?

QUASS: It said. (*Draws breath.*) It said: 'Poor old Emmanuel. Bowled out by Nathaniel.'

DANIEL: Who's Emmanuel?

QUASS: My brother. Older brother. Eleven years older.

DANIEL: What does it mean, 'bowled out by Nathaniel'?

QUASS: I bowled him out of the window. (*Points to french windows*) Killed him.

DANIEL: Why?

QUASS: He was trying to teach me the rules of cricket.

DANIEL: And that's why you killed him?

QUASS: Yes – no – I mean he was different from Nellie and me. Made himself into a perfect English type. Tall. Slim. Muscular. A head of hair. So, of course, he was accepted into the best public school. No mere Amplesides for him. One afternoon I was in here, scraping away at the violin, in he came, with a cricket bat. 'Now,' he said. 'Let me show you.' I said, 'Come on. Emmanuel, I'm practising violin, not cricket.' He said, 'It's time you bloody learnt the rules and the fundamentals of the game, at least.' 'I don't want to know about cricket,' I said. 'I'm happy with this.' Showing him my bow. He snatched it away from me and I tried to snatch it back and it went into his eye and suddenly there he was running backwards, skipping and jumping backwards, yowling, swinging his bat, right through the windows, over the porch, on to the terrace on to his head. It was an accident, Davenport.

DANIEL: Have you ever told anyone?

QUASS: I had a collapse. Nellie had to put me in hospital. I don't know what I said to the doctors, the other patients.

(DANIEL *shakes his head.*)

DANIEL: (*Gently*) You're lying, Quass.

QUASS: What, you think I killed him on purpose?

DANIEL: No. I expect it was an accident all right. That's why it doesn't make sense. It's nothing for you to commit suicide for. After all these years. But you might commit suicide to protect Nellie.

(QUASS *bows his head.*)

336

QUASS: It happened just as I said. (*Little pause.*) He took away my bow. Nellie was just trying to get it back.

DANIEL: And that's what you might have told the doctors, the other patients? That Nellie killed him?

(QUASS *looks at him pathetically, nods. There is a pause.*)

QUASS: (*Tentatively*) So. So what about you, Davenport? No death in it, I hope?

DANIEL: Yes. Death in it.

QUASS: But you – you haven't killed anyone?

(DANIEL *puts another piece of fudge in his mouth abstractedly.*)

DANIEL: (*Slowly and painfully, chewing*) As a matter of fact, yes.

QUASS: (*After a little pause*) Miss Wright?

DANIEL: Her husband.

QUASS: You killed Miss Wright's husband?

DANIEL: She wasn't Miss Wright then. She was Mrs Hopjoy. Before that she was Miss Wright. Then later – after I killed her husband – she went back to being Miss Wright again. He was a university lecturer. He taught social sciences. No, social studies. One of those useless subjects –

(*He gestures. There is a pause.*)

QUASS: (*Waits.*) But that's not why you killed him? Because he taught a useless subject?

DANIEL: He was unbalanced, you see. Definitely unbalanced. When he somehow got wind that she and I were – he became very possessive. Very jealous.

QUASS: Well, isn't that, um, normal? With husbands. When their wives –

DANIEL: He wasn't her husband. Not when I came on the scene. Except in name. He'd left her a couple of years before. For one of his students. Several of his students as a matter of fact. But he still felt he had a claim on Davina. Used to follow her. And me. I have an idea he actually employed private detectives – anyway . . . (*Pause.*) He gave me no choice.

QUASS: (*Encouragingly*) How did you do it?

337

DANIEL: I – ran over him.

QUASS: (*Nods.*) Ran him over.

DANIEL: No, I didn't run him over. I ran over him. Quite
different.

QUASS: Yes? In what respect?

DANIEL: One night I roared up to her door and felt this bump. A
sort of soft bump. So I looked under the wheels. And there
he was. He must've just laid himself out on the street and –
waited for me to go over him. It was suicide really. But at
my expense. Of course I should have gone to the police. But
then he was the husband, I was the lover, Davina was the
only witness, nobody would have believed – although I
don't know. I've discovered since then that juries can be
very perverse. I might have got one that believed the truth.
Especially with a good QC. Carstairs, for instance. He was
in his prime then. Before he took to buying race horses –
but still it would have ruined me, even if I'd been acquitted.
I'd certainly never have had the slightest chance of ending
up a judge.

QUASS: So that's what you want, is it?

DANIEL: Well, one day – it's possible – was possible.
(QUASS *nods.*)

QUASS: (*After a little pause*) What did you do?

DANIEL: Got his body into the car and drove it down to the Mile
End Road. Left it outside his college. Queen Mary College.
Lots of traffic, you see. Especially at dawn. Apparently
quite a lot of it went over him before anyone noticed – so he
was quite hard to identify. Took them weeks.

QUASS: How long ago did this happen?

DANIEL: Nine years ago. Ten. Ten years ago. June 6th, 1979.

QUASS: Well, even if you were followed, they wouldn't wait ten
years, would they?

DANIEL: No, they wouldn't. It must be somebody who's found
out *now*. Look – let's look at the whole thing logically.
There must be a motive. What are the usual motives for

338

destroying people? Money? But they haven't asked for
money. Revenge?

QUASS: (*Breaking out suddenly*) But why death for me and
Shulman, and only gaol for you and Jackaboots? And the
rest. You know why. (*As if realizing*) I'll tell you why.
Because Shulman and I are Jewish. That's why! It's
discrimination.

(DANIEL *shakes his head.*)

How do you know?

DANIEL: Because I'm Jewish. And as they know everything else
about me, they're bound to know that, aren't they?

QUASS: (*Astonished*) You're Jewish?

(DANIEL *nods.*)

But I used to see you going into chapel every morning, to
sing hymns, why, you even got confirmed, didn't you?

DANIEL: Yes. But it didn't mean anything. For some reason
everyone assumed I was of C. of E. And of course I never
quite got around to explaining – I just did what the others
did.

QUASS: (*Muttering*) Well, one does have to conform. Or try to. As
they say.

DANIEL: What?

QUASS: And are you still C. of E.?

DANIEL: No, of course not.

QUASS: Jewish again, then?

DANIEL: I regard myself first and foremost as a barrister.

QUASS: Well, shortly you may be regarding yourself as a
gaolbird.

(NELLIE *enters, carrying two letters and a bowl of toffee.*)

NELLIE: Here you are, one each, delivered by hand. Isn't that
nice?

QUASS: (*Taking his letter*) Where – where did you get these?

NELLIE: From the mat, of course. I saw them lying on it when I
was coming to give Daniel a refill. I knew he'd be ready for
one. (*Putting down bowl*) This time, toffee, Daniel. Give

your jaws something to work on. Well, go on, why don't
you open them? Who are they from?

(QUASS *and* DANIEL *open their letters.*)

QUASS: (*As he does so*) Oh, chaps from the old school that
Davenport and I have asked to help in a little charity
project. I'll tell you about it later, Nellie.

NELLIE: As long as it's not goat's cheeses and frozen turkeys to
people who don't want them, eh, Daniel?

(NELLIE *exits. There is a pause.*)

QUASS: What's – what's yours?

DANIEL: Mostly it's a signed statement from (*Looks at end*)
Mavis and Donald Carper. (*Frowns as if a hint of memory
at the name.*) Private investigators working on behalf of
Geoffrey Hopjoy – (*His eye skimming through text*) –
assigned to watch his wife, Davina Hopjoy's residence –
did witness the death of our client, Geoffrey Hopjoy, at
one a.m. June 6th, 1979 – they say – they say I did it
on purpose! Swerved on to the pavement – hit him –
reversed over him – several times – (*Voice shaking*) –
followed me to the forecourt of Queen Mary College,
University of London – they've got – they say they've
got photographs which they will send with a copy of this
statement to the police, the bar association, every
national newspaper, and to Mrs Davina Hopjoy *née*
Wright, unless I comply with their instructions, which
are *en route*. (*Looks up at* QUASS.) And yours?

QUASS: Signed statements from people at one of the – the homes
I had to stay in. That I said that – that Nellie had killed
Emmanuel. (*Looks at* DANIEL, *stricken.*) How could I, oh
how could I – copies will be sent to Miss Nellie Quass to –
(*Counting*) – every rabbi in London, and the Chief Rabbi of
Leeds – why Leeds? And the police of course. Unless I
comply with their instructions which are *en route*.

(*They stare at each other.*)

Instructions for what? Instructions to me to commit suicide?

Instructions to you to get yourself sent to gaol? What can
they want, Davenport?

(*Doorbell rings.* QUASS *and* DANIEL *look at each other.* QUASS
gets up, goes over to the window, looks down. DANIEL *joins
him. We see from* QUASS's *and* DANIEL's *point of view a*
MESSENGER *in helmet, goggles and gauntlets, holding two
envelopes. The door opens. The* MESSENGER *hands over the two
envelopes and a board with pencil. The board is handed back.
The* MESSENGER *continues to stand there with the board.*)
What's going on? What's she doing? Why's he still there?

(*The* MESSENGER *takes off a gauntlet, bends forward towards
the doorway, takes something between his fingers, puts it in his
mouth, nods, turns. We see from* DANIEL's *point of view the*
MESSENGER *stopping for a moment, putting his finger in his
mouth, trying to fish something out with his finger, gives up. The*
MESSENGER *goes around the corner. Sound of motorbike over
the sound of* NELLIE *coming upstairs.*)

NELLIE: (*Out of shot*) Two more! One for each of you. (*Enters.*)
Oh, look at you, such friends you've become all over again.
(*Gives them an envelope each.*) After these years – too many
years you don't see each other – what I want is you bring your
wife and twins around, Daniel, all of us together –
(*She is becoming emotional, turns, goes out hurriedly.* DANIEL *and*
QUASS *rip open their envelopes.* QUASS *stares at* DANIEL *radiantly.*)

QUASS: Money. Only money they want. And so little. (*Claps his
hands.*) Who would have believed it!

DANIEL: How much?

QUASS: Twenty thousand, that's all. And you?

DANIEL: (*Ashen, not sharing* QUASS's *jubilation*) Twenty-five
thousand. (*Repeats*) Twenty-five thousand. (*Reading*) The
monies will be in denominations of five-pound notes. We
will take delivery at the gate to platform ten, Waterloo
Station, at one p.m. tomorrow. You will carry for both
parties. There will be a telephone call immediately after
receipt of this communication with further details.

QUASS: (*Reads*) You will accompany the carrier to Waterloo
Station and then wait at the gate of platform nine until the
transaction is completed.

(DANIEL *puts a toffee into his mouth.*)

Once you have begun the journey to Waterloo Station you
will not make any contact with the monies. You will also
control your wheezing and so avoid making a public
spectacle of yourself. There will be a telephone call
immediately on receipt of this communication giving further
details.

(*The telephone rings.* QUASS *reaches for telephone, goes on
reading,* CARPER *is on the other end.*)

Which your accomplice must answer.

(QUASS *hands the telephone to* DANIEL.)

Answer it, Davenport, answer it.

(DANIEL, *struggling desperately with the toffee in his mouth,
makes gagging noises down the telephone of* 'Yes', 'I understand',
and 'Right'. QUASS *snatches the telephone from him.*)

(*Babblingly*) I'm sorry for my friend, his mouth is full of
toffee.

(DANIEL, *swallowing the toffee, snatches the telephone back.*)

DANIEL: Hello, yes. (*Listens.*) Yes, yes, I've got all that, but
listen – please – (*listens*) – you've already said all that, a man
in a green cap, yes, but how – (*listens*) yes, I've got it –
(*Looks at* QUASS.) He keeps repeating the same thing.

QUASS: It must be a recording.

DANIEL: Oh. (*Listens again as the voice goes metallically on.*)
Yes – (*He puts the telephone down.*)

QUASS: What did he say?

DANIEL: (*Listlessly*) That a man in a green cap would be waiting
at the gate to the platform. I'm to identify myself by saying,
'I'm carrying the agreed sum. Here it is.' Then I give it to
him and say, 'Thank you. Goodbye.' So – so just common
criminals after all. We ought to go – (*tries to draw himself up*)
– we have a duty to go. To the police.

342

QUASS: The police! (*Squawking*) The police – when they've got
  this – (*Shaking his statements*) – if anything happened to
  Nellie – they're right. I'd – I'd kill myself.

DANIEL: But they're just blackmailers and everybody knows
  blackmailers never stop after the first payment. In fact it
  encourages them to go on. I defended a chap once. An
  absolute swine. He blackmailed illegal immigrants. Charged
  them *weekly*. That's the way they operate.

QUASS: What happened to him?

DANIEL: Oh. I got him off.

QUASS: And the illegal immigrants. What happened to them?

DANIEL: They got sent back to – (*Remembers where they got sent
  back to*) – a country recognized by Her Majesty's
  Government. (*Slams his hand down on the desk.*) For God's
  sake, Quass, what does it matter what happened to them,
  what matters is, what matters is – (*Swelling, then subsiding*) –
  what matters is I haven't got twenty-five thousand pounds.
  Not available in cash, anyway.

QUASS: (*Disbelieving*) But surely you could raise it?

DANIEL: Not easily. I've got commitments – the mortgage,
  heavy insurance. And the car, of course. That bloody car.
  Why did I ever allow myself? Bootsie warned me. But
  everything was beginning to go so well. More and more
  cases. Getting quite a reputation at last. (*Stops.*) Of course,
  if they give me time, three weeks, a month. (*Pause. Gets
  up.*) I'd better go. I've got to be in court tomorrow. Possibly
  for the last time, eh? Or rather the last time in a professional
  capacity. The next time I suppose I'll be in the dock. And
  now I must go home to my wife. (*Looks at* QUASS.) Good
  luck for tomorrow. I'll be – be very pleased for you if it's the
  end of it. My best to Nellie.
  (*He turns, goes out.* QUASS *sits for a moment, then gets up, hurries
  out. We see* DANIEL *just about to go out through the door.*)

QUASS: Wait – wait a minute, Davenport!
  (*He hurries down.*)

343

EXT. QUASS'S HOUSE. NIGHT

DANIEL, *who has stepped outside, turns.* QUASS *closes the door behind him.*

QUASS: (*In a low voice*) You're giving up? Just because you haven't got the money?

DANIEL: What else can I do if I haven't got the money? By tomorrow, remember, one p.m.

QUASS: Ssssh. (*Points to entry phone.*) You could ask me.

DANIEL: (*Relief visible*) But I – I might not be able to repay it for years.

QUASS: Repay when you can. If you can't, don't.
(DANIEL *makes to speak emotionally. Checks himself.*)

DANIEL: (*Formally*) It's really very good of you, Quass.

QUASS: No, it's not. It's easy. Easy isn't good. Simply easy.

DANIEL: (*Smiling*) That sounded – sounded extremely like Nellie.

QUASS: Then I was at my best. Money I can afford. More of this – (*Putting his hand to chest, shakes his head.*) So no more about the money except what we've got to do tomorrow. I'll go to the bank and draw out forty-five thousand pounds in cash –
(DANIEL *flinches slightly*)
– and then meet you. Where do I meet you?

DANIEL: I've got to be in court until twelve thirty. Old Bailey. Court number five. We should just do it from there to Waterloo.

QUASS: I'll come in a hired car. We'll go straight on –

DANIEL: No, by tube. The traffic at lunchtime – we're much safer by tube. Don't forget to take a bag – a big one –

QUASS: Two. I'll take two. Forty-five thousand in fivers –

NELLIE: (*Voice over, entry phone*) Is that you two whispering away down there?

QUASS: Just saying good night, Nellie.

NELLIE: (*Voice over, entry phone*) What about a good night to me, shame to you, Daniel.
DANIEL: Sorry, Nellie. Good night.
    (*They shake hands.*)
QUASS: (*Solemnly*) Tomorrow then.
DANIEL: Tomorrow then. And – thank you, Nathaniel.

EXT. DANIEL'S HOUSE. NIGHT

DANIEL *arriving in front of his house. One light on in the sitting room. He opens the front door.*

INT. DANIEL'S HOUSE: HALL. NIGHT

Slightly eerie sensation. DANIEL *composes himself, goes upstairs, opens sitting-room door.*

INT. DANIEL'S HOUSE: SITTING ROOM. NIGHT

The television is on. There are signs of recent lolling on the sofa, but the room is empty. DANIEL *sees the study door half open, light on. He goes in.*

INT. DANIEL'S HOUSE: STUDY. NIGHT

DANIEL: Bootsie?
    (*It is empty. He sees one message on the machine. He turns, goes out, goes on up to the bedroom.*)

INT. DANIEL'S HOUSE: BEDROOM. NIGHT

Clothes spilled across the floor. Bed unmade. DANIEL, *clearly getting anxious, goes to bathroom. It is empty.*

OLD FLAMES

INT. DANIEL'S HOUSE. NIGHT

Montage:
DANIEL opening door on twins' room.
Calling, 'Bootsie! Bootsie!' with increasing desperation as he goes on to kitchen, laundry room.
He goes back to the sitting room, panic-stricken.
Enters the study again.

INT. DANIEL'S HOUSE: STUDY. NIGHT

DANIEL *sees the telephone answering machine, is about to go out, then stops, turns, plays the message.*

SOPHIE: (*On machine, pathetically*) Oh, Popsie, I didn't know
    where to get hold of you. You didn't even leave a number.
    I've tried everywhere, and now they're coming to get me
    and you won't even be there to help –
    (*The message is obviously continuing, but:*)

INT. HOSPITAL CORRIDOR. NIGHT

DANIEL, *hurrying down hospital corridor to maternity-ward desk. A*
NURSE *or whatever is sitting at it, crisp-looking, efficient.*

DANIEL: Mrs Davenport, please. I'm her husband.
    (*He is breathless, sweating.*)
NURSE: (*Looking down list*) Ah, yes. (*Smiles.*) Congratulations,
    Mr Davenport. You're the father of an eight-pound six-
    ounce girl.
DANIEL: Only one. (*Still fighting for breath*) But there are meant
    to be two. (*Little pause.*) Twins.
    (*The NURSE frowns, looks at the list again.*)
NURSE: Well, only one's been delivered. So far, anyway.

INT. HOSPITAL CORRIDOR. NIGHT

Cut to DANIEL *and* NURSE *going down another corridor. They stop before a door. The* NURSE *is about to push the door open.* DANIEL *sees, through window, a baby in a cot.*

DANIEL: That's not mine.
  (*The* NURSE *looks at him.*)
NURSE: How do you know?
DANIEL: Because – because – (*Gestures towards the woman in the bed*) – that's not my wife.
  (*The* NURSE *looks at her list.*)
NURSE: (*Firmly*) Dandidop. D–6.
DANIEL: No, Davenport. Davenport.

INT. HOSPITAL CORRIDOR. NIGHT

DANIEL *and the* NURSE *hurrying down another corridor, stopping before a private room.* DANIEL *goes in.*

INT. HOSPITAL PRIVATE ROOM. NIGHT

SOPHIE: (*Seeing* DANIEL) Oh, Popsie, Popsie, where have you been?
  (*He goes to her, takes her hand, kisses her.*)
DANIEL: The important thing is I'm here in time. (*Moved*) Oh, my Bootsie!
  (*He kisses her on the forehead.*)

INT. HOSPITAL PRIVATE ROOM. NIGHT

Montage:
SOPHIE *in mild labour,* DANIEL *sitting beside her.*
SOPHIE *sleeping seraphically,* DANIEL *in chair,* SOPHIE *in mild labour,* DANIEL *staring anxiously,* SOPHIE *asleep again,* SOPHIE *in*

labour, then shot after shot of SOPHIE *at seemingly the same stage of labour.*

INT. HOSPITAL PRIVATE ROOM. DAY

Later. We come in on DANIEL *asleep on a chair by the bed, snoring slightly. The bed is empty. A* DOCTOR *enters, comes over, shakes* DANIEL's *arm.* DANIEL *lurches into consciousness, stares up, clearly unaware of where he is.*

DOCTOR: They're on their way, Mr Davenport. They'll be here any minute.
DANIEL: Who?

INT. HOSPITAL CORRIDOR. DAY

As they walk along the corridor:

DOCTOR: Your wife's in tip-top form – well, considering she's been at it for fourteen hours or so.
DANIEL: What, fourteen – !
(*He looks at his watch. Cut to watch: it is twelve ten.*)
(*Staring in panic at the* DOCTOR) Oh, my God – I've got to go.
DOCTOR: But your babies will be here –
DANIEL: No, no. (*Beginning to run off*) I've got to be somewhere important by twelve thirty. Matter of life and –
(*He jogs off along hospital corridor.*)

INT. COURT CORRIDOR. DAY

DANIEL *is jogging desperately along the court corridor, various solicitors, barristers, clients conferring, among them* COOKSON, ZELDA *and* STRAUSS, *all obviously worried. They see* DANIEL *coming.* STRAUSS *comes towards* DANIEL.

STRAUSS: (*In an angry whisper*) Where the hell have you been? Zelda's been making a dreadful hash of the cross-examination –

(DANIEL, *not listening, spots* QUASS *looking absolutely frantic, tapping his watch, two enormous overnight bags in front of him.*)

DANIEL: (*To* STRAUSS) It's Sophie – she's having the babies – I've got to get back to the hospital – come on, man, come on –

(*He gestures to* QUASS. QUASS *hurries over.* DANIEL *takes* QUASS's *arm.*)

QUASS: Where have you been?

DANIEL: (*For* STRAUSS's *benefit*) We've got to get to the hospital –

QUASS: Hospital! Waterloo. We've got to get to Waterloo. What's the matter with you –

(STRAUSS *hears this.* DANIEL *pulls* QUASS *away, and we see them, from* STRAUSS's *point of view jogging along the corridor.* COOKSON *has come over to him.*)

COOKSON: I haven't got a chance, have I? (*Bitterly, gazing after retreating* QUASS *and* DANIEL) I'm going to do that bastard. When I get out.

EXT. WATERLOO UNDERGROUND: STAIRS TO MAIN
STATION. DAY

DANIEL *and* QUASS *struggling up the stairs with other passengers.*

QUASS: What are you going to call them?

(DANIEL *looks at his watch.*)

DANIEL: Seven minutes to. Should have gone by taxi – never trust London Transport. Never.

QUASS: What a pity – what a pity you missed the birth, eh?

DANIEL: (*Stops suddenly.*) Give me the bags!

QUASS: What?

DANIEL: Give me the bags! I'm meant to be carrying them, remember!

QUASS: Oh – oh God, yes!
> (*He pushes them at* DANIEL, *begins to wheeze, fumbling in his pocket.*)

DANIEL: Oh no, not now. Please not now!

QUASS: Just – just one second. They said I'm not to wheeze –
> (*He has taken out his inhaler, is trying to break the seal.*
> DANIEL *takes it from him, breaks the seal, hands the inhaler back to* QUASS.
> *Squirts*) There. There. Right – right, Davenport.
> (*They move off,* DANIEL *surging ahead with bags,* QUASS *shakily labouring after him.*)

INT. WATERLOO STATION. DAY

DANIEL *and* QUASS. *We see the clock from their point of view. It is six minutes to one. Cut to* QUASS, *staring at* DANIEL, *his expression one of dreadful tension as he tries to control his wheezing.* DANIEL *hesitates, suddenly reaches out his hand, squeezes* QUASS'S *arm.* DANIEL *turns away, and we see him from* QUASS'S *point of view walking to platform ten, then cut to* DANIEL'S *point of view, eyes flicking around as he stands with his bag, clocking various faces. We see them from his point of view and also* QUASS *watching, from* DANIEL'S *point of view and then cut to* QUASS, *and we see from his point of view* DANIEL *waiting. He takes in a number of* MEN, *one seen by him, not by* DANIEL, *and then* TWO MEN *together.* DANIEL *looking at the* TWO MEN, *then looking past them, then we see, also from* QUASS'S *point of view,* CARPER *talking to the* CAMERA LADY *and* PARKES. CARPER *takes a green cap out of his pocket, pulls it low over his eyes, begins to edge towards* DANIEL. QUASS *begins to wheeze and reaches for his inhaler. Cut to* DANIEL, *and we see from his point of view* QUASS *about to use his inhaler.* QUASS *is suddenly jostled and the inhaler falls from his hand.* QUASS *tries to pick it up, is jostled again by* LARGE MAN, *(camera lady's companion), then falls. All this seen from* DANIEL'S *point of view. We see* MAN *picking up the inhaler, then helping* QUASS *to his feet, dusting him down.*

There is something odd in the whole sequence. Then DANIEL *spots Carper's green cap pulled very low, partly but not properly recognizes* CARPER, *who is moving towards him. Then* DANIEL *sees, loitering some way behind* CARPER, PARKES, *then the* CAMERA WOMAN. CARPER *comes up to* DANIEL, *his face lowered.* DANIEL *stares at him, says nothing.*

CARPER: (*Head still down*) There's something you're meant to
    say to me. (*Pause.*) Shall I take these, Mr Davenport?
    (*He reaches for the bags.*)
DANIEL: Don't touch them! If you don't stop molesting me, I
    shall call a policeman.
    (CARPER *lifts his head, stares at him. We see* CARPER *full face.*
    DANIEL *turns, hurries over to* QUASS.)
    Come on, come on, we've got to get away. It's a trap. There
    are people all around –
    (*He shoves a bag into* QUASS's *hand, takes his arm, strides off.*
    QUASS *stumbles beside him, breathing heavily.*)
    Keep walking!

INT. TAXI. DAY

QUASS *slumped in a corner,* DANIEL *sitting tensely.*

QUASS: (*Wheezing slightly*) Who – who were they?
DANIEL: The one in the green cap – the other day he gave me
    some information about the other one – and asked for
    twenty-five thousand pounds. I thought it was a joke – I
    suppose the others were police. And the woman with a
    camera – a reporter, I suppose. So police and press. That's
    who they were. If I'd handed over the money – (*Gestures.*)
    My God! A barrister! Bribing a witness! That's the sort of
    thing *solicitors* do! But a barrister! Never! Do you realize
    what it means? The sheer cold *planning* that's gone into it –
    just to get me into gaol! Such lengths – such lengths! I

wonder what they'd planned for you. Push you under a train? I saw that man, the one who knocked you over. He was up to something.

(*He looks at* QUASS, *sees him properly.* QUASS *is lying back helpless, struggling for breath, feebly groping in his pocket for his inhaler. His condition is clearly desperate.* DANIEL, *in a panic, reaches over, fumbles in Quass's pocket, pulls out the inhaler, turns to* QUASS, *who is lying back, mouth agape, fighting for breath.* DANIEL *makes to apply the inhaler, then snatches it away in horror, looks at it.*)

But this one's got a cap! That man trod on it at Waterloo. I saw. This isn't the same one. He must have substituted it.

(QUASS, *unable to reply, sits fighting for breath, his hand flapping loosely towards the inhaler, then letting it flap back.* DANIEL *leans forward.*)

(*To* TAXI DRIVER) Hurry, please hurry!

INT. QUASS'S HOUSE: HALL. DAY

NELLIE *and* DANIEL *dragging* QUASS *along.*

NELLIE: Oh, look at him – look at him – I warned him – why didn't he use his spray? Why?

DANIEL: There was something wrong with it.

NELLIE: With both of them, impossible!

DANIEL: (*Panting*) Both of them?

NELLIE: I always put two in his pocket, in case. Two fresh ones. Every morning.

(*Cut to* DANIEL's *face, appalled.*)

(*Out of shot*) In here – get him in here –

(*She is drawing them to a door that hasn't been opened before.*)

(*To* QUASS, *crooningly*) Oh, my *Liebchen, hier, mein Liebchen, Nellie ist mit dir, Nell ist mit dir* –

INT. QUASS'S HOUSE: SICKROOM. DAY

They struggle into a large room with a bed in it, an oxygen tent, all sorts of medical equipment, in fact a small emergency ward. There is a trestle.

NELLIE: (*As they get* QUASS *on to the bed*) Get his clothes off.
    (DANIEL *begins to undress* QUASS *awkwardly.* QUASS *is now unconscious, in a coma.*)
DANIEL: Surely – surely what he needs – (*As he continues the undressing*) – is to be able to breathe?
NELLIE: I know what he needs.
    (DANIEL *is in a panic, which he attempts to control.*)
DANIEL: He's going, Nellie. Going.
NELLIE: Be quiet, be quick!
    (*She comes back with an oxygen mask, which she clamps over* QUASS's *mouth.* DANIEL *has now got* QUASS *down to his underpants.*)
    (*Indicating oxygen mask*) Here. Hold this.
    (DANIEL *takes the mask as* NELLIE *peels down* QUASS's *underpants speedily, goes to the trestle. Cut between* QUASS's *face, with the mask over it;* DANIEL's *face, intent;* NELLIE *bustlingly arranging the trestle.*)
    Now. (*Coming back*) Let's bring him over.
    (*They lift* QUASS *with difficulty over to the trestle,* DANIEL *just managing to keep the mask on, though it slips once or twice. They arrange him face forward over the trestle.* NELLIE *attaches the mask securely, with a strap.* NELLIE *goes to a shelf, opens a bottle.*)
    Here. Rub this in with your hand.
DANIEL: Where?
NELLIE: Everywhere. Touch him, stroke him, soothe him – that's what he needs. Your body's warmth. Your body's tenderness. Your body's love. Give him your love through your fingers. Everywhere, Davenport.

353

(DANIEL *opens the bottle, rubs the ointment on* QUASS's *back, shoulders.* NELLIE *goes to the hi-fi set, sorts out a tape, puts it on: Mozart. It fills the room.*)
This also he needs. So – rub underneath – around – every little patch, reach it with your love and care, Daniel.
(DANIEL *continues to rub, intensely.* NELLIE *comes over to him.*)
Now I'll do the rest. (*Takes the bottle from* DANIEL.) Thank you, Daniel. Now you go. Wait outside.
(*She begins to rub the ointment into* QUASS. *As she does so, she croons to the music.* DANIEL *goes to the door, turns; we see from his point of view* NELLIE *rubbing, crooning. She turns to him. Her eyes are full of panic. Then she goes back to crooning, her voice as if inspired.*)

INT. QUASS'S HOUSE: HALL. DAY

DANIEL *closes the door. Clearly deeply exhausted, he stands, then turns, goes almost automatically into the study.*

INT. QUASS'S HOUSE: STUDY. DAY

DANIEL *hesitates, looks around, sees a cupboard. Through this, faintly, the sound of* NELLIE *singing to Mozart.* DANIEL *goes to the cupboard, finds bottles of alcohol, takes out a bottle of whisky, looks around for a glass, can't see one, takes a swig from the bottle. Rocks slightly. Puts the bottle down, then picks it up again, takes a small gulp. Mozart and* NELLIE, *over, stop.* DANIEL *rubs his eyes, yawns, takes another gulp. As he lowers the bottle, he stops, listening. Slight noises off of a door opening. Low voices. Footsteps. He puts down the bottle and goes to the door, looks down the corridor and we see from his point of view.*

INT. QUASS'S HOUSE: HALL. DAY

The CAMERA WOMAN *(but without camera) coming out of a room down the hall, followed by* PARKES *and* CARPER *and her* COMPANION *from the wine bar. As they approach the sickroom, that door opens as if they have been summoned. They file in. The door closes.* DANIEL *blinks, dazed. He goes to the sickroom, stands for a moment, then sees that the door of the room from which the* CAMERA WOMAN, CARPER *and* PARKES *and the* COMPANION *have come is open. He goes to it.*

INT. QUASS'S HOUSE: BUGGING CENTRE. DAY

It is a highly sophisticated bugging centre for the house. There is a television screen, on which is a picture of the room that DANIEL *has just left, the bottle of whisky in evidence. On the table in the bugging centre, a board of buttons with labels for each button:* STUDY, DINING ROOM, STAIRS, LIVING ROOM, FRONT HALL, *etc., and a button marked* VIDEO. *On another table there are mugs of half-drunk tea, a bottle of whisky and some glasses, gauntlets and helmet and* CARPER'S *green cap.* DANIEL *stares around him, then presses a button marked* STUDY. *We see Quass's study on the screen. Then he presses the button marked* FRONT HALL, *then stabs his finger randomly down on each button in quick succession so we see shots of different parts of the house on the screen. The last button he presses is* VIDEO. DANIEL *and* QUASS *appear on the screen.*

QUASS: (*On screen*) So. So what about you, Davenport? No death in it, I hope?

DANIEL: (*On screen*) Yes. Death in it.

QUASS: (*On screen*) But you – you haven't killed anyone?

(DANIEL *on the screen. He puts a piece of fudge into his mouth.*)

DANIEL: (*Chewing*) As a matter of fact, yes.

(*Cut to* DANIEL'S *finger stabbing down the button. The screen goes blank. He turns, looks around wildly, sees a stack of files on a shelf, then spots one on the desk under the shelf marked*

355

JACKABOY.J. *He opens it. There is a caricature of* JACKABOY, *doing a nazi salute as he marches unheedingly towards an open manhole. He flicks on, a few photographs of* JACKABOY *at school, receiving his degree, etc. Then a small clipping:* 'PROMINENT GYNAECOLOGIST EXONERATED', *then a series of papers, marked* CONFIDENTIAL: *hospital reports on the competence of* JACKABOY. DANIEL *looks up, takes in a row of files on the shelf marked* DAVENPORT. D. 1965–1975 *and* DAVENPORT. D. 1976–1989. *He plucks the one down marked* 1965–1975, *opens it. We see from* DANIEL's *point of view photographs from Amplesides' house yearbook: shots of* DANIEL *playing cricket, receiving an award, etc. Cut to* DANIEL. *He puts the file back, seizes the other one. Cut to picture of* DAVINA *and* DANIEL *walking in the park, holding hands. Then newspaper cuttings, small, with such headlines as:* MYSTERY DEATH OF UNIVERSITY DON, *and* MILE END HORROR ACCIDENT, *and* RUN OVER – AT LEAST TWELVE TIMES! *with photographs of Queen Mary College, and, on the first one, a photograph of a man in his mid-thirties, bespectacled; under it* DOCTOR GEOFFREY HOPJOY. *Then a number of photographs, one of which is* DANIEL *laying the corpse on Mile End Road, and a recent one of* DANIEL *walking with* SOPHIE, *then one of the birthday dinner at Luigi's,* DANIEL *blowing out the candles on the cake,* SOPHIE *smiling and pregnant. As* DANIEL *looks at the last photograph, file in hand, the door opens.* NELLIE *enters.*)

NELLIE: Would you like to come and see him, Daniel? He's ready for you.

DANIEL: (*Almost as if he hasn't heard*) You've been following me, watching me all these years? Years and years?

NELLIE: Oh. (*Looks around.*) Yes, that's right, Daniel.

DANIEL: And those people – Parkes and that other one. Committing bribery, perjury. They're just your hirelings.

NELLIE: Oh, no. They're our *friends*, Daniel – Sidney, Donald, Mavis and Harold. Part of the team.

DANIEL: All this – all this just to ruin my life?

NELLIE: Ruin? Is your life ruined? I don't see ruin, Daniel, I see unshaven, bewildered, and I smell – um, well, not surprising, no change of clothes for two days. But ruin – do you think Nathaniel could *ruin* anyone, anything?

DANIEL: (*After a small pause*) He ruined all the others. Got them into gaol. Had one of them killed.

NELLIE: Just cases we found in the papers. The right age to have been with you at Amplesides is all. What, run over old-age pensioners and a social worker? The idea!

DANIEL: But Jackaboots. Boy. I saw with my own eyes what you did to him.

NELLIE: Oh, we didn't do much. Little things. Stole his trousers. Imitated the police now and then. The rest he did to himself. We never meant for him to go mad with knives and such. Just a little breakdown, we hoped. To convince you, you see, Daniel.

DANIEL: Are you saying that everything – everything you did – (*Gestures around room*) – was really because of me?

NELLIE: Because of you, Daniel, yes.

DANIEL: Why, Nellie? Why?

NELLIE: You still don't remember?

(DANIEL *shakes his head*.)

One afternoon he's in the music room, pouring himself out through his violin. When the door bursts open and in come some boys. Well-fed English chaps, with beaming faces, and drag him off to the locker room and stuff him into a locker and lock it.

DANIEL: Not me, Nellie. Not me. I couldn't do such a thing. Even at Amplesides.

NELLIE: Then you and Jackaboots come in and hear him crying. And Jackaboots unlocks the locker and laughs and you, Daniel, the older brother he never had, look down on Nathaniel and you smile. And then you wink. A lovely look

357

and smile and wink, perfect Church of English, and you say
– you say – (*Little pause.*)

DANIEL: Oh dear, well one does have to conform . . . (*After a
long pause*) But that was twenty-five years ago, Nellie.
Twenty-five years.

NELLIE: Twenty-five years of heart trouble, asthma, steroids,
hair falling out – twenty-five years of never to be a musician,
never to play in public, and now dead. (*Gently*) *That*'s a
ruined life, Daniel.

DANIEL: (*Swaying slightly*) So I see! It was revenge after all.

NELLIE: Revenge! Oh, that must be the way I told it, Daniel.
Don't think revenge. Think instead Nathaniel. Think love.
Hope. Fun and games. With a touch of revenge mixed in.
Like pepper. To add salt. There. Now you have it. Anyway,
it's finished, Daniel. All over. So come and say your
goodbyes to Nathaniel.

(*She turns, goes out of the door.* DANIEL *follows her,
will-less.*)

INT. QUASS'S HOUSE: HALL/STAIRS. DAY

NELLIE *leads him past the room* QUASS *was in, to the living room.
She opens the door.*

INT. QUASS'S HOUSE: LIVING ROOM. DAY

We come in on QUASS *dead, his body arranged in a hard-backed
chair. He is wearing a very smart, well-tailored dinner-jacket. He is
gripping his violin and bow. The bow is resting against the strings of
his violin. His eyes are open. His mouth is set in a slight smile.*
DANIEL *stands, mesmerized.* QUASS's *bow twitches. A slight sound
from the violin. The bow twitches again. Pause. Twitches again.
Pause. Twitches again. Each time a sound from the violin. Then
twitch again, but go on from twitch into playing, but mechanically,
as if* QUASS *were a doll. The piece is the piece that he choked on*

earlier, when playing to NELLIE *and* DANIEL. *As* QUASS *continues to play, he becomes less and less wooden, though his expression remains as in death. When he is playing dexterously, fluently, he rises from the chair. Flickers of life begin to appear on* QUASS's *face, transforming it by fleeting stages into one of delighted concentration, the music soaring past the point at which he abandoned it previously.* QUASS's *wig begins to slip a little, as he plays feverishly. Then hold on him for the finale. At the conclusion, the music still trembling in the air, he stops. He is drenched with sweat. He steps forward, shaking, takes a little bow. There is a pause.*

DANIEL: Thank you.

INT. QUASS'S HOUSE: LIVING ROOM/MATERNITY ROOM. DAY

DANIEL *turns, looks at* NELLIE, *goes to the door, opens it, and we see from his point of view as if the door has opened directly on to the maternity room,* SOPHIE *in bed, a baby in each arm. She smiles from one to the other and then towards* DANIEL. *He closes the door behind him, steps forward, goes over to the bed and we move back to take in the Davenport family as a group.*

They Never Slept

For Kenith Trodd

They Never Slept was first broadcast by BBC Television on 19 January 1991. The cast included:

MONK	Edward Fox
PRUNELLA MERRIMAN	Emily Morgan
BOB	James Fleet
PETUNIA	Patricia Lawrence
THE ADMIRAL	Francois Chaumette
NINETTE	Maria Laborit
HELEN WATSON	Alison Fielding
MAURICE	Maurice Risch
AMELIA CLEVERLY/CAT-LADY	Harriet Walter
BBC COMMISSIONAIRE	Pete Postlethwaite
THE PRODUCER	Imelda Staunton
HEINDRICH	Patrick Fierry
ELAINE	Yvette Petit
Director	Udayan Prasad
Producer	Kenith Trodd

MONTAGE SEQUENCE: ARCHIVE NEWSREEL FOOTAGE

AMELIA CLEVERLY, *on radio, voice over as montage sequence. She has a strong, warm, throbbing voice.*

AMELIA: (*Voice over, radio*) I've talked so often about the debt that we, here at home, owe to all our chaps who are fighting this war. Some up in the skies, in their small planes, protecting our homes. Other chaps flying across the channel, to drop bombs on the evil factories where the Germans make the weapons with which they are trying to destroy us. Chaps on the ground in tanks, and on foot with simple weapons. Chaps on the water, and chaps under the water, all of them so far from their homes, and those that love them.
(*Montage during the above: newsreel footage, illustrating as referred to, i.e. chaps in planes, submarines, etc., intercut with pictures of devoted radio listeners, old people, young people, etc.*)

INT. MONTAGE: HQ. CLAPHAM PSYCHIATRIC HOSPITAL: CANTEEN. DAY

AMELIA: (*Voice over, radio*) And then, of course, there are chaps who fight with their brains, driving themselves on, working day and night, night and day, concentrating every ounce of their minds, every last ounce of their physical energy, working out ways to save thousands of lives by out-thinking and out-manoeuvring the enemy.
(*Montage during this: Clapham Psychiatric Hospital. People working in heavily-barred small wards, some with earphones on, etc., some on telephones, all active.*
Then cut to BOB *in canteen, studying a file, other files on table as he sips tea, munches sandwich, then cut to:*)

365

INT. MONTAGE: HQ. MEETING ROOM. DAY

MONK, *standing before a blackboard, on which there is a map of Bordeaux. Above the map, on the blackboard, is written 'Lucifer' with a chalk drawing of the face of Lucifer beside it. On the map itself there are two clusters of arrows encircling two towns. There are thick lines leading to one cluster, hyphenated lines leading to the other. The thick lines have written boldly 'True', the hyphenated lines 'Phoney' at the top of the lines.*
Surrounding MONK *are two high-ranking officers of the British and American forces. Both are listening attentively, the American clearly finding it difficult to follow* MONK, *scratching his head, frowning, etc., the British nodding in approval and admiration, as* MONK, *speaking at high speed, with rapid movements of his pointer, follows the lines, arrows, gestures, whips around to another blackboard, on which a number of photographs: outside shot of the Café Libre, of* MAURICE, HEINDRICH, *the* ADMIRAL, NINETTE, PETUNIA HUMBERT, SALLY, *his pointer flying from one to the other, the American becoming even more bewildered. On the blackboard, two chalk caricatures of a fat man's face, a thin man's face, above written in chalk:* OP: FATTYPUFF/THINNIFER.

AMELIA: (*Voice over, radio*) Let us never forget that they too, like the chaps at the front, the chaps in the air and on the ground, the chaps above and under the sea – like the chaps they send on deadly missions all over Europe, like the chaps all over Europe whose loyalty they command – the noble partisans of Greece, France, Italy, Yugoslavia, Poland, Hungary, Czechoslovakia, Holland, Albania, Roumania, Russia – they too, they too never sleep!
(*Montage during this of* MONK *throwing down pointer, glaring triumphantly at British officer, who wags his head in admiring astonishment, American looking confused, then* MONK *glancing at his watch.*
Cut to him walking at enormous speed through Clapham

*Psychiatric Hospital, passing small wards in which people
working, listening on headphones, etc., bursting into his office,
looking at other desk, looks at his watch again, turning on radio,
throwing himself into chair of own desk. (N.B. Two desks
therefore*
Voice over, radio) But now let us turn our minds to those
others of us who must not be forgotten during the war. We
women. We who spend so much time thinking of the brave
chaps who are risking their lives, and yes, losing their lives,
but who have themselves their own, very important work to
do. Some of it is simple, but because of our country's great
need of it, it is never, no never, a drudgery. Some of it is
highly skilled, almost as highly skilled as the chaps' work,
yes, top secret even –
(Montage during this, cutting between PRUNELLA MERRIMAN
dressing in her WVS *uniform, tying tie, etc., in a forthright,
eager, practical manner, and* SALLY, *applying make-up
meticulously, but has a raffish, slightly feckless manner about
her, between these two scenes,* PRU's *at beginning,* SALLY *at
end, a rapid sequence of shots of women working in factories,
cleaning offices, digging in fields, etc., but end with* SALLY
turning triumphantly away from mirror, as:
Voice over, radio) – and some of it, for all we know,
may even be highly dangerous! But the truth is, isn't it,
that whatever the nature of our work, in whatever our
walk of life, whether we're young women or
grandmothers –
(Montage: PRU *checking herself for efficiency in mirror, then cut
to:)*

EXT. STREET BY TUBE STATION. DAY

SALLY *strutting quickly through London street, cutting on
'grandmothers' to* PETUNIA HUMBERT, *a woman in her seventies,
waiting anxiously at Gloucester Road tube station.*

AMELIA: (*Voice over, radio*) – with a simple daily task, or a
skillful and dangerous one –
(*Montage*: SALLY *sees* PETUNIA *on the other side of the road,
waves eagerly, steps off the pavement, and is run over by a bus.*
PETUNIA *stares in shock, as people scream, a crowd gathers,
etc., then turns and hurries into tube station, makes bee-line for
telephone, clutching her chest, as*:
Voice over, radio) – all of you know what I mean when I say
that there are precious few moments in our day, our busy,
busy woman's day, when somewhere in our hearts we aren't
thinking of our chaps, there in front lines, above us in the
sky, on and under the great seas, or scheming for our
preservation in their lonely offices –
(*During last part of the above, cut to:*)

INT. HQ. MONK'S OFFICE. DAY

MONK *is sitting, rapt, dabbing emotionally at his eyes with his
handkerchief,* AMELIA's *voice coming directly from his radio.*

AMELIA: (*Voice over, radio*) May God be with you.
MONK: (*Huskily, sniffing*) May God be with you too, Amelia.
RADIO ANNOUNCER: (*Voice over, radio*) That was Amelia
Cleverly with a midday thought in war-time. She will be
back this evening with an evening thought in war-time. And
now for some music from that fine old England-loving
composer, Handel.
(BOB, *from the canteen, enters. He has only one arm, in his mid-
thirties, with an appearance of muffled affability. He is carrying
files that he was studying in canteen.*)
MONK: (*Blowing his nose to conceal his emotions as music starts*)
Fine old England-loving, I suppose that means he wasn't
English, was he?
BOB: Dutch I think, Monk.
MONK: Then why don't they say so, nothing wrong with being

Dutch at the moment, not their fault – (*Turns radio off.*) But where have you been, you were meant to wait for Ted's call about Heindrich –

BOB: It came, Monk. Heindrich's coming back tonight for his briefing as ordered, Monk – oh, (*Holding file*) and I was checking in his file, it's his birthday.
(MONK *takes tennis ball out of drawer, throws it against wall.* BOB *drops file, catches it, throws it back against the wall. During the following a high-speed game of office squash follows, the ball being hurled at the walls, being caught by either* BOB *or* MONK.)

MONK: Is it, by God, is it, then we'll give him a surprise, bit of a party, champagne so forth, I tell you I've got a good feeling about this op, Bob, in spite of the Yankee at the briefing, foolish face, didn't seem to understand a word, not a word, but still all we have to do is wait for Petunia and her girlie and the Café Libre – and then in nine days, nine days from now, lives saved, war shortened – (*Also during above* BOB, *amazingly agile in spite of only one arm, is exclaiming 'Well caught, sir!'*) it's the waiting, the waiting I can't stand – (*Telephone rings.*)

MONK: (*Simultaneously catching ball and snatching up telephone*) Clapham Psychiatric Hospital, Section 18, Monk – Petunia – just talking about you – what's the matter – where's the girlie, don't say she's unpunctual again – I warned that girlie – (*Stops, listens.*) A bus! A bus! Run over by a bus! Hope to God you're just teasing, Petunia! What? No – no – you can't go back to bloody Lyme Regis, the whole op depends – (*Stops, thinks rapidly*) we'll get you another niece, we've got another one lined up for back-up, a perfectly good girlie, she'll do just as well – now you wait there, Petunia – what, no, all right, don't wait, but be back in – in two hours, yes, two hours to the minute, she'll be there, I promise you! (*Hangs up. To* BOB) What are you waiting for – didn't you hear what's happened – get the files – the files, quick, man! –

(BOB *plucks files, hands one to* MONK.)
– has to speak French fluently, but otherwise a simple,
patriotic, dim-witted girl, an amateur – not this –
(*Discarding photograph of knowing-looking girl*) or this – or
this – (*Discarding photographs*) – ah, this one – this one has
the look – does she speak French? (*Turns the photograph over
to read attached c.v. on back.*)

BOB: (*Seeing photograph, stares at it*) Good lord, isn't that Ingrid?
Yes – we had her hanged last month. Sorry, Monk, wrong
file – (*Takes it from him.*) Enemy girls. This must be the one
we want – no, these are chaps – now where's the one –

MONK: Oh, for God's sakes, Bob, for God's sakes – (*Bouncing
ball savagely.*)

BOB: Sorry, Monk. The trouble is we had a hard job finding one
in the first place – not many to choose from –

MONK: A bus, a bus, and not even pushed, Petunia says, that's
more than dim-witted, that's imbecile, why, why the hell
did we choose her in the first place (*Bouncing ball*) oh, come
on, Bob, come on, man, we've got two hours, less than two
hours – damn Petunia and Lyme Regis, I've got a mind to
pull her pension – what are you doing, what are you doing?

BOB: Here, Monk, got it. French speakers. All volunteers. No
experience in intelligence –
(MONK *is staring at the door.*
PRU *is standing there in her* WVS *uniform, holding file.*)

MONK: Who the hell are you?

PRU: Corporal Merriman reporting to Commander Scott, sir.

MONK: What for?

PRU: Driving duties, Commander. (*Holds out file.*
BOB *takes it.*)

MONK: Don't be ridiculous, girlie, we've got a perfectly good
driver, now clear out, can't you see we're busy?

BOB: Actually Monk, actually – we haven't got a driver.

MONK: What do you mean, of course we have, old Alec or Alfred
or whatever his name is.

BOB: No, but Monk – I'm sure I told you – yesterday evening –
he's been taken to hospital –

MONK: Malingering again, you mean. Well, get him out.

BOB: He's had a stroke this time, Monk. Paralysed down the left
hand side of his body. Can't talk. Or walk. That's why I put
in a requy for a new one. Didn't ask for a – a – (*Gestures
with his head at* PRU.)

MONK: Well, we haven't got time to mess about with drivers
now, you'll have to do (*To* PRU) until we get a proper one,
go and sit somewhere, we'll call you when we need you.

BOB: I'll just have to ask her a few questions, Monk. Security.
You know. All that.

MONK: Make it quick then – make it quick – (*Snatching Pru's file
from* BOB *by mistake*) at least I can get on with what's
important, while you're buggering about security. What the
hell's this, is this all we've got, just this one –

BOB: No, no – that's the Corporal's file, Monk. This is the one –

MONK: (*Looking into file*) You taught French?

PRU: Yes, Commander. At Cheltenham Ladies' College. Though
my main teaching was games. Gym, lacrosse, hockey,
tennis –

MONK: (*In dreadful French*) Et vous parlez français, n'est-ce-pas?

PRU: *Mais oui*, Commander (*All the rest in French*) my mother
was French, you see, so I'm half French, she made me
speak it at home because she wanted me to be bilingual –

MONK: (*Holding up hand to stop her as he studies file*) Not married?

PRU: No, Commander.

MONK: No fiancée? Nothing of that sort?

PRU: Well, I was engaged to a chap the year after I went to
Cheltenham, but he was killed in a skiing accident in the
Engladine. There was a freak avalanche –

MONK: Bloody fool. What about habits, vices, what are they?

PRU: Well – well – I don't drink. I tried to once, at the first end-
of-term staff party, but I made such an ass of myself and got
a headache –

MONK: Why'd you join up? For the glamour?

PRU: No – no, Commander! I just wanted to do anything I can to help win the war, and I heard there was a shortage of drivers, and as I used to drive the school bus to all the away matches –

MONK: Well, don't think that just because you used to drive a lot of little girlies about with hockey sticks, that's all you have to do for me. You're not here to spend the day sitting around on your fanny waiting for some fun at the wheel, understood?

(PRU *nods*.)

Right. Now it just happens that I have a little op going on at the moment I can use you for. So what you have to do is this. Get into some civvies, pretty yourself up, then prattle away at some Free French – your mother was French, you soft on them?

PRU: No, well I mean I'm glad they're our allies of course but I'm English through and –

MONK: Listen. Could you just listen for a moment, instead of breaking in all the time? Your job is to find out what they want you to do for 'em, and agree to do it, they know you're working for Section 18 and they know I'm your boss and I know what it is they want to know and that's the only thing you're not to let 'em know, follow, that you're doing what they want you to do for me and not for them, it's all quite simple, the whole thing's been set up for you by our top female agent, only female agent, you're lucky to have a chance to work for her, she's your aunt by the way, which makes you her niece, she'll be waiting for you at Gloucester Road underground station in an hour and three-quarters, name's Petunia, Petunia Humbert, call her Pet or Pettie, something like that, above all be natural, be yourself, don't put a foot wrong, and you'll be perfectly all right, and at least it'll give you something useful to do until we need you for the driving, off you go then.

PRU: (*Dazed but determined to keep up*) Gloucester Road tube, three and a quarter hours.

MONK: An hour and three-quarters, an hour and three-quarters, an hour and three-quarters, looking pretty, where do you live?

PRU: Forty-seven Oakley Gardens, Chelsea –

MONK: Gives you forty-five minutes there, twenty minutes to get pretty, forty minutes to Gloucester Road, you can do it in ten running on foot, take an extra ten for pretty, still plenty of time if you stop dilly-dallying and get a move on.

PRU: Right, Commander! (*Salutes.*)

MONK: Don't do that, don't do that, never do that again. (*Face twitching.*) This is meant to be a secret service, we don't go around hail hitlering each other, one more thing, Fattypuffs and Thinnifers, they probably won't come up until round two, but if they do, look blank, play dumb, say you'll try to find out – understood and out?

PRU: Understood, Commander! (*Just restrains herself from saluting, turns, hurries out of door.*)

BOB: Well – (*Whistles*) think she'll be all right?

MONK: Why not? Can't see much difference between her and the other one, except she doesn't look as if she's going to end up under a bus. (*Takes ball out, begins to bounce it.*) Told you I had a good feeling about this one.
(*Throws ball at* BOB, *who catches and returns it.*)
Except the waiting. Heindrich's birthday, eh? Champagne. Oysters. No, no oysters – waiting. Bloody waiting! (*Hurling ball.*
Cut to:)

EXT. STREET BY TUBE STATION. DAY

PETUNIA *looking at her watch outside Gloucester Road tube station. She sees* PRU *hurrying along in civvies towards her.* PRU *steps into the road, and cut to, from* PETUNIA's *point of view, a bus whipping*

373

around corner, as before with SALLY, *screams, etc. from pavement.*
PETUNIA *puts her hand to her chest as before, turns, makes for
underground telephone, then sees* PRU *cantering towards her, from
behind the bus.*

PRU: Golly, that was a near one, I was jolly lucky, wasn't I? You
are my aunt, aren't you, Aunt – Aunt –
PETUNIA: (*Only partially concealing her disappointment*) I suppose
it was too much to expect it to happen twice in the same
day, especially when a person is meant to be in Lyme Regis
for her health – well, (*walking along street*) well – you don't
look at all like my niece, I've been telling them all you're tall
and blonde and English rose and you look almost
continental, you're far too short as well, you know! Far, far,
too short – I say tall and blonde and then here I am turning
up with short and swarthy – but of course they've become so
mad recently there's a chance they won't even notice, she
just wants to pass you on as quickly as she can and stay out
of it, and he with his (*Makes drinking movements with her
arm*) here we are, we're there, the rest is up to you! (*Pushes
open the door of the Café Libre, as she does so clutches
dramatically at her chest.*) Oh, your name, your name, don't
forget to change your name – oh – oh – (*Wheezing hideously*)
unless it's the same one – same one –
(*They go inside the restaurant.*)
Sit down – I've got to sit down – the Admiral – there's the
Admiral –
(*Take in* ADMIRAL, *sitting alone at an otherwise full restaurant.
On the walls photographs and posters of De Gaulle. The*
ADMIRAL *is slumped, his chin resting mournfully on his hand.
At tables near by, assorted English and French people. At two
other tables, Polish émigrés.*
ADMIRAL, *clearly slightly drunk, but hangs on to his cunning,
looks up as* PETUNIA *sinks into chair.*)
ADMIRAL: Oh, it's you, Ninette's in a frenzy, she's been waiting

for you over an hour, two hours, three – (*Gestures*) look at
her! (*Nods his head, and cut to:*
NINETTE, *at back of café, by kitchen. She is in her early
forties, and is talking and gesticulating hysterically, stamping
her foot and shaking her fist at a young and pretty waitress –*
HELEN WATSON – *who is standing with her head lowered.*)

ADMIRAL: And with that new girl, so nice, so kind, so *mignon*, as
soon as her rage comes because of you she goes to make the
bêtises with her –

NINETTE: (*Has seen* PETUNIA, *comes steaming over. Savagely, to*
ADMIRAL) I tell you she is *méchante*, *méchante*, I can smell
her lying and thieving here, in my nostrils, why are you late,
why (*To* PETUNIA), do you think I have nothing better to do
with my time, it makes my head swim and thump – the risk,
the danger –

ADMIRAL: (*In French*) Be quiet, be quiet, everyone can hear you.

NINETTE: What? (*Looks around.*) Yes, yes, look at them.
(*Laughs.*) In half an hour they'll be singing and dancing,
they'd do that even if I was swinging and dancing – (*Puts her
hand around her throat to illustrate being hanged.*)

PRU: I'm very sorry, it's my fault we're late, I had to stay on in
the office, you see –

NINETTE: You're the girl? This is your niece?

PETUNIA: Yes, yes, Sally, this is Ninette –

NINETTE: But you said she was blonde. Blonde and fat.

PETUNIA: No, tall. Blonde and tall, I said.

NINETTE: But she is small and dark.

PETUNIA: Oh, don't confuse me, Ninette, please, your temper,
you know, it makes it so difficult to keep things straight in
one's head when you go at a person like that, especially with
a dicky heart and a train to catch, what I said was that when
she was a child she was tall and blonde, but she grew up –
grew up to be small and dark, in the way that children do, it
just shows – just shows how much notice you take –

NINETTE: What's your name?

375

PRU: (*After a fraction of ghastly indecision*) Poochy.
PETUNIA: (*Simultaneously*) Sally.
  (NINETTE *looks from one to the other, with ferocious suspicion.*)
PRU: Since school people have always called me Poochy, except
  for Aunt um, um – Patsy (*Very quickly*) she still calls me
  Sally –
NINETTE: The English and their blasted stupid names – Patsy,
  Poochy, Sally – you come with me, and you (*To* ADMIRAL,
  *bends over, turns, whispers commands into his ear, hurries
  towards the kitchen.*
  PRU *looks desperately at* PETUNIA, *who gestures her angrily
  after* NINETTE. NINETTE *and* PRU *head into kitchen.*)

INT. CAFÉ LIBRE: KITCHEN. DAY

HELEN WATSON *is washing up at sink. A number of old women,
stirring soup, etc., one of whom is pouring salt into a tureen.*

NINETTE: (*Who is making for some stairs at the back, spots this,
  stops, wags a finger at the old woman, shouting*) Pas du sel, pas
  du sel, pas du *blasted* sel, no damned salt, I put in the salt, I,
  Ninette, put in the salt, I tell you a thousand times, *entendu!*
  (*There is a crash from the sink.* NINETTE *whirls, and see from
  her's, and* PRU's *point of view,* HELEN WATSON, *terrified, a
  broken plate at her feet.*)
  Oh you – yes, yes, it would be you –
HELEN: I'm sorry, Miss, sorry, it just fell from – from –
NINETTE: Get out, go away, you leave at the end of the week,
  entendu, entendu, now go in there, go, this comes from your
  money (*Kicking at shards of plate*), go in there and do the
  tables, out – out!
  (HELEN WATSON *runs out into the restaurant.*
  In French) This is England, this is what we have to put up
  with, disgusting people, no manners, no style, coarse,
  stupid – here, don't stand there, help me, help me –

(*Picking up shards and putting them into bin.*)
(PRU *helps.*
As she continues to pick up shards, in a whisper) Listen to me
carefully. I only tell you because I am surrounded, you
understand? (*In French.*)

PRU: *Oui, mademoiselle.*

NINETTE: Tomorrow morning you go at seven thirty to Waterloo
Station. To the ladies' waiting room. First class. There you
will meet a young woman. You will be able to identify her
because of her cat. She will be stroking it. You understand?
(*All this in French.*)

PRU: *Oui, mademoiselle.*

NINETTE: She will tell you what you have to do next. Also – this
is important, this is serious – she will give you a package.
You bring it straight back here to me. Understand? (*In
French*) You don't open it, you don't look – (*Stands facing
PRU, a jagged shard in her hand*) you don't even feel. You
bring. Understand?

PRU: *Oui, mademoiselle.* (*Looking at shard, which is between her
breasts and her throat.*)

NINETTE: If you don't do exactly – exactly – I will – I will – (*In
French, making ripping movement with the shard.*)

PRU: (*In French*) I will do exactly – exactly – Waterloo Station,
lady with a cat – a package for you – no looking, nothing –

NINETTE: So you say, so you say, but how do I trust you, how?
They are everywhere, everywhere, why not you, too? (*In
French.*)

PRU: But I want to help the Free French, *mademoiselle*. I'll do
anything you say, anything – (*Voice rising slightly, in French.*)

NINETTE: Sssh, sssh, idiot! (*Looking around. She studies* PRU,
then attempts a smile, ghastly in its effect, of warmth.) Yes, yes,
I trust you – I can see that you're a good girl, Bootchy, a
good loyal girl, now our business is ended (*With equally
ghastly jocularity*) you go back to your auntie Patsy and my
papa and tell Papa – tell him to give you a nice Polish treat,

377

you have deserved it. Understood, my child. A nice Polish
treat. There! (*Touches her on cheek with hand.*) I will come
and join you soon. Amuse yourself well! (*All this in French.*)

PRU: Thank you. Thank you, *mademoiselle!*
(*She turns, hurries out of kitchen into restaurant and towards*
ADMIRAL's *table.* PETUNIA *is sitting back, hand to her chest.*
ADMIRAL *is talking to* HELEN WATSON *dotingly, not aware
immediately of* PRU.)

ADMIRAL: No, no, my poor sweet child, you are not to distress
yourself because of my daughter, she is only a little – little –
(*Taps his forehead*) but I will look after you, protect you, I
promise you you will stay here with me – (*Sees* PRU.)

PRU: Excuse me, Admiral, your daughter said I was to – well,
she said something about a polish treat –

ADMIRAL: Ah, how well I know her. I have anticipated. It is
here! Already here! (*Tapping jug.*) Thanks to our émigré
friends there! (*Lifting jug towards them.*)

POLES: Café Libre, Café Libre, Café Libre! (*Lifting their glasses.*)

ADMIRAL: (*Stands up and bows*) Time to present them with a bill.
Charge them half, my cherub! (*To* HELEN WATSON)
Because of their present of vodka! And then treble it,
because of my daughter's soup! (*Bows again.*)

POLES: (*Laugh, clap*) Café Libre, Café Libre, Café Libre!
(HELEN *goes off, as:*)

ADMIRAL: Now watch! I give you an exhibition how to drink
Polish potato water. You raise the glass so – close your eyes
so – dream of Mother Poland, fat landlords flogging
peasants, a landscape of bones and ice – and then you throw
it down your throat so! (*Doing so.*) And then do you know
what you do, if you are a Pole? You do it again. And again.
And again. (*Doing it.*) Until you fall over. This is their
culture. Are you ready, *mademoiselle* (*Filling her glass*) to lift
your glass so! (*Lifting his own.*)

PRU: Oh, I'm terribly sorry (*With a laugh*), but you see I don't
drink, not since the end-of-term party –

ADMIRAL: My daughter says a Polish treat! You drink! You drink! (*Glaring at her with drunken command.*)

(PETUNIA *raises her elbow rapidly and angrily, miming drink.*)

PRU: – but as it's a special occasion – (*Raises glass, sips.*)

ADMIRAL: No! No, no, no! Did you not watch! (*Banging table with fist.*) There! Look at them! They are waiting! Do not insult them! (*Gestures to* POLES, *who are in fact studying bill brought by* HELEN, *depressed, puzzled, muttering as they pass it about.*) Café Libre, Café Libre, Café Libre!

POLES: (*Look up, startled, then dully*) Café Libre, Café Libre, Café Libre!

ADMIRAL: You throw – throw – (*Throws contents of glass down his throat.*)

(PRU *follows suit, winces from the effect, coughs.*)

ADMIRAL: (*Fills her glass immediately*) Now that is just to start. Now we begin the treat!

PETUNIA: (*Rising*) I really must be getting along – train to catch – tell everybody I've done everything I can, please – and – and – (*Puts hand to chest*) there's nothing more for me – me – goodbye, goodbye – Admiral – and you of course – (*Aims a kiss at* PRU's *cheek, hurries out.*

PRU, *her eyes following* PETUNIA *in panic.*)

ADMIRAL: (*Shouting after* PETUNIA) Goodbye, my dear, my sweet, my darling – Café Libre, Café Libre, Café Libre! (*Throws down drink, glaring at* PRU, *who again follows suit as:*)

POLES: (*Perking up*) Café Libre, Café Libre, Café Libre! (*Tossing drinks down their throats.*
Cut to:)

INT. MONTAGE: CAFÉ LIBRE: RESTAURANT. DAY

ADMIRAL, POLES, PRU *throwing vodka down their throats, shouting,* 'Café Libre, Café Libre, Café Libre!'
Cut to PRU, ADMIRAL *dancing on the table,* POLES *gathered around*

clapping their hands to a Polish drinking song which the POLES *are also singing, seen from* NINETTE's *point of view at the back of the restaurant, coming towards them. She stops briefly to berate* HELEN WATSON *who is also clapping her hands to the song, sends her into the kitchen, then comes on to the table. She slips a pill into glass, pours vodka into glass, hands it up to* PRU, *who is kicking up her legs Russian style.* PRU *tosses it down her throat to cheers and laughter as song continues,* NINETTE *joining ferociously in, clapping and singing, and cut to:*

A little later. PRU *still dancing and singing, but in slow motion, her legs buckling, her eyes rolling,* ADMIRAL *drunkenly catching her, passing her down to* NINETTE, *amidst applause from* POLES. *They carry her off towards the kitchen, and cut to:*

INT. CAFÉ LIBRE: UPSTAIRS ROOM. DUSK

PRU *lying on sofa.* NINETTE's *fingers at her clothing.* ADMIRAL *sitting slumped in a chair.*

NINETTE: (*In French*) Get yourself ready, prepare yourself!
(ADMIRAL *gets up rockily, begins to undress unsteadily as* NINETTE *continues to undress* PRU.
A series of frozen frames of the ADMIRAL, *naked in various positions, with* PRU *naked. Blinding lights. Angry whispers from* NINETTE, *drunken mumbles from* ADMIRAL, *then cut to* NINETTE's *face, mad with attention.*)
NINETTE: There is somebody at the door! At the door! (*In French, runs to door, flings it open. There is nobody there. She turns.*) I tell you – that filthy girl of yours – at the keyhole – I am sure of it!
(*Cut to: a little later.* PRU *lying on sofa, eyes closed. Cold water is poured over her face. Her eyes open.* NINETTE *is standing over her, with an empty glass and a sponge. She attacks* PRU's *face with the sponge, vigorously.*)
PRU: Wha – ? Where? Please – please – (*Attempts to defend herself.*)

NINETTE: (*Gives her a few last punches with the sponge*) You awake then?

PRU: Yes – yes – what – what happened?

NINETTE: What happened! What happened! You got drunk and made a spectacle of the Café Libre, that's what happened! Look at yourself, look! (*In French.*)
(PRU *sees her body from her point of view. Blouse buttons undone, skirt hiked up past her knees.*)
If the police had come by they'd have closed us down – or worse. Far, far worse. (*In French. Then in English*) Lewd and disgusting behaviour. And in the Café Libre! Now get up! Up!
(NINETTE *takes* PRU *by the ear, tugs her to her feet.*)

PRU: I'm sorry – sorry if I made a bit of an ass – ow!

NINETTE: Where do you go tomorrow?

PRU: Waterloo Station. Ladies' waiting room.

NINETTE: (*Gives her ear a little jerk*) What time?

PRU: Seven thirty.

NINETTE: (*Gives a little jerk*) And the young woman – what about her?

PRU: Stroking a cat.

NINETTE: And then what – then what – the important thing – the thing my life depends on? (*Jerk, jerk, jerk.*)

PRU: The package. I bring it straight to you. (*Her head is turned so that she is looking into a corner, in which photographic equipment, tripod, etc. lying.*)

NINETTE: Straight to me. Straight to me. (*Jerk, jerk. Then lets her go.*) There! There! (*Patting* PRU's *cheek in a grisly show of affection.*) I do that only to make sure your head is clear and that you remember everything. From now on I believe you will be a very good girl. A very good girl. Now go home. Go to bed. And the next time you come here – no vodka. No vodka, eh? (*Wags her finger.*
PRU *turns, wavers out. As she does so, takes in photographic equipment, tripod, etc. again.*

Following her) What's the matter with you, get along with you – home to bed! (*Slaps* PRU *angrily on the bottom, and as* PRU *stumbles out, slams the door.*

PRU *stands for a second, trying to pull herself together, then hears, and feebly tries to follow* NINETTE's *voice through the door.*

Voice over, evidently on telephone) Hello, hello, blast it, hello, are you there? It's done, Papa will leave them for you tonight but you have to have the thing, do you understand, the thing! – I can't go on without it, they are everywhere, I tell you – what? I don't care what you blasted think, I do nothing more until I have it, nothing! So you make sure you give it to her! Now no more – it is dangerous on the telephone – go away! (*Slams down telephone.*

There is a slight pause, then NINETTE *emits sudden terrible sobs and moans of anguish.*

Voice over) Oh, mon dieu! Mon Dieu! (*Silence.*) Who's there? Somebody's there! (*As sound of her moving towards the door.*

PRU *hurries, almost falling, down the stairs, as sound of door opening. She makes it to the bottom, in shadow, where* NINETTE *can't see her, looks up.* NINETTE's *face at the door, peering madly out. She hurries into kitchen. It is deserted, except for one old lady, asleep in a chair.*

PRU *goes on into restaurant. Also deserted except for a couple of* POLES, *lying drunk across the table, and* HELEN WATSON, *bent over a table, loading dishes onto an already over-loaded tray. She turns just as* PRU *is about to pass her. There is a brief dance of uncertainty,* HELEN *lurches, crockery slides off the tray and crashes to the floor.*)

HELEN: Oh no! Oh no! Oh – oh, look what you've made me do, you slut, you stupid slut!

(*One of the* POLES, *woken by noise, looks towards them, recognizes* PRU, *raises glass.*)

POLE: Café Libre!

OTHER POLES: (*Mutter in sleep*) Café Libre.
>   (HELEN *looks at* PRU, *as if suddenly conscious of her loss of control. Makes to say something, then pushes past her, runs to the kitchen.* PRU *stares after her, then goes to the door, opens it, steps on to the pavement.*)

EXT. STREET OUTSIDE CAFÉ LIBRE. NIGHT

PRU *stands for a moment, desperately trying to pull herself together. As she does so a car parked down the street starts up, drives towards her, very fast and erratically.* PRU *is about to step into the street when she becomes suddenly aware of it. Manages to step back as the car slows to a stop beside her.*

MONK: (*Leaning out of passenger window*) Get in, get in, girlie! We're in a hurry!
>   (PRU *makes for the back door as* BOB *gets out from the driving side.*)

>   Not there – you're meant to be our driver, aren't you, drive!
BOB: (*Apologetically, gesturing to his absent arm*) I'm afraid I still haven't quite mastered the art – (*Getting into the back beside* MONK.

>   PRU *gets into the driving seat.*)
MONK: Come on, girlie! Get going!
>   (PRU *starts the car as:*)

>   We've been waiting outside a good eleven, twelve minutes, and don't tell me – (*Lets out an exclamation of annoyance as car jumps forward*) what are you doing – thought you were meant to be trained – don't tell me that you were working on Ninette, Petunia phoned from the station, gave me a full report, you'd already had your little session with Ninette, and you were back in the restaurant swilling down vodka and dancing on the table, well I'm glad *you've* had yourself a good evening – where the hell do you think you're going?
PRU: I – I don't know, Commander.

383

MONK: Epsom. Now keep your mind on your driving and fill me
    in. Who's your round two? Where do you meet? When?
    Watch it – watch it –
    (*Cut to:*)

INT. CAR. NIGHT

MONK *has his arm around back of* PRU's *seat, his face pressed
intently close to hers.* PRU *is straining to look alert and to drive
alertly, in spite of her physical and mental condition.*

MONK: A cat, eh? What sort of cat?
PRU: I don't know, Commander. Only that she'll be stroking it.
MONK: Supposing there's a woman there with a cat. And she *isn't*
    stroking it. What then?
PRU: I don't know, Commander.
MONK: (*Imitating*) You don't know, Commander. And didn't
    think to ask. Well, this is what she meant. Pay attention –
    and to the road, and to the road – she meant that if she was
    stroking it, it was safe to go and speak to her, that's what
    she meant – (*turning to* BOB) now we're going to have this
    cat-lady under surveillance, somebody already there when
    she arrives, and then to keep on her tail until we know who
    she is, who *her* contact is –
BOB: There's Rupert free at the moment –
MONK: Six foot three with jowels. Perfect for the ladies' first-
    class waiting room, thanks Bob, thanks.
BOB: No, of course, um foolish – it's the old problem then of
    finding a girl.
PRU: (*Blinking to attention*) Perhaps I can help, Commander.
MONK: Now there's a thought, girlie! You have your
    conversation with Cat-lady and then follow her home, is that
    it? How could she be expected to notice that, eh?
PRU: Sorry – sorry, Commander –
MONK: Your job is to drive, not to help plan the details of a

highly sophisticated top secret op, understood and out? It'll
have to be Petunia again (*Turning back to* BOB) – phone her
up as soon as we get back, tell her to catch the milk train,
Lyme Regis gets in at Waterloo so she can get straight off
and into the ladies' waiting room, then she sticks with Cat-
lady until she's found out who, where, who with, and then
report back and then she can go home, positively her last
job, tell her, so no natter, natter, natter about her heart,
'yes' and her pension's safe, 'no' and I'll see to it that she's
parachuting into France this time next week, that'll give her
heart something to think about, now what else (*Turning to*
PRU) happened at the Café Libre, you're holding back on
something, come on out with it and for God's sake! – (*As*
PRU *swerves*) What is it? What else happened at the Café
Libre besides the dancing and the drinking?

PRU: Nothing else happened, Commander. Well, except that I
   got a bit – a bit faint – overcome by the heat and – and had
   to lie down for a while. And – and – (*Sudden images of*
   ADMIRAL, *naked, etc.*)

MONK: Watch it!

PRU: (*Swerves to avoid a truck*) Sorry, Commander.

MONK: Could you stop – could you please stop – calling me
   Commander? Why do you call me Commander?

PRU: They told me at the pool that you insisted on being called
   Commander or Commander Stott –

MONK: Stott! I'm not Stott! I'm Scott! They sent you to the
   wrong bloody Commander, girlie! I told you – (*Slapping
   back of seat*) told you that I had a good feeling about this
   one, didn't I, Bob? Something goes wrong, and there's an
   accident to set it right immediately. Well, well. Well, well!
   (*To* PRU) Stott's an old imbecile. All he thinks about is
   rank. With me you stick to plain 'sir', got that?

PRU: Yes, sir.

MONK: Back to the Café Libre! You say you got drunk, had to lie
   down – there we are, there it is, don't overshoot – look out,

(*As they swerve off road down a side road*) look out, there's a
nasty bend ahead, and there he is (*Pointing out of window to
plane coming in to land*) Heindrich's coming in, we've only
just made it – (*Flings door open and starts to run towards
hangar, shouting as he does so*) Hope to God they've
remembered the champagne! Come on, come on, you too,
girlie! you can lend a hand in the singing and drinking,
you're good at that! (*Goes on running.*
BOB *runs after him.* PRU *gets out, runs after them, and cut to:*)

INT. EPSOM AIRFIELD: HANGAR. NIGHT

MONK *bursts in, passes a table on which a bottle of champagne, in a
bucket.*

MONK: (*Plucks the bottle out of the bucket, tosses it behind him to
BOB*) Here, you deal with that – he'll be coming through the
back – glasses, girlie, get them on the table – in the crate
there –
(*Goes to back doors, pushes them open, as* BOB, *who has caught
the bottle deftly, is now staring down at it in some confusion,
then decides to work on it with his teeth. Meanwhile,* PRU *has
located crate and takes out some grubby, used, unwashed
glasses.*)
PRU: How many? (*To* BOB.)
BOB: (*Taking bottle out of his mouth*) Oh, just the four, old girl, I
suppose.
(PRU *puts them on the table, wiping them with her sleeve as she
does so, and see from their point of view, the doors wide open.
Plane taxis to a stop beside doors: a figure, not visible because of
the light and darkness, leaps out, comes towards them.*)
MONK: (*Surges back*) Come on, come on, it's his birthday, give
him a greeting – haven't you got that open yet?
(*Snatches bottle from between* BOB's *jaws, wrestles with it,
singing:*)

Happy birthday to you/ Happy birthday to you –
(PRU *and* BOB *join in,* PRU *blurring over the name.*)
MONK/BOB/PRU: Happy birthday, dear Heindrich –
(*The cork flies off the champagne bottle, foams over* PRU, *who is standing next to* MONK, *who is staring aghast, as is* BOB, *at* MAURICE, *a rather roly-poly figure, reminiscent of Roy Kinnear, emerging into the full light of the hangar. He is unbelievably grubby, utterly exhausted.*)
PRU: (*On her own*) Happy birthday to you!
MONK: Maurice! What the hell are you doing here! (*Strides over to him.*) Where's Heindrich?
MAURICE: (*Swaying, close to passing out, but deeply happy at being back*) Oh, don't worry – at the moment he is all right – not like me – (*gestures*) he has the luck, old Heindrich – sleeps every night in a café – I have not slept for two weeks except with pigs in a ditch – so we decided to change with each other – I know – he next time –
MONK: You decided! You decided!
(*Grips* MAURICE *by the lapels, then brings himself under control.*)
And what about my info? Did you get it to all the right people? Did you?
(*Restrains himself from shaking* MAURICE *again, tries smiling calmly.*)
MAURICE: Ah, the info. The info. Monk. There is the problem. Exactly there. I tell them in Lyons – yes, the three in Lyons – and they were very frightened, Monk – terrified – they tell me to shut up, to go away, to hide, and then they vanish – perhaps the Bosch – or like me, with the pigs in ditches –
MONK: Only Lyons – only Lyons – but they weren't important – I told you that it was Bordeaux that mattered – Bordeaux – all fifteen of them – that's why I gave you three weeks – three whole weeks – so you could get to all of them – it has to come from you – *you* – they've been told not to trust any other source. Not even me! Didn't you understand that, man, and we've got – nine – nine – only nine –

MAURICE: A little rest – a few days – then I go back – yes, to
    Bordeaux – do what you wish, Monk – I swear – I swear –
    (*Passes out.*)

INT. CAR. NIGHT

PRU *driving.* MAURICE *is lying against her. He is obviously
extremely smelly, from the twitching of* PRU's *nostrils, who is leaning
as far away from him as possible.* MONK *and* BOB *are in the back.*

MONK: What's the first rule? Don't panic! Take it step by step!
    What's the first problem? Maurice over here when he
    should be over there – solution, get him back immediately,
    tomorrow morning – tomorrow morning, eh? Your
    department, Bob.
BOB: Right, Monk. But if he'll crack up without a rest and he's
    got to make fifteen contacts when he gets back, all miles
    apart –
MONK: Don't be bloody ridiculous, he doesn't have to, the
    contacts don't matter, *he's* what matters – as long as we get
    him back he can spend his time there with his pigs in a ditch
    if he likes – now, second problem, we've got to put him
    somewhere for the night and get him a bath or they'll smell
    him coming before he's across the Channel – solution, hey
    girlie –
    (*Leans forward, taps* PRU *on the shoulder.* PRU *jumps. Car
    swerves. Cut to:*)

INT. PRU'S FLAT: BATHROOM. NIGHT

MAURICE *standing, swaying, as* PRU *finishes undressing him. Takes
in, in her almost somnambulist state, his smells, from his body, clothes.*

PRU: (*Dully*) In. (*Gestures heavily to bath.*)
MAURICE: (*Dazed*) Quoi?

PRU: (*In French*) Into the bath.

MAURICE: *Ah, oui maman.* (*Clambers infantilely into the bath.* PRU *carries clothes out of the bathroom, into kitchen, shoves them into rubbish, goes back into bathroom.* MAURICE *is asleep in the bath.* PRU *takes soap, begins to wash him.* MAURICE *makes little mewling noises of pleasure, and cut to* MAURICE, *standing naked, asleep on his feet,* PRU *drying him.*)

PRU: Now to bed. (*In French, taking his hand.*)

MAURICE: But where are my pyjamas, *maman*?

PRU: (*In French*) No pyjamas, *mon petit.*

MAURICE: (*As he is led into Pru's bedroom*) Ah, no pyjamas, *maman. Merci, maman.*

INT. PRU'S FLAT: BEDROOM. NIGHT

MAURICE *asleep,* PRU *tucking him in. She tiptoes to cupboard, selects clothes for morning. Cut to:*

INT. PRU'S FLAT: SITTING-ROOM. NIGHT

Clothes arranged on chair by sofa. Old clothes discarded in a heap. PRU *finishes making up small and uncomfortable sofa, sets alarm for half-past six, is about to clamber into bed, when a sudden, terrible cry from* MAURICE. PRU *runs to bedroom.*

INT. PRU'S FLAT: BEDROOM. NIGHT

MAURICE *is sitting bolt upright, shaking with fear, in a nightmare.*

MAURICE: (*In French*) I know nothing – nothing – my name is Maurice Le Grand, mechanic, supporter of Vichy, God bless Pétain, I know nothing, I know nothing, help me, help me –

PRU: (*Puts her arms around him, and in French*) It's all right, it's all right, here is *maman*, she will save you.

MAURICE: Hold me, maman. Hold me tight. Keep them away.
   They will kill me. I know nothing. I am Maurice Le Grand,
   mechanic, supporter of Vichy –
   (PRU *gets into bed, puts her arms around* MAURICE. *He shakes
   for a while, then falls asleep.*
   Cut to: later. PRU, *exhausted, awake, holding* MAURICE *who
   is deeply asleep. Cut to:*)

INT. PRU'S FLAT: BEDROOM. DAY

Later: early morning. MAURICE *still clutching.* PRU's *eyes fluttering,
close to sleep. Distant sound of alarm.* PRU's *eyes open. She makes to
get out of* MAURICE's *clutch. He pulls her back in his sleep, her eyes
flutter, her head nods, almost goes to sleep.*
There is an imperious ring at the doorbell. PRU *jerks awake, looks
around in panic, pulls her dress over her head as another ring, runs to
the door, as another ring. She opens the door.*
Cut to: MONK *and* BOB.

MONK: (*Takes in her dishevelled state, including bare legs and feet*)
   Just getting dressed, are we? Six thirty means six thirty in
   our line of work even if it means giving up a few minutes
   sleep (*pushing past,* BOB *following*) – where is he?
   (PRU *nods to her bedroom.* MONK *goes in, followed by* BOB,
   and see briefly from PRU's *point of view* MAURICE *curled up,
   thumb in his mouth, eyes flickering.*)
   'Morning, Maurice, everything's taken care of, nothing for
   you to worry about –
   (PRU *desperately dressing, and see from her point of view* BOB
   coming out of bedroom, his hand around MAURICE's *arm.*
   MAURICE *is being pulled along, dressed in Pru's dressing-gown
   and a pair of Pru's slippers, one of which he loses in the hall.*
   MONK *is riding herd, squeezing against him.*)
MAURICE: This is not just – this is not English – always we have
   a holiday – four days – three – that's all I ask – (*Sees* PRU,

turns towards her imploringly.) Ah, petite maman, mon ange,
help me –
        (*Is jostled out into the passage towards the door.*)
MONK: Well, don't just stand there – you've got a job to do –
        come and do it –
        (PRU *grabs handbag, coat, runs after them, down the hall, out
        on to the pavement.*)

EXT. STREET IN FRONT OF PRU'S FLAT. DAY

There are two cars parked: the one PRU *drove the night before and
another one, atrociously parked, its wheels on pavement.*
BOB *is standing with his only arm around* MAURICE'S *chest.* MONK *is
standing in front of* MAURICE, *who is twitching in struggle.* MONK *is
talking earnestly and very fast and very low to* MAURICE, *both hands
on* MAURICE'S *shoulders, in restraint.* MAURICE *is listening, in spite
of himself.* PRU *watches, not able to hear properly, marooned
between the two cars, unsure of what she's meant to do.*

MAURICE: You promise!
MONK: I promise!
MAURICE: All right then, Monk. I agree. But if it does not
        happen, Monk, I swear, I swear to God –
MONK: There's a good chap!
        (*Gives him a little shake, strides towards* PRU.)
        Get in, get in, why aren't you behind the wheel, I've got
        work to do, you've got Waterloo to get to –
        (PRU *hurries to car, gets in.* MONK *gets into back.*)
MAURICE: But you're not letting him drive – he's not driving
        me –
MONK: Bob's an excellent driver. He drove me here! Why aren't
        we moving? (*To* PRU.
        PRU *starts the engine.*)
MAURICE: (*He is at the window*) I go with Bob to the airfield. It is
        madness, but I go. I go to Bordeaux. It is madness, but I go.

But in eight days – eight days at the most late – I return. I return. That is our agreement? Before this – this sacred witness.

MONK: My agreement, pledge and solemn promise. Eight days at the most. That's all I ask.

MAURICE: Good. Then for eight days I shall think of nothing but *mon ange! Ma petite maman!* Thus I shall survive.
(*Seizes* PRU's *hand, raises it reverently to his lips.*)
You shall be my life. In here. (*Touches her hand to his head.*)
And in here.
(*Turns, walks with dignity to car, which* BOB *is now standing beside, door opens.* MAURICE *gets in.*)

PRU: (*Has started moving the car out*) Where to, sir?
(PRU *drives past* BOB, *who has leapt into driver's seat, is making an appalling hash of setting off.* PRU *takes this in as* MONK *leans forward, propping elbows on passenger seat next to* PRU.)

MONK: Oh come, girlie, you already know the schedule, me to the loony-bin, then you by tube to Waterloo (*checking watch*) in forty-three minutes! So foot down and keep it there – now, this is round two, remember, so don't forget for a second that Cat-lady's a professional and you're just an amateur, so if you put a foot wrong you'll end up with a bullet between your eyes or barbed wire around your neck and I'll have a ruined op with at least two thousand dead Englishmen on my conscience, now your main objective is to get her on to Fattypuffs and Thinnifers – what was that bump, did you run over something? (*As* PRU *slows down.*) No, keep going, keep going, probably only a dog – and don't forget Petunia Humbert will be there, but don't worry about her, that woman can make herself so invisible she can virtually follow you into your lavatory without your noticing – and another thing, very important –
(*Cut to:*)

INT. WATERLOO STATION: LADIES' WAITING ROOM. DAY

From PRU's *point of view, dimly lit. A number of women sitting about. Her eyes go from one to the other, taking in* PETUNIA, *who is knitting viciously away in a corner, several women, one sitting in the corner, whom she can't see very clearly, her eyes travel on, rest on a young woman, glamorous but slightly furtive looking. She has a fur bundle on her lap. One of her hands is concealed, the other resting on the fur bundle.*

PRU *looking about unconcernedly, her eyes going to fur bundle, she hurries over to her, makes to speak, woman withdraws hand from bundle, revealing it as a muff,* PRU *veers away, her eyes settle on woman in corner who lights a cigarette, illuminating her face, dark and mysterious. But the rest of her is not properly visible.* PRU *stares towards her, when she suddenly becomes aware of a woman at the door, staring in, clutching a handbag with a cat for a clasp, which she is stroking. She is young, big, horsey, wearing country clothes. Their eyes meet.* CAT-LADY *turns, goes out.*

PRU *gets up, follows her.* CAT-LADY *strides rapidly to bench, unoccupied. Sits down.* PRU *follows, sits down beside her.*

PETUNIA *flounders out of waiting room, attempting to gather up wool trailing all around her, clutching at her chest. Sits down at nearby bench, resumes knitting, though with great difficulty.*

PRU: Excuse me, I think we have a friend in common, Ninette.

CAT-LADY: (*She has a pronounced little girl lisp completely at odds with her clothes and manner. Slightly artificial*) What the hell's kept you! I sat in that bloody place for fifteen minutes, do you think this is some sort of game, (*Lighting a cigarette*) we could both end up swinging by our necks, don't you know that?

PRU: I'm sorry, I had a bit of trouble getting away from my boss –

CAT-LADY: Oh la la, I bet you did. (*Lets out a coarse, explosive laugh at variance with her lisp.*) Well, I haven't time for your sex life, my train's due in five minutes, let's get to business, Fattypuffs and Thinnifers, ever heard of them?

PRU: Oh yes, I know the book almost word for word, the French one, *Patapoufs et Fillifers*, Mummy used to read it to me almost every night for years – two pages and then my prayers in English was the ritual! (*Laughs.*)

CAT-LADY: How absolutely disgusting, what can they do, the forces of the Hun, against a single English child at prayer, blow it up, that's what they can bloody do! (*This comes out in a surge of viciousness that the lisp makes more grotesque. She checks herself, as if realizing she's made a mistake, and hurriedly*) You know perfectly well what I mean, Fattypuffs and Thinnifers in your Section 18, from your Commander Scott.
(PRU *hesitates.*)
You have, haven't you? So get on with it.

PRU: I've heard them mentioned once or twice – I don't know who they are –

CAT-LADY: You don't have to know. All you have to do is to find out how much they weigh this month, to the exact ounce.

PRU: But that must be top secret info. If I get caught –

CAT-LADY: You'll hang. So don't get caught.

PRU: But I don't even know how –

CAT-LADY: Yes, you do. We know you're sleeping with Scott, that phoney aunt of yours told Ninette, besides you've just admitted it, what else would you be doing with him at seven in the morning – look, this is a waste of time, I've got about two minutes – (*Takes envelope out of her bag, unclasping cat-clasp with a sharp noise as she does so.*) Take a look!
(PRU *extracts from the envelope a heap of photographs. See quickly a succession of photographs of* CAT-LADY *in jodhpurs, holding a dog,* CAT-LADY *on a horse,* CAT-LADY *at a point-to-point,* CAT-LADY *on a horse, holding a trophy.*
Sees them, snatches them) No, no, not those – (*Upset*) these, these are yours! (*Hands back half photographs from underneath.*)

(PRU *looks at them. They are of herself, naked, cradled in the* ADMIRAL'*s arms, and variations on this.*)
What would your Commander Scott say to those? You get the negatives back the moment you pass over the info, and it's got to be soon, in the next couple of days, or they go elsewhere, including Scott and the police. It's your own fault – you should just have agreed to do it – you're half French, we're Free French, it's your bloody duty – the moment you've found out tell Ninette, she'll arrange another meeting – (*Turns away, stuffing envelope into handbag, sees something.*) Oh damn, there's this. (*Taking package out*) And tell her from me she's being a bloody fool, tell her to pull herself together or she'll do for us all, there are six in it, we're not getting her any more.
(*Turns, strides off, past* PETUNIA, *who desperately gathers together her knitting.*
PRU *looks down at photographs again, the last one is of* CAT-LADY *on a horse. She puts them and package in her own handbag, looks again towards* CAT-LADY *striding along concourse,* PETUNIA *still sitting on bench.*
PRU *gets up, walks quickly off in the other direction, clearly in emotional turmoil. Cut to:*)

EXT. STREET OUTSIDE CAFÉ LIBRE. DAY

Car parked outside Café Libre, TWO MEN *in it, unnoticed by* PRU. *She goes to the door, pushes. It is locked. She looks around, finds bell, pushes it. There is a pause. Door opens.* HELEN WATSON *is standing there, in apron, etc., a mop in her hand. She is surprised to see* PRU, *then smiles ingratiatingly as she lets* PRU *pass.*

HELEN: I'm very sorry about what I said last night, m'um. I was that upset –
PRU: (*Making effort*) That's all right. Where's Ninette, please?
HELEN: Upstairs, m'um – and if you could put in a word for me –

(PRU *nods, turns, hurries through Café, chairs on tables, bucket*
HELEN *working from in evidence, otherwise empty. She does not
notice that* HELEN *has stayed at the door, is gesturing quickly
across the street.*)

INT. CAFÉ LIBRE: RESTAURANT. DAY

PRU *goes up the stairs, opens the door.*

INT. CAFÉ LIBRE: UPSTAIRS ROOM. DAY

ADMIRAL *is lying seemingly naked on the sofa, face down.* NINETTE
*is straddling him, her skirt hiked up, pumping up and down as she
twists away at his neck. The first impression is one of bizarre sex.*
PRU *stands staring.*

NINETTE: (*Becomes aware of her, clambers off*) There – that is
what you did to him with your dancing and drinking – his
neck and his back – of course he deserves it too, the blasted
old bugger, but for me it is exhausting – well, my package,
you have it, where is it?
(PRU *takes it out of the bag, hands it to her.* ADMIRAL *rises
ropily off sofa. He is unshaven, looks disgusting. He is also
wearing a pair of voluminous underpants, previously unseen. He
goes to his clothes as:*)
PRU: She says she's given you six, she won't give you any more,
you're to pull yourself together. (*In French.*)
NINETTE: Pshaw! What does she know? She is not me, she
doesn't have him, she's not surrounded by spies and traitors
– (*In French, unwrapping package with eager hands, half-
turned from* PRU.)
PRU: When I have the information she wants me to tell you. You
will arrange our next meeting. (*In French.*)
NINETTE: Yes, yes – (*As she continues excitedly unwrapping
package.*) It will be done, it will be done!

PRU: And she gave me these. To make sure I'd do what she says. (*Holding out photographs.*
NINETTE *and* ADMIRAL *look at them,* ADMIRAL *while struggling into corset,* NINETTE *still pre-occupied with unwrapping package.*
Her voice shaking) I didn't know people could do such disgusting things to people! (*In English.*)

ADMIRAL: I assure you, *mademoiselle*, there was no impropriety – (*In English.*)

NINETTE: Well? And so? Do you think we can just accept you without protection, do you think I trust anyone? Anyone? Why do you think you are special? We are all threatened, all in danger – yes, now you too (*Wagging the contents of the package under* PRU's *nose. It is a small but lethal-looking pistol.*) You are threatened with photographs, and I threaten you with this if you do anything – anything – anyone – I do not go alone, no, no – now. Now. (*Steadying herself*) You understand, eh? Good. So go away and come back when you have your blasted information –
(*Door opens.* HELEN WATSON *is standing at it.*
Swiftly lowering pistol, concealing it) Oh you, of course you don't know to knock on doors, but still you are finished, you horrible English thing, you don't stay until the end of the week, you leave now, understand! *Mis à la porte*, out, out!

HELEN: (*With authority, and an improved accent*) With pleasure, Miss Lelièvre. But first there are some gentlemen who'd like a word with you. (*Turns*) Come in, chaps!
(*The* TWO MEN *from the car outside enter. One is bald, fat, smiling. The other tall, bespectacled, academic.*)

BALDY: Well, well. (*To* ADMIRAL, *who is frozen, about to step into his trousers*) Been up to something French, have we, sir?

ACADEMIC: (*Looks at him with distaste*) Thank you, Dennis, I'll do this bit. Mademoiselle Ninette Lelièvre, Monsieur Claud Lelièvre, you will please accompany us.

HELEN: The girl too. She's part of it.

(PRU, *aware of photographs in her hand, is trying to sneak them back into her handbag.*)

BALDY: (*Smoothly chuckling*) Name's Derek, not Dennis, wish you'd get that straight, Basil.
(*Stepping across, takes pictures from* PRU *after a slight skirmish, looks down at them, chuckles, hands them to* ACADEMIC.)

ACADEMIC: (*Looks down at them with distaste, then looks at* PRU *with distaste, then to* ADMIRAL) Hurry up! Get dressed!

NINETTE: (*To* ADMIRAL) I told you – I told you that blasted girl –

HELEN: That blasted girl's going to finish you. I can't wait to give evidence –

NINETTE: Can't you? Can't you (*Shoots* HELEN *dead.*)
(ACADEMIC, BALDY, *freeze.* NINETTE *swings gun backwards and forwards between them, her expression demented with triumph.*)

NINETTE: Now – now you see, you English – lewd and disgusting English –

ACADEMIC: *Je vous – je vous assure, ma chère mademoiselle –*
(*Suddenly springs.*)
(NINETTE *shoots him dead.*)

NINETTE: Ha ha! Ha ha ha!
(BALDY *stares aghast, then chuckles placatingly, raises his hands.* NINETTE *shoots him dead.*)
Ha ha! Ha ha ha!
(*Swings the gun on* PRU. PRU *stands absolutely immobile, convinced that her last moment has come.*)

ADMIRAL: Oh Ninette, Ninette, Ninette. (*Sadly*)

NINETTE: (*Gradually comes to herself, looks around at the carnage*) *Alors, c'est fini.* (*In a mutter.*
ADMIRAL *comes to her, trousers still around his ankles, takes gun from her.*)

ADMIRAL: (*To* PRU) *Allez, mon enfante! Tout de suite!*
(PRU *turns to go, then checks herself, stoops, picks up the photographs, among them* CAT-LADY *on a horse, then goes to*

door, turns, sees ADMIRAL *and* NINETTE *standing, looking at each other. She closes the door, runs down the stairs.*
PRU, *as she runs down the stairs, nearly stumbling, hears a shot. She falters. A slight pause. Then another shot. She continues down rest of stairs, out through the kitchen, the restaurant, in a state of shock.*
Cut to:)

EXT. STREET. DAY

PRU *walking along in a state of shock, makes to cross road, nearly steps under a taxi. Driver skids to a halt inches from her, leans out.*

DRIVER: What are you trying to do, get yourself to hospital?
PRU: (*Blankly*) Yes, that's right. The Psychiatric Hospital in
    Clapham, please. (*Gets in.*
    Cut to:)

INT. HQ. PSYCHIATRIC HOSPITAL. DAY

PRU *walking along corridors, approaching Monk's office. From within there come extraordinary yelps, banging noises. She blinks as if achieving a slightly clearer degree of consciousness, frowns, puzzled, opens the door.*

INT. HQ. MONK'S OFFICE. DAY

MONK *and* BOB *are engaged in a ferocious game of office squash, both their faces intense with concentration,* BOB's *as always affably,* MONK's *savagely. They continue playing, as if unaware that* PRU *is in the room, the ball zinging around her until hurled by* MONK *it bounces closer to her than to* BOB. PRU *catches it by reflex, the skilful ball player, and without thinking hurls it at the wall. She is immediately included in the game,* MONK *still not seeming to notice that she is there, although playing to her as much as to* BOB (*whose*

*one-armed agility, by the way, is phenomenal). The game continues
between the three of them at great speed, during the following:*

MONK: (*Suddenly, the game still going on*) How long do we have to
    wait, girlie! Cat-lady, Cat-lady, out with it!
PRU: Yes, sir. (*Catching, throwing, etc.*) Perhaps I should begin
    with recent events at the Café Libre, sir.
MONK: Bugger the Café Libre, get on with Cat-lady, don't say
    you didn't meet, don't say that!
PRU: No, sir. We met, sir. (*Catching ball, a very difficult one.*)
BOB: Oh well caught, sir!
MONK: And? And? And?
PRU: It was just as you said, sir. They wanted to know about
    Fattypuffs and Thinnifers. Their weight this month.
MONK: (*To* BOB) Well, that's that then. Virtually all done! And
    when do you see her again?
PRU: She wants us to meet as soon as I've found out, sir.
MONK: That'll be in two minutes' time! (*Laughs.*) No, make it –
    now we've got a bit of breathing space – for tomorrow
    morning. Keep 'em on edge, eh?
PRU: Yes, sir. How, sir?
MONK: How? Well, presumably you made an arrangement,
    girlie?
PRU: Yes, sir. I'm to go to the Café Libre and tell Ninette I've
    got the info. And then Ninette will fix up the meeting. But
    you see, sir –
MONK: There you are then! What could be simpler?
PRU: Ninette's – Ninette's dead, sir.
    (MONK *stares at her. Ball ricochets off wall. He catches it
    without looking at it.*)
BOB: Oh, well caught, sir!
    (*Cut to Monk's office, later.* BOB *is sitting on desk, mopping at
    himself with a handkerchief,* PRU *also, both still slightly
    breathless, but come straight in on* MONK *on telephone.*)
MONK: (*On telephone, sweating profusely, not mopping himself*)

Vodka! You planted that girl in the Café Libre to keep an
eye out for the black market vodka! (*Listens.*) Oh, and last
night she uncovered a pornography racket – well,
Commissioner, I can see that that's very serious – stopping
the sale of black market vodka, stamping out the production
of dirty postcards – far more important than winning the –
(*Listens*) but it wasn't murder, was it, Commissioner, until
your two chaps went trampling in and got themselves
murdered, until then your only concerns were vodka and
filth, in spite of the fact that I warned you, warned you to
steer clear of the Café Libre, I needed it, needed it –
(*Listens*) what do you mean! Nonsense! I sent over a chit,
signed by myself, three weeks ago –
(*Stops, stares at* BOB, *who has spotted something on his desk,
picked it up, looked at it, is now showing it to* MONK, *shame-
faced. It is a chit.* MONK *slams down the phone, stares at* BOB.)

BOB: (*After a pause*) Sorry, Monk. Don't know how it slipped my
– my

MONK: Perhaps if you spent less time feeling sorry for yourself,
and more time on your duties – and as for you, girlie, there
you were with a mad woman and a gun, a perfectly simple
situation, didn't they teach you unarmed combat at
Cheltenham Ladies' College?

PRU: I'm sorry, sir – it was so quick, you see – and I still don't
understand why she did it – and then that her father – her
own father –

MONK: Why do people say that? *Own* father! *Own* father! A
father's a father, *own* doesn't come into it, anyway he wasn't
her father, he was her uncle, common-law uncle, filthy
couple, they *would* be doing pornography on the side, and
the reason she shot everybody was because she thought the
game was up, that our idiot police were arresting her for
spying, which meant that she would have been first
interrogated, then hanged, isn't that obvious, I thought that
was obvious!

PRU: But why did she think that, sir? Surely we don't hang the
Free French, even for spying, after all we're on the same
side –

MONK: Free French! Do your really think the Free French go
around shooting police officers in the middle of London,
even the Free French aren't that lunatic, she was Vichy,
working for the Hun, but I haven't got time to sit back and
take you through your mental muddles and
misunderstandings, the fact is that between the two of you
you've landed us plonk into a crisis, a crisis, without
Ninette we can't make contact with Cat-girl, without Cat-
girl I can't get the wrong Fattypuff/Thinnifer info through
to the Huns, and – (*Slaps desk*) Petunia! Thank God I had
the foresight to stick Pentunia on Cat-girl's tail!
(*Telephone rings.*
Snatches it up) Clapham Psychiatric Hospital, Section 18,
Monk. (*Little pause.*) Yes, that's right, Commander Scott,
what is it, who is this? (*Listens.*) I see. Where exactly?
(*Listens.*) I see. How long ago? (*Listens.*) I see. Well, thank
you very, very much for letting me know. (*Hangs up
thoughtfully, looks at* PRU *almost gently*) Petunia Humbert is
dead. Her corpse was found sitting on a bench at Waterloo
Station.

BOB: Oh Lord!

MONK: Now I'm being very calm about this, and not allowing
myself to grieve for Petunia, whom I adored, adored,
because I want you to be calm too, girlie. You're our only
hope now.

PRU: Sir.

MONK: Our only hope is you.

PRU: Sir.

MONK: What we need is a clear and vivid description of Cat-
girlie. And remember, many, many chaps may die if you
fail. Ready?

PRU: Sir.

MONK: Right. Close your eyes. Concentrate . Fire away.

PRU: (*Closing eyes*) Well, it was a very short meeting, about five minutes in all because of her train but – but she – the main thing I remember about her was her voice – her voice, she had a lisp like a little girl but it sounded all wrong, perhaps because she was so big and – and – she hates children and – and – oh, of course! she loves dogs and horses, yes, she's the horsey type, won a trophy at a point-to-point, goes to hunts – got a beautiful grey mare, a brown chestnut – the dog's a spaniel, and there was also a poodle –

MONK: (*Sharply*) Just a moment. You say you had a few minutes with her?

PRU: Sir.

MONK: And she spent them lisping away about hating children and telling you about her dogs and horses and point-to-points? Sounds very odd to me, girlie, very odd.

PRU: Well, sir, she didn't actually talk about them but I saw some pictures –

MONK: She showed you pictures? Of herself?

PRU: Sir. But – these are the ones she really wanted me to see – (*With sudden, desperate resolve, snatches up her handbag, opens it, takes out pictures, hands them to* MONK.) These, sir.

MONK: (*Looks down at the top one*) And this is Cat-lady? This is actually Cat-lady? (*Holding up picture of* CAT-LADY *on a horse.*)

PRU: I'd forgotten that one, sir, because – because of the others.

MONK: (*As he begins to look at others*) But why in God's name didn't you show them to me at once instead of – (*stops, stares*) and why show you pictures of herself cavorting about in the nude with some old crone during a five minute conversation – there's something very wrong here – a trick of some sort –

BOB: (*Staring over his shoulder*) Um, no, Monk, those others are of – of – (*Nods his head towards* PRU.)

MONK: (*Peers closely, checking photograph with* PRU's *face*) So it is, so it is! Then who's the old crone?

BOB: The uncle, isn't it?

MONK: So it is! So she was blackmailing you, eh, girlie?

PRU: Yes, sir. You see, she – she thinks we're sleeping together –

MONK: Who? Who?

PRU: You and – you and I, sir. Because that's what Petunia told Ninette and then Ninette –

MONK: That's what made Petunia so special! Her little flashes of inspiration – could make people believe anything, however grotesque – God, I'm going to miss that old rascal – well, well, she's left us a legacy – (*Rapping photos*) what a legacy – and Cat-lady has bungled, bungled her way to the end of a rope probably, eh, now we've got this we're bound to find her – (*Holding up* CAT-LADY *photo*) and now we know she's got these (*Holding up photos of* PRU) she's handed girlie here exactly the right motive for going looking for her, I mean if girlie here just turns up at some hunt or point-to-point we've tracked Cat-girl down to and says, 'Here I am, I've found out who you are and where you live' – (*Doing coarse imitation of* PRU) 'so that I can give you the relevant info on Fattypuffs and Thinnifers, their weight this month', Cat-girlie would tell her to bugger off, she wasn't having any of it, but now girlie can turn up and say, 'I've found out who you are and where you live because I'm so desperate, please, please give me my photos back and I'll give you the info' – (MONK *wringing his hands as he does the imitation*) Cat-girlie won't think twice – so all we have to do is find her and then we've got her – and I'm not overlooking your part in this, girlie, it's true that if you hadn't agreed to pose in the nude with that filthy old man the bobbies wouldn't have ruined my op and got themselves killed into the bargain, but it's also because of you that it's going to turn out all right, and I'll tell you this for nothing, most girls would rather have

404

died than debase themselves as you did, girlie, it almost
makes up for all your other blunders!

PRU: Thank you, sir. (*Bursts into tears.*)

MONK: But what did I – what did I – I mean, you pay them a
compliment and they – they –

BOB: Well, I expect from her point of view she's been having
rather a strange time, Monk – you know, murders, suicide,
posing for dirty pictures, blackmail –

MONK: Yes, yes, but that's all part of the job. I told you at the
beginning it wouldn't be just driving about having a good
time, didn't I?

PRU: Yes, sir. I'm sorry, sir. Very, very sorry. (*Struggling to
bring herself under control.*)

MONK: Apology accepted, accepted! But please don't do it again.
It muddles my mind up, and it has to be kept clear, lives
depend on its clarity, Petunia never cried, never, did she,
Bob?

(BOB *shakes his head.*)

Nag, nag, natter, natter, but no tears ever. You see, girlie?

PRU: Sir. (*In a whisper.*)

MONK: Right, good, now we've cleared that up, here's what we
do, this is what we do, you girlie – (*Tossing photos on table.*)
(*From* PRU's *point of view see photos swimming before her
eyes.*

Out of shot) – and you, Bob, you two go straight down to the
library, get out copies of all relevant magazines, *Horse and
House*, *Country Life*, *Tatler*, etc. While I contact the Home
Office – (*Picking up telephone.*

Cut to PRU *from his point of view staring at photographs
listlessly.*)

But what's the matter, why aren't you on your way?

PRU: Sir. (*Clambers shakily to her feet, swaying slightly.*)

BOB: I think she may be a bit, um, peckish, Monk. Probably
hasn't had much chance for a bite.

PRU: (*Feebly*) No, no, I'm –

MONK: (*Cutting across*) Oh for – ! Very well then, stop off on the way to the library and feed her – but no dallying about over cups of tea! (*Looking at his watch.*
BOB *supports* PRU *out of office, closes the door.*
MONK *crosses quickly to radio, rather furtively, puts it on, and at first crackling is heard, then:*)

RADIO ANNOUNCER: (*Voice over, radio*) – Amelia Cleverly, with her afternoon thought in war-time.

AMELIA: (*Voice over, radio*) In these dreadful days, when there's very much to worry about, with bombs falling on our cities and chaps risking and losing their lives, so far from all who love them –
(MONK *sits down with a sigh, takes out his handkerchief.*
Voice over, radio) – we don't often allow ourselves time to think about the many little things that give us pleasure, but let us pause for a second –
(*Cut to:*)

INT. HQ. CANTEEN. DAY

PRU *is gobbling down the last of a sandwich, swigging down from a mug of tea, watched by* BOB. *She then crams a jam roll into her mouth, swigs down more tea.*
At other tables, an assortment of personnel sitting, while over, on the radio, AMELIA's *talk, to which they are all listening in rapture and reverence.*

AMELIA: (*Voice over, radio*) – the continuing beauty of our native English flowers, even though so many have vanished. The roses and hollyhocks that have had to make way for the necessary potatoes and spinach in our favourite spots of our gardens.

BOB: (*During the above*) God, you really were peckish, weren't you?

PRU: (*Nods, gulps down more tea*) Loss of sugar, you see. Always

used to tell my girls – after a big game – get sugar down
you –
(*People at nearby tables glance towards her with disgust, as they
try to listen.*)

BOB: You know, old girl – you know – I think – I mean given
that Monk just chucked you in the deep end – well, I just
want you to know –

WOMAN: (*Nearby table*) Sssh!

BOB: Oh sorry, sorry – (*In a whisper to* PRU) of course it's old
Amelia Cleverly. Monk likes her too, though he never really
admits it.

PRU: For me – for me she's the real voice of England. Do you
mind if I – if you don't want –
(*Takes Bob's mug, drinks and listens as:*)

AMELIA: (*Voice over, radio*) Ah, but look harder about you, those
of you who know and love our native countryside, and your
eye can still fall on the daisies and dandelions growing in the
same spots they grew in centuries ago, those little miracles
of our timeless history –
(PRU *sits with mug in hand, then lowers it reverentially, puts
hand to her eyes.* BOB, *also moved, smiles at her.*
Voice over, radio*) – the small, self-perpetuating tokens from
the very soil of our dear, blessed land that no bombs,
bayonets or tanks can ever destroy. And then think of our
children.
(PRU *catches* BOB's *smile, smiles back at him.*
Voice over, radio*) What can they do, all the forces of the
Hun, against a single English child at prayer.

PRU: (*Stares at* BOB) Blow him up, that's the least they can
bloody do! (*In a loud lisp.*
Sounds of disbelief, outrage, etc. from all around.*
Gets up*) That's her, that's her, the cat-lady!

BOB: Oh come now, old girl! (*Also getting up*) You're still a little
light-headed, I expect –
(*From all around: 'Sssh!', 'Disgraceful!', 'How dare you', etc.*)

AMELIA: (*Voice over, radio, continuing through this*) Let me give
you my favourite picture of this. I expect it is yours, too.
The words are as simple as the picture, and brief, so very
brief – I first heard them from my mother, when I and my
twin sister used to sit at the ends of our beds, after tea and
bath and toothbrushing were over, and sleep ahead, back
there in those old days when bombs never fell and sirens
never screamed and all was safe and warm and English
sunshine, English sleep.

PRU: (*During this*) We have to tell Monk – have to tell Monk –
straight away –
(*Turns, runs out of the canteen, followed by* BOB, *followed by
the angry eyes and exclamations of the listeners, and cut to:*)

INT. HQ. MONK'S OFFICE. DAY

MONK, *tears streaming down his face, as:*

AMELIA: (*Voice over, radio*) Gentle Jesus, meek and mild/ Look
upon this little child/ Pity my simplicity/ Teach me Lord to
come to thee.
(*There is a pause, during which* MONK *blows his nose violently*.)

RADIO ANNOUNCER: That was Amelia Cleverly, with one of her
afternoon thoughts in war-time. She'll be back this evening,
at the usual hour of seven o'clock, with her evening thought
in war-time. And now for a little music, from that most
patriotic of English composers, Sir Edward Elgar.
(*As music commences, the door bursts open,* PRU *and* BOB
enter.)

MONK: (*Desperately trying to adjust his emotional clothing*) Elgar,
Elgar, doesn't sound English to me, more like another Hun
– (*Turning radio off.*) Just hoping to catch the news – missed
it – (*blows nose again*) but what are you two doing here,
you're meant to be down with the magazines – looking for
Catty-girl!

BOB: Well, Monk, um, that's just it – (*Glances worriedly at the radio.*) Corporal Merriman thinks – thinks she knows who Cat-girlie is.
(MONK *looks eagerly towards* PRU. PRU *makes to speak, and cut to Monk's office, a few minutes later.*)

MONK: (*Struggling hard not to believe*) Lots of women have lisps. Small women, big women, hunting women, poisoners – why shouldn't Cat-lady?

PRU: Well, because she hasn't, sir. She's got the most famous voice in England, strong, warm, vibrant – that's why she had to disguise it, and that's why it sounded so false –

BOB: It does make sense, Monk.

PRU: And what she said on the radio about an English child at prayer – that's what she said to me word for word – except she added the bit about blowing it up, but she looked horrified, sir, just for a second, as if afraid she'd done something stupid –

BOB: I did see Corporal Merriman's face, Monk –

MONK: Quiet, let me think, I'm thinking – (*In a rapid mutter in which only certain sentences are audible*) Supposing it's true – just a minute – Waterloo and train – could be a blind – a blind – straight to Broadcasting House – morning Amelia – but there's the voice – wonderful voice – sustained me through dark hours – but then face it, face it – female and the BBC – perfect recipe for treachery so sentimentality put aside, put aside – reason insists – time running out – no choice, no choice – (*Looks at* PRU) You realize we've a mere week to pull off one of the most sophisticated ops in the history of intelligence, we can't afford any more blunders or to go off down sidetracks, you sure about this, girlie? (*Gives her a gimlet stare.*)
(PRU *hesitates. The telephone rings.*
Snatching it) Clapham Psychiatric Hospital, Section 18, Monk. Ted, hello, make it quick, nothing trivial. (*Listens.*) All right, Ted (*Sweetly*) we'll expect him tomorrow at

midnight. (*Puts telephone down, looks at* BOB *and* PRU) It appears that I made a little mistake. I haven't got a mere week to pull off one of the most sophisticated ops in the history of intelligence. I've got a whole day and a half, day and a half! (*Pause, face showing great strain*) So if you're wrong about this, girlie –

PRU: Sir, Amelia Cleverly is the cat-lady. (*Voice shaking slightly.*)

MONK: (*After a pause, nods*) Then here's what we do, this is what we do –
(*Cut to:*)

INT. BROADCASTING HOUSE: RECEPTION. DAY

Various people sitting around, a number of commissionaires in evidence, one standing by the reception desk, to which PRU *hurries. The* RECEPTIONIST *is dealing with a girl, the* COMMISSIONAIRE *clearly listening in.*

GIRL: (*To* RECEPTIONIST) My name's Muriel. I've got a script for Mr Cumbridge from Mr Thomas. Poetry and Drama. He's expecting me.

RECEPTIONIST: Who? (*Checking list.*)

GIRL: Muriel. Mr Cumbridge. Poetry and Drama. Script from Mr Thomas.

RECEPTIONIST: (*Nods, ticks name off list*) You can go up.

COMMISSIONAIRE: Lifts over there, Miss.

PRU: Prunella Merriman for Mr Panter, Security, please.

RECEPTIONIST: Who? (*Checking list.*)

PRU: Prunella Merriman. Mr Panter of Security.

RECEPTIONIST: (*Checks list again*) No such person.

PRU: Well, there must be – I'm sure there is –

RECEPTIONIST: Harry, know a Panter in Security?

COMMISSIONAIRE: Who's asking, may I ask, Miss?

PRU: Prunella Merriman.

COMMISSIONAIRE: And who are you from?

PRU: Well, my employers – they're – actually, as it's a security matter, I'm not at liberty to say.

COMMISSIONAIRE: Oh, aren't you? Your employers, who shall be nameless, ask you to pop over to British Broadcasting Corporation and demand an interview with a non-existent Mr Panter of the Security Department, have I got it right, Miss?

PRU: It's extremely important that I speak to Mr Panter.

COMMISSIONAIRE: It's certainly extremely important that you speak to *somebody* in Security (*taking her by the arm*), come this way, please, Miss. (*Escorting her firmly to the lifts, one of which has just opened its doors.*)
(COMMISSIONAIRE *hustles* PRU *in, and as a few people attempt to follow:*
Holding up free hand to check them) I'll have to ask you to take another lift, reasons of security. (*Presses button five.*)

PRU: (*As lift doors close*) I'm here on urgent business – if you just find Panter he'll clear me –

COMMISSIONAIRE: I'm Panter and you're cleared, Miss. My problem is the only way I can get you into the building is by arresting you virtually, what I keep trying to tell them at the loony-bin is if I'm meant to be undercover why stick me in a uniform at the front desk, where they don't even know my name, to them I'm just Harry, what they should have done is put me in as a producer or director or writer even, now all I've found out is that her talks are just a small part of it, she's hush-hush top security propaganda, fifth floor stuff, her office number isn't listed, her telephone number isn't listed, nobody even knows what she really looks like because she won't let herself be photographed even, all they know is she's the most popular woman in England after Winnie himself – (*Lift stops.*) There you are, Miss, the unlisted offices are at the end of the corridor, you tell Section 18 what I said and keep your eye on the ball, this is a restricted area.

(*Lift door closes as* PRU *steps out, on* COMMISSIONAIRE *looking a menacing warning at her.*

PRU *turns, walks along corridor, looking quickly at the door of each office. They all have numbers until the last four, two on either side of the corridor.* PRU *listens at the door of the first one on the right. Opens it gently.*

Two men absorbed, facing each other in chairs. One is reading rapidly from a script in German; the other, also absorbed, is nodding and muttering with a continuous laugh: 'Ja, ja, sehr gut, sehr gut, Hans.'

PRU *withdraws quietly. Listens at the door opposite, opens it gently. A man is sitting, with his feet up on the desk. He is wearing dark glasses. He is obviously rehearsing, in Polish. Correcting himself. Suddenly stops, stares towards* PRU.)

POLE: Is there somebody there? (*Obviously blind.*

PRU *closes the door softly, moves on to the next, then sees that the door opposite is slightly open. Decides to do that one first. Goes to it, pushes it wider open. The room is empty, but there is a room, off, through which the sound of women's voices, indistinguishable, but ill-tempered.* PRU *looks around, sees on desk the handbag, with cat-clasp on it.*

The door off opens, and a PRODUCER, *a small, fat, almost dwarf-like woman, comes steaming out, shouting as she does so:*)

PRODUCER: – the trouble ith that you're getting too big for your booth!

(*Her lisp is clearly the basis of Cat-lady's imitation. She slams the door, sees* PRU.)

And who the hell are you?

PRU: Is this – is this the office for Amelia Cleverly's *Thoughts in War-time*?

PRODUCER: Yeth, I'm the produther, what do you want?

PRU: Well, I just wanted to pay my respects to Miss Cleverly and say how much – how much I enjoy her programme –

PRODUCER: Do you, how bloody thweet, the fact ith thith part of the buildingth ith rethricted, how did you find uth?

412

THEY NEVER SLEPT

PRU: Well, I was just dropping off a script for – for Mr Cumbridge from Mr Thomas and I mentioned *Thoughts in War-time* and he said to come and tell you – is Miss Cleverly here? (*Glancing towards door.*)

PRODUCER: (*Seizing telephone*) Cumbridge, and what's your name?

PRU: Oh, Muriel – if I could have just a few words with Miss Cleverly –

PRODUCER: (*As she dials*) And thith Cumbridge told you where to go?

PRU: Well, he said fifth floor at the end –
(*Stops as* CAT-LADY *opens door of inner office.*)

CAT-LADY: For God's sakes, Daisy, I'm trying to write a bloody peace thought, can't you keep your –
(*Sees* PRU, *freezes.*)

PRODUCER: One of your ardent fanth, darling, tho much for thecurity! – (*Into telephone*) Thecurity, 'Knocking the Hun' thpeaking!
(CAT-LADY *makes urgent, angry push-off movements of the head to* PRU, PRU *making imploring gestures back. Into telephone*) Apparently there'th an imbethile called Cumbridge on the third floor who'th found out where our offith ith and ith actually thending people along to pay their respecth –
(CAT-LADY *signals to* PRU, *mouths 'Ladies' lav – ladies' lav', gestures direction with her head.* PRU *nods, turns, hurries out, as:*)

PRODUCER: (*Into telephone*) – she'th up here now, named Muriel, hey, hey there – (*To* PRU) they want to talk to you –
(PRU *continues out of office.*)

CAT-LADY: I'll get her – you – come back – come back at once –
(*Following* PRU *out as:*)

PRODUCER: (*Out of shot*) She's running away, it'th all very fithy –
(*Follow* PRU *walking rapidly down corridor, overtaken by* CAT-

413

LADY, *who takes her by the arm, jerks her along a few more paces, opens door of ladies' lavatory, pushes* PRU *roughly into it.*)

CAT-LADY: (*Giving us the full range of her exciting voice*) How dare you – how *dare* you come here – I told you to go through Ninette!

PRU: Ninette's dead. The Admiral shot her. And then himself. With that gun you sent her.

CAT-LADY: The Admiral! The Admiral – but why? Why?

PRU: There was a – a hideous row over one of the waitresses –

CAT-LADY: How typically bloody French! But how the hell did you find me?

PRU: I heard you on our afternoon peace thought. I recognized that line – about the Hun and the English child –

CAT-LADY: Well, I hope you're here because you've got what I want!

(PRU *nods.*)

Let's have it then!

PRU: When I get the negatives back.

CAT-LADY: Don't be ridiculous, do you think I carry the disgusting things around with me!

PRU: Then we meet later. You give me the negatives, I'll give you the info.

CAT-LADY: Then how could I be sure it's true? Once you've got them you could say anything you wanted.

PRU: No negatives, no info.

CAT-LADY: Listen, you little twerp! –

(*Seizes* PRU *by the collar, drags her to her*)

this corridor's swarming with security because of you – so you give me the information, if it's true I'll get you the negatives! (*Shaking her about as she talks.*

PRU *thumps* CAT-LADY *in the stomach twice, quite savagely.* CAT-LADY *lurches back with a yelp.*)

PRU: I'm sick to death of being shaken about by people like you and Ninette – I offered to help and all I get is horrible

414

bullying – (*squaring up to* CAT-LADY) and blackmailing and –
and – I don't give a pickle about security, I want those
negatives!

CAT-LADY: I wish I had time – time to teach you – you say you
want to help, give me the information, and – and – I swear
to you – cross my heart and hope to die – (*Doing it.*)

PRU: How are you going to transmit it?

CAT-LADY: Why?

PRU: If I have something on you that I can prove – then it won't
be so bad you're having these photos on me. But I'll want
them back tomorrow.

CAT-LADY: (*Thinks, nods*) I'll send it in some sort of code. In a
night thought.

PRU: (*Stares at her*) On the – on the radio!

CAT-LADY: Now give me the weights of Fattypuff and Thinnifer!

PRU: When will you transmit it?

CAT-LADY: Tell me the weights, then I'll know.

PRU: Thinnifer is weighing in at twenty-four pounds eleven
ounces, no weight this month for Fattypuff!

CAT-LADY: (*Working it out*) Twenty-four eleven – oh God, I'll
have to transmit it tonight, I'll have to change the script –
look, you've got to go, you've got to go – (*Opens door, looks
out.*
See from her point of view and PRU's *peering over her shoulder
two men at Cat-lady's office door,* PRODUCER *at the door,
talking to them excitedly.*)
I told you!

PRU: The negatives tomorrow – where do we meet?

CAT-LADY: Lyons Corner House. Eight a.m.
(*In an impulse of hatred, seizes* PRU's *hair, gives it a jerk.*)
Little rat!
(PRU, *suppressing yelp, turns, kicks* CAT-LADY's *ankle, then
scurries out into corridor, whips along towards lift, presses
button.*
SECURITY MAN *sees her, saying something to* PRODUCER.

PRODUCER *looks, all this as* PRU *tries to stand nonchalantly at the lift.*

PRODUCER: Yeth – yeth, thatth her!

SECURITY MAN: (*Turns, runs towards* PRU) Miss – hey, Miss! (PRU *pretends deafness as lift arrives. She gets into it, presses ground-floor button. Lift door closes just as* SECURITY MAN *skids in front of it.*)

INT. BROADCASTING HOUSE: LIFT. DAY

PRU, *tense, watches indicator as it passes fourth, then stops at third. Lift door opens.*

COMMISSIONAIRE – PANTER – *and a* MAN IN CIVVIES *get in, shepherding between them a third man –* CUMBRIDGE – *distraught.*

COMMISSIONAIRE *presses basement button, ignoring* PRU.

CUMBRIDGE: Look, this is a nonsense, a nonsense! All I know is that a girl called Muriel delivered a package of new poems from Dylan Thomas and went away – why should I tell her to go and see Amelia Cleverly, I don't know her office number, I don't even know what floor she's on – all I know about the bloody woman is that she does those revolting little peace talks, morning, noon and night –

MAN IN CIVVIES: Revolting? Did you say revolting? (*Menacingly.*

Lift stops at ground floor.)

CUMBRIDGE: I only meant – I only meant – look, I've got a meeting with Dylan Thomas himself in half an hour – I've got to have at least glanced at his poems –

(*Lift door opens at ground floor.* PRU *steps hurriedly out. Other people try to get in.*)

COMMISSIONAIRE: Take another lift, please. This is a security matter. We're going down. (*As doors close.*

PRU *begins to walk quickly through lobby. Aware of commotion behind her. A* SECURITY MAN *has come hurtling*

down the stairs, is now sprinting across the lobby towards her.
PRU, *aware of him, breaks into a run.*)
SECURITY MAN: Here – stop that girl – stop that girl –
(PRU, *as she reaches the door, has her arms grabbed, one on
either side.* MONK *has one,* BOB *the other.*)
MONK: (*as he escorts* PRU *out*) It's all right – we've been looking
for this lady – she's wanted by Scotland Yard – thank you
for helping us detain her, thank you, thank you – (*Pushing
door open, he and* BOB *pulling* PRU *out.*)
(*Various* SECURITY MEN *stop in confusion as* MONK, BOB
bundle PRU *towards waiting car, dreadfully parked.* PRU *is
bundled into driving seat,* MONK *gets in beside her,* BOB *in the
back,* PRU *starts the car, drives off, this shot from the point of
view of* COMMISSIONAIRES, SECURITY, *etc. on the other side
of the doors, spilling on to the pavement.*)

INT. MONK'S CAR. DAY

MONK: (*To* PRU) Epsom airstrip!
(*Cut to:*)

INT.EXT. CAR/COUNTRY LANE. DAY

MONK: Now listen, girlie, you've had a lot of fun being a chap or
a Petunia, spying about the place, infiltrating here,
infiltrating there, time you went back to being a – a fragrant
young female again, that's what we need now –
PRU: Sir.
MONK: Which doesn't mean you can be a woman driver, eye on
the road, tongue and mind on a tight leash, this is what's
happened, Ted was fed false info, Maurice isn't coming
back at midnight, he's actually on his way here now,
something's going on over there, don't know what, and not
your concern anyway, but if we can trust Cat-lady to get the
info out, on her evening thought, can we trust her?

PRU: Yes, sir.

MONK: Hope to God you're right, thousands of lives depend on it, future course of the war, whole allied cause, that's why you've got to look at your prettiest, you see, turn his head. Right back to where he's just come from so however much he gibbers, whines, weeps, even if he goes down on all fours and barks like a dog, you make sure he goes straight back to Bordeaux – pity you couldn't have slipped into something a little more alluring – all your clothes seem to look the same – Amelia Cleverly, eh? Amelia Cleverly. (*His expression briefly tragic. Little pause.*) Get a move on. (*Little pause.*) Careful on the – the –

(PRU *glances at him. His eyes are full of tears, and cut to:*)

EXT. EPSOM AIRFIELD: HANGAR. DUSK

Plane arrival almost exactly as before. Plane coming in to land as car pulls up, MONK *flings open door, runs off towards hangar,* BOB *and then* PRU *following, and cut to:*

INT. HANGAR. DUSK

MONK *bursting in, passing table on which champagne in bucket, plucking bottle out of bucket, flinging it backwards to* BOB, *who catches it, begins to work on it.*

MONK: (*As he runs to the back*) The glasses, girlie!

(PRU *hurries to crate, takes out glasses, wipes them on her sleeve as before.*

MONK *pushing doors open as plane taxis in beside door. Again the figure of man not visible because of the light and darkness, comes towards them.*)

MONK: (*Surges back*) Come on, come on, give him a song – you, girlie – you're the one he wants to hear from – God, Bob, do you have to be so cack-handed!

(*Snatches champagne from* BOB's *jaws, begins to open it as:*)
PRU: (*Hesitates, then breaks into*) Oh God our help in ages past/
    Our hope for years to come –
MONK: No, no, not a hymn, for God's sake, not a hymn!
PRU: Um, um – (*Stares at him hopelessly, as suddenly:*
    Figure advancing breaks into 'La Marseillaise' at the top of his
    voice. He struts towards them, singing away, and as he emerges
    into the full light of the hangar, reveals himself to be a tall,
    gangling fellow, not MAURICE *but* HEINDRICH. *He struts up to*
    them, still singing, as cork flies off champagne bottle, dousing
    MONK, *who is gaping.*)
HEINDRICH: (*Laughs joyfully*) Maurice tells me you greet him
    with a song – so I decide to greet you with one! Oh my
    Monk, how good to see you again –
    (*Pinches* MONK's *cheeks, turns, throws his arms around* BOB,
    gives him a cuddle and a shaking.)
    My Bob, old chap – and this, I cannot be mistaken, is the
    angel – (*takes* PRU's *hand reverentially*) the little mother of
    Maurice – oh, the story he tells about you – (*Kisses her*
    head.) Now some champagne, please –
MONK: (*Pours him a glass, hands it to him*) And where is Maurice,
    Heindrich? (*Keeping himself under firm control, attempting to*
    exude warmth.)
HEINDRICH: (*Raises glass in toast*) *Salut!*
BOB: *Salut!* (*No glass.*)
PRU: *Salut!* (*No glass.*)
MONK: (*No glass*) Yes, yes, *salut, salut!*
    (*As* HEINDRICH *drains his glass*) Heindrich, we were
    expecting Maurice, you know.
HEINDRICH: I know. Poor Maurice. That information you gave
    him about the American troops has driven him completely
    mad. He thinks that either the Germans will capture him
    and torture him for it, or that the Americans and now even
    you, Monk, will assassinate him to stop him being captured
    – he took me by the throat, like this – and shouted it all into

my face, every detail, and then told me if he saw me again
he'd kill me, yes, kill me, his old *copain*, Heindrich – he
hopes *I'll* be captured, you see, and then they won't trouble
with him – and that's why I was so happy to take his place
in the plane, let him stay hidden in his filthy cellar until the
war ends. Then he will come out, bath himself, cross the
channel, and marry his angel, his little *maman*. (*Bows to*
PRU.) That is his plan. I mention it to you, *maman*, to
prepare you for the wait! (*Laughs.*)

MONK: And you know where this filthy cellar is, do you?

HEINDRICH: Of course. I alone know. (*Laughs.*) But do not
think, my dear Monk, (*helps himself to more champagne*) that
if I tell you, you can go yourself and bring him back. He
will shoot you if you try. Also he'll shoot old chap Bob here
if he tries. So forget Maurice until *la guerre est finie*. Think
of Heindrich, and the little holiday he has deserved, eh?
Now where do I go tonight? (*His eyes go meaningfully to*
PRU) For food, a bath, a sweet sleep –
(*Stops, as he takes in first* PRU's *face, grave; then* BOB's,
worried; then MONK's, *full of intent. And cut to:*)

INT. EPSOM AIRFIELD: AEROPLANE HOLD. DUSK

HEINDRICH *being buckled down by* BOB *and* MONK, *from* PRU's
point of view on tarmac.

HEINDRICH: (*Struggling against buckles*) This is not a joke, then,
you are serious, but I tell you, Monk, he is mad, mad,
madder than you even, if he sees I have come back he will
suspect me, he will shoot me –

MONK: Nonsense, nonsense, you'll be perfectly safe, I've worked
it all out, I tell you, you'll be back here in a few hours, all of
you, then you can sleep, drink, do what you like as far as
I'm concerned –

HEINDRICH: (*Writhes desperately*) No, no, I refuse, refuse –

MONK: It's either that or a bullet in the back of your head. Your choice, Heindrich. (*Stares at him coldly, then takes one of his hands, trapped under the straps.*) A few hours. (*Shakes hand.*) There. You have my word for it.

HEINDRICH: Your word – your word – the word of Albion – perfidious Albion – !

MONK: There's a good chap, knew you had it in you – (*Turns to* BOB) everything covered? (*Meaningfully.*)

BOB: Yes, I think so, Monk, thanks.

MONK: Every detail, Bob? (*Even more meaningfully.*)

BOB: Why yes, I – oh, oh – (*Realizing, fumbles in his pocket, takes out two pills, one a slightly darker colour than the other, looks at them in momentary confusion, then as if remembering, puts one back in his pocket, turns to* HEINDRICH) Mustn't forget this, eh, old chap? Only routine, I know, but – (*Putting pill into little pocket in* HEINDRICH's *belt.*)

HEINDRICH: Oh, *ça alors*, no don't forget that! Why not put it straight into my mouth – (*mimes savage bite*) save time, eh? (*Laughs crazily.*)

BOB: Oh, really, old chap, don't make one of your dramas. (*Turns back to* MONK.)

HEINDRICH: (*Muttering over, as* BOB *talking to* MONK) Drama, drama, because I'm a frog, old chap, we make dramas when we are sent by Englishmen to our certain death – (*Throws head back in despair.*)

BOB: Don't worry, Monk. I'll look after everything.

MONK: Just remember – remember how much depends on it. The lives at stake. Don't go soft on us, Bob.
(BOB, *swallowing, shakes his head.*
Claps BOB *on his armless shoulder, leaps down*) Well, girlie – it's up to you now. This is what you've got to do, here is what you've got to do –

PRU: I know what I've got to do, sir.

MONK: (*After a pause, nods*) Time you stopped calling me sir. Time you started calling me Monk.

PRU: Thank you, Monk.

EXT. EPSOM AIRFIELD. DUSK

See from MONK's *point of view plan taking off, as over, traditional RAF film music.*
As MONK *watches, his face taut with emotion, a puppyish young* RAF OFFICER *gambols up to him, holding a slip of paper.*

RAF OFFICER: Message for Commander Scott, sir. (*Rather jolly.*)
MONK: (*His eyes still fixed on plane*) Well, read it out, read it out!
RAF OFFICER: Um – (*Clearing throat, unfolding slip*) um –
  (MONK, *almost unaware of him, and as if in spite of himself, salutes plane now approaching horizon.*)
  (*In a clear, jolly voice*) 'Urgent attention Monk. Owing typical Yankee mess-up' (*chuckles*) 'imperative abort, repeat abort, Operation Fattypuff/Thinnifer. Good luck. Lucifer.
  (MONK *has been standing, frozen in disbelief, still saluting. Plane vanishing over horizon. He turns slowly, stares at* RAF OFFICER.)
  Got all that, sir, or shall I –
MONK: When – when did this come in?
RAF OFFICER: Oh, about five minutes ago, sir, but I thought I'd wait until your friends left before interrupting you.
MONK: Because of you – because of you – three fine men, one of them a woman, will probably go to hideous deaths and for nothing! For nothing! No, worse than that – their deaths will actually advance the German war effort!
  (*Stares at* RAF OFFICER, RAF OFFICER's *face fills with horror. Cut to:*)

EXT. NIGHT

Aircraft flying. Searchlights, etc. in background. Cut to:

THEY NEVER SLEPT

EXT. FRANCE. AIRFIELD. NIGHT

A light flickering on and off, to guide plane.
Cut to FRENCH PARTISAN – JEAN-LUC – *wagging the light,*
muttering obscenities under his breath.
Cut to plane landing. BOB *throws open hold door.*

HEINDRICH: Yes. Now it begins, eh? (*Quietly*) Very well. We
    live or we die. (*Leaps down.*)
BOB: (*Looks at* PRU) We'll see you in half an hour, old girl.
    (*Cut to* JEAN-LUC's *point of view, wagging light, sees* PRU,
    BOB *shaking hands. Obscenities increase.* PRU *jumps down.*
    HEINDRICH *and* PRU *run towards him. As they approach, he*
    turns, goes through woods. HEINDRICH *and* PRU *follow, and*
    cut to:)

EXT. FRANCE. CLEARING IN WOODS. NIGHT

JEAN-LUC, PRU, HEINDRICH, *out of breath, beside a small van.*
JEAN-LUC *runs his light up and down* PRU, *shakes his head in*
disbelief, muttering incredulous obscenities, turns, gets into back of
van. HEINDRICH *and* PRU *climb into front of van, drive off, and*
cut to:

INT. FRANCE. VAN. NIGHT

Driving down country road. PRU *briskly combing her hair, applying*
make-up, etc., checking herself in mirror.
[*The following scenes are spoken in French until stated.*]

HEINDRICH: (*Shaking his head*) At any moment you may be
    stopped by the Bosch, hung up nude by your thumbs, and
    have your toe-nails pulled from you, and yet you concern
    yourself – (*Stops, realizing.*) No, of course you are right,
    forgive me – Maurice must see you at your best – I would

advise a piece of hair hang over your eye – a little more
lipstick at the side of the mouth – undo a button on the
blouse – no, no, again you are right, it is not a woman he
yearns for, it is his angel and *maman* – pure, but soft and
loving – oh, I hope you do not disappoint him. (*Looks at her
doubtfully.*
Van rattles up a farm drive, stops before a dark farmhouse.
HEINDRICH *gets out,* PRU *climbs after him.* JEAN-LUC *gets
down, strolls off, unbuttoning his flies.*)

EXT. FRANCE. FARMHOUSE. NIGHT

HEINDRICH *goes to door, knocks complicatedly. A very dim light
discernible. The door opens cautiously to a crack.*

HEINDRICH: It's all right, Elaine – it's only Heindrich.
ELAINE: (*An elderly, work-ravaged French peasant, carrying a
    lamp*) Why have you come back, he will shoot you.
HEINDRICH: I have brought him his angel, to take him to London.
ELAINE: He will shoot her too.
HEINDRICH: No, no, he dreams of her –
ELAINE: He will shoot her, then he will go on dreaming of her.
PRU: Show me where he is, please. I will go alone. You will be
    quite safe, I promise.
    (ELAINE *hesitates, shrugs, leads* PRU *into kitchen.*)

INT. FRANCE. FARMHOUSE: KITCHEN. NIGHT

ELAINE *pulls open a concealed trap-door in floor, stands back,
beckons* PRU, *hands* PRU *the lamp. Cut to:*

INT. FRANCE. FARMHOUSE: CELLAR. NIGHT

PRU *descending into cellar. She moves across cellar uncertainly, until
light catches* MAURICE. *He is lying asleep on straw, food by him, a*

slop bucket visible. The smell is clearly appalling. A rat slouches past PRU. *She lets out an involuntary squeal.*
MAURICE, *his eyes jerk open, his gun jerks up, points at* PRU. *Cut to* MAURICE, *an expression of growing awe and reverence, and cut to, from his point of view,* PRU, *bathed in the glow of the lamp, an image of angelic radiance and softness. Religious music plays, of course.* MAURICE *arranges himself in a posture of devotion.*

PRU: (*Reaches down, holds out her hand*) Come, my child. It is time for you to go home.
MAURICE: (*Looks at her, eyes filled with tears of adoration and gratitude*) I knew you would come. (*In a whisper. Rises*) Knew.
(PRU *leads him by the hand out of the cellar, suppressing another shriek at the sight of another rat, and cut to:*)

INT. FRANCE. FARMHOUSE: KITCHEN. NIGHT

PRU *and* MAURICE *surfacing in kitchen,* MAURICE *moving in mystical trance, past* ELAINE, *through kitchen, outside.*

EXT. FRANCE. FARMHOUSE. NIGHT

HEINDRICH *stares at them in joy, as they move to the van.* PRU *guides* MAURICE *in,* HEINDRICH *following.*

HEINDRICH: Where's Jean-Luc? (*As he gets into van, starts engine.*
To ELAINE, *who is hurrying towards them*) Where's Jean-Luc?
ELAINE: What about my money?
HEINDRICH: What?

425

EXT. FRANCE. AIRFIELD. NIGHT

BOB *and* PILOT *standing by plane which is parked right at the edge of the field next to trees.*

BOB: (*To* PILOT) Time to go, old chap.
PILOT: Sir?
BOB: (*Firmly*) Time to go.
    (*They clamber aboard, engine starts.*)

EXT. FRANCE. FARMHOUSE. NIGHT

ELAINE: (*To* HEINDRICH, *indicating* MAURICE) He took a lease on the apartment for two years. Also he has had three bottles of wine, eight loaves, charcuterie and cheese – he owes me 143 francs, 27 centimes – also one franc fifty centimes for cleaning and laundry –
    (*A shot rings out and* ELAINE *drops dead, a bullet in her head. More shots follow, the windscreen of the van shatters,* HEINDRICH *is hit in the shoulder.* HEINDRICH, MAURICE *and* PRU *try and take cover on the floor of the van as spotlights spring on from two points in the surrounding area, illuminating them. These are figures silhouetted in patrol cars, on which the spots are mounted. One of them is holding a megaphone.*)
MEGAPHONE: Stop! Surrender! One more move and we shoot!
    (MAURICE *looks completely bewildered.* HEINDRICH *clutches at his wounded shoulder, frozen with fear. A number of* GERMAN SOLDIERS *are running towards them.*)
MAURICE: Who are they?
HEINDRICH: (*Laughs viciously*) They're Bosch, you imbecile. And they've come to take you away from your *maman*, your angel.
MAURICE: What?
    (*He looks at* PRU, *then in a series of lightning moves, almost superhuman, he leaps from the back of the van and shoots three*

(or four?) of the advancing soldiers. One of the spotlights
desperately tries to find him as he runs, while stuffing pistol in
belt and picks up a dead soldier's rifle. MAURICE *shoots at the*
lamps, knocking them both out, just as he is hit in the shoulder.
HEINDRICH *starts the van and races towards* MAURICE. PRU
helps MAURICE *aboard and the van hurtles past the* GERMANS
who set off in hot pursuit, firing continuously. MAURICE *returns*
fire, leaning dangerously out of the window.)

EXT. FRANCE. AIRFIELD. NIGHT

The plane is taxiing to the start of its take-off run. As it is about to
start its run, the van bursts through woods at far end of field, heads
straight for plane, forcing it to stop. The Germans come out of woods
as HEINDRICH, PRU *and* MAURICE *jump out and run/hobble to*
plane, which is beginning to taxi slowly around van.

MAURICE: *(Runs to* PRU, *pulls her to plane)* Come, *maman*, come!
    *(*HEINDRICH *is shot in the leg just before he reaches the hold.*
    PRU *runs to him, struggles to help him.* MAURICE *has turned, is*
    firing with demonic intensity and accuracy.)
    [The following is spoken in English unless specified]
BOB: *(To* PRU, *holding his hand out to her)* Up, old girl – up!
PRU: Him first – him first!
    *(*BOB *hesitates, an expression of indecision on his face. His eyes*
    meet HEINDRICH's, *then pulls* HEINDRICH *on board.)*
BOB: Now you! *(Grabs her hand, begins to pull her up.)*
PRU: Maurice – Maurice! Come on!
    *(*MAURICE *turns, sees her, sees the plane moving away, belts*
    after it. He is shot in the leg. Continues to hobble after plane.
    PRU *is reaching for him.* MAURICE *is shot in the arm, drops*
    automatic rifle, manages to grab PRU's *hand.)*
    (To BOB*)* Help me! Help me!
    *(*BOB *again for a second an expression on his face of*
    indecisiveness, more apparent this time, not seen by MAURICE,

whose eyes are fixed on PRU's *with intense yearning, but seen by* HEINDRICH.)

Help me, Bob!

(BOB *bends, between them they hoist* MAURICE *aboard. He and* PRU *tumble backwards, as plane takes off over the heads of* GERMANS *who fire at it.*)

BOB: (*To* HEINDRICH) The door – the door!

(HEINDRICH *gazing at* BOB *with recognition, goes over, helps with the door as the plane takes off.*)

Well, phew! eh, chaps? (*Attempts a smile at* HEINDRICH.)

INT. AEROPLANE HOLD: INFLIGHT. NIGHT

BOB *and* HEINDRICH *are standing.* MAURICE *is lying, clutching* PRU's *hand.*

HEINDRICH: Phew, phew, phew! Phew, phew, phew *à vous, monsieur* old chap! (*Spits in* BOB's *face.*)

(BOB *lurches back.*)

I saw you – saw your face – you wanted to leave us – wanted to leave us! Oh yes, it is all clear! I knew, I knew before we left that Monk planned something very bad – but I did not believe that even that Englishman – even *that* Englishman – had arranged to give us alive to the Bosch!

BOB: Oh, for goodness sake's, Heindrich –

HEINDRICH: (*In French*) Give me the pistol, Fattypuff.

MAURICE: (*In French*) But why, Thinnifer?

HEINDRICH: (*In French*) Because – because, Fattypuff, he plotted to have the Bosch capture us – and *petite maman*! and torture her to death!

(MAURICE *whips out pistol, presses it against* BOB's *head.*)

(*In French*) A moment, Fattypuff. (*To* BOB) Well, old chap, do you deny it?

BOB: Of course I deny it, old – (*stops himself*) complete and utter nonsense! for one thing, Monk could never do a thing like

428

that – and for another – I mean, do you think that even Monk can phone up some Hun in Bordeaux and say, 'Oh, by the way, Fattypuff and Thinnifer are in your neighbourhood, and Fattypuff's got some top secret info about the American raid we think you ought to have – (*stops, attempts to laugh with jolly contempt, is suddenly aware of* PRU's *eyes on him*) and anyway – anyway (*quickly*) he's got too much faith in you two, he knows you'd never let them take you alive –

HEINDRICH: What? Oh, this – this you mean eh? (*Wrestling pill out of his belt.*) If you're caught, just one little bite – one little bite, like a good little French frog – and pouf! well played, monsieur, *bien joué*, old chap, eh? Ha, ha, ha, one little dead frog! But I don't think so, no. I don't think so – there's nothing in this but sugar and water – or something to make us more brave as they pull out our nails and flog us – go on, show us, show us what's in it! (*Pressing capsule against* BOB's *sealed mouth.*)

PRU: (*In French*) Give it to me – (*trying to force capsule out of* HEINDRICH's *hand*) mon ange – (*To* MAURICE) make him! (MAURICE, *clearly bewildered by all this, points pistol at* HEINDRICH.)

HEINDRICH: (*In French*) Idiot!

PRU: (*To* HEINDRICH) If it's really so important to you I'll do it. At least I'm not particularly valuable. Nothing like as valuable as Bob. I don't believe Monk betrayed you, but even if he did, even if his op was as horrible and cruel as you believe – then I'm still sorry it didn't work – yes, I am. Because if it had worked, then I'm sure good would have come of it. Perhaps lots and lots of lives would have been saved, and this dreadful war would have been over that much quicker. And that's what we all want, isn't it? Even if we lose our own lives doing it. We've known from the beginning we may have to sacrifice ourselves (*goes on, completely unaware that she is doing so, in English. Her tone is*

strongly reminiscent of AMELIA CLEVERLY'S) just as the chaps
at the front, the chaps who fly planes, chaps above the sea
and even under the sea know it! Just as the girls and
mothers who are waiting for them to come home know in
their hearts they may never come home. And that there may
not even be homes to come back to. We accept the risk, we
have to accept the risk, or we shan't survive, and we'll
never, never have our two countries safe again, for our
children and their children to grow up in, our green and
lovely England, *notre belle France*! For your sakes, I gladly
accept the risk. And Monk – whatever the outcome – I
salute you, sir! (*Raises the capsule to her mouth.*)

MAURICE: (*Gently, in French*) But what are you doing?
(*Takes capsule from her.*)
(HEINDRICH *snatches the capsule from* MAURICE.)

HEINDRICH: (*In French*) Oh, you fool, Fattypuff, oh you fool –
it's all a farce, a nonsense! There is nothing in it, I tell you –
(*Crams cyanide capsule into his mouth, bites, goes into hideous
spasm, dies.*
There is a long, ghastly pause. PRU *attempts to smile beatifically
at* MAURICE, *whose pistol is still pointing at* HEINDRICH. *She
pushes pistol down.*)

PRU: (*Gently, in French*) There you are, *mon enfant*. Everything
is all right. No-one betrayed us.

MAURICE: (*Beatifically, in French*) No one betrayed us, *maman*.
(*Cut to* BOB, *as:*)

PRU: (*Out of shot*) Is there a lavatory on the plane, by any chance?

BOB: Um. I'm afraid not, old girl.
(*Cut to:*)

INT. EPSOM AIRFIELD: HANGAR. DAWN

The doors are open, as when we last saw them, for HEINDRICH'S
arrival. The champagne is still on the table, glasses as left. MONK *is
sitting in a state of complete collapse.*

430

There is the sudden drone of the approaching airplane. MONK *lifts his head wearily, his despair even worse.*
Sound of the plane getting closer and closer. Landing. Then taxiing up beside the hangar. MONK *stares towards it, unable, as before, to see clearly through the darkness. The hold opens, figures get out, move through the darkness, into the light of the hangar. First* BOB, *then* PRU *and* MAURICE, MAURICE *clutching tightly to* PRU'S *hand, his face turned adoringly towards her, his clothes covered in blood from his wounds.*
Cut to MONK'S *face, at first an expression of incredulous joy, as he takes them in one after another, and then as a group, as music soars.*

MONK: (*Almost beyond speech*) My God – my God – (*In a whisper, as they continue towards him.*
    When close to him, the group stops. There is a pause.)
    So here you are back, just as I promised! So what was all the fuss, eh? (*Then, realizing*) But Heindrich, where's Heindrich?
    (*Cut to:*)

INT. MONK'S CAR. DAY

PRU *driving.* MONK *beside her.* BOB *in the back. The last strains of the music dying away. There is a period of tension, then:*

MONK: (*In exasperation*) Put the wrong capsule in his belt! Put the wrong capsule in his belt! Good God, man, I sometimes wonder whether you lost some of your wits when you lost your arm – and as for you, girlie, (*swinging over to* PRU) don't think you're going to spend the rest of the war holding hands with Maurice, for one thing the funny doctors will soon knock all that nonsense out of him, for another I've got plans for him – and I've got plans for you too, girlie – there's a rabbit! (*Car swerves violently.*) Don't swerve, don't

swerve, don't swerve for rabbits – now listen to me, this is a briefing – there's this Dutch ballet company – all speak French – you know the type, easy for you to infiltrate – (*Spreading himself, to keep attention of both* BOB *and* PRU) now, here's what we'll do, this is what we'll do –
(*Cut to:*)

EXT. MONK'S CAR. DAY

Long shot of car on country road. MONK, PRU, BOB *seen through window.*

MONK: (*Voice over*) Firstly Amelia Cleverly, our cat-lady. I've decided not to hang her. Yet. We'll use her to send messages to the Huns in Holland – my messages – eye and mind on the road, girlie – there's not a word she'll send out that won't have been thought up by me. Every time she says 'tulip' a hundred Bosch will die –
(*Cut to:*)

INT. BROADCASTING HOUSE: STUDIO. DAY

AMELIA: So let our hearts turn to that peaceful land of canals and windmills and its fields and fields of tulips – pink tulips, white tulips, and my own favourite, the simple crimson tulip, nodding in the breeze. And now that little land and all its tulips lie crushed under the Nazi jackboot. But don't despair, our Dutch friends, we are with you as we have been with every oppressed nation during the long course of our island's history –

MONK: (*Voice over*) By the time I've finished with her she'll know the meaning of all the important words in the English language, eh?

432

AMELIA: Let's remind ourselves – honour, duty, courage, loyalty and sacrifice.

(*As* MONK *appears behind her.*)

MONK: And that's when I'll hang her.